Lineberger Memorial

Library

STRABO

VII

LCL 241

STRABO

GEOGRAPHY

BOOKS 15–16

WITH AN ENGLISH TRANSLATION BY

HORACE LEONARD JONES

HARVARD UNIVERSITY PRESS

CAMBRIDGE, MASSACHUSETTS

LONDON, ENGLAND

First published 1930
Reprinted 1954, 1961, 1966, 1983, 1995, 2000

LOEB CLASSICAL LIBRARY® is a registered trademark
of the President and Fellows of Harvard College

ISBN 0-674-99266-0

*Printed in Great Britain by St Edmundsbury Press Ltd,
Bury St Edmunds, Suffolk, on acid-free paper.
Bound by Hunter & Foulis Ltd, Edinburgh, Scotland.*

CONTENTS

THE

GEOGRAPHY OF STRABO

BOOK XV

ΣΤΡΑΒΩΝΟΣ ΓΕΩΓΡΑΦΙΚΩΝ

ΙΕ΄

Ι

1. Τὰ περιλειπόμενα τῆς Ἀσίας ἐστὶ τὰ ἐκτὸς
τοῦ Ταύρου, πλὴν Κιλικίας καὶ Παμφυλίας καὶ
Λυκίας, τὰ[1] ἀπὸ τῆς Ἰνδικῆς μέχρι Νείλου μεταξὺ
τοῦ Ταύρου καὶ τῆς ἔξω θαλάττης τῆς νοτίου[1]
κείμενα. μετὰ δὲ τὴν Ἀσίαν ἡ Λιβύη ἐστί, περὶ
ἧς ἐροῦμεν ὕστερον, νῦν δ᾽ ἀπὸ τῆς Ἰνδικῆς
ἀρκτέον· πρώτη γὰρ ἔκκειται πρὸς ταῖς ἀνατολαῖς
καὶ μεγίστη.

2. Δεῖ δ᾽ εὐγνωμόνως ἀκούειν περὶ αὐτῆς· καὶ
γὰρ ἀπωτάτω ἐστί, καὶ οὐ πολλοὶ τῶν ἡμετέρων
κατώπτευσαν αὐτήν· οἱ δὲ καὶ ἰδόντες μέρη τινὰ
εἶδον, τὰ δὲ πλείω λέγουσιν ἐξ ἀκοῆς· καὶ ἃ εἶδον
δέ, ἐν παρόδῳ στρατιωτικῇ καὶ δρόμῳ κατέμαθον·
διόπερ οὐδὲ τὰ αὐτὰ περὶ τῶν αὐτῶν ἐξαγγέλ-
λουσι, καὶ ταῦτα συγγράψαντες ὡς ἂν πεφροντισ-
μένως ἐξητασμένα, τινὲς δ᾽ αὐτῶν καὶ συστρατεύ-
σαντες ἀλλήλοις καὶ συνεπιδημήσαντες, καθάπερ
οἱ Ἀλεξάνδρῳ συγκαταστρεψάμενοι τὴν Ἀσίαν·
ἀλλ᾽ ἕκαστος ἑκάστῳ τἀναντία λέγει πολλάκις.

---

[1] δ᾽, before ἀπό, the editors omit.

[1] *i.e.* the Indian Ocean.

THE GEOGRAPHY OF STRABO

BOOK XV

I

1. THE parts still left of Asia are those outside the Taurus except Cilicia and Pamphylia and Lycia, I mean the parts extending from India as far as the Nile and lying between the Taurus and the outer sea on the south.[1] After Asia one comes to Libya, which I shall describe later, but I must now begin with India, for it is the first and largest country that lies out towards the east.

2. But it is necessary for us to hear accounts of this country with indulgence, for not only is it farthest away from us, but not many of our people have seen it; and even those who have seen it, have seen only parts of it, and the greater part of what they say is from hearsay; and even what they saw they learned on a hasty passage with an army through the country. Wherefore they do not give out the same accounts of the same things, even though they have written these accounts as though their statements had been carefully confirmed. And some of them were both on the same expedition together and made their sojourns together, like those who helped Alexander to subdue Asia; yet they all frequently contradict one

3

ὅπου δὲ περὶ τῶν ὁραθέντων οὕτω διαφέρονται, τί δεῖ νομίζειν περὶ τῶν ἐξ ἀκοῆς ;

3. Καὶ μὴν οὐδ' οἱ πολλοὶ[1] πολλοῖς χρόνοις ὕστερον συγγράψαντές τι περὶ τούτων, οὐδ' οἱ νῦν πλέοντες ἐκεῖσε, ἀποφαίνονταί τι ἀκριβές. C 686 Ἀπολλόδωρος γοῦν ὁ τὰ Παρθικὰ ποιήσας, μεμνημένος καὶ τῶν τὴν Βακτριανὴν ἀποστησάντων Ἑλλήνων παρὰ τῶν Συριακῶν βασιλέων τῶν ἀπὸ Σελεύκου τοῦ Νικάτορος, φησὶ μὲν αὐτοὺς αὐξηθέντας ἐπιθέσθαι καὶ τῇ Ἰνδικῇ· οὐδὲν δὲ προσανακαλύπτει τῶν πρότερον ἐγνωσμένων, ἀλλὰ καὶ ἐναντιολογεῖ, πλείω τῆς Ἰνδικῆς ἐκείνους ἢ Μακεδόνας καταστρέψασθαι λέγων. Εὐκρατίδαν γοῦν πόλεις χιλίας ὑφ' ἑαυτῷ ἔχειν· ἐκεῖνοι δέ γε αὐτὰ τὰ μεταξὺ ἔθνη τοῦ τε Ὑδάσπου καὶ τοῦ Ὑπάνιος τὸν ἀριθμὸν ἐννέα, πόλεις τε σχεῖν πεντακισχιλίας, ὧν μηδεμίαν εἶναι Κῶ τῆς Μεροπίδος ἐλάττω· ταύτην δὲ πᾶσαν τὴν χώραν καταστρεψάμενον Ἀλέξανδρον παραδοῦναι Πώρῳ.

4. Καὶ οἱ νῦν δὲ ἐξ Αἰγύπτου πλέοντες ἐμπορικοὶ τῷ Νείλῳ καὶ τῷ Ἀραβίῳ κόλπῳ μέχρι τῆς Ἰνδικῆς σπάνιοι μὲν καὶ[2] περιπεπλεύκασι μέχρι τοῦ Γάγγου, καὶ οὗτοι δ' ἰδιῶται καὶ οὐδὲν πρὸς ἱστορίαν τῶν τόπων χρήσιμοι. κἀκεῖθεν δὲ ἀφ' ἑνὸς τόπου καὶ παρ' ἑνὸς βασιλέως, Πανδίονος, καὶ ἄλλου[3] Πώρου, ἧκεν ὡς Καίσαρα τὸν Σεβαστὸν δῶρα καὶ πρεσβεῖα

---

[1] πολλοί, which Corais and the later editors eject, Jones restores.

[2] καί, omitted by Cmoxz.

[3] Before καὶ ἄλλου Groskurd inserts ἤ, at the same time

another. But if they differ thus about what was seen, what must we think of what they report from hearsay?

3. Moreover, most of those who have written anything about this region in much later times, and those who sail there at the present time, do not present any accurate information either. At any rate, Apollodorus, who wrote *The Parthica*, when he mentions the Greeks who caused Bactriana to revolt from the Syrian kings who succeeded Seleucus Nicator, says that when those kings had grown in power they also attacked India, but he reveals nothing further than what was already known, and even contradicts what was known, saying that those kings subdued more of India than the Macedonians; that Eucratidas, at any rate, held a thousand cities as his subjects. Those other writers, however, say that merely the tribes between the Hydaspes and the Hypanis were nine in number, and that they had five thousand cities, no one of which was smaller than the Meropian Cos, and that Alexander subdued the whole of this country and gave it over to Porus.

4. As for the merchants who now sail from Aegypt by the Nile and the Arabian Gulf as far as India, only a small number have sailed as far as the Ganges; and even these are merely private citizens and of no use as regards the history of the places they have seen. But from India, from one place and from one king, I mean Pandion, or another Porus, there came to Caesar Augustus presents and gifts

---

conjecturing κατ' ἄλλους, which latter is followed by Kramer and Meineke; but the ἄλλου seems needed in view of the Porus mentioned in § 3 above.

καὶ ὁ κατακαύσας ἑαυτὸν ᾿Αθήνησι σοφιστὴς
᾿Ινδός, καθάπερ καὶ ὁ Κάλανος ᾿Αλεξάνδρῳ τὴν
τοιαύτην θέαν ἐπιδειξάμενος.

5. Εἰ τοίνυν ταῦτ' ἀφείς τις τὴν πρὸ τῆς
᾿Αλεξάνδρου στρατείας ἐπιβλέποι μνήμην, πολὺ
ἂν εὕροι τούτων τυφλότερα. ᾿Αλέξανδρον μὲν
οὖν πιστεύειν τοῖς τοιούτοις εἰκός, τετυφωμένον
ταῖς τοσαύταις εὐτυχίαις. φησὶ γοῦν Νέαρχος
φιλονεικῆσαι αὐτὸν διὰ τῆς Γεδρωσίας ἀγαγεῖν
τὴν στρατιάν, πεπυσμένον διότι καὶ Σεμίραμις
ἐστράτευσεν ἐπὶ ᾿Ινδοὺς καὶ Κῦρος, ἀλλ' ἡ μὲν
ἀνέστρεψε, φεύγουσα μετὰ εἴκοσι ἀνθρώπων,
ἐκεῖνος δὲ μεθ' ἑπτά· ὡς σεμνὸν τό,[1] ἐκείνων
τοσαῦτα παθόντων, αὐτὸν καὶ[2] στρατόπεδον
διασῶσαι μετὰ νίκης διὰ τῶν αὐτῶν ἐθνῶν τε καὶ
τόπων· ἐκεῖνος μὲν δὴ ἐπίστευσεν.

6. ῾Ημῖν δὲ τίς ἂν δικαία γένοιτο πίστις περὶ
τῶν ᾿Ινδικῶν ἐκ τῆς τοιαύτης στρατείας τοῦ
Κύρου ἢ τῆς Σεμιράμιδος; συναποφαίνεται δέ
πως καὶ Μεγασθένης τῷ λόγῳ τούτῳ, κελεύων
ἀπιστεῖν ταῖς ἀρχαίαις περὶ ᾿Ινδῶν ἱστορίαις· οὔτε
γὰρ παρ' ᾿Ινδῶν ἔξω σταλῆναί ποτε στρατιάν,
οὔτ' ἐπελθεῖν ἔξωθεν καὶ κρατῆσαι, πλὴν τῆς
μεθ' ῾Ηρακλέους καὶ Διονύσου καὶ τῆς νῦν μετὰ
Μακεδόνων. καίτοι Σέσωστριν μὲν τὸν Αἰγύπτιον
καὶ Τεάρκωνα τὸν Αἰθίοπα ἕως Εὐρώπης προελ-
C 687 θεῖν· Ναβοκοδρόσορον δὲ τὸν παρὰ Χαλδαίοις

---

[1] For σεμνὸν τό Capps conj. σεμνόν τι.
[2] καί, omitted by Cmoz.

---

[1] See 15. 1. 73.
[2] For a similar statement, see 15. 2. 5.

of honour and the Indian sophist who burnt himself up at Athens,[1] as Calanus had done, who made
a similar spectacular display of himself before
Alexander.

5. If, however, one should dismiss these accounts
and observe the records of the country prior to the
expedition of Alexander, one would find things still
more obscure. Now it is reasonable to suppose that
Alexander believed such records because he was
blinded by his numerous good fortunes; at any
rate, Nearchus says that Alexander conceived an
ambition to lead his army through Gedrosia when
he learned that both Semiramis and Cyrus had
made an expedition against the Indians, and that
Semiramis had turned back in flight with only
twenty people and Cyrus with seven; and that
Alexander thought how grand it would be, when
those had met with such reverses, if he himself
should lead a whole victorious army safely through
the same tribes and regions.[2] Alexander, therefore,
believed these accounts.

6. But as for us, what just credence can we
place in the accounts of India derived from such an
expedition made by Cyrus, or Semiramis ? And
Megasthenes virtually agrees with this reasoning
when he bids us to have no faith in the ancient
stories about the Indians; for, he says, neither
was an army ever sent outside the country by the
Indians nor did any outside army ever invade their
country and master them, except that with Heracles
and Dionysus and that in our times with the
Macedonians. However, Sesostris, the Aegyptian,
he adds, and Tearco the Aethiopian advanced as far
as Europe; and Nabocodrosor, who enjoyed greater

εὐδοκιμήσαντα. Ἡρακλέους μᾶλλον καὶ ἕως
Στηλῶν ἐλάσαι· μέχρι μὲν δὴ δεῦρο καὶ Τεάρκωνα[1]
ἀφικέσθαι· ἐκεῖνον δὲ καὶ ἐκ τῆς Ἰβηρίας εἰς τὴν
Θράκην καὶ τὸν Πόντον ἀγαγεῖν τὴν στρατιάν·
Ἰδάνθυρσον δὲ τὸν Σκύθην ἐπιδραμεῖν τῆς Ἀσίας
μέχρι Αἰγύπτου· τῆς δὲ Ἰνδικῆς μηδένα τούτων
ἄψασθαι· καὶ Σεμίραμιν δ᾽ ἀποθανεῖν πρὸ τῆς
ἐπιχειρήσεως· Πέρσας δὲ μισθοφόρους μὲν ἐκ τῆς
Ἰνδικῆς μεταπέμψασθαι Ὕδρακας, ἐκεῖ δὲ μὴ
στρατεῦσαι, ἀλλ᾽ ἐγγὺς ἐλθεῖν μόνον, ἡνίκα Κῦρος
ἤλαυνεν ἐπὶ Μασσαγέτας.

7. Καὶ τὰ περὶ Ἡρακλέους δὲ καὶ Διονύσου
Μεγασθένης μὲν μετ᾽ ὀλίγων πιστὰ ἡγεῖται, τῶν
δ᾽ ἄλλων οἱ πλείους, ὧν ἐστι καὶ Ἐρατοσθένης,
ἄπιστα καὶ μυθώδη, καθάπερ καὶ τὰ παρὰ τοῖς
Ἕλλησιν. ὁ μὲν γὰρ ἐν ταῖς Βάκχαις ταῖς
Εὐριπίδου Διόνυσος τοιαῦτα νεανιεύεται·

> λιπὼν δὲ Λυδῶν τὰς πολυχρύσους γύας
> Φρυγῶν τε Περσῶν θ᾽ ἡλιοβλήτους πλάκας
> Βάκτριά τε τείχη τήν τε δύσχειμον χθόνα
> Μήδων ἐπῆλθον Ἀραβίαν εὐδαίμονα
> Ἀσίαν τε πᾶσαν.

παρὰ Σοφοκλεῖ δέ τίς ἐστι τὴν Νῦσαν[2] καθυμνῶν
ὡς τὸ Διονύσῳ καθιερωμένον ὄρος·

> ὅθεν κατεῖδον τὴν βεβακχιωμένην
> βροτοῖσι κλεινὴν Νῦσαν,[3] ἣν ὁ βούκερως
> Ἴακχος αὑτῷ μαῖαν ἡδίστην νέμει,
> ὅπου τίς ὄρνις οὐχὶ κλαγγάνει;

καὶ τὰ ἑξῆς. καὶ Μηροτραφὴς δὲ λέγεται·[4] καὶ

---

[1] Τεάρκον, F. [2] Νῦσαν, C, Νύσσαν other MSS.
[3] Νῦσαν, the editors, for Νύσσαν.

repute among the Chaldaeans than Heracles, led an army even as far as the Pillars. Thus far, he says, also Tearco went; and Sesostris also led his army from Iberia to Thrace and the Pontus; and Idanthyrsus the Scythian overran Asia as far as Aegypt; but no one of these touched India, and Semiramis too died before the attempt; and, although the Persians summoned the Hydraces as mercenary troops from India, the latter did not make an expedition to Persia, but only came near it when Cyrus was marching against the Massagetae.

7. As for the stories of Heracles and Dionysus, Megasthenes with a few others considers them trustworthy; but most other writers, among whom is Eratosthenes, consider them untrustworthy and mythical, like the stories current among the Greeks. For instance, in the *Bacchae* [1] of Euripides Dionysus says with youthful bravado as follows: " I have left behind me the gold-bearing glades of Lydia and of Phrygia, and I have visited the sun-stricken plains of Persia, the walled towns of Bactria, the wintry land of the Medes, and Arabia the Blest, and the whole of Asia." [2] In Sophocles, also, there is someone who hymns the praises of Nysa as the mountain sacred to Dionysus: " Whence I beheld the famous Nysa, ranged in Bacchic frenzy by mortals, which the horned Iacchus roams as his own sweetest nurse, where—what bird exists that singeth not there?" And so forth. And he is also called " Merotraphes." And Homer says of

[1] 13 ff.
[2] Quoted also in 1. 2. 20.

---

[4] καὶ . . . λέγεται, Meineke ejects.

ὁ ποιητὴς περὶ Λυκούργου τοῦ Ἠδωνοῦ φησιν
οὕτως·

ὅς ποτε μαινομένοιο Διωνύσοιο τιθήνας
σεῦε κατ᾽ ἠγάθεον Νυσήιον.

τοιαῦτα μὲν τὰ περὶ Διονύσου· περὶ δὲ Ἡρακλέους
οἱ μὲν ἐπὶ τἀναντία μόνον μέχρι τῶν ἑσπερίων
περάτων ἱστοροῦσιν, οἱ δ᾽ ἐφ᾽ ἑκάτερα.
8. Ἐκ δὲ τῶν τοιούτων Νυσαίους δή τινας
ἔθνος προσωνόμασαν καὶ πόλιν παρ᾽ αὐτοῖς
Νῦσαν,[1] Διονύσου κτίσμα, καὶ ὄρος τὸ ὑπὲρ τῆς
πόλεως Μηρόν, αἰτιασάμενοι καὶ τὸν αὐτόθι
κισσὸν καὶ ἄμπελον, οὐδὲ ταύτην τελεσίκαρπον·
ἀπορρεῖ γὰρ ὁ βότρυς πρὶν περκάσαι διὰ τοὺς
ὄμβρους τοὺς ἄδην· Διονύσου δ᾽ ἀπογόνους τοὺς
Συδράκας,[2] ἀπὸ τῆς ἀμπέλου τῆς παρ᾽ αὐτοῖς καὶ
τῶν πολυτελῶν ἐξόδων, βακχικῶς τάς τε ἐκστρα-
C 688 τείας πυιουμένων τῶν βασιλέων καὶ τὰς ἄλλας
ἐξόδους μετὰ τυμπανισμοῦ καὶ εὐανθοῦς στολῆς·
ὅπερ ἐπιπολάζει καὶ παρὰ τοῖς ἄλλοις Ἰνδοῖς.
Ἄορνον δέ τινα πέτραν, ἧς τὰς ῥίζας ὁ Ἰνδὸς
ὑπορρεῖ πλησίον τῶν πηγῶν, Ἀλεξάνδρου κατὰ
μίαν προσβολὴν ἑλόντος, σεμνύνοντες ἔφασαν,
τὸν Ἡρακλέα τρὶς μὲν προσβαλεῖν τῇ πέτρᾳ
ταύτῃ, τρὶς δ᾽ ἀποκρουσθῆναι. τῶν δὲ κοινωνη-
σάντων αὐτῷ τῆς στρατείας ἀπογόνους εἶναι
τοὺς Σίβας, σύμβολα τοῦ γένους σώζοντας, τό τε
δορὰς ἀμπέχεσθαι, καθάπερ τὸν Ἡρακλέα, καὶ
τὸ σκυταληφορεῖν καὶ ἐπικεκαῦσθαι βουσὶ καὶ
ἡμιόνοις ῥόπαλον. βεβαιοῦνται δὲ τὸν μῦθον

---

[1] Νύσσαν D.
[2] Συδράκας, C, Ὀξύδρακας Σύδρακας, s, Ὀξυδράκας other MSS.

Lycurgus the Edonian as follows: " who once drove the nurses of frenzied Dionysus down over the sacred mount of Nysa."[1] So much for Dionysus. But, regarding Heracles, some tell the story that he went in the opposite direction only, as far as the extreme limits on the west, whereas others say that he went to both extreme limits.

8. From such stories, accordingly, writers have named a certain tribe of people " Nysaeans," and a city among them " Nysa," founded by Dionysus; and they have named a mountain above the city " Merus," alleging as the cause of the name the ivy that grows there, as also the vine, which latter does not reach maturity either; for on account of excessive rains the bunches of grapes fall off before they ripen; and they say that the Sydracae are descendants of Dionysus, judging from the vine in their country and from their costly processions, since the kings not only make their expeditions out of their country in Bacchic fashion, but also accompany all other processions with a beating of drums and with flowered robes, a custom which is also prevalent among the rest of the Indians. When Alexander, at one assault, took Aornus, a rock at the foot of which, near its sources, the Indus River flows, his exalters said that Heracles thrice attacked this rock and thrice was repulsed; and that the Sibae were descendants of those who shared with Heracles in the expedition, and that they retained badges of their descent, in that they wore skins like Heracles, carried clubs, and branded their cattle and mules with the mark of a club. And they further confirm this

---

[1] *Iliad* 6. 132.

STRABO

τοῦτον καὶ ἐκ τῶν περὶ τὸν Καύκασον καὶ τὸν
Προμηθέα· καὶ γὰρ ταῦτα μετενηνόχασιν ἐκ τοῦ
Πόντου δεῦρο ἀπὸ μικρᾶς προφάσεως, ἰδόντες
σπήλαιον ἐν τοῖς Παροπαμισάδαις ἱερόν· τοῦτο
γὰρ ἐνεδείξαντο Προμηθέως δεσμωτήριον, καὶ
δεῦρο ἀφιγμένον τὸν Ἡρακλέα ἐπὶ τὴν ἐλευθέρω-
σιν τοῦ Προμηθέως, καὶ τοῦτον εἶναι τὸν
Καύκασον, ὃν Ἕλληνες Προμηθέως δεσμωτήριον
ἀπέφηναν.

9. Ὅτι δ᾽ ἐστὶ πλάσματα ταῦτα τῶν κολα-
κευόντων Ἀλέξανδρον, πρῶτον μὲν ἐκ τοῦ μὴ
ὁμολογεῖν ἀλλήλοις τοὺς συγγραφέας δῆλον, ἀλλὰ
τοὺς μὲν λέγειν, τοὺς δὲ μηδ᾽ ἁπλῶς μεμνῆσθαι·
οὐ γὰρ εἰκός, τὰ οὕτως ἔνδοξα καὶ τύφου πλήρη
μὴ πεπύσθαι, ἢ πεπύσθαι μέν, μὴ ἄξια δὲ μνήμης
ὑπολαβεῖν, καὶ ταῦτα τοὺς πιστοτάτους αὐτῶν·
ἔπειτα ἐκ τοῦ μηδὲ τοὺς μεταξύ, δι᾽ ὧν ἐχρῆν τὴν
ἐς Ἰνδοὺς ἄφιξιν γενέσθαι τοῖς περὶ τὸν Διόνυσον
καὶ τὸν Ἡρακλέα, μηδὲν ἔχειν τεκμήριον δεικνύ-
ναι τῆς ἐκείνων ὁδοῦ διὰ τῆς σφετέρας γῆς. καὶ
ἡ τοῦ Ἡρακλέους δὲ στολὴ ἡ τοιαύτη πολὺ
νεωτέρα τῆς Τρωικῆς μνήμης ἐστί, πλάσμα τῶν
τὴν Ἡράκλειαν ποιησάντων, εἴτε Πείσανδρος ἦν,
εἴτ᾽ ἄλλος τις· τὰ δ᾽ ἀρχαῖα ξόανα οὐχ οὕτω
διεσκεύασται.

10. Ὡς ἐν τοῖς τοιούτοις οὖν ἀποδέχεσθαι δεῖ
πᾶν τὸ ἐγγυτάτω πίστεως. ἐποιησάμεθα δ᾽ ἡμεῖς
καὶ ἐν τοῖς πρώτοις λόγοις τοῖς περὶ γεωγραφίας
δίαιταν, ἣν δυνατὸν ἦν, περὶ τούτων· καὶ νῦν
ἐκείνοις τε ἐξ ἑτοίμου χρησόμεθα, καὶ ἕτερα

---

[1] Adventures of Heracles.

myth by the stories of the Caucasus and Prometheus, for they have transferred all this thither on a slight pretext, I mean because they saw a sacred cave in the country of the Paropamisadae; for they set forth that this cave was the prison of Prometheus and that this was the place whither Heracles came to release Prometheus, and that this was the Caucasus the Greeks declared to be the prison of Prometheus.

9. But that these stories are fabrications of the flatterers of Alexander is obvious; first, not only from the fact that the historians do not agree with one another, and also because, while some relate them, others make no mention whatever of them; for it is unreasonable to believe that exploits so famous and full of romance were unknown to any historian, or, if known, that they were regarded as unworthy of recording, and that too by the most trustworthy of the historians; and, secondly, from the fact that not even the intervening peoples, through whose countries Dionysus and Heracles and their followers would have had to pass in order to reach India, can show any evidence that these made a journey through their country. Further, such accoutrement of Heracles is much later than the records of the Trojan War, being a fabrication of the authors of the *Heracleia*,[1] whether the author was Peisander or someone else. The ancient statues of Heracles are not thus accoutred.

10. So, in cases like these, one must accept everything that is nearest to credibility. I have already in my first discussion of the subject of geography[2] made decisions, as far as I could, about these matters. And now I shall unhesitatingly use those decisions

[2] 2. 1. 1 ff.

προσθήσομεν, ὅσων ἂν δεῖν δόξῃ πρὸς τὴν σαφή-
νειαν. μάλιστα δ' ἐκ[1] τῆς διαίτης ἐδόκει τῆς
τότε πιστότατα εἶναι τὰ ὑπὸ τοῦ Ἐρατοσθένους
ἐν τῷ τρίτῳ τῶν γεωγραφικῶν ἐκτεθέντα κεφα-
λαιωδῶς περὶ τῆς τότε νομιζομένης Ἰνδικῆς,
ἡνίκα Ἀλέξανδρος ἐπῆλθε· καὶ ἦν ὁ Ἰνδὸς ὅριον
ταύτης τε καὶ τῆς Ἀριανῆς, ἣν ἐφεξῆς πρὸς τῇ
C 689 ἑσπέρᾳ[2] κειμένην Πέρσαι κατεῖχον· ὕστερον γὰρ
δὴ καὶ τῆς Ἀριανῆς πολλὴν ἔσχον οἱ Ἰνδοὶ
λαβόντες παρὰ τῶν Μακεδόνων. ἔστι δὲ τοιαῦτα,
ἃ λέγει ὁ Ἐρατοσθένης.

11. Τὴν Ἰνδικὴν περιώρικεν ἀπὸ μὲν τῶν
ἄρκτων τοῦ Ταύρου τὰ ἔσχατα ἀπὸ τῆς Ἀριανῆς
μέχρι τῆς ἑῴας θαλάττης, ἅπερ οἱ ἐπιχώριοι
κατὰ μέρος Παροπάμισόν τε καὶ Ἠμωδὸν καὶ
Ἴμαον[3] καὶ ἄλλα ὀνομάζουσι, Μακεδόνες δὲ
Καύκασον· ἀπὸ δὲ τῆς ἑσπέρας ὁ Ἰνδὸς ποταμός·
τὸ δὲ νότιον καὶ τὸ προσεῷον πλευρόν, πολὺ
μείζω τῶν ἑτέρων ὄντα, προπέπτωκεν εἰς τὸ
Ἀτλαντικὸν πέλαγος, καὶ γίνεται ῥομβοειδὲς τὸ
τῆς χώρας σχῆμα, τῶν μειζόνων πλευρῶν ἑκα-
τέρου πλεονεκτοῦντος παρὰ τὸ ἀπεναντίον πλευρὸν καὶ τρισχιλίοις σταδίοις, ὅσων[4] ἐστὶ τὸ
κοινὸν ἄκρον τῆς τε ἑωθινῆς παραλίας καὶ τῆς
μεσημβρινῆς, ἔξω προπεπτωκὸς ἐξ ἴσης ἐφ' ἑκάτερον παρὰ τὴν ἄλλην ἠιόνα. τῆς μὲν οὖν ἑσπε-
ρίου πλευρᾶς ἀπὸ τῶν Καυκασίων ὀρῶν ἐπὶ τὴν
νότιον θάλατταν στάδιοι μάλιστα λέγονται μύριοι

---

[1] δ' ἐκ, Corais, for ἐκ ; so Meineke.
[2] ἑσπέρᾳ F, ἑσπερίᾳ other MSS.
[3] Ἴμαον, E, Μᾶον CF, Μάον Dhxz.
[4] ὅσων, F, ὅσον other MSS.

as accepted, and shall also add anything else that seems required for the purpose of clearness. It was particularly apparent from my former discussion that the summary account set forth in the third book of his geography by Eratosthenes of what was in his time regarded as India, that is, when Alexander invaded the country, is the most trustworthy; and the Indus River was the boundary between India and Ariana, which latter was situated next to India on the west and was in the possession of the Persians at that time; for later the Indians also held much of Ariana, having received it from the Macedonians. And the account given by Eratosthenes is as follows:

11. India is bounded on the north, from Ariana to the eastern sea, by the extremities [1] of the Taurus, which by the natives are severally called " Paropamisus " and " Emodus " and " Imäus " and other names, but by the Macedonians " Caucasus "; on the west by the Indus River; but the southern and eastern sides, which are much greater than the other two, extend out into the Atlantic sea, and thus the shape of the country becomes rhomboidal, each of the greater sides exceeding the opposite side by as much as three thousand stadia, which is the same number of stadia by which the cape [2] common to the eastern and southern coast extends equally farther out in either direction than the rest of the shore. Now the length of the western side from the Caucasian Mountains to the southern sea is generally called thirteen thousand stadia,

---

[1] See 11. 8. 1 and footnote 3.
[2] *i.e.* Cape Comorin.

τρισχίλιοι παρὰ τὸν Ἰνδὸν ποταμὸν μέχρι τῶν
ἐκβολῶν αὐτοῦ· ὥστ᾽ ἀπεναντίον ἡ ἑωθινὴ προσ-
λαβοῦσα τοὺς τῆς ἄκρας τρισχιλίους ἔσται
μυρίων καὶ ἑξακισχιλίων σταδίων. τοῦτο μὲν
οὖν πλάτος τῆς χώρας τό τ᾽ ἐλάχιστον καὶ τὸ
μέγιστον. μῆκος δὲ τὸ ἀπὸ τῆς ἑσπέρας ἐπὶ τὴν
ἕω· τούτου δὲ τὸ μὲν μέχρι Παλιβόθρων ἔχοι
τις ἂν βεβαιοτέρως εἰπεῖν, καταμεμέτρηται γὰρ
σχοινίοις,¹ καὶ ἔστιν ὁδὸς βασιλικὴ σταδίων
μυρίων·² τὰ δ᾽ ἐπέκεινα στοχασμῷ λαμβάνεται
διὰ τῶν ἀνάπλων τῶν ἐκ θαλάττης διὰ τοῦ
Γάγγου ποταμοῦ μέχρι Παλιβόθρων· εἴη δ᾽ ἄν
τι³ σταδίων ἑξακισχιλίων. ἔσται δὲ τὸ πᾶν,
ᾗ βραχύτατον, μυρίων ἑξακισχιλίων, ὡς ἔκ τε
τῆς ἀναγραφῆς τῶν σταθμῶν τῆς πεπιστευμένης
μάλιστα λαβεῖν Ἐρατοσθένης φησί· καὶ ὁ Μεγασθένης οὕτω συναποφαίνεται, Πατροκλῆς δὲ
χιλίοις ἔλαττόν φησι. τούτῳ δὴ πάλιν τῷ διαστήματι προστεθὲν τὸ τῆς ἄκρας διάστημα τὸ
προπῖπτον⁴ ἐπὶ πλέον πρὸς τὰς ἀνατολάς, οἱ
τρισχίλιοι στάδιοι ποιήσουσι τὸ μέγιστον μῆκος·
ἔστι δὲ τοῦτο τὸ ἀπὸ τῶν ἐκβολῶν τοῦ Ἰνδοῦ
ποταμοῦ παρὰ τὴν ἑξῆς ἠιόνα, μέχρι τῆς λεχθείσης
ἄκρας καὶ τῶν ἀνατολικῶν αὐτῆς τερμόνων· οἰκοῦσι
δ᾽ ἐνταῦθα οἱ Κωνιακοὶ καλούμενοι.

12. Ἐκ δὲ τούτων πάρεστιν ὁρᾶν ὅσον διαφέ-
ρουσιν αἱ τῶν ἄλλων ἀποφάσεις, Κτησίου μὲν
οὐκ ἐλάττω τῆς ἄλλης Ἀσίας τὴν Ἰνδικὴν λέ-

---

¹ σχοινίοις, Corais emends to σχοίνοις.
² μυρίων, Casaubon, for δισμυρίων; so the later editors.
³ δ᾽ ἀντί, CDFh; τι omitted by moxz.
⁴ προπῖπτον, Corais, for προσπῖπτον: so the later editors.

I mean along the Indus River to its outlets, so that the length of the opposite side, the eastern, if one adds the three thousand of the cape, will be sixteen thousand stadia. These, then, are the minimum and maximum breadths of the country. The lengths are reckoned from the west to the east; and, of these, that to Palibothra can be told with more confidence, for it has been measured with measuring-lines,[1] and there is a royal road of ten thousand stadia. The extent of the parts beyond Palibothra is a matter of guess, depending upon the voyages made from the sea on the Ganges to Palibothra; and this would be something like six thousand stadia. The entire length of the country, at its minimum, will be sixteen thousand stadia, as taken from the *Register of Days' Journeys* that is most commonly accepted, according to Eratosthenes; and, in agreement with him, Megasthenes states the same thing, though Patrocles says a thousand stadia less. If to this distance, however, one adds the distance that the cape extends out into the sea still farther towards the east, the extra three thousand stadia will form the maximum length;[2] and this constitutes the distance from the outlets of the Indus River along the shore that comes next in order thereafter, to the aforesaid cape, that is, to the eastern limits of India. Here live the Coniaci, as they are called.

12. From this one can see how much the accounts of the other writers differ. Ctesias says that India is not smaller than the rest of Asia; Onesicritus that

---

[1] Or, by a slight emendation of the text, "in terms of the schoenus" (see critical note and cf. 11. 14. 11).

[2] *i.e.* 19,000 stadia.

γοντος, Ὀνησικρίτου δὲ τρίτον μέρος τῆς οἰκουμένης, Νεάρχου δὲ μηνῶν ὁδὸν τεττάρων τὴν δι'
C 690 αὐτοῦ[1] τοῦ πεδίου, Μεγασθένους δὲ καὶ Δηιμάχου
μετριασάντων μᾶλλον, ὑπὲρ γὰρ δισμυρίους
τιθέασι σταδίους τὸ ἀπὸ τῆς νοτίου θαλάττης
ἐπὶ τὸν Καύκασον, Δήιμαχος δ' ὑπὲρ τοὺς
τρισμυρίους κατ' ἐνίους τόπους· πρὸς οὓς ἐν τοῖς
πρώτοις λόγοις εἴρηται. νῦν δὲ τοσοῦτον εἰπεῖν
ἱκανόν, ὅτι καὶ ταῦτα συνηγορεῖ τοῖς αἰτουμένοις
συγγνώμην, ἐάν τι περὶ τῶν Ἰνδικῶν λέγοντες μὴ
διισχυρίζωνται.

13. Ἅπασα δ' ἐστὶ κατάρρυτος ποταμοῖς ἡ
Ἰνδική, τοῖς μὲν εἰς δύο τοὺς μεγίστους συρρηγνυ-
μένοις, τόν τε Ἰνδὸν καὶ τὸν Γάγγην, τοῖς δὲ κατ'
ἴδια στόματα ἐκδιδοῦσιν εἰς τὴν θάλατταν·
ἅπαντες δ' ἀπὸ τοῦ Καυκάσου τὴν ἀρχὴν ἔχουσι
καὶ φέρονται μὲν ἐπὶ τὴν μεσημβρίαν τὸ πρῶτον,
εἶθ' οἱ μὲν μένουσιν ἐπὶ τῆς αὐτῆς φορᾶς, καὶ
μάλιστα οἱ εἰς τὸν Ἰνδὸν συμβάλλοντες, οἱ δ'
ἐπιστρέφονται πρὸς ἕω, καθάπερ καὶ ὁ Γάγγης
ποταμός. οὗτος μὲν οὖν καταβὰς ἐκ τῆς ὀρεινῆς
ἐπειδὰν ἅψηται τῶν πεδίων, ἐπιστρέψας πρὸς ἕω
καὶ ῥυεὶς παρὰ τὰ Παλίβοθρα, μεγίστην πόλιν,
πρόεισιν ἐπὶ τὴν ταύτῃ θάλατταν καὶ μίαν
ἐκβολὴν ποιεῖται, μέγιστος ὢν τῶν κατὰ τὴν
Ἰνδικὴν ποταμῶν. ὁ δὲ Ἰνδὸς δυσὶ στόμασιν εἰς
τὴν μεσημβρινὴν ἐκπίπτει θάλατταν, ἐμπερι-
λαμβάνων τὴν Παταληνὴν καλουμένην χώραν,
παραπλησίαν τῷ κατ' Αἴγυπτον Δέλτα. ἐκ δὲ
τῆς ἀναθυμιάσεως τῶν τοσούτων ποταμῶν καὶ
ἐκ τῶν ἐτησίων, ὡς Ἐρατοσθένης φησί, βρέχεται

---

[1] αὐτοῦ, Meineke omits.

18

it is a third part of the inhabited world: Nearchus that the march merely through the plain itself takes four months; but Megasthenes and Deïmachus are more moderate in their estimates, for they put the distance from the southern sea to the Caucasus at "above twenty thousand stadia," although Deïmachus says that "at some places the distance is above thirty thousand stadia;" but I have replied to these writers in my first discussion of India.[1]   At present it is sufficient to say that this statement of mine agrees with that of those writers who ask our pardon if, in anything they say about India, they do not speak with assurance.

13. The whole of India is traversed by rivers. Some of these flow together into the two largest rivers, the Indus and the Ganges, whereas others empty into the sea by their own mouths. They have their sources, one and all, in the Caucasus; and they all flow first towards the south, and then, though some of them continue to flow in the same direction, in particular those which flow into the Indus, others bend towards the east, as, for example, the Ganges.   Now the Ganges, which is the largest of the rivers in India, flows down from the mountainous country, and when it reaches the plains bends towards the east and flows past Palibothra, a very large city, and then flows on towards the sea in that region and empties by a single outlet.   But the Indus empties by two mouths into the southern sea, encompassing the country called Patalenê, which is similar to the Delta of Aegypt.   It is due to the vapours arising from all these rivers and to the Etesian winds, as Eratosthenes says, that India is

[1] 2. 1. 4 ff.

τοῖς θερινοῖς ὄμβροις ἡ Ἰνδική, καὶ λιμνάζει τὰ
πεδία· ἐν μὲν οὖν τούτοις τοῖς ὄμβροις λίνον
σπείρεται καὶ κέγχρος· πρὸς τούτοις σήσαμον,
ὄρυζα, βόσμορον. τοῖς δὲ χειμερινοῖς καιροῖς πυ-
ροί, κριθαί, ὄσπρια καὶ ἄλλοι καρποὶ ἐδώδιμοι,
ὧν ἡμεῖς ἄπειροι. σχεδὸν δέ τι τοῖς ἐν Αἰθιοπίᾳ
καὶ κατ' Αἴγυπτον τὰ αὐτὰ φύεται καὶ ἐν τῇ
Ἰνδικῇ, καὶ τῶν ἐν τοῖς ποταμοῖς, πλὴν ἵππου
ποταμίου, τὰ ἄλλα φέρουσι καὶ οἱ Ἰνδικοί·
Ὀνησίκριτος δὲ καὶ τοὺς ἵππους γίνεσθαί φησι.
τῶν δ' ἀνθρώπων οἱ μὲν μεσημβρινοὶ τοῖς
Αἰθίοψίν εἰσιν ὅμοιοι κατὰ τὴν χροιάν, κατὰ δὲ
τὴν ὄψιν καὶ τὴν τρίχωσιν τοῖς ἄλλοις (οὐδὲ γὰρ
οὐλοτριχοῦσι διὰ τὴν ὑγρότητα τοῦ ἀέρος), οἱ δὲ
βόρειοι τοῖς Αἰγυπτίοις.

14. Τὴν δὲ Ταπροβάνην πελαγίαν εἶναί φασι
νῆσον, ἀπέχουσαν τῶν νοτιωτάτων τῆς Ἰνδικῆς
τῶν κατὰ τοὺς Κωνιακοὺς πρὸς μεσημβρίαν
ἡμερῶν ἑπτὰ πλοῦν, μῆκος μὲν ὡς ὀκτακισχιλίων[1]
σταδίων ἐπὶ τὴν Αἰθιοπίαν· ἔχειν δὲ καὶ ἐλέφαντας. τοιαῦται μὲν αἱ τοῦ Ἐρατοσθένους ἀποφάσεις. προστεθεῖσαι δὲ καὶ αἱ τῶν ἄλλων, εἴ
C 691 πού τι προσακριβοῦσιν, ἰδιοποιήσουσι[2] τὴν
γραφήν.

15. Οἷον περὶ τῆς Ταπροβάνης Ὀνησίκριτός
φησι, μέγεθος μὲν εἶναι πεντακισχιλίων σταδίων,
οὐ διορίσας μῆκος οὐδὲ πλάτος, διέχειν δὲ τῆς
ἠπείρου πλοῦν ἡμερῶν εἴκοσι· ἀλλὰ κακοπλοεῖν

---

[1] ὀκτακισχιλίων, Meineke, following Groskurd, emends to
πεντακισχιλίων (see Groskurd, Vol. III, p. 117, note 2).
[2] For ἰδιοποιήσουσι, Corais and Meineke read εἰδοποιή-
σουσι.

20

watered by the summer rains and that the plains
become marshes. Now in the rainy seasons flax
is sown, and also millet, and, in addition to these,
sesame and rice and bosmorum,[1] and in the winter
seasons wheat and barley and pulse and other edibles
with which we are unacquainted. I might almost say
that the same animals are to be found in India as
in Aethiopia and Aegypt, and that the Indian rivers
have all the other river animals except the hippopotamus, although Onesicritus says that the hippopotamus is also to be found in India. As for the
people of India, those in the south are like the
Aethiopians in colour, although they are like the rest
in respect to countenance and hair (for on account
of the humidity of the air their hair does not curl),
whereas those in the north are like the Aegyptians.

14. As for Taprobanê,[2] it is said to be an island
situated in the high sea within a seven days' sail
towards the south from the most southerly parts of
India, the land of the Coniaci; that it extends in
length about eight thousand stadia [3] in the direction
of Aethiopia, and that it also has elephants. Such
are the statements of Eratosthenes; but my own
description will be specially characterised by the
addition of the statements of the other writers,
wherever they add any accurate information.

15. Onesicritus, for example, says of Taprobanê
that it is " five thousand stadia in size," without
distinguishing its length or breadth; and that it is a
twenty days' voyage distant from the mainland, but

[1] See § 18 following.
[2] On Taprobanê (Ceylon), cf. Pliny 24 (22) ff.
[3] See 2. 1.14, where Strabo says five thousand (see critical
note).

21

τὰς ναῦς, φαύλως μὲν ἱστιοπεποιημένας, κατε-
σκευασμένας δὲ ἀμφοτέρωθεν[1] ἐγκοιλίων μητρῶν[2]
χωρίς· εἶναι δὲ καὶ ἄλλας νήσους αὐτῆς μεταξὺ
καὶ τῆς Ἰνδικῆς, νοτιωτάτην δ᾽ ἐκείνην. κήτη δ᾽
ἀμφίβια περὶ αὐτὴν γίνεσθαι, τὰ μὲν βουσί, τὰ
δ᾽ ἵπποις, τὰ δ᾽ ἄλλοις χερσαίοις ἐοικότα.

16. Νέαρχος δὲ περὶ τῆς ἐκ τῶν ποταμῶν ἐπι-
χοῆς παραδείγματα φέρει τὰ τοιαῦτα, ὅτι καὶ τὸ
Ἕρμου, καὶ Καΰστρου πεδίον καὶ Μαιάνδρου καὶ
Καΐκου παραπλησίως εἴρηται, διὰ τὸ[3] τὴν ἐπιφο-
ρουμένην τοῖς πεδίοις χοῦν αὔξειν αὐτά, μᾶλλον δὲ
γεννᾶν, ἐκ τῶν ὀρῶν καταφερουμένην, ὅση εὔγεως
καὶ μαλακή· καταφέρειν δὲ τοὺς ποταμούς, ὥστε
τούτων ὡς ἂν γεννήματα ὑπάρχειν τὰ πεδία, καὶ
εὖ λέγεσθαι, ὅτι τούτων ἐστὶ τὰ πεδία. τοῦτο δὲ
ταὐτόν ἐστι τῷ ὑπὸ τοῦ Ἡροδότου λεχθέντι ἐπὶ
τοῦ Νείλου καὶ τῆς ἐπ᾽[4] αὐτῷ γῆς, ὅτι ἐκείνου
δῶρόν ἐστι· διὰ τοῦτο δ᾽ ὀρθῶς καὶ ὁμώνυμον τῇ
Αἰγύπτῳ φησὶ λεχθῆναι τὸν Νεῖλον ὁ Νέαρχος.

17. Ἀριστόβουλος δὲ μόνα καὶ ὕεσθαι καὶ
νίφεσθαι τὰ ὄρη καὶ τὰς ὑπωρείας φησί, τὰ πεδία
δὲ καὶ ὄμβρων ὁμοίως ἀπηλλάχθαι καὶ νιφετῶν,
ἐπικλύζεσθαι δὲ μόνον κατὰ τὰς ἀναβάσεις
τῶν ποταμῶν· νίφεσθαι μὲν οὖν τὰ ὄρη
κατὰ χειμῶνα, τοῦ δὲ ἔαρος ἀρχομένου καὶ

---

[1] Before ἐγκοιλίων Meineke inserts πρώραις.
[2] μήτρων, DF[h].
[3] τό, Corais inserts ; so the later editors.
[4] ἐπ᾽, Kramer, for ὑπ᾽ ; so the later editors.

---

[1] Pliny (6. 24 [22]) says, "navibus utrimque prorae, ne per
angustias alvei circumagi sit necesse" ("the ships have prows

that it is a difficult voyage for ships that are poorly furnished with sails and are constructed without belly-ribs on both sides;[1] and that there are also other islands between Taprobanê and India, though Taprobanê is farthest south; and that amphibious monsters are to be found round it, some of which are like kine, others like horses, and others like other land-animals.

16. Nearchus, speaking of the alluvia deposited by the rivers, gives the following examples: that the Plain of the Hermus River, and that of the Cayster, as also those of the Maeander and the Caïcus, are so named because they are increased, or rather created, by the silt that is carried down from the mountains over the plains—that is all the silt that is fertile and soft; and that it is carried down by the rivers, so that the plains are, in fact, the offspring, as it were, of these rivers; and that it is well said that they belong to these. This is the same as the statement made by Herodotus in regard to the Nile and the land that borders thereon, that the land is the gift of the Nile;[2] and for this reason Nearchus rightly says that the Nile was also called by the same name as the land Aegyptus.

17. Aristobulus says that only the mountains and their foothills have both rain and snow, but that the plains are free alike from rain and snow, and are inundated only when the rivers rise; that the mountains have snow in the winter-time, and at the

at either end, in order that it may not be necessary to tack while navigating the narrow passages of the channel "). Meineke, following the conjecture of Kramer, emends the words of Strabo to make them more in accord with those of Pliny (see critical note).

[2] Cp. 1. 2. 29.

τοὺς ὄμβρους ἐνάρχεσθαι, καὶ ἀεὶ καὶ μᾶλλον
λαμβάνειν ἐπίδοσιν, τοῖς δ' ἐτησίαις[1] καὶ
ἀδιαλείπτως νύκτωρ καὶ μεθ' ἡμέραν ἐκχεῖσθαι
καὶ λάβρους ἕως ἐπιτολῆς Ἀρκτούρου· ἔκ τε
δὴ τῶν χιόνων καὶ τῶν ὑετῶν πληρουμένους
ποταμοὺς[2] ποτίζειν τὰ πεδία. κατανοηθῆναι δὲ
ταῦτα καὶ ὑφ' ἑαυτοῦ καὶ ὑπὸ τῶν ἄλλων φησίν,
ὡρμηκότων μὲν εἰς τὴν Ἰνδικὴν ἀπὸ Παροπαμισαδῶν μετὰ δυσμὰς Πληιάδων, καὶ διατριψάντων
κατὰ τὴν ὀρεινὴν ἔν τε τῇ Ὑπασίων καὶ τῇ
Ἀσσακανοῦ[3] γῇ τὸν χειμῶνα, τοῦ δ' ἔαρος
ἀρχομένου καταβεβηκότων εἰς τὰ πεδία καὶ πόλιν
Τάξιλα εὐμεγέθη, ἐντεῦθεν δ' ἐπὶ Ὑδάσπην καὶ
τὴν Πώρου χώραν· τοῦ μὲν οὖν χειμῶνος ὕδωρ
οὐκ ἰδεῖν, ἀλλὰ χιόνας μόνον· ἐν δὲ τοῖς Ταξίλοις
πρῶτον ὑσθῆναι, καὶ ἐπειδὴ καταβᾶσιν ἐπὶ τὸν
Ὑδάσπην καὶ νικήσασι Πῶρον ὁδὸς ἦν ἐπὶ τὸν
Ὕπανιν πρὸς ἕω κἀκεῖθεν ἐπὶ τὸν Ὑδάσπην
πάλιν, ὕεσθαι συνεχῶς, καὶ μάλιστα τοῖς ἐτησίαις, ἐπιτείλαντος δὲ Ἀρκτούρου, γενέσθαι
παῦλαν· διατρίψαντας δὲ περὶ τὴν ναυπηγίαν
ἐπὶ τῷ Ὑδάσπῃ καὶ πλεῖν ἀρξαμένους πρὸ δύσεως
Πληιάδος οὐ πολλαῖς ἡμέραις, καὶ τὸ φθινόπωρον
πᾶν καὶ τὸν χειμῶνα καὶ τὸ ἐπιὸν ἔαρ καὶ θέρος
C 692 ἐν τῷ κατάπλῳ πραγματευθέντας ἐλθεῖν εἰς τὴν
Παταληνὴν περὶ Κυνὸς ἐπιτολήν· δέκα μὲν δὴ
τοῦ κατάπλου γενέσθαι μῆνας, οὐδαμοῦ δ' ὑετῶν
αἰσθέσθαι, οὐδ' ὅτε ἐπήκμασαν οἱ ἐτησίαι, τῶν δὲ
ποταμῶν πληρουμένων τὰ πεδία κλύζεσθαι, τὴν

---

[1] τοῖς δ' ἐτησίαις, Tyrwhitt, for τοῖς δὲ τῆς ἀσίας; so the
later editors.

[2] ποταμούς, inserted by Groskurd; so the later editors.

[3] Ἀσσακανοῦ, Corais, for Μουσικανοῦ; so the later editors.

beginning of spring-time the rains also set in and
ever increase more and more, and at the time of
the Etesian winds the rains pour unceasingly and
violently from the clouds, both day and night, until
the rising of Arcturus; and that, therefore, the
rivers, thus filled from both the snows and the rains,
water the plains. He says that both he himself and
the others noted this when they had set out for
India from Paropamisadae, after the setting of the
Pleiades, and when they spent the winter near the
mountainous country in the land of the Hypasians
and of Assacanus, and that at the beginning of
spring they went down into the plains and to Taxila,
a large city, and thence to the Hydaspes River and
the country of Porus; that in winter, however, no
water was to be seen, but only snow; and that it
first rained at Taxila; and that when, after they
had gone down to the Hydaspes River and had
conquered Porus, their journey led to the Hypanis
River towards the east and thence back again to
the Hydaspes, it rained continually, and especially
at the time of the Etesian winds; but that when
Arcturus rose, the rain ceased; and that after tarry-
ing while their ships were being built on the Hydaspes
River, and after beginning their voyage thence only
a few days before the setting of the Pleiades, and,
after occupying themselves all autumn and winter
and the coming spring and summer with their
voyage down to the seacoast, they arrived at Patalenê at about the time of the rising of the Dog Star;
that the voyage down to the seacoast therefore took
ten months, and that they saw rains nowhere, not
even when the Etesian winds were at their height,
and that the plains were flooded when the rivers

25

δὲ θάλατταν ἄπλουν εἶναι τῶν ἀνέμων ἀντιπνεόντων, ἀπογαίας[1] δὲ μηδεμιᾶς πνοῆς ἐκδεξαμένης.

18. Τοῦτο μὲν οὖν αὐτὸ[2] καὶ ὁ Νέαρχος λέγει, περὶ δὲ τῶν θερινῶν ὄμβρων οὐχ ὁμολογεῖ, ἀλλά φησιν ὕεσθαι τὰ πεδία θέρους, χειμῶνος δ' ἄνομβρα εἶναι. λέγουσι δ' ἀμφότεροι καὶ τὰς ἀναβάσεις τῶν ποταμῶν. ὁ μέν γε Νέαρχος τοῦ Ἀκεσίνου πλησίον στρατοπεδεύοντάς[3] φησιν ἀναγκασθῆναι μεταλαβεῖν τόπον ἄλλον ὑπερδέξιον κατὰ τὴν ἀνάβασιν, γενέσθαι δὲ τοῦτο κατὰ θερινὰς τροπάς· ὁ δ' Ἀριστόβουλος καὶ μέτρα τῆς ἀναβάσεως ἐκτίθεται τετταράκοντα πήχεις, ὧν τοὺς μὲν εἴκοσιν ὑπὲρ τὸ προϋπάρχον βάθος πληροῦν μέχρι χείλους τὸ ῥεῖθρον, τοῖς δ'[4] εἴκοσιν ὑπέρχυσιν εἶναι εἰς τὰ πεδία. ὁμολογοῦσι δὲ καὶ διότι συμβαίνει νησίζειν τὰς πόλεις ἐπάνω χωμάτων ἱδρυμένας, καθάπερ καὶ ἐν Αἰγύπτῳ καὶ Αἰθιοπίᾳ, μετὰ δὲ Ἀρκτοῦρον παύεσθαι τὴν πλήμμυραν, ἀποβαίνοντος τοῦ ὕδατος· ἔτι ἡμίψυκτον σπείρεσθαι τὴν γῆν, ὑπὸ[5] τοῦ τυχόντος[6] ὀρύκτου χαραχθεῖσαν, καὶ ὅμως φύεσθαι τὸν καρπὸν τέλειον καὶ καλόν. τὴν δ' ὄρυζάν φησιν ὁ Ἀριστόβουλος ἑστάναι ἐν ὕδατι κλειστῷ, πρασιὰς δ' εἶναι τὰς ἐχούσας αὐτήν· ὕψος δὲ τοῦ φυτοῦ τετράπηχυ, πολύσταχύ τε καὶ πολύκαρπον· θερίζεσθαι δὲ περὶ δύσιν Πληιάδος καὶ

---

[1] ἀπογαίας, Corais, for ἀπὸ γαίας ; so the later editors.
[2] αὐτό, Xylander, for αὐτοί ; so the later editors.
[3] στρατοπεδεύοντας, Tzschucke, for στρατεύοντα E, στρατοπεδεύοντος other MSS. ; so the later editors.
[4] τοὺς δέ F(?)xz Tzschucke and Corais.

were filled, and the sea was not navigable when the winds were blowing in the opposite direction, and that no land breezes succeeded them.

18. Now this is precisely what Nearchus says too, but he does not agree with Aristobulus about the summer rains, saying that the plains have rains in summer but are without rains in winter. Both writers, however, speak also of the risings of the rivers. Nearchus says that when they were camping near the Acesines River they were forced at the time of the rising to change to a favourable place higher up, and that this took place at the time of the summer solstice; whereas Aristobulus gives also the measure of the height to which the river rises, forty cubits, of which cubits twenty are filled by the stream above its previous depth to the margin and the other twenty are the measure of the overflow in the plains. They agree also that the cities situated on the top of mounds become islands, as is the case also in Aegypt and Aethiopia, and that the overflows cease after the rising of Arcturus, when the waters recede; and they add that although the soil is sown when only half-dried, after being furrowed by any sort of digging-instrument,[1] yet the plant comes to maturity and yields excellent fruit. The rice, according to Aristobulus, stands in water enclosures and is sown in beds; and the plant is four cubits in height, not only having many ears but also yielding much grain; and the harvest is about the time of the setting of the Pleiades, and

---

[1] Cf. 7. 4. 6 and footnote on " digging-instrument."

[5] ὑπό, Corais, for ἀπό; so the later editors.
[6] τυχόντος, E, ψύχοντος other MSS.

27

πτίσσεσθαι[1] ὡς τὰς ζειάς· φύεσθαι δὲ καὶ ἐν τῇ
Βακτριανῇ καὶ Βαβυλωνίᾳ καὶ Σουσίδι, καὶ ἡ
κάτω δὲ Συρία φύει. Μέγιλλος δὲ τὴν ὄρυζαν
σπείρεσθαι μὲν πρὸ τῶν ὄμβρων φησίν, ἀρδείας
δὲ καὶ φυτείας[2] δεῖσθαι, ἀπὸ τῶν κλειστῶν
ποτιζομένην ὑδάτων. περὶ δὲ τοῦ βοσμόρου[3]
φησὶν Ὀνησίκριτος, διότι σῖτός[4] ἐστι μικρότερος
τοῦ πυροῦ· γεννᾶται δ' ἐν ταῖς μεσοποταμίαις.
φρύγεται δ', ἐπὰν ἀλοηθῇ, προομνύντων μὴ
ἀποίσειν ἄπυρον ἐκ τῆς ἅλω τοῦ μὴ ἐξάγεσθαι
σπέρμα.

19. Τὴν δ' ὁμοιότητα τῆς χώρας ταύτης πρός
τε τὴν Αἴγυπτον καὶ τὴν Αἰθιοπίαν καὶ πάλιν
τὴν ἐναντιότητα παραθεὶς ὁ Ἀριστόβουλος, διότι
τῷ Νείλῳ μὲν ἐκ τῶν νοτίων ὄμβρων ἐστὶν ἡ
πλήρωσις, τοῖς Ἰνδικοῖς δὲ ποταμοῖς ἀπὸ τῶν
C 693 ἀρκτικῶν, ζητεῖ, πῶς οἱ μεταξὺ τόποι οὐ κατομ-
βροῦνται· οὔτε γὰρ ἡ Θηβαῒς μέχρι Συήνης καὶ
τῶν ἐγγὺς Μερόης, οὔτε τῆς Ἰνδικῆς τὰ ἀπὸ τῆς
Παταληνῆς μέχρι τοῦ Ὑδάσπου. τὴν δ' ὑπὲρ
ταῦτα τὰ μέρη χώραν, ἐν ᾗ καὶ ὄμβροι καὶ
νιφετοί, παραπλησίως ἔφη γεωργεῖσθαι τῇ ἄλλῃ
τῇ ἔξω τῆς Ἰνδικῆς χώρᾳ· ποτίζεσθαι γὰρ ἐκ τῶν
ὄμβρων καὶ χιόνων. εἰκὸς δ' οἷς εἴρηκεν οὗτος
καὶ εὔσειστον εἶναι τὴν γῆν, χαυνουμένην ὑπὸ τῆς
πολλῆς ὑγρασίας καὶ ἐκρήγματα λαμβάνουσαν,
ὥστε καὶ ῥεῖθρα ποταμῶν ἀλλάττεσθαι. πεμφθεὶς
γοῦν ἐπί τινα χρείαν ἰδεῖν φησιν ἐρημωθεῖσαν

---

[1] πτίσσεσθαι, sec. man. in D, for πτίζεσθαι CEF*xz*, πίζεσθαι
siw, βαπτίζεσθαι *m*.
[2] Corais inserts μή before δεῖσθαι; so Meineke.
[3] ὄν, after βοσμόρου, Corais ejects; so later editors.

the grain is winnowed like barley; and rice grows also in Bactriana and Babylonia and Susis, as also in Lower Syria. Megillus says that rice is sown before the rains, but requires irrigation and transplanting,[1] being watered from tanks. Bosmorum, according to Onesicritus, is a smaller grain than wheat; and it grows in lands situated between rivers. It is roasted when it is threshed out, since the people take an oath beforehand that they will not carry it away unroasted from the threshing-floor, to prevent the exportation of seed.

19. Aristobulus, comparing the characteristics of this country that are similar to those of both Aegypt and Aethiopia, and again those that are opposite thereto, I mean the fact that the Nile is flooded from the southern rains, whereas the Indian rivers are flooded from the northern, inquires why the intermediate regions have no rainfall; for neither the Thebaïs as far as Syenê and the region of Meroê nor the region of India from Patalenê as far as the Hydaspes has any rain. But the country above these parts, in which both rain and snow fall, are cultivated, he says, in the same way as in the rest of the country that is outside India; for, he adds, it is watered by the rains and snows. And it is reasonable to suppose from his statements that the land is also quite subject to earthquakes, since it is made porous by reason of its great humidity and is subject to such fissures that even the beds of rivers are changed. At any rate, he says that when he was sent upon a certain mission he saw a country

---

[1] See critical note.

---

[4] σῖτος, Epit., σεπτός other MSS. ; so the editors.

χώραν πλειόνων ἢ χιλίων πόλεων σὺν κώμαις,
ἐκλιπόντος τοῦ Ἰνδοῦ τὸ οἰκεῖον ῥεῖθρον, ἐκτραπο-
μένου δ' εἰς τὸ ἕτερον ἐν ἀριστερᾷ κοιλότερον
πολύ, καὶ οἷον καταρράξαντος, ὡς τὴν ἀπολειφθεῖσαν ἐν δεξιᾷ χώραν μηκέτι ποτίζεσθαι ταῖς
ὑπερχύσεσι, μετεωροτέραν οὖσαν οὐ τοῦ ῥείθρου
τοῦ καινοῦ μόνον, ἀλλὰ καὶ τῶν ὑπερχύσεων.
20. Ταῖς δὲ τῶν ποταμῶν πληρώσεσι καὶ τῷ
τοὺς ἀπογαίους μὴ πνεῖν ὁμολογεῖ καὶ τὸ λεχθὲν
ὑπὸ τοῦ Ὀνησικρίτου· τεναγώδη γάρ φησιν εἶναι
τὴν παραλίαν, καὶ μάλιστα κατὰ τὰ στόματα τῶν
ποταμῶν, διά τε τὴν χοῦν καὶ τὰς πλημμυρίδας
καὶ τὴν τῶν πελαγίων ἀνέμων ἐπικράτειαν.
Μεγασθένης δὲ τὴν εὐδαιμονίαν τῆς Ἰνδικῆς
ἐπισημαίνεται τῷ δίκαρπον εἶναι καὶ δίφορον·
καθάπερ καὶ Ἐρατοσθένης ἔφη, τὸν μὲν εἰπὼν
σπόρον χειμερινόν, τὸν δὲ θερινόν, καὶ ὄμβρον
ὁμοίως· οὐδὲν γὰρ ἔτος εὑρίσκεσθαί φησι πρὸς
ἀμφοτέρους καιροὺς ἄνομβρον· ὥστ' εὐετηρίαν ἐκ
τούτου συμβαίνειν, ἀφόρου μηδέποτε τῆς γῆς
οὔσης· τούς τε ξυλίνους καρποὺς γεννᾶσθαι
πολλοὺς καὶ τὰς ῥίζας τῶν φυτῶν, καὶ μάλιστα
τῶν μεγάλων καλάμων, γλυκείας καὶ φύσει καὶ
ἑψήσει, χλιαινομένου τοῦ ὕδατος τοῖς ἡλίοις τοῦ
τ' ἐκπίπτοντος ἐκ Διὸς καὶ τοῦ ποταμίου. τρόπον
δή τινα λέγειν βούλεται, διότι ἡ παρὰ τοῖς ἄλλοις
λεγομένη πέψις καὶ καρπῶν καὶ χυμῶν παρ'
ἐκείνοις ἕψησίς ἐστι, καὶ κατεργάζεται τοσοῦτον
εἰς εὐστομίαν, ὅσον καὶ ἡ διὰ πυρός· διὸ καὶ τοὺς
κλάδους φησὶν εὐκαμπεῖς εἶναι τῶν δένδρων, ἐξ

of more than a thousand cities, together with villages, that had been deserted because the Indus had abandoned its proper bed, and had turned aside into the other bed on the left that was much deeper, and flowed with precipitous descent like a cataract, so that the Indus no longer watered by its overflows the abandoned country on the right, since that country was now above the level, not only of the new stream, but also of its overflows.

20. The flooding of the rivers and the absence of land breezes is confirmed also by the statement of Onesicritus; for he says that the seashore is covered with shoal-water, and particularly at the mouths of the rivers, on account of the silt, the flood-tides, and the prevalence of the winds from the high seas. Megasthenes indicates the fertility of India by saying that it produces fruit and grain twice a year. And so says Eratosthenes, who speaks of the winter sowing and the summer sowing, and likewise of rain; for he says that he finds that no year is without rain in both seasons; so that, from this fact, the country has good seasons, never failing to produce crops; and that the trees there produce fruits in abundance, and the roots of plants, in particular those of large reeds, which are sweet both by nature and by heating, since the water from the sky as well as that of the rivers is warmed by the rays of the sun. In a sense, therefore, Eratosthenes means to say that what among other peoples is called " the ripening," whether of fruits or of juices, is called among those people a " heating," and that ripening is as effective in producing a good flavour as heating by fire. For this reason also, he adds, the branches of the trees from which the wheels of carriages are

31

ὧν οἱ τροχοί· ἐκ δὲ τῆς αὐτῆς αἰτίας ἐνίοις καὶ
ἐπανθεῖν ἔριον. ἐκ τούτου δὲ Νέαρχός φησι τὰς
εὐητρίους ὑφαίνεσθαι σινδόνας, τοὺς δὲ Μακεδόνας ἀντὶ κναφάλλων[1] αὐτοῖς χρῆσθαι καὶ τοῖς
C 694 σάγμασι σάγης·[2] τοιαῦτα δὲ καὶ τὰ Σηρικά, ἔκ
τινων φλοιῶν ξαινομένης βύσσου. εἴρηκε δὲ καὶ
περὶ τῶν καλάμων, ὅτι ποιοῦσι μέλι, μελισσῶν
μὴ οὐσῶν· καὶ[3] γὰρ[4] δένδρον εἶναι καρποφόρον,
ἐκ δὲ τοῦ καρποῦ συντίθεσθαι μέλι, τοὺς δὲ
φαγόντας ὠμοῦ τοῦ καρποῦ[5] μεθύειν.

21. Πολλὰ γὰρ δὴ καὶ δένδρα παράδοξα ἡ
Ἰνδικὴ τρέφει, ὧν ἐστι καὶ τὸ κάτω νεύοντας
ἔχον τοὺς κλάδους, τὰ δὲ φύλλα ἀσπίδος οὐκ
ἐλάττω. Ὀνησίκριτος δὲ καὶ περιεργότερον τὰ
ἐν τῇ Μουσικανοῦ διεξιών, ἅ φησι νοτιώτατα
εἶναι τῆς Ἰνδικῆς, διηγεῖται μεγάλα δένδρα τινά,
ὧν τοὺς κλάδους αὐξηθέντας ἐπὶ πήχεις καὶ
δώδεκα, ἔπειτα τὴν λοιπὴν αὔξησιν καταφερῆ
λαμβάνειν, ὡς ἂν κατακαμπτομένους, ἕως ἂν
ἅψωνται τῆς γῆς· ἔπειτα κατὰ γῆς διαδοθέντας
ῥιζοῦσθαι ὁμοίως ταῖς κατώρυξιν, εἶτ’ ἀναδοθέντας
στελεχοῦσθαι· ἐξ οὗ πάλιν ὁμοίως τῇ αὐξήσει
κατακαμφθέντας[6] ἄλλην κατώρυγα ποιεῖν εἶτ’
ἄλλην, καὶ οὕτως ἐφεξῆς, ὥστ’ ἀφ’ ἑνὸς δένδρου
σκιάδιον γίνεσθαι[7] μακρόν, πολυστύλῳ σκηνῇ

---

[1] κναφάλλων, CF, κναφίλων other MSS.
[2] σάγης, Tzschucke, for σάγην; so the later editors.
[3] καί, EFx, οὐ other MSS.
[4] γάρ x omits; so Tzschucke and Corais.
[5] συντίθεσθαι . . . καρποῦ omitted by all MSS. except EF,
but quoted by Eustathius (note on *Dionysius* 1125).
[6] κατακαμφθέντας, Corais, for κατακαμφθέντα.
[7] γίνεσθαι, Corais, for γενέσθαι; so the later editors.

made are flexible; and for the same reason even
wool [1] blossoms on some. From this wool, Nearchus
says, finely threaded cloths are woven, and the
Macedonians use them for pillows and as padding
for their saddles. The Serica [2] also are of this kind,
Byssus [3] being dried out of certain barks. He states
also concerning the reeds,[4] that they produce honey,
although there are no bees, and in fact that there is
a fruit-bearing tree from the fruit of which honey
is compounded, but that those who eat the fruit raw
become intoxicated.

21. In truth, India produces numerous strange
trees, among which is the one whose branches bend
downwards and whose leaves are no smaller than a
shield. Onesicritus, who even in rather superfluous
detail describes the country of Musicanus, which, he
says, is the most southerly part of India, relates that
it has some great trees whose branches have first
grown to the height of twelve cubits, and then, after
such growth, have grown downwards, as though
bent down, till they have touched the earth; and
that they then, thus distributed, have taken root
underground like layers, and then, growing forth,
have formed trunks; and that the branches of these
trunks again, likewise bent down in their growth,
have formed another layer, and then another, and
so on successively, so that from only one tree there
is formed a vast sunshade, like a tent with many

[1] i.e. cotton.
[2] i.e. the threads of which the Seres make their garments
(see Pausanias 6. 26. 4 and Frazer's note thereon).
[3] By " Byssus " Strabo undoubtedly means *silk*, supposing
it to be a kind of *cotton* (see Miss Richter's article on " Silk
in Greece," *Am. Jour. Arch.*, Jan.–March, 1929, pp. 27–33).
[4] i.e. sugar-cane.

ὅμοιον. λέγει δὲ καὶ μεγέθη δένδρων, ὥστε πέντε
ἀνθρώποις δυσπερίληπτα εἶναι τὰ στελέχη. κατὰ
δὲ τὸν Ἀκεσίνην καὶ τὴν συμβολὴν τὴν πρὸς
Ὑάρωτιν καὶ Ἀριστόβουλος εἴρηκε περὶ τῶν
κατακαμπτομένους ἐχόντων τοὺς κλάδους καὶ
περὶ τοῦ μεγέθους, ὥσθ᾽ ὑφ᾽ ἑνὶ δένδρῳ μεσημ-
βρίζειν σκιαζομένους ἱππέας πεντήκοντα· οὗτος
δὲ τετρακοσίους. λέγει δὲ ὁ Ἀριστόβουλος καὶ
ἄλλο δένδρον οὐ μέγα, λοποὺς¹ ἔχον, ὡς ὁ κύαμος,
δεκαδακτύλους τὸ μῆκος, πλήρεις μέλιτος· τοὺς
δὲ φαγόντας οὐ ῥᾳδίως σώζεσθαι. ἅπαντας δ᾽
ὑπερβέβληνται περὶ τοῦ μεγέθους τῶν δένδρων
οἱ φήσαντες ἑωρᾶσθαι πέραν τοῦ Ὑαρώτιδος
δένδρον ποιοῦν σκιὰν ταῖς μεσημβρίαις πεντα-
στάδιον. καὶ τῶν ἐριοφόρων δένδρων φησὶν οὗτος
τὸ ἄνθος ἔχειν πυρῆνα· ἐξαιρεθέντος δὲ τούτου,
ξαίνεσθαι τὸ λοιπὸν ὁμοίως ταῖς ἐρέαις.

22. Ἐν δὲ τῇ Μουσικανοῦ καὶ σῖτον αὐτοφυῆ
λέγει πυρῷ παραπλήσιον καὶ ἄμπελον, ὥστ᾽
οἰνοφορεῖν, τῶν ἄλλων ἄοινον λεγόντων τὴν
Ἰνδικήν· ὥστε μηδ᾽ αὐλὸν εἶναι κατὰ τὸν Ἀνά-
χαρσιν, μήτ᾽ ἄλλο² τῶν μουσικῶν ὀργάνων μηδὲν
πλὴν κυμβάλων καὶ τυμπάνων καὶ κροτάλων, ἃ
τοὺς θαυματοποιοὺς κεκτῆσθαι. καὶ πολυφάρ-
μακον δὲ καὶ πολύρριζον τῶν τε σωτηρίων καὶ
τῶν ἐναντίων, ὥσπερ καὶ πολυχρώματον καὶ
οὗτος εἴρηκε, καὶ ἄλλοι γε. προστίθησι δ᾽ οὗτος,
ὅτι καὶ νόμος εἴη τὸν ἀνευρόντα τι τῶν ὀλεθρίων,
ἐὰν μὴ προσανεύρῃ καὶ τὸ ἄκος αὐτοῦ, θανα-
C 695 τοῦσθαι· ἀνευρόντα δὲ τιμῆς τυγχάνειν παρὰ τοῖς

¹ οὐ μεγαλολεπισματαπους CDFh.
² F reads τι after ἄλλο.

supporting columns.[1] He says also of the size of the trees that their trunks could hardly be embraced by five men. Aristobulus also, where he mentions the Acesines and its confluence with the Hyarotis, speaks of the trees that have their branches bent downwards and of such size that fifty horsemen—according to Onesicritus, four hundred—can pass the noon in shade under one tree. Aristobulus mentions also another tree, not large, with pods, like the bean, ten fingers in length, full of honey, and says that those who eat it cannot easily be saved from death. But the accounts of all writers of the size of the trees have been surpassed by those who say that there has been seen beyond the Hyarotis a tree which casts a shade at noon of five stadia. And as for the wool-bearing trees, Aristobulus says that the flower contains a seed, and that when this is removed the rest is combed like wool.

22. Aristobulus speaks also of a self-grown grain, similar to wheat, in the country of Musicanus, and of a vine from which wine is produced, although the other writers say that India has no wine; and therefore, according to Anacharsis, it also has no flutes, or any other musical instruments except cymbals and drums and castanets, which are possessed by the jugglers. Both he and other writers speak of this country as abounding in herbs and roots both curative and poisonous, and likewise in plants of many colours. And Aristobulus adds that they have a law whereby any person who discovers anything deadly is put to death unless he also discovers a cure for it, but if that person discovers a

---

[1] The banyan tree (*Ficus Bengalensis*).

βασιλεῦσιν. ἔχειν δὲ καὶ κιννάμωμον καὶ νάρδον
καὶ τὰ ἄλλα ἀρώματα τὴν νότιον γῆν τὴν Ἰνδικήν,
ὁμοίως ὥσπερ τὴν Ἀραβίαν καὶ τὴν Αἰθιοπίαν,
ἔχουσάν τι ἐμφερὲς ἐκείναις κατὰ τοὺς ἡλίους·
διαφέρειν δὲ τῷ πλεονασμῷ τῶν ὑδάτων, ὥστ'
ἔνικμον εἶναι τὸν ἀέρα καὶ τροφιμώτερον παρὰ
τοῦτο καὶ γόνιμον μᾶλλον, ὡς δ' αὕτως καὶ τὴν
γῆν καὶ τὸ ὕδωρ· ᾗ δὴ [1] καὶ μείζω τά τε χερσαῖα
τῶν ζῴων καὶ τὰ καθ' ὕδατος τὰ ἐν Ἰνδοῖς τῶν
παρ' ἄλλοις εὑρίσκεσθαι· καὶ τὸν Νεῖλον δ' εἶναι
γόνιμον μᾶλλον ἑτέρων καὶ μεγαλοφυῆ [2] γεννᾶν
καὶ τἆλλα καὶ τὰ ἀμφίβια, τάς τε γυναῖκας
ἔσθ' ὅτε καὶ τετράδυμα τίκτειν τὰς Αἰγυπτίας.
Ἀριστοτέλης δέ τινα καὶ ἑπτάδυμα [3] ἱστορεῖ
τετοκέναι, καὶ αὐτὸς πολύγονον καλῶν τὸν Νεῖλον
καὶ τρόφιμον διὰ τὴν ἐκ τῶν ἡλίων μετρίαν ἔψησιν,
αὐτὸ καταλειπόντων [4] τὸ τρόφιμον, τὸ δὲ περιττὸν
ἐκθυμιώντων.

23. Ἀπὸ δὲ τῆς αὐτῆς αἰτίας καὶ τοῦτο συμβαίνειν εἰκός, ὅπερ φησὶν οὗτος, ὅτι τῷ ἡμίσει
πυρὶ ἔψει τὸ [5] τοῦ Νείλου ὕδωρ ἢ τὰ ἄλλα. ὅσῳ
δέ γέ φησι τὸ μὲν τοῦ Νείλου ὕδωρ δι' εὐθείας
ἔπεισι πολλὴν χώραν καὶ στενὴν καὶ μεταβάλλει
πολλὰ κλίματα καὶ πολλοὺς ἀέρας, τὰ δ' Ἰνδικὰ
ῥεύματα ἐς πεδία ἀναχεῖται μείζω καὶ πλατύτερα,
ἐνδιατρίβοντα πολὺν χρόνον τοῖς αὐτοῖς κλίμασι,

---

[1] ᾗ δή, Corais, for ἤδη ; so the later editors.
[2] μεγαλοφυῆ, Xylander, for μεγαλοφυεῖν ; so the later editors.
[3] For ἑπτάδυμα, Corais reads πεντάδυμα, following Gellius 10. 2, and Aristotle's *Hist. An.* 7. 4 and *De Generat.* 4. 4.
[4] καταλειπόντων, Corais, for καταλιπόντων ; so the later editors.

cure he receives a reward from the king. And he says that the southern land of India, like Arabia and Aethiopia, bears cinnamon, nard, and other aromatic products, being similar to those countries in the effect of the rays of sun, although it surpasses them in the copiousness of its waters; and that therefore its air is humid and proportionately more nourishing and more productive; and that this applies both to the land and to the water, and therefore, of course, both land and water animals in India are found to be larger than those in other countries; but that the Nile is more productive than other rivers, and produces huge creatures, among others the amphibious kind; and that the Aegyptian women sometimes actually bear four children. Aristotle reports that one woman actually bore seven; and he, too, calls the Nile highly productive and nourishing because of the moderate heat of the sun's rays, which, he says, leave the nourishing element and evaporate merely the superfluous.

23. It is probably from the same cause, as Aristotle says, that this too takes place—I mean that the water of the Nile boils with one-half the heat required by any other. But in proportion, he says, as the water of the Nile traverses in a straight course a long and narrow tract of country and passes across many "climata"[1] and through many atmospheres, whereas the streams of India spread into greater and wider plains, lingering for a long time in the same "climata," in the same proportion those of India are more nourishing than those of the Nile; and on

[1] *i.e.* "belts of latitude" (see Vol. I, p. 22, footnote 2).

[5] πυρὶ ἕψει τό, Kramer, for περιεψεῖτο F, πυρὶ ἐψεῖτο Di πυρὶ ἐψεῖται other MSS.

τοσῷδε ἐκεῖνα τούτου τροφιμώτερα, διότι καὶ τὰ
κήτη μείζω τε καὶ πλείω· καὶ ἐκ τῶν νεφῶν δὲ
ἐφθὸν ἤδη χεῖσθαι τὸ ὕδωρ.

24. Τοῦτο δ' οἱ μὲν περὶ Ἀριστόβουλον οὐκ
ἂν συγχωροῖεν οἱ φάσκοντες μὴ ὕεσθαι τὰ πεδία.
Ὀνησικρίτῳ δὲ δοκεῖ τόδε τὸ ὕδωρ αἴτιον εἶναι
τῶν ἐν τοῖς ζῴοις ἰδιωμάτων, καὶ φέρει σημεῖον
τὸ καὶ τὰς χρόας τῶν πινόντων βοσκημάτων
ξενικῶν ἀλλάττεσθαι πρὸς τὸ ἐπιχώριον. τοῦτο
μὲν οὖν εὖ· οὐκέτι δὲ καὶ τὸ τοῦ μέλανας εἶναι
καὶ οὐλότριχας τοὺς Αἰθίοπας ἐν ψιλοῖς τοῖς
ὕδασι τὴν αἰτίαν τιθέναι, μέμφεσθαι δὲ τὸν Θεο-
δέκτην εἰς αὐτὸν τὸν ἥλιον ἀναφέροντα τὸ αἴτιον,
ὅς φησιν οὕτως·

> οἷς ἀγχιτέρμων ἥλιος διφρηλατῶν
> σκοτεινὸν ἄνθος ἐξέχρωσε λιγνύος
> εἰς σώματ' ἀνδρῶν, καὶ συνέστρεψεν κόμας
> μορφαῖς ἀναυξήτοισι συντήξας πυρός.

ἔχοι δ' ἄν τινα λόγον· φησὶ γὰρ μήτε ἐγγυτέρω
τοῖς Αἰθίοψιν εἶναι τὸν ἥλιον ἢ τοῖς ἄλλοις, ἀλλὰ
μᾶλλον κατὰ κάθετον εἶναι καὶ διὰ τοῦτο ἐπι-
καίεσθαι πλέον, ὥστ' οὐκ εὖ λέγεσθαι ἀγχιτέρ-
μονα αὐτοῖς τὸν ἥλιον, ἴσον πάντων διέχοντα,
μήτε τὸ θάλπος εἶναι τοῦ τοιούτου πάθους αἴτιον·
C 696 μηδὲ γὰρ τοῖς ἐν γαστρί, ὧν οὐχ ἅπτεται ἥλιος.
βελτίους δὲ οἱ τὸν ἥλιον αἰτιώμενοι καὶ τὴν ἐξ
αὐτοῦ[1] ἐπίκαυσιν, κατ' ἐπίλειψιν σφοδρὰν τῆς
ἐπιπολῆς ἰκμάδος· καθ' ὃ καὶ τοὺς Ἰνδοὺς μὴ

---

[1] τὴν ἐξ αὐτοῦ, Casaubon, for τὴν ἑαυτοῦ, CDF*hiw*, τὴν οὐτοῦ
E*moxz*.

this account their river animals are also larger and more numerous; and further, he says, the water is already heated when it pours from the clouds.

24. To this statement Aristobulus and his followers, who assert that the plains are not watered by rain, would not agree. But Onesicritus believes that rain-water is the cause of the distinctive differences in the animals; and he adduces as evidence that the colour of foreign cattle which drink it is changed to that of the native animals. Now in this he is correct; but no longer so when he lays the black complexion and woolly hair of the Aethiopians on merely the waters and censures Theodectes,[1] who refers the cause to the sun itself, saying as follows: " Nearing the borders of these people the Sun, driving his chariot, discoloured the bodies of men with a murky dark bloom, and curled their hair, fusing it by unincreasable forms of fire." But Onesicritus might have some argument on his side; for he says that, in the first place, the sun is no nearer to the Aethiopians than to any other people, but is more nearly in a perpendicular line with reference to them and on this account scorches more, and therefore it is incorrect to say, " Nearing the borders . . . the sun," since the sun is equidistant from all peoples; and that, secondly, the heat is not the cause of such a discoloration, for it does not apply to infants in the womb either, since the rays of the sun do not touch them. But better is the opinion of those who lay the cause to the sun and its scorching, which causes a very great deficiency of moisture on the surface of the skin. And I assert that it is in accordance

---

[1] " Theodectas " is probably the correct spelling (see I. G. II, 977).

οὐλοτριχεῖν φαμεν, μηδ᾿ οὕτως ἀπεφεισμένως [1]
ἐπικεκαῦσθαι τὴν χρόαν, ὅτι ὑγροῦ κοινωνοῦσιν
ἀέρος. ἐν δὲ τῇ γαστρὶ ἤδη κατὰ σπερματικὴν
διάδοσιν [2] τοιαῦτα γίνεται, οἷα τὰ γεννῶντα· καὶ
γὰρ πάθη συγγενικὰ οὕτω λέγεται καὶ ἄλλαι
ὁμοιότητες. καὶ τὸ πάντων δ᾿ ἴσον ἀπέχειν τὸν
ἥλιον πρὸς αἴσθησιν λέγεται, οὐ πρὸς λόγον· καὶ
πρὸς αἴσθησιν, οὐχ ὡς ἔτυχεν, ἀλλ᾿ ὥς φαμεν
σημείου λόγον ἔχειν τὴν γῆν πρὸς τὴν τοῦ ἡλίου
σφαῖραν· ἐπεὶ πρός γε τὴν τοιαύτην αἴσθησιν,
καθ᾿ ἣν θάλπους ἀντιλαμβανόμεθα, ἐγγύθεν μὲν
μᾶλλον, πόρρωθεν δὲ ἧττον, οὐκ ἴσον· οὕτω δ᾿
ἀγχιτέρμων ὁ ἥλιος λέγεται τοῖς Αἰθίοψιν, οὐχ
ὡς Ὀνησικρίτῳ δέδοκται.[3]

25. Καὶ τοῦτο δὲ τῶν ὁμολογουμένων ἐστὶ καὶ
τῶν σωζόντων τὴν πρὸς τὴν Αἴγυπτον ὁμοιότητα
καὶ τὴν Αἰθιοπίαν, ὅτι, τῶν πεδίων ὅσα μὴ
ἐπίκλυστα, ἄκαρπά ἐστι διὰ τὴν ἀνυδρίαν.
Νέαρχος δὲ τὸ ζητούμενον πρότερον ἐπὶ τοῦ
Νείλου, πόθεν ἡ πλήρωσις αὐτοῦ, διδάσκειν ἔφη
τοὺς Ἰνδικοὺς ποταμους, ὅτι ἐκ τῶν θερινῶν
ὄμβρων συμβαίνει· Ἀλέξανδρον δ᾿ ἐν μὲν τῷ
Ὑδάσπῃ κροκοδείλους ἰδόντα, ἐν δὲ τῷ Ἀκεσίνῃ
κυάμους Αἰγυπτίους, εὑρηκέναι δόξαι τὰς τοῦ
Νείλου πηγάς, καὶ παρασκευάζεσθαι στόλον εἰς
τὴν Αἴγυπτον, ὡς τῷ ποταμῷ τούτῳ μέχρι ἐκεῖσε

---

[1] ἀπεφεισμένως, Meineke, for πεπυσμένως Dh, πεπεισμένους
xz, πεπεισμένως other MSS.
[2] διάδοσιν, F, διάθεσιν other MSS.

with this fact that the Indians do not have woolly hair, and also that their skin is not so unmercifully scorched, I mean the fact that they share in an atmosphere that is humid. And already in the womb children, by seminal impartation, become like their parents in colour; for congenital affections and other similarities are also thus explained. Further, the statement [1] that the sun is equidistant from all peoples is made in accordance with observation, not reason; and, in accordance with observations that are not casual, but in accordance with the observation, as I put it, that the earth is no larger than a point as compared with the sun's globe; since in accordance with the kind of observation whereby we feel differences in heat—more heat when the heat is near us and less when it is far away—the sun is not equidistant from all; and it is in this sense that the sun is spoken of [2] as " nearing the borders " of the Aethiopians, not in the sense Onesicritus thinks.

25. The following, too, is one of the things agreed upon by all who maintain the resemblance of India to Aegypt and Aethiopia: that all plains which are not inundated are unproductive for want of water. Nearchus says that the question formerly raised in reference to the Nile as to the source of its floodings is answered by the Indian rivers, because it is the result of the summer rains; but that when Alexander saw crocodiles in the Hydaspes and Aegyptian beans in the Acesines, he thought he had found the sources of the Nile and thought of preparing a fleet for an expedition to Aegypt, thinking that he would sail as

---

[1] *i.e.* of Onesicritus.   [2] *i.e.* by Theodectes.

[3] δέδεκται, CDh*igrxz.*

πλευσόμενον, μικρὸν δ' ὕστερον γνῶναι διότι οὐ
δύναται ὃ ἤλπισε·

μέσσῳ[1] γὰρ μεγάλοι ποταμοὶ καὶ δεινὰ
ῥέεθρα,
'Ωκεανὸς μὲν πρῶτον,

εἰς ὃν ἐκδιδόασιν οἱ 'Ινδικοὶ πάντες ποταμοί·
ἔπειτα ἡ 'Αριανὴ καὶ ὁ Περσικὸς κόλπος καὶ ὁ
'Αράβιος καὶ αὐτὴ ἡ 'Αραβία καὶ ἡ Τρωγλοδυ-
τική.
Τὰ μὲν οὖν περὶ τῶν ἀνέμων καὶ τῶν ὄμβρων
τοιαῦτα λέγεται καὶ τῆς πληρώσεως τῶν ποταμῶν καὶ τῆς ἐπικλύσεως τῶν πεδίων.
26. Δεῖ δὲ καὶ τὰ καθ' ἕκαστα περὶ τῶν
ποταμῶν εἰπεῖν, ὅσα πρὸς τὴν γεωγραφίαν χρήσιμα καὶ ὅσων ἱστορίαν παρειλήφαμεν. ἄλλως
τε γὰρ οἱ ποταμοί, φυσικοί τινες ὅροι καὶ μεγεθῶν
καὶ σχημάτων τῆς χώρας ὄντες, ἐπιτηδειότητα
πολλὴν παρέχουσι πρὸς ὅλην τὴν νῦν ὑπόθεσιν·
C 697 ὁ δὲ Νεῖλος καὶ οἱ κατὰ τὴν 'Ινδικὴν πλεονέκτημά
τι ἔχουσι παρὰ τοὺς ἄλλους διὰ τὸ τὴν χώραν
ἀοίκητον εἶναι χωρὶς αὐτῶν, πλωτὴν ἅμα καὶ
γεωργήσιμον οὖσαν, καὶ μήτ' ἐφοδεύεσθαι δυναμένην ἄλλως, μήτ' οἰκεῖσθαι τὸ παράπαν. τοὺς
μὲν οὖν εἰς τὸν 'Ινδὸν καταφερομένους ἱστοροῦμεν
τοὺς ἀξίους μνήμης καὶ τὰς χώρας, δι' ὧν ἡ φορά,
τῶν δ' ἄλλων ἐστὶν ἄγνοια πλείων ἢ γνῶσις.
'Αλέξανδρος γὰρ ὁ μάλιστα ταῦτ' ἀνακαλύψας
κατ' ἀρχὰς μέν, ἡνίκα οἱ Δαρεῖον δολοφονήσαντες
ὥρμησαν ἐπὶ τὴν τῆς Βακτριανῆς ἀπόστασιν,
ἔγνω προυργιαίτατον ὂν διώκειν καὶ καταλύειν

far as there by this river, but he learned a little later
that he could not accomplish what he had hoped;
" for between are great rivers and dreadful streams,
Oceanus first," [1] into which all the Indian rivers
empty; and then intervene Ariana, and the Persian
and the Arabian Gulfs and Arabia itself and the
Troglodyte country.

Such, then, are the accounts we have of the winds
and the rains, and of the flooding of the rivers, and
of the inundation of the plains.

26. But I must tell also the several details concerning the rivers, so far as they are useful for the
purposes of geography and so far as I have learned
their history. For the rivers in particular, being a
kind of natural boundary for both the size and the
shape of countries, are very convenient for the purposes of the whole of our present subject; but the
Nile and the Indian rivers offer a certain advantage
as compared with the rest because of the fact that
apart from them the countries are uninhabitable,
being at the same time navigable and tillable, and
that they can neither be travelled over otherwise nor
inhabited at all. Now as for the rivers worthy of
mention that flow down into the Indus, I shall tell
their history, as also that of the countries traversed
by them; but as for the rest there is more ignorance
than knowledge. For Alexander, who more than any
other uncovered these regions, at the outset, when
those who had treacherously slain Dareius set out to
cause the revolt of Bactriana, resolved that it would
be most desirable to pursue and overthrow them.

[1] *Odyssey* 11. 157.

---

[1] μέσσῳ, Corais, for μέσον *moxz*, μέσῳ other MSS.

ἐκείνους. ἧκε μὲν οὖν τῆς Ἰνδικῆς πλησίον δι᾽ Ἀριανῶν, ἀφεὶς δ᾽ αὐτὴν ἐν δεξιᾷ ὑπερέβη τὸν Παροπάμισον εἰς τὰ προσάρκτια μέρη καὶ τὴν Βακτριανήν· καταστρεψάμενος δὲ τἀκεῖ πάντα, ὅσα ἦν ὑπὸ Πέρσαις, καὶ ἔτι πλείω, τότ᾽ ἤδη καὶ τῆς Ἰνδικῆς ὠρέχθη, λεγόντων μὲν περὶ αὐτῆς πολλῶν, οὐ σαφῶς δέ. ἀνέστρεψε δ᾽ οὖν ὑπερθεὶς τὰ αὐτὰ ὄρη κατ᾽ ἄλλας ὁδοὺς ἐπιτομωτέρας, ἐν ἀριστερᾷ ἔχων τὴν Ἰνδικήν, εἶτ᾽ ἐπέστρεψεν εὐθὺς ἐπ᾽ αὐτὴν καὶ τοὺς ὅρους τοὺς ἑσπερίους αὐτῆς καὶ¹ τὸν Κώφην ποταμὸν καὶ τὸν Χοάσπην, ὃς εἰς τὸν Κώφην ἐμβάλλει ποταμὸν κατὰ Πλημύριον² πόλιν, ῥυεὶς παρὰ Γώρυδα,³ ἄλλην πόλιν, καὶ διεξιὼν τήν τε Βανδοβηνὴν καὶ τὴν Γανδαρῖτιν. ἐπυνθάνετο δ᾽ οἰκήσιμον εἶναι μάλιστα καὶ εὔκαρπον τὴν ὀρεινὴν καὶ προσάρκτιον· τὴν δὲ νότιον τὴν μὲν ἄνυδρον, τὴν δὲ ποταμόκλυστον καὶ τελέως ἔκπυρον, θηρίοις τε μᾶλλον ἢ ἀνθρώποις σύμμετρον. ὥρμησεν οὖν τὴν ἐπαινουμένην κατακτᾶσθαι πρότερον, ἅμα καὶ τοὺς ποταμοὺς εὐπερατοτέρους νομίσας τῶν πηγῶν πλησίον, οὓς ἀναγκαῖον ἦν διαβαίνειν, ἐπικαρσίους ὄντας καὶ τέμνοντας ἣν ἐπῄει γῆν. ἅμα δὲ καὶ ἤκουσεν εἰς ἓν πλείους συνιόντας ῥεῖν, καὶ τοῦτ᾽ ἀεὶ καὶ μᾶλλον συμβαῖνον, ὅσῳ πλεῖον εἰς τὸ πρόσθεν προΐοιεν,⁴ ὥστ᾽ εἶναι δυσπερατοτέραν, καὶ ταῦτα ἐν πλοίων ἀπορίᾳ. δεδιὼς οὖν τοῦτο διέβη τὸν Κώφην, καὶ κατεστρέφετο τὴν ὀρεινήν, ὅση ἐτέτραπτο πρὸς ἔω.

¹ κατά, after καί, Corais ejects ; so the later editors.
² Πλιγύριον s and on margin of CF, Πληχήριον moxz.
³ Γώρυδα i, Γώρυδι other MSS. ; so Corais and later editors.
⁴ προΐοιεν, Corais, for προΐη E, προιδεῖν other MSS.

He therefore approached India through Ariana, and, leaving India on the right, crossed over Mt. Paropamisus to the northerly parts and Bactriana; and, having subdued everything there that was subject to the Persians and still more, he then forthwith reached out for India too, since many men [1] had been describing it to him, though not clearly. Accordingly he returned, passing over the same mountains by other and shorter roads, keeping India on the left, and then turned immediately towards India and its western boundaries and the Cophes River and the Choaspes, which latter empties into the Cophes River near a city Plemyrium, after flowing past Gorys, another city, and flowing forth through both Bandobenê and Gandaritis. He learned by inquiry that the mountainous and northerly part was the most habitable and fruitful, but that the southerly part was partly without water and partly washed by rivers and utterly hot, more suitable for wild beasts than for human beings. Accordingly, he set out to acquire first the part that was commended to him, at the same time considering that the rivers which it was necessary to cross, since they flow transversely and cut through the country which he meant to traverse, could more easily be crossed near their sources. At the same time he also heard that several rivers flowed together into one stream, and that this was always still more the case the farther forward they advanced, so that the country was more difficult to cross, especially in the event of lack of boats. Afraid of this, therefore, he crossed the Cophes and began to subdue all the mountainous country that faced towards the east.

[1] Historians and geographers who accompanied him.

27. Ἦν δὲ μετὰ τὸν Κώφην ὁ Ἰνδός, εἶθ᾽ ὁ Ὑδάσπης, εἶθ᾽ ὁ Ἀκεσίνης καὶ ὁ Ὑάρωτις, ὕστατος δ᾽ ὁ Ὕπανις. περαιτέρω γὰρ προελθεῖν ἐκωλύθη, τοῦτο μὲν μαντείοις τισὶ προσέχων, τοῦτο δ᾽ ὑπὸ τῆς στρατιᾶς ἀπηγορευκυίας ἤδη πρὸς τοὺς πόνους ἀναγκασθείς· μάλιστα δ᾽ ἐκ τῶν ὑδάτων ἔκαμνον, συνεχῶς ὑόμενοι. ταῦτ᾽ οὖν ἐγένετο γνώριμα ἡμῖν τῶν ἑωθινῶν τῆς Ἰνδικῆς C 698 μερῶν, ὅσα ἐντὸς τοῦ Ὑπάνιος, καὶ εἴ τινα προσιστόρησαν οἱ μετ᾽ ἐκεῖνον περαιτέρω τοῦ Ὑπάνιος προελθόντες μέχρι τοῦ Γάγγου καὶ Παλιβόθρων. μετὰ μὲν οὖν τὸν Κώφην ὁ Ἰνδὸς ῥεῖ· τὰ δὲ μεταξὺ τούτων τῶν δυεῖν ποταμῶν ἔχουσιν Ἀστακηνοί τε καὶ Μασιανοὶ[1] καὶ Νυσαῖοι καὶ Ὑπάσιοι·[2] εἶθ᾽ ἡ Ἀσσακανοῦ, ὅπου Μασόγα[3] πόλις, τὸ βασίλειον τῆς χώρας. ἤδη δὲ πρὸς τῷ Ἰνδῷ πάλιν ἄλλη πόλις Πευκολαῖτις, πρὸς ᾗ ζεῦγμα γενηθὲν ἐπεραίωσε τὴν στρατιάν.

28. Μεταξὺ δὲ τοῦ Ἰνδοῦ καὶ τοῦ Ὑδάσπου Τάξιλά ἐστι, πόλις μεγάλη καὶ εὐνομωτάτη, καὶ ἡ περικειμένη χώρα συχνὴ καὶ σφόδρα εὐδαίμων, ἤδη συνάπτουσα καὶ τοῖς πεδίοις. ἐδέξαντό τε δὴ φιλανθρώπως τὸν Ἀλέξανδρον οἱ ἄνθρωποι καὶ ὁ βασιλεὺς αὐτῶν Ταξίλης· ἔτυχόν τε πλειόνων ἢ αὐτοὶ παρέσχον, ὥστε φθονεῖν τοὺς Μακεδόνας καὶ λέγειν ὡς οὐκ εἶχεν, ὡς ἔοικεν, Ἀλέξανδρος, οὓς εὐεργετήσει πρὶν ἢ διέβη τὸν Ἰνδόν. φασὶ δ᾽ εἶναί τινες τὴν χώραν ταύτην Αἰγύπτου μείζονα.

[1] Βασιανοί Dhi.

[2] Ὑπάσιοι, Tzschucke emends to Ἱππάσιοι, Corais to Ἀσπάσιοι.

[3] Μασόγα, Tzschucke and Corais emend to Μάσσαγα; the MSS. of Arrian (Indica 8) read Μάσσακα.

27. After the Cophes he went to the Indus, then
to the Hydaspes, then to the Acesines and the
Hyarotis, and last to the Hypanis; for he was prevented from advancing farther, partly through
observance of certain oracles and partly because he
was forced by his army, which had already been
worn out by its labours, though they suffered most
of all from the waters, being continually drenched
with rain. Of the eastern parts of India, then,
there have become known to us all those parts which
lie this side the Hypanis, and also any parts beyond
the Hypanis of which an account has been added by
those who, after Alexander, advanced beyond the
Hypanis, as far as the Ganges and Palibothra. Now
after the Cophes follows the Indus; and the region
between these rivers is occupied by Astaceni, Masiani,
Nysaei, and Hypasii; and then one comes to the
country of Assacanus, where is a city Mesoga, the
royal seat of the country; and now near the Indus
again, one comes to another city, Peucolaïtis, near
which a bridge that had already been built afforded
a passage for the army.

28. Between the Indus and the Hydaspes lies
Taxila, a city which is large and has most excellent
laws; and the country that lies round it is spacious
and very fertile, immediately bordering also on the
plains. Both the inhabitants and their king, Taxiles,
received Alexander in a kindly way; and they
obtained from Alexander more gifts than they
themselves presented, so that the Macedonians were
envious and said that Alexander did not have anyone, as it seemed, on whom to bestow his benefac-
tions until he crossed the Indus. Some say that this
country is larger than Aegypt. Above this country

47

ὑπὲρ δὲ ταύτης ἐν τοῖς ὄρεσιν ἡ τοῦ Ἀβισάρου χώρα, παρ' ᾧ δύο δράκοντας ἀπήγγελλον οἱ παρ' αὐτοῦ πρέσβεις τρέφεσθαι, τὸν μὲν ὀγδοήκοντα πηχῶν, τὸν δὲ τετταράκοντα πρὸς τοῖς ἑκατόν, ὡς εἴρηκεν Ὀνησίκριτος· ὃν οὐκ Ἀλεξάνδρου μᾶλλον ἢ τῶν παραδόξων ἀρχικυβερνήτην προσείποι τις ἄν. πάντες μὲν γὰρ οἱ περὶ Ἀλέξανδρον τὸ θαυμαστὸν ἀντὶ τἀληθοῦς ἀπεδέχοντο μᾶλλον, ὑπερβάλλεσθαι δὲ δοκεῖ τοὺς τοσούτους ἐκεῖνος τῇ τερατολογίᾳ. λέγει[1] δ' οὖν τινα καὶ πιθανὰ καὶ μνήμης ἄξια, ὥστε καὶ ἀπιστοῦντα μὴ παρελθεῖν αὐτά. περὶ δ' οὖν τῶν δρακόντων καὶ ἄλλοι λέγουσιν, ὅτι ἐν τοῖς Ἠμωδοῖς ὄρεσι θηρεύουσι καὶ τρέφουσιν ἐν σπηλαίοις.

29. Μεταξὺ δὲ τοῦ Ὑδάσπου καὶ τοῦ Ἀκεσίνου ἥ τε τοῦ Πώρου ἐστί, πολλὴ καὶ ἀγαθή, σχεδόν τι καὶ τριακοσίων πόλεων, καὶ ἡ πρὸς τοῖς Ἠμωδοῖς ὄρεσιν ὕλη, ἐξ ἧς Ἀλέξανδρος κατήγαγε τῷ Ὑδάσπῃ κόψας ἐλάτην τε πολλὴν καὶ πεύκην καὶ κέδρον καὶ ἄλλα παντοῖα στελέχη ναυπηγήσιμα, ἐξ ὧν στόλον κατεσκευάσατο ἐπὶ τῷ Ὑδάσπῃ πρὸς ταῖς ἐκτισμέναις ὑπ' αὐτοῦ πόλεσιν ἐφ' ἑκάτερα τοῦ ποταμοῦ ὅπου τὸν Πῶρον ἐνίκα διαβάς· ὧν τὴν μὲν Βουκεφαλίαν ὠνόμασεν ἀπὸ τοῦ πεσόντος ἵππου κατὰ τὴν μάχην τὴν πρὸς τὸν Πῶρον (ἐκαλεῖτο δὲ Βουκεφάλας ἀπὸ τοῦ πλάτους τοῦ μετώπου· πολεμιστὴς δ' ἦν ἀγαθός, C 699 καὶ ἀεὶ τούτῳ ἐκέχρητο κατὰ τοὺς ἀγῶνας), τὴν δὲ Νίκαιαν ἀπὸ τῆς νίκης ἐκάλεσεν. ἐν δὲ τῇ λεχθείσῃ ὕλῃ καὶ τὸ τῶν κερκοπιθήκων διηγοῦν-

---

[1] λέγει, Corais, for λέγειν; so the later editors.

in the mountains lies the country of Abisarus, who,
according to the ambassadors that came from him,
kept two serpents, one eighty cubits in length and
another one hundred and forty, according to Onesicritus, who cannot so properly be called arch-pilot
of Alexander as of things that are incredible; for
though all the followers of Alexander preferred to
accept the marvellous rather than the true, Onesicritus seems to surpass all those followers of his in
the telling of prodigies. However, he tells some
things that are both plausible and worthy of mention,
and therefore they are not passed by in silence even
by one who disbelieves them. At any rate, others
too speak of the serpents, saying that they are
caught in the Emodi mountains and kept in caves.

29. Between the Hydaspes and the Acesines is,
first, the country of Porus, extensive and fertile,
containing about three hundred cities; and, secondly,
the forest near the Emodi mountains, from which
Alexander cut, and brought down on the Hydaspes,
a large quantity of fir, pine, cedar, and other logs
of all kinds fit for shipbuilding, from which he built
a fleet on the Hydaspes near the cities founded by
him on either side of the river where he crossed and
conquered Porus. Of these cities, he named one
Bucephalia, after Bucephalas, the horse which fell
during the battle with Porus (the horse was called
Bucephalas [1] from the width of his forehead; he
was an excellent war-horse and was always used by
Alexander in his fights); and he called the other
Nicaea, after his victory. In the forest above-
mentioned both the number and the size of the long-

[1] *i.e.* Oxhead.

ται πλῆθος ὑπερβάλλον καὶ τὸ μέγεθος ὁμοίως,
ὥστε τοὺς Μακεδόνας ποτέ, ἰδόντας ἔν τισιν
ἀκρολοφίαις ψιλαῖς ἑστῶτας ἐν τάξει κατὰ
μέτωπον πολλούς (καὶ γὰρ ἀνθρωπονούστατον
εἶναι τὸ ζῷον, οὐχ ἧττον τῶν ἐλεφάντων), στρατο-
πέδου λαβεῖν φαντασίαν καὶ ὁρμῆσαι μὲν ἐπ᾽
αὐτούς, ὡς πολεμίους, μαθόντας δὲ παρὰ Ταξίλου,
συνόντος τότε τῷ βασιλεῖ, τὴν ἀλήθειαν παύσασ-
θαι. ἡ δὲ θήρα τοῦ ζῷου διττή· μιμητικὸν δὲ
καὶ ἐπὶ τὰ δένδρα ἀναφευκτικόν· οἱ οὖν θηρεύοντες,
ἐπὰν ἴδωσιν ἐπὶ δένδρων ἱδρυμένον, ἐν ὄψει θέντες
τρυβλίον ὕδωρ ἔχον, τοὺς ἑαυτῶν ὀφθαλμοὺς
ἐναλείφουσιν ἐξ αὐτοῦ· εἶτ᾽, ἀντὶ τοῦ ὕδατος
ἰξοῦ τρυβλίον θέντες, ἀπίασι καὶ λοχῶσι πόρρω-
θεν· ἐπὰν δὲ καταπηδῆσαν τὸ θηρίον ἐγχρίσηται
τοῦ ἰξοῦ, καταμύσαντος δ᾽ ἀποληφθῇ[1] τὰ βλέ-
φαρα, ἐπιόντες ζωγροῦσιν. εἷς μὲν οὖν[2] τρόπος
οὗτος, ἄλλος δέ· ὑποδυσάμενοι θυλάκους, ὡς
ἀναξυρίδας, ἀπίασιν, ἄλλους καταλιπόντες
δασεῖς, τὰ ἐντὸς κεχρισμένους ἰξῷ· ἐνδύντας δὲ
εἰς αὐτοὺς ῥᾳδίως αἱροῦσι.

30. Καὶ τὴν Κάθαιαν[3] δέ τινες καὶ[4] τὴν
Σωπείθους, τῶν νομαρχῶν τινος, κατὰ τήνδε τὴν
μεσοποταμίαν τιθέασιν· ἄλλοι δὲ καὶ τοῦ
Ἀκεσίνου πέραν καὶ τοῦ Ὑαρώτιδος, ὅμορον τῇ
Πώρου τοῦ ἑτέρου, ὃς ἦν ἀνεψιὸς τοῦ ὑπ᾽ Ἀλε-
ξάνδρου ἁλόντος· καλοῦσι δὲ Γανδαρίδα τὴν ὑπὸ

---

[1] Instead of ἀποληφθῇ, CDhixw read ἀπολειφθῇ (corrected
to ἀπολήφθη in Dh); ἀλειφθῇ mo, Casaubon and Tzschucke;
ἐπαλειφθῇ, Corais.
[2] οὖν omitted by all MSS. except Dhi.
[3] Κάθαιαν, Tzschucke, for Καθέαν; so the later editors.
[4] καί, Corais inserts (citing Diodorus 17. 91).

tailed apes [1] are alike described as so extraordinary that once the Macedonians, seeing many of these standing as in front-line array on some bare hills (for this animal is very human-like in mentality, no less so than the elephant), got the impression that they were an army of men; and they actually set out to attack them as human enemies, but on learning the truth from Taxiles, who was then with the king, desisted. The capture of the animal is effected in two ways. It is an imitative animal and takes to flight up in the trees. Now the hunters, when they see an ape seated on a tree, place in sight a bowl containing water and rub their own eyes with it; and then they put down a bowl of bird-lime instead of the water, go away, and lie in wait at a distance; and when the animal leaps down and besmears itself with the bird-lime, and when, upon winking, its eyelids are shut together, the hunters approach and take it alive. Now this is one way, but there is another. They put on baggy breeches like trousers and then go away, leaving behind them others that are shaggy and smeared inside with bird-lime; and when the animals put these on, they are easily captured.

30. Some put both Cathaea and the country of Sopeithes, one of the provincial chiefs, between these two rivers,[2] but others on the far side of the Acesines and the Hyarotis, as bordering on the country of the second Porus, who was a cousin [3] of the Porus captured by Alexander. The country that was subject

[1] The species *cercopitheces* (for a fuller description see 15. 1. 37).

[2] The Hydaspes and Acesines.

[3] Or " nephew."

τούτῳ χώραν. ἐν δὲ τῇ Καθαίᾳ¹ καινότατον
ἱστορεῖται τὸ περὶ τοῦ κάλλους, ὅτι τιμᾶται
διαφερόντως, ὡς ἵππων καὶ κυνῶν· βασιλέα τε
γὰρ τὸν κάλλιστον αἱρεῖσθαί φησιν Ὀνησίκριτος,
γενόμενόν τε παιδίον μετὰ δίμηνον κρίνεσθαι
δημοσίᾳ, πότερον ἔχοι τὴν ἔννομον μορφὴν καὶ
τοῦ ζῆν ἀξίαν, ἢ οὔ· κριθέντα δ' ὑπὸ τοῦ ἀπο-
δειχθέντος ἄρχοντος ζῆν ἢ θανατοῦσθαι· βάπτεσ-
θαί τε πολλοῖς εὐανθεστάτοις χρώμασι τοὺς
πώγωνας αὐτοῦ τούτου χάριν, καλλωπιζομένους·
τοῦτο δὲ καὶ ἄλλους² ποιεῖν ἐπιμελῶς συχνοὺς
τῶν Ἰνδῶν (καὶ γὰρ δὴ φέρειν τὴν χώραν χρόας
θαυμαστὰς) καὶ θριξὶ καὶ ἐσθῆσι· τοὺς δ' ἀνθρώπους τὰ ἄλλα μὲν εὐτελεῖς εἶναι, φιλοκόσμους δέ.
ἴδιον δὲ τῶν Καθαίων³ καὶ τοῦτο ἱστορεῖται, τὸ
αἱρεῖσθαι νυμφίον καὶ νύμφην ἀλλήλους καὶ τὸ
συγκατακαίεσθαι τεθνεῶσι τοῖς ἀνδράσι τὰς
γυναῖκας κατὰ τοιαύτην αἰτίαν, ὅτι ἐρῶσαί ποτε
C 700 τῶν νέων ἀφίσταιντο⁴ τῶν ἀνδρῶν ἢ φαρμακεύοιεν
αὐτούς· νόμον οὖν θέσθαι τοῦτον, ὡς παυσομένης
τῆς φαρμακείας. οὐ πιθανῶς μὲν οὖν ὁ νόμος,
οὐδ' ἡ αἰτία λέγεται. φασὶ δ' ἐν τῇ Σωπείθους
χώρᾳ ὀρυκτῶν ἁλῶν ὄρος εἶναι, ἀρκεῖν δυνάμενον
ὅλῃ τῇ Ἰνδικῇ· καὶ χρυσεῖα δὲ καὶ ἀργυρεῖα οὐ
πολὺ ἄπωθεν ἐν ἄλλοις ὄρεσιν ἱστορεῖται καλά,
ὡς ἐδήλωσε Γόργος ὁ μεταλλευτής. οἱ δ' Ἰνδοὶ
μεταλλείας καὶ χωνείας ἀπείρως ἔχοντες, οὐδ' ὧν

---

¹ Καθαίᾳ, Tzschucke and later editors, for Καθέα.
² ἄλλους, his, ἄλλως other MSS.
³ Καθαίων, Tzschucke and later editors, for Καθέων.
⁴ ἀφίσταιντο, Corais and later editors, for ἀφίστατο.

to him is called Gandaris. As for Cathaea, a most
novel regard for beauty there is reported; I mean
that it is prized in an exceptional manner, as, for
example, for the beauty of its horses and dogs; and,
in fact, Onesicritus says that they choose the hand-
somest person as king, and that a child is judged in
public after it is two months old as to whether it has
the beauty of form required by law and is worthy
to live or not; and that when it is judged by the
appointed magistrate it is allowed to live or is put
to death; and that the men dye their beards with
many most florid colours for the sole reason that
they wish to beautify themselves; and that this
practice is carefully followed by numerous other
Indian peoples also (for the country produces marvellous colours, he says), who dye both their hair
and their garments; and that the people, though
shabby in every other way, are fond of adornment.
The following too is reported as a custom peculiar
to the Cathaeans: the groom and bride choose one
another themselves, and wives are burned up with
their deceased husbands for a reason of this kind—
that they sometimes fell in love with young men
and deserted their husbands or poisoned them; and
therefore the Cathaeans established this as a law,
thinking that they would put a stop to the poison-
ing. However, the law is not stated in a plausible
manner, nor the cause of it either. It is said that
in the country of Sopeithes there is a mountain of
mineral salt sufficient for the whole of India. And
gold and silver mines are reported in other mountains not far away, excellent mines, as has been
plainly shown by Gorgus the mining expert. But
since the Indians are inexperienced in mining and

53

εὐποροῦσιν ἴσασιν, ἀλλ᾽ ἁπλούστερον μεταχειρί-
ζονται τὸ πρᾶγμα.

31. Ἐν δὲ τῇ Σωπείθους καὶ τὰς τῶν κυνῶν
ἀρετὰς διηγοῦνται θαυμαστάς· λαβεῖν γοῦν τὸν
Ἀλέξανδρον παρὰ τοῦ Σωπείθους κύνας πεντήκοντα καὶ ἑκατόν· διαπείρας δὲ χάριν λέοντι
προσαφέντας[1] δύο, κρατουμένων[2] αὐτῶν, δύο
ἄλλους ἐπαφεῖναι· τότε δ᾽ ἤδη καθεστώτων εἰς
ἀντίπαλα, τὸν μὲν Σωπείθη κελεῦσαι τῶν κυνῶν
ἕνα ἀποσπᾶν τοῦ σκέλους τινὰ λαβόμενον, ἐὰν
δὲ μὴ ὑπακούῃ, ἀποτεμεῖν· τὸν Ἀλέξανδρον δὲ
κατ᾽ ἀρχὰς μὲν οὐ συγχωρεῖν ἀποτεμεῖν, φειδόμενον
τοῦ κυνός, εἰπόντος δ᾽, ὅτι Τέτταρας ἀντιδώσω
σοι, συγχωρῆσαι, καὶ τὸν κύνα περιιδεῖν ἀποτμη-
θέντα τὸ σκέλος βραδείᾳ τομῇ, πρὶν ἀνεῖναι τὸ
δῆγμα.

32. Ἡ μὲν οὖν μέχρι τοῦ Ὑδάσπου ὁδὸς
τὸ πλέον ἦν ἐπὶ μεσημβρίαν, ἡ δ᾽ ἐνθένδε
πρὸς ἕω μᾶλλον μέχρι τοῦ Ὑπάνιος, ἅπασα
δὲ τῆς ὑπωρείας μᾶλλον ἢ τῶν πεδίων ἐχο-
μένη. ὁ δ᾽ οὖν Ἀλέξανδρος ἀπὸ τοῦ Ὑπάνιος
ἀναστρέψας ἐπὶ τὸν Ὑδάσπην καὶ τὸν ναύ-
σταθμον, ἠρτικρότει[3] τὸν στόλον, εἶτ᾽ ἔπλει
τῷ Ὑδάσπῃ, πάντες δ᾽ οἱ λεχθέντες ποταμοὶ συμ-
βάλλουσιν εἰς ἕνα τὸν Ἰνδόν· ὕστατος δ᾽ ὁ Ὑπανις·
πεντεκαίδεκα δὲ τοὺς σύμπαντας συρρεῖν φασι,
τούς γε ἀξιολόγους· πληρωθεὶς δ᾽ ἐκ πάντων
ὥστε καὶ ἐφ᾽ ἑκατὸν σταδίους, ὡς οἱ μὴ μετριά-
ζοντές φασιν, εὐρύνεσθαι κατά τινας τόπους,

---

[1] προσαφέντος CFwx, προσαφέντα moz.
[2] δ᾽, before αὐτῶν, Corais and later editors omit.
[3] Instead of ἠρτικρότει, F reads ἠρτικροτι (sic), C ἠρτικότι

smelting, they also do not know what their resources are, and handle the business in a rather simple manner.

31. Writers narrate also the excellent qualities of the dogs in the country of Sopeithes. They say, at any rate, that Alexander received one hundred and fifty dogs from Sopeithes; and that, to prove them, two were let loose to attack a lion, and, when they were being overpowered, two others were let loose upon him, and that then, the match having now become equal, Sopeithes bade someone to take one of the dogs by the leg and pull him away, and if the dog did not yield to cut off his leg; and that Alexander would not consent to cutting off the dog's leg at first, wishing to spare the dog, but consented when Sopeithes said that he would give him four instead; and that the dog suffered the cutting off of his leg by slow amputation before he let go his grip.

32. Now the march to the Hydaspes was for the most part towards the south, but from there to the Hypanis it was more towards the east, and as a whole it kept to the foothills more than to the plains. At all events, Alexander, when he returned from the Hypanis to the Hydaspes and the naval station, proceeded to make ready his fleet and then to set sail on the Hydaspes. All the above-mentioned rivers, last of all the Hypanis, unite in one river, the Indus; and it is said that the Indus is joined by fifteen noteworthy rivers all told, and that after being filled so full by all that it is widened in some places, according to writers who are immoderate, even to the extent of one hundred stadia, but, according to the more

(corrected to συνεκρότει), D*h* ἠρτικρότη, *i* ἀρτικρότη, and other MSS. and editors before Kramer συνεκρότει.

ὡς δ' οἱ μετριώτεροι, πεντήκοντα τὸ πλεῖστον,
ἐλάχιστον δὲ ἑπτά (καὶ πολλὰ ἔθνη καὶ πόλεις
εἰσὶ[1] πέριξ[2]), ἔπειτα δυσὶ στόμασιν εἰς τὴν νοτίαν
ἐκδίδωσι θάλατταν καὶ τὴν Παταληνὴν προσα-
γορευομένην ποιεῖ νῆσον. ταύτην δ' ἔσχε τὴν
διάνοιαν Ἀλέξανδρος, ἀφεὶς τὰ πρὸς ἕω μέρη
πρῶτον μὲν διὰ τὸ κωλυθῆναι διαβῆναι τὸν
Ὕπανιν, ἔπειτα καὶ ψευδῆ καταμαθὼν τῇ πείρᾳ
τὸν προκατέχοντα λόγον, ὡς ἔκπυρα εἴη καὶ
θηρίοις μᾶλλον οἰκήσιμα τὰ ἐν τοῖς πεδίοις ἢ
ἀνθρωπείῳ γένει· διόπερ ὥρμησεν ἐπὶ ταῦτα,
ἀφεὶς ἐκεῖνα, ὥστε καὶ ἐγνώσθη ταῦτα ἀντ'
ἐκείνων ἐπὶ πλέον.

33. Ἡ μὲν οὖν μεταξὺ τοῦ Ὑπάνιος καὶ τοῦ
C 701 Ὑδάσπου λέγεται ἐννέα ἔχειν ἔθνη, πόλεις δὲ
εἰς πεντακισχιλίας οὐκ ἐλάττους Κῶ τῆς Μερο-
πίδος· δοκεῖ δὲ πρὸς ὑπερβολὴν εἰρῆσθαι τὸ
πλῆθος. ἡ δὲ μεταξὺ τοῦ Ἰνδοῦ καὶ τοῦ Ὑδάσπου,
εἴρηται σχεδόν τι, ὑφ' ὧν οἰκεῖται τῶν ἀξίων
μνήμης. κάτω δ' ἑξῆς εἰσιν οἵ τε Σίβαι λεγόμενοι,
περὶ ὧν καὶ πρότερον ἐμνήσθημεν, καὶ Μαλλοὶ
καὶ Συδράκαι,[3] μεγάλα ἔθνη. καὶ Μαλλοὶ μέν,
παρ' οἷς ἀποθανεῖν ἐκινδύνευσεν Ἀλέξανδρος,
τρωθεὶς ἐν ἁλώσει πολίχνης τινός, Συδράκαι[4]
δέ, οὓς τοῦ Διονύσου συγγενεῖς ἔφαμεν μεμυ-
θεῦσθαι. πρὸς αὐτῇ δ' ἤδη τῇ Παταληνῇ τήν
τε τοῦ Μουσικανοῦ λέγουσι καὶ τὴν Σάβου, οὗ

[1] εἰσί DF, εἶναι other MSS.
[2] καὶ πολλὰ . . . πέριξ, Meineke ejects, following conj. of
Kramer.
[3] Σιδράκαι Dhi, Ὀξυδράκαι E.
[4] Συδράκαι F (corrected in margin to Ὀξυδράκαι), Ὀξυδράκαι
other MSS.

moderate, fifty at the most and seven at the least
(and there are many tribes and cities all about it),[1]
it then empties into the southern sea by two mouths
and forms the island called Patalenê. Alexander
conceived this purpose [2] after dismissing from his
mind the parts towards the east; first, because he
had been prevented from crossing the Hypanis, and,
secondly, because he had learned by experience the
falsity of the report which had preoccupied his mind,
that the parts in the plains were burning hot and
more habitable for wild beasts than for a human
race; [3] and therefore he set out for these parts,
dismissing those others, so that the former became
better known than those others.

33. Now the country between the Hypanis and the
Hydaspes is said to contain nine tribes, and also cities
to the number of five thousand—cities no smaller than
Cos Meropis,[4] though the number stated seems to be
excessive. And as for the country between the Indus
and the Hydaspes, I have stated approximately the
peoples worthy of mention by which it is inhabited; [5]
and below them, next in order, are the people called
Sibae, whom I have mentioned before,[6] and the
Malli and the Sydracae, large tribes. It was in the
country of the Malli that Alexander was in peril of
death, being wounded in the capture of some small
city; and as for the Sydracae, I have already spoken
of them as mythically akin to Dionysus.[7] Near
Patalenê, they say, one comes at once to the country
of Musicanus, and to that of Sabus, where is Sindo-

---

[1] The words in parenthesis are probably a gloss.
[2] *i.e.* to turn back from the Hypanis.   [3] See § 26.
[4] See 14. 2. 19.   [5] § 28 above.
[6] § 8 above.   [7] § 8 above.

τὰ Σινδόμανα,¹ καὶ ἔτι τὴν Πορτικανοῦ καὶ ἄλλων, ὧν ἐκράτησεν ἁπάντων Ἀλέξανδρος, τὴν τοῦ Ἰνδοῦ παροικούντων ποταμίαν, ὑστάτης δὲ τῆς Παταληνῆς, ἣν ὁ Ἰνδὸς ποιεῖ, σχισθεὶς εἰς δύο προχοάς. Ἀριστόβουλος μὲν οὖν εἰς χιλίους σταδίους διέχειν ἀλλήλων φησὶν αὐτάς, Νέαρχος δ' ὀκτακοσίους προστίθησιν, Ὀνησίκριτος δὲ τὴν πλευρὰν ἑκάστην τῆς ἀπολαμβανομένης νήσου τριγώνου τὸ σχῆμα δισχιλίων, τοῦ δὲ ποταμοῦ τὸ πλάτος, καθ' ὃ σχίζεται εἰς τὰ στόματα, ὅσον διακοσίων·² καλεῖ δὲ τὴν νῆσον Δέλτα, καί φησιν ἴσην εἶναι τοῦ κατ' Αἴγυπτον Δέλτα, οὐκ ἀληθὲς τοῦτο λέγων. τὸ γὰρ κατ' Αἴγυπτον Δέλτα χιλίων καὶ τριακοσίων λέγεται σταδίων ἔχειν τὴν βάσιν, τὰς δὲ πλευρὰς ἑκατέραν ἐλάττω τῆς βάσεως. ἐν δὲ τῇ Παταληνῇ πόλις ἐστὶν ἀξιόλογος τὰ Πάταλα, ἀφ' ἧς καὶ ἡ νῆσος καλεῖται.

34. Φησὶ δ' Ὀνησίκριτος τὴν πλείστην παραλίαν τὴν ταύτῃ πολὺ τὸ τεναγῶδες ἔχειν, καὶ μάλιστα κατὰ τὰ στόματα τῶν ποταμῶν, διά τε τὴν χοῦν καὶ τὰς πλημμυρίδας καὶ τὸ μὴ πνεῖν ἀπογαίους,³ ἀλλ' ὑπὸ τῶν πελαγίων ἀνέμων κατέχεσθαι τούτους τοὺς τόπους τὸ πλέον. λέγει δὲ καὶ περὶ τῆς Μουσικανοῦ χώρας ἐπὶ πλέον ἐγκωμιάζων αὐτήν, ὧν τινα κοινὰ καὶ ἄλλοις Ἰνδοῖς ἱστόρηται, ὡς τὸ μακρόβιον, ὥστε καὶ τριάκοντα ἐπὶ τοῖς ἑκατὸν προσλαμβάνειν (καὶ

¹ σαβούτα σινδοναλίαν *moz*; σαβούτα σινδολίαν *sw*; σάβου τὰ σινδονάλια CDF*h*, Tzschucke and Corais; Σάβου, τὰ Σινδόμανα Meineke, and so Kramer, who, however, inserts οὗ after Σάβου.
² For διακοσίων Groskurd conj. εἴκοσι, Kramer (citing Arrian 5. 20) ἑκατόν.

mana, and also to the country of Porticanus and others, who, one and all, were conquered by Alexander, these peoples dwelling along the river-lands of the Indus; but last of all to Patalenê, a country formed by the Indus, which branches into two mouths. Now Aristobulus says that these mouths are one thousand stadia distant from one another, but Nearchus adds eight hundred; and Onesicritus reckons each of the two sides of the included island, which is triangular in shape, at two thousand, and the width of the river, where it branches into the mouths, at about two hundred; and he calls the island Delta, and says that it is equal in size to the Aegyptian Delta, a statement which is not true. For it is said that the Aegyptian Delta has a base of one thousand three hundred stadia, though each of the two sides is shorter than the base. In Patalenê there is a noteworthy city, Patala, after which the island is named.

34. Onesicritus says that most of the seaboard in this part of the world abounds in shoals, particularly at the mouths of the rivers, on account of the silt and the overflows and also of the fact that no breezes blow from the land, and that this region is subject for the most part to winds that blow from the high sea. He describes also the country of Musicanus, lauding it rather at length for things of which some are reported as common also to other Indians, as, for example, their length of life, thirty years beyond one hundred (and indeed some say

---

[3] ἀπογαίους, Casaubon, for ἀπὸ γέας CF*moz*, ἀπὸ γαίας D*i*, ὑπογαίας *i*, ἀπογαίας *sx*.

γὰρ τοὺς Σῆρας ἔτι τούτων μακροβιωτέρους τινές φασι) καὶ τὸ λιτόβιον καὶ τὸ ὑγιεινόν, καίπερ τῆς χώρας ἀφθονίαν ἁπάντων ἐχούσης. ἴδιον δὲ τὸ συσσίτιά τινα Λακωνικὰ αὐτοῖς εἶναι δημοσίᾳ σιτουμένων, ὄψα δ' ἐκ θήρας ἐχόντων· καὶ τὸ χρυσῷ μὴ χρῆσθαι, μηδ' ἀργύρῳ, μετάλλων ὄντων· καὶ τὸ ἀντὶ δούλων τοῖς ἐν ἀκμῇ χρῆσθαι νέοις, ὡς Κρῆτες μὲν τοῖς Ἀφαμιώταις, Λάκωνες δὲ τοῖς Εἵλωσι· μὴ ἀκριβοῦν δὲ τὰς ἐπιστήμας πλὴν ἰατρικῆς· ἐπί τινων γὰρ κακουργίαν εἶναι C 702 τὴν ἐπὶ πλέον ἄσκησιν, οἷον ἐπὶ τῆς πολεμικῆς[1] καὶ τῶν ὁμοίων· δίκην δὲ μὴ εἶναι πλὴν φόνου καὶ ὕβρεως· οὐκ ἐπ' αὐτῷ γὰρ τὸ μὴ παθεῖν ταῦτα, τὰ δ' ἐν τοῖς συμβολαίοις ἐπ' αὐτῷ ἑκάστῳ, ὥστε ἀνέχεσθαι δεῖ, ἐάν τις παραβῇ τὴν πίστιν, ἀλλὰ καὶ προσέχειν, ὅτῳ πιστευτέον, καὶ μὴ δικῶν πληροῦν τὴν πόλιν. ταῦτα μὲν οἱ μετ' Ἀλεξάνδρου στρατεύσαντες λέγουσιν.

35. Ἐκδέδοται δέ τις καὶ Κρατεροῦ πρὸς τὴν μητέρα Ἀριστοπάτραν ἐπιστολή, πολλά τε ἄλλα παράδοξα φράζουσα καὶ οὐχ ὁμολογοῦσα οὐδενί, καὶ δὴ καὶ τὸ μέχρι τοῦ Γάγγου προελθεῖν τὸν Ἀλέξανδρον. αὐτός τέ φησιν ἰδεῖν τὸν ποταμὸν καὶ κήτη τὰ ἐπ' αὐτῷ καὶ μεγέθος καὶ πλάτους καὶ βάθους πόρρω πίστεως μᾶλλον ἢ ἐγγύς. ὅτι μὲν γὰρ μέγιστος τῶν μνημονευομένων κατὰ τὰς τρεῖς ἠπείρους, καὶ μετ' αὐτὸν ὁ Ἰνδός, τρίτος δὲ καὶ τέταρτος ὁ Ἴστρος καὶ ὁ Νεῖλος, ἱκανῶς

---

[1] τῆς πολεμικῆς EF, τοῖς πολεμικοῖς other MSS.

---

[1] See 10. 4. 16, 20.

that the Seres live still longer than this), and their
healthfulness, and simple diet, even though their
country has an abundance of everything. Peculiar
to them is the fact that they have a kind of Laconian
common mess,[1] where they eat in public and use as
food the meat of animals taken in the chase; and
that they do not use gold or silver, although they
have mines; and that instead of slaves they use
young men in the vigour of life, as the Cretans use
the Aphamiotae and the Laconians the Helots;[2]
and that they make no accurate study of the sciences
except that of medicine, for they regard too much
training in some of them as wickedness; for example,
military science and the like; and that they have
no process at law except for murder and outrage, for
it is not in one's power to avoid suffering these,
whereas the content of contracts is in the power of
each man himself, so that he is required to endure
it if anyone breaks faith with him, and also to consider carefully who should be trusted and not to fill
the city with lawsuits. This is the account of those
who made the expedition with Alexander.

35. But there has also been published a letter of
Craterus to his mother Aristopatra, which alleges
many other strange things and agrees with no one
else, particularly in saying that Alexander advanced
as far as the Ganges. And he says that he himself
saw the river and monsters on its banks, and a magni-
tude both of width and of depth which is remote
from credibility rather than near it. Indeed, it is
sufficiently agreed that the Ganges is the largest of
known rivers on the three continents, and after it
the Indus, and third and fourth the Ister and the

[2] See 8. 5. 4 and 12. 3. 4.

STRABO

συμφωνεῖται· τὰ καθ' ἕκαστα δ' ἄλλοι ἄλλως
περὶ αὐτοῦ λέγουσιν, οἱ μὲν τριάκοντα σταδίων
τοὐλάχιστον πλάτος, οἱ δὲ καὶ τριῶν, Μεγασθένης
δέ, ὅταν ᾖ μέτριος καὶ εἰς ἑκατὸν εὐρύνεσθαι,
βάθος δὲ εἴκοσι ὀργυιῶν τοὐλάχιστον.

36. Ἐπὶ δὲ τῇ συμβολῇ τούτου τε καὶ τοῦ
ἄλλου ποταμοῦ[1] τὰ Παλίβοθρα ἱδρῦσθαι, σταδίων
ὀγδοήκοντα τὸ μῆκος, πλάτος δὲ πεντεκαίδεκα,
ἐν παραλληλογράμμῳ σχήματι, ξύλινον περίβολον ἔχουσαν κατατετρημένον, ὥστε διὰ τῶν
ὀπῶν τοξεύειν· προκεῖσθαι δὲ καὶ τάφρον φυλακῆς
τε χάριν καὶ ὑποδοχῆς τῶν ἐκ τῆς πόλεως ἀπορ-
ροιῶν· τὸ δ' ἔθνος, ἐν ᾧ ἡ πόλις αὕτη, καλεῖσθαι
Πρασίους, διαφορώτατον τῶν πάντων· τὸν δὲ
βασιλεύοντα ἐπώνυμον δεῖν[2] τῆς πόλεως εἶναι,
Παλίβοθρον καλούμενον πρὸς τῷ ἰδίῳ τῷ ἐκ
γενετῆς ὀνόματι, καθάπερ τὸν Σανδρόκοττον, πρὸς
ὃν ἧκεν ὁ Μεγασθένης πεμφθείς. τοιοῦτο δὲ καὶ
τὸ παρὰ τοῖς Παρθυαίοις· Ἀρσάκαι γὰρ καλοῦνται
πάντες, ἰδίᾳ δὲ ὁ μὲν Ὀρώδης,[3] ὁ δὲ Φραάτης, ὁ
δ' ἄλλο τι.

37. Ἀρίστη δ' ὁμολογεῖται πᾶσα ἡ τοῦ Ὑπάνιος
πέραν· οὐκ ἀκριβοῦνται δέ, ἀλλὰ διὰ τὴν ἄγνοιαν
καὶ τὸν ἐκτοπισμὸν λέγεται πάντ' ἐπὶ τὸ μεῖζον

[1] After ποταμοῦ Meineke inserts Ἐραννοβόα, following
Arrian, Indica 10.
[2] δεῖν F, δεῖ other MSS.
[3] Ἡρώδης moxz.

[1] More than twelve miles.
[2] About 120 feet. " According to the latest calculations,
the length of the main stream of the Ganges is 1540 m., or
with its longest affluent, 1680; breadth at true entrance into

Nile; but the several details concerning it are stated differently by different writers, some putting its minimum breadth at thirty stadia and others even at three, whereas Megasthenes says that when its breadth is medium it widens even to one hundred stadia [1] and that its least depth is twenty fathoms.[2]

36. It is said that Palibothra lies at the confluence of the Ganges and the other river,[3] a city eighty stadia in length and fifteen in breadth, in the shape of a parallelogram, and surrounded by a wooden wall that is perforated so that arrows can be shot through the holes; and that in front of the wall lies a trench used both for defence and as a receptacle of the sewage that flows from the city; and that the tribe of people amongst whom this city is situated is called the Prasii and is far superior to all the rest; and that the reigning king must be surnamed after the city, being called Palibothrus in addition to his own family name, as, for example, King Sandrocottus to whom Megasthenes was sent on an embassy.[4] Such is also the custom among the Parthians; for all are called Arsaces, although personally one king is called Orodes, another Phraates, and another something else.

37. Writers are agreed that the country as a whole on the far side of the Hypanis is best; but they do not describe it accurately, and because of their ignorance and of its remoteness magnify all things

the sea, 20 m.; breadth of channel in dry season, $1\frac{1}{4}$ to $2\frac{1}{4}$ m.; depth in dry season, 30 ft." (Holdich, in *Encyc. Britannica*.)
   [3] The Erannoboas (now the Sone), according to Groskurd (who cites Arrian, *Indica* 10) and the later editors (see critical note).
   [4] See 2. 1. 9.

ἢ τὸ τερατωδέστερον· οἶα τὰ τῶν χρυσωρύχων
μυρμήκων καὶ ἄλλων θηρίων τε καὶ ἀνθρώπων
ἰδιομόρφων καὶ δυνάμεσί τισιν ἐξηλλαγμένων·
ὡς τοὺς Σῆρας μακροβίους φασί, πέρα καὶ
διακοσίων ἐτῶν παρατείνοντας. λέγουσι δὲ καὶ
ἀριστοκρατικήν τινα σύνταξιν πολιτείας αὐτόθι
ἐκ πεντακισχιλίων βουλευτῶν συνεστῶσαν, ὧν
C 703 ἕκαστον παρέχεσθαι τῷ κοινῷ ἐλέφαντα. καὶ
τίγρεις δ᾽ ἐν τοῖς Πρασίοις φησὶν ὁ Μεγασθένης
μεγίστους γίνεσθαι, σχεδὸν δέ τι καὶ διπλασίους
λεόντων, δυνατοὺς δέ, ὥστε τῶν ἡμέρων τινά,
ἀγόμενον ὑπὸ τεττάρων, τῷ ὀπισθίῳ σκέλει δραξά-
μενον ἡμιόνου, βιάσασθαι καὶ ἑλκύσαι πρὸς
ἑαυτόν· κερκοπιθήκους δὲ μείζους τῶν μεγίστων
κυνῶν, λευκοὺς πλὴν τοῦ προσώπου· τοῦτο δ᾽
εἶναι μέλαν (παρ᾽ ἄλλοις δ᾽ ἀνάπαλιν), τὰς δὲ
κέρκους μείζους δυεῖν πήχεων, ἡμερωτάτους δὲ
καὶ οὐ κακοήθεις περὶ ἐπιθέσεις καὶ κλοπάς·
λίθους δ᾽ ὀρύττεσθαι λιβανόχρους, γλυκυτέρους
σύκων ἢ μέλιτος· ἀλλαχοῦ δὲ διπήχεις ὄφεις
ὑμενοπτέρους, ὥσπερ αἱ νυκτερίδες, καὶ τούτους
δὲ νύκτωρ πέτεσθαι, σταλαγμοὺς ἀφιέντας οὔρων,
τοὺς δὲ ἱδρώτων, διασήποντας τὸν χρῶτα τοῦ μὴ
φυλαξαμένου· καὶ σκορπίους εἶναι πτηνούς, ὑπερβάλλοντας μεγέθεσι· φύεσθαι δὲ καὶ ἔβενον·
εἶναι δὲ καὶ κύνας ἀλκίμους, οὐ πρότερον μεθιέν-
τας τὸ δηχθέν, πρὶν εἰς τοὺς ῥώθωνας ὕδωρ κατα-

---

[1] See 2. 1. 9.
[2] Apparently an imaginary creature (sometimes called " ant-
lion ") with the fore-parts of a lion and the hind-parts of an
ant. Herodotus (3. 102) describes it as " smaller than a dog

or make them more marvellous.[1] For example, the stories of the ants that mine gold[2] and of other creatures, both beasts and human beings, which are of peculiar form and in respect to certain natural powers have undergone complete changes, as, for example, the Seres, who, they say, are long-lived, and prolong their lives even beyond two hundred years. They tell also of a kind of aristocratic order of government that was composed outright of five thousand counsellors, each of whom furnishes the new commonwealth with an elephant. Megasthenes says that the largest tigers are found among the Prasii, even nearly twice as large as lions, and so powerful that a tame one, though being led by four men, seized[3] a mule by the hind leg and by force drew the mule to itself; and that the long-tailed apes are larger than the largest dogs, are white except their faces, which are black (the contrary is the case elsewhere), that their tails are more than two cubits long, and that they are very tame and not malicious as regards attacks and thefts; and that stones are dug up of the colour of frankincense and sweeter than figs or honey; and that in other places there are reptiles two cubits long with membranous wings like bats, and that they too fly by night, discharging drops of urine, or also of sweat, which putrefy the skin of anyone who is not on his guard; and that there are winged scorpions of surpassing size; and that ebony is also produced; and that there are also brave dogs, which do not let go the object bitten till water is poured down into their nostrils;

but larger than a fox." Strabo elsewhere (16. 4. 15) refers to " lions called ants."

[3] The Greek word suggests seizing *with the claws*, not *with the teeth*.

χυθῆναι· ἐνίους δ' ὑπὸ προθυμίας ἐν τῷ δήγματι διαστρέφεσθαι τοὺς ὀφθαλμούς, τοῖς δὲ καὶ ἐκπίπτειν· κατασχεθῆναι δὲ καὶ λέοντα ὑπὸ κυνὸς καὶ ταῦρον, τὸν δὲ ταῦρον καὶ ἀποθανεῖν, κρατούμενον τοῦ ῥύγχους, πρότερον ἢ ἀφεθῆναι.

38. Ἐν δὲ τῇ ὀρεινῇ Σίλαν[1] ποταμὸν εἶναι, ᾧ μηδὲν ἐπιπλεῖ· Δημόκριτον μὲν οὖν ἀπιστεῖν, ἅτε πολλὴν τῆς Ἀσίας πεπλανημένον· καὶ Ἀριστοτέλης δὲ ἀπιστεῖ, καίπερ[2] ἀέρων ὄντων λεπτῶν, οἷς οὐδὲν ἐποχεῖται πτηνόν· ἔτι δὲ τῶν ἀναφερομένων ἀτμῶν ἐπισπαστικοί τινές εἰσι πρὸς ἑαυτοὺς καὶ οἷον ῥοφητικοὶ τοῦ ὑπερπετοῦς, ὡς τὸ ἤλεκτρον τοῦ ἀχύρου καὶ ἡ σιδηρῖτις τοῦ σιδήρου· τάχα δὲ καὶ καθ' ὕδατος τοιαῦταί τινες εἶεν ἂν δυνάμεις. ταῦτα μὲν οὖν φυσιολογίας ἔχεταί τινος καὶ τῆς περὶ τῶν ὀχουμένων πραγματείας, ὥστε ἐν ἐκείνοις ἐπισκεπτέον· νυνὶ δ' ἔτι καὶ ταῦτα προσληπτέον καὶ ὅσα ἄλλα τῆς γεωγραφίας ἐγγυτέρω.

39. Φησὶ δὴ τὸ τῶν Ἰνδῶν πλῆθος εἰς ἑπτὰ μέρη διῃρῆσθαι, καὶ πρώτους μὲν τοὺς φιλοσόφους εἶναι κατὰ τιμήν, ἐλαχίστους δὲ κατ' ἀριθμόν· χρῆσθαι δ' αὐτοῖς, ἰδίᾳ μὲν ἑκάστῳ τοὺς θύοντας ἢ τοὺς ἐναγίζοντας, κοινῇ δὲ τοὺς βασιλέας κατὰ τὴν μεγάλην λεγομένην σύνοδον, καθ' ἣν τοῦ νέου ἔτους ἅπαντες οἱ φιλόσοφοι τῷ βασιλεῖ συνελθόντες ἐπὶ θύρας, ὅ τι ἂν αὐτῶν

---

[1] Σίλαν Epitome, Σιλίαν other MSS.
[2] DF*w* omit καί before ἀέρων.

---

[1] This clause is obviously ironical, unless, as others suggest, the text is corrupt.

and that some bite so vehemently that their eyes
become distorted and sometimes actually fall out;
and that even a lion was held fast by a dog, and
also a bull, and that the bull was actually killed,
being overpowered through the dog's hold on his
nose before he could be released.

38. Megasthenes goes on to say that in the mountainous country there is a River Silas on which nothing
floats; that Democritus, however, disbelieves this,
inasmuch as he had wandered over much of Asia.[1]
But Aristotle also disbelieves it, although there are
atmospheres so thin that no winged creature can fly
in them. Besides, certain rising vapours tend to
attract to themselves and " gulp down," as it were,
whatever flies over them, as amber does with chaff
and the magnet with iron; and perhaps there might
also be natural powers of this kind in water. Now
these things border, in a way, on natural philosophy
and on the science of floating bodies, and therefore
should be investigated there; but in this treatise
I must add still the following, and whatever else is
closer to the province of geography.

39. He says, then, that the population of India is
divided into seven castes:[2] the one first in honour,
but the fewest in number, consists of the philosophers; and these philosophers are used, each indi-
vidually, by people making sacrifice to the gods or
making offerings to the dead, but jointly by the
kings at the Great Synod, as it is called, at which,
at the beginning of the new year, the philosophers,
one and all, come together at the gates of the king;
and whatever each man has drawn up in writing or

[2] On the caste system in India see " Caste " in *Encyc.
Britannica.*

ἕκαστος συντάξῃ τῶν χρησίμων ἢ τηρήσῃ πρὸς
εὐετηρίαν καρπῶν τε καὶ ζώων καὶ περὶ πολιτείας,[1] προφέρει[2] τοῦτ᾽ εἰς τὸ μέσον· ὃς δ᾽ ἂν
τρὶς ἐψευσμένος ἁλῷ, νόμος ἐστὶ σιγᾶν διὰ βίου·
C 704 τὸν δὲ κατορθώσαντα ἄφορον καὶ ἀτελῆ κρίνουσι.

40. Δεύτερον δὲ μέρος εἶναι τὸ τῶν γεωργῶν,
οἳ πλεῖστοί τέ εἰσι καὶ ἐπιεικέστατοι, ἀστρα-
τείᾳ καὶ ἀδείᾳ τοῦ ἐργάζεσθαι, πόλει μὴ προσιόντες μηδ᾽ ἄλλῃ χρείᾳ μηδ᾽ ὀχλήσει κοινῇ·
πολλάκις γοῦν ἐν τῷ αὐτῷ χρόνῳ καὶ τόπῳ τοῖς
μὲν παρατετάχθαι συμβαίνει καὶ διακινδυνεύειν
πρὸς τοὺς πολεμίους, οἱ δ᾽ ἀροῦσιν ἢ[3] σκάπτουσιν
ἀκινδύνως, προμάχους ἔχοντες ἐκείνους. ἔστι δ᾽
ἡ χώρα βασιλικὴ πᾶσα· μισθοῦ δ᾽ αὐτὴν ἐπὶ
τετάρταις ἐργάζονται τῶν καρπῶν.

41. Τρίτον τὸ τῶν ποιμένων καὶ θηρευτῶν,
οἷς μόνοις ἔξεστι θηρεύειν καὶ θρεμματοτροφεῖν,
ὤνιά τε παρέχειν καὶ μισθοῦ ζεύγη· ἀντὶ δὲ τοῦ
τὴν γῆν ἐλευθεροῦν θηρίων καὶ τῶν σπερμολόγων
ὀρνέων μετροῦνται παρὰ τοῦ βασιλέως σῖτον,
πλάνητα καὶ σκηνίτην νεμόμενοι βίον. ἵππον
δὲ καὶ ἐλέφαντα τρέφειν οὐκ ἔξεστιν ἰδιώτῃ·
βασιλικὸν δ᾽ ἑκάτερον νενόμισται τὸ κτῆμα, καί
εἰσιν αὐτῶν ἐπιμεληταί.

[1] καὶ ζῴων καὶ περὶ πολιτείας, Corais and the later editors,
for καὶ ζῴων καὶ πολιτείας.
[2] προφέρει, Corais and later editors, for προσφέρει.
[3] Instead of ἤ, w and Corais read καί.

[1] Perhaps the more natural interpretation of the Greek
would be, " the farmers cultivate it for wages, on condition
of receiving a fourth part of the produce," whether " wages "
and " fourth part " are appositional, or " on condition of "
means, as it might, " in addition to."   But Diodorus Siculus

observed as useful with reference to the prosperity of either fruits or living beings or concerning the government, he brings forward in public; and he who is thrice found false is required by law to keep silence for life, whereas he who has proved correct is adjudged exempt from tribute and taxes.

40. The second caste, he says, is that of the farmers, who are not only the most numerous, but also the most highly respected, because of their exemption from military service and right of freedom in their farming; and they do not approach a city, either because of a public disturbance or on any other business; at any rate, he says, it often happens that at the same time and place some are in battle array and are in peril of their lives against the enemy, while the farmers are ploughing or digging without peril, the latter having the former as defenders. The whole of the country is of royal ownership; and the farmers cultivate it for a rental in addition to paying a fourth part of the produce.[1]

41. The third caste is that of the shepherds and hunters, who alone are permitted to hunt, to breed cattle, and to sell or hire out beasts of burden; and in return for freeing the land from wild beasts and seed-picking birds, they receive proportionate allowances of grain from the king, leading, as they do, a wandering and tent-dwelling life. No private person is permitted to keep a horse or elephant. The possession of either is a royal privilege, and there are men to take care of them.

(2. 40. 5) says, (" the rentals of the country they pay to the king . . . but apart from the rental they pay a fourth part into the royal treasury "). Hence the translator agrees with Tozer (*Selections from Strabo*, p. 317), who quotes Lassen (*Indische Alterthumskunde* II, p. 721).

42. Θήρα δὲ τῶν θηρίων τούτων τοιάδε. χωρίον ψιλὸν ὅσον τεττάρων ἢ πέντε σταδίων τάφρῳ περιχαράξαντες βαθείᾳ γεφυροῦσι τὴν εἴσοδον στενωτάτῃ γεφύρᾳ· εἶτ᾽ εἰσαφιᾶσι θηλείας τὰς ἡμερωτάτας τρεῖς ἢ τέτταρας, αὐτοὶ δ᾽ ἐν καλυ-βίοις κρυπτοῖς ὑποκάθηνται λοχῶντες. ἡμέρας μὲν οὖν οὐ προσίασιν οἱ ἄγριοι, νύκτωρ δ᾽ ἐφ᾽ ἕνα ποιοῦνται τὴν εἴσοδον· εἰσιόντων δέ, κλείουσι τὴν εἴσοδον λάθρα, εἶτα τῶν ἡμέρων ἀθλητῶν τοὺς ἀλκιμωτάτους εἰσάγοντες διαμάχονται πρὸς αὐτούς, ἅμα καὶ λιμῷ καταπονοῦντες· ἤδη δὲ καμνόντων, οἱ εὐθαρσέστατοι τῶν ἡνιόχων λάθρα καταβαίνοντες ὑποδύνουσιν ἕκαστος τῇ γαστρὶ τοῦ οἰκείου ὀχήματος· ὁρμώμενος δ᾽ ἐνθένδε ὑπο-δύνει τῷ ἀγρίῳ καὶ σύμποδα δεσμεῖ· γενομένου δὲ τούτου, κελεύουσι τοῖς τιθασοῖς τύπτειν τοὺς συμποδισθέντας, ἕως ἂν πέσωσιν εἰς τὴν γῆν, πεσόντων δ᾽ ὠμοβοΐνοις ἱμᾶσι προσλαμβάνονται τοὺς αὐχένας αὐτῶν πρὸς τοὺς τῶν τιθασῶν· ἵνα δὲ μὴ σειόμενοι τοὺς ἀναβαίνειν ἐπ᾽ αὐτοὺς ἐπιχειροῦντας ἀποσείοιντο, τοῖς τραχήλοις αὐτῶν ἐμβάλλονται κύκλῳ τομάς, καὶ κατ᾽ αὐτὰς τοὺς ἱμάντας περιτιθέασιν, ὥσθ᾽ ὑπ᾽ ἀλγηδόνων εἴκειν τοῖς δεσμοῖς καὶ ἡσυχάζειν· τῶν δ᾽ ἁλόντων ἀπολέξαντες τοὺς πρεσβυτέρους ἢ νεωτέρους τῆς χρείας τοὺς λοιποὺς ἀπάγουσιν εἰς τοὺς σταθ-μούς, δήσαντες δὲ τοὺς μὲν πόδας πρὸς ἀλλή-λους, τοὺς δὲ αὐχένας πρὸς κίονα εὖ πεπηγότα, C 705 δαμάζουσι λιμῷ· ἔπειτα χλόῃ καλάμου καὶ πόας ἀναλαμβάνουσι· μετὰ δὲ ταῦτα πειθαρχεῖν δι-

42. The chase of the elephant is conducted as follows: they dig a deep ditch round a treeless tract about four or five stadia in circuit and bridge the entrance with a very narrow bridge; and then, letting loose into the enclosure three or four of their tamest females, they themselves lie in wait under cover in hidden huts. Now the wild elephants do not approach by day, but they make the entrance one by one at night; and when they have entered, the men close the entrance secretly; and then, leading the most courageous of their tame combatants into the enclosure, they fight it out with the wild elephants, at the same time wearing them down also by starvation; and, once the animals are worn out, the boldest of the riders secretly dismount and each creeps under the belly of his own riding-elephant, and then, starting from here, creeps under the wild elephant and binds his feet together; and when this is done, they command the tamed elephants to beat those whose feet have been bound until they fall to the ground; and when they fall, the men fasten their necks to those of the tamed elephants with thongs of raw ox-hide; and in order that the wild elephants, when they shake those who are attempting to mount them, may not shake them off, the men make incisions round their necks and put the thongs round at these incisions, so that through pain they yield to their bonds and keep quiet. Of the elephants captured, they reject those that are too old or too young for service and lead away the rest to the stalls; and then, having tied their feet to one another and their necks to a firmly planted pillar, they subdue them by hunger; and then they restore them with green cane and grass. After this the elephants are

71

δάσκουσι, τοὺς μὲν διὰ λόγου, τοὺς δὲ μελισμῷ
τινι καὶ τυμπανισμῷ κηλοῦντες· σπάνιοι δ' οἱ
δυστιθάσευτοι· φύσει γὰρ διάκεινται πράως καὶ
ἡμέρως, ὥστ' ἐγγὺς εἶναι λογικῷ ζώῳ· οἱ δὲ[1] καὶ
ἐξαίμους τοὺς ἡνιόχους ἐν τοῖς ἀγῶσι πεσόντας
ἀνελόμενοι σώζουσιν ἐκ τῆς μάχης, τοὺς[2] δὲ[3]
ὑποδύντας μεταξὺ τῶν προσθίων ποδῶν ὑπερμα-
χόμενοι διέσωσαν· τῶν δὲ χορτοφόρων καὶ διδα-
σκάλων εἴ τινα παρὰ θυμὸν ἀπέκτειναν, οὕτως
ἐπιποθοῦσιν, ὥσθ' ὑπ' ἀνίας ἀπέχεσθαι τροφῆς,
ἔστι δ' ὅτε καὶ ἀποκαρτερεῖν.

43. Βιβάζονται δὲ καὶ τίκτουσιν, ὡς ἵπποι,
τοῦ ἔαρος μάλιστα· καιρὸς δ' ἐστὶ τῷ μὲν ἄρρενι,
ἐπειδὰν οἴστρῳ κατέχηται καὶ ἀγριαίνῃ· τότε
δὴ καὶ λίπους τι διὰ τῆς ἀναπνοῆς ἀνίησιν, ἣν
ἔχει[4] παρὰ τοὺς κροτάφους· ταῖς δὲ θηλείαις,
ὅταν ὁ αὐτὸς οὗτος πόρος ἀνεῳγὼς τυγχάνῃ.
κύουσι δὲ τοὺς μὲν πλείστους ὀκτωκαίδεκα μῆνας,
ἐλαχίστους δ' ἑκκαίδεκα· τρέφει δ' ἡ μήτηρ ἐξ
ἔτη· ζῶσι δ' ὅσον μακροβιώτατοι ἄνθρωποι οἱ
πολλοί, τινὲς δὲ καὶ ἐπὶ διακόσια διατείνουσιν
ἔτη· πολύνοσοι δὲ καὶ δυσίατοι. ἄκος δὲ πρὸς
ὀφθαλμίαν μὲν βόειον γάλα προσκλυζόμενον,
τοῖς πλείστοις δὲ τῶν νοσημάτων ὁ μέλας οἶνος
πινόμενος, τραύμασι δὲ ποτὸν μὲν βούτυρον

---

[1] Instead of οἱ δέ, moz and Corais read τινὲς γάρ.
[2] Instead of τούς, moz and Tzschucke read οἱ.
[3] Before ὑποδύντας Dhimoz insert καί.
[4] Instead of ἔχει, F and Meineke read ἴσχει.

---

[1] The so-called "must" (frenzied male) elephant discharges
an abundance of dark oily matter from two pores in the
forehead (see "Elephant" in Encyc. Britannica). "True,

taught to obey commands, some through words of command and others through being charmed by tunes and drum-beating. Those that are hard to tame are rare; for by nature the elephant is of a mild and gentle disposition, so that it is close to a rational animal; and some elephants have even taken up their riders who had fallen from loss of blood in the fight and carried them safely out of the battle, while others have fought for, and rescued, those who had crept between their fore-legs. And if in anger they have killed one of their feeders or masters, they yearn after him so strongly that through grief they abstain from food and sometimes even starve themselves to death.

43. They copulate and bear young like horses, mostly in the spring. It is breeding-time for the male when he is seized with frenzy and becomes ferocious; at that time he discharges a kind of fatty matter through the breathing-hole which he has beside his temples.[1] And it is breeding-time for the females when this same passage is open. They are pregnant eighteen months at the most and sixteen at the least; and the mother nurses her young six years. Most of them live as long as very long-lived human beings, and some continue to live even to two hundred years, although they are subject to many diseases and are hard to cure. A remedy for eye diseases is to bathe the eyes with cow's milk; but for most diseases they are given dark wine to drink; and, in the case of wounds, melted butter

on occasion male elephants get into the stage called *musth*, the symptoms of which, and possibly the cause, are certain head glands. *Musth* has no connection with sex, although this is commonly thought to be the case " (Major A. W. Smith, *Atlantic Monthly*, November 1928, p. 632).

(ἐξάγει γὰρ τὰ σιδήρια), τὰ δ' ἕλκη σαρξὶν ὑείαις
πυριῶσιν. Ὀνησίκριτος δὲ καὶ ἕως τριακοσίων
ἐτῶν ζῆν φησι, σπάνιον δὲ καὶ ἕως πεντακοσίων,
κρατίστους δ' εἶναι περὶ τὰ διακόσια ἔτη, κυΐ-
σκεσθαι δὲ δεκαετίαν. μείζους δὲ τῶν Λιβυκῶν
καὶ ἐρρωμενεστέρους ἐκεῖνός τε εἴρηκε καὶ ἄλλοι·
ταῖς οὖν προβοσκίσιν ἐπάλξεις καθαιρεῖν καὶ
δένδρα ἀνασπᾶν πρόρριζα, διανισταμένους εἰς
τοὺς ὀπισθίους πόδας. Νέαρχος δὲ καὶ ποδάγρας
ἐν ταῖς θήραις τίθεσθαι κατά τινας συνδρόμους
φησί, συνελαύνεσθαι δ' ὑπὸ τῶν τιθασῶν τοὺς
ἀγρίους εἰς ταύτας, κρειττόνων ὄντων καὶ ἡνιο-
χουμένων. οὕτως δ' εὐτιθασεύτους εἶναι, ὥστε
καὶ λιθάζειν ἐπὶ σκοπὸν μανθάνειν καὶ ὅπλοις
χρῆσθαι· νεῖν τε κάλλιστα· μέγιστόν τε νομίζεσθαι κτῆμα ἐλεφάντων ἅρμα· ἄγεσθαι δ' ὑπὸ
ζυγὸν[1] ὡς[2] καὶ καμήλους· γυναῖκα δ' εὐδοκιμεῖν,
εἰ λάβοι παρὰ ἐραστοῦ δῶρον ἐλέφαντα. οὗτος
ὁ λόγος οὐχ ὁμολογεῖ τῷ φήσαντι μόνων[3] βασιλέων εἶναι κτῆμα ἵππον καὶ ἐλέφαντα.[4]

44. Τῶν δὲ μυρμήκων τῶν χρυσωρύχων δέρματα
ἰδεῖν φησιν οὗτος παρδαλέαις ὅμοια. Μεγασθένης
C 706 δὲ περὶ τῶν μυρμήκων οὕτω φησίν, ὅτι ἐν Δέρδαις,
ἔθνει μεγάλῳ τῶν προσεῴων καὶ ὀρεινῶν Ἰνδῶν,
ὀροπέδιον εἴη τρισχιλίων πως τὸν κύκλον στα-

[1] ζυγόν CDF*h*, ζυγῶν other MSS.
[2] ὡς, Jones inserts from conj. of Tzschucke and Groskurd ;
Corais emends καὶ καμήλους to ἀχαλίνους (" without bridles ") ;
Kramer and Meineke merely place an asterisk before the two
words.
[3] μόνων F, μόνον other MSS.
[4] οὗτος . . . . . ἐλέφαντα, omitted by *moz*, is probably a
gloss.

74

is applied to them (for it draws out the bits of iron), while ulcers are poulticed with swine's flesh. Onesicritus says that they live as long as three hundred years and in rare cases even as long as five hundred; but that they are most powerful when about two hundred years of age, and that females are pregnant for a period of ten years. And both he and others state that they are larger and stronger than the Libyan elephants; at any rate, standing up on their hind feet, they tear down battlements and pull up trees by the roots by means of the proboscis. Nearchus says that in the hunt for them foot-traps also are put at places where tracks meet, and that the wild elephants are driven together into these by the tamed ones, which latter are stronger and guided by riders; and that they are so easy to tame that they learn to throw stones at a mark and to use weapons; and that they are excellent swimmers; and that a chariot drawn by elephants is considered a very great possession, and that they are driven under yoke like camels;[1] and that a woman is highly honoured if she receives an elephant as a gift from a lover. But this statement is not in agreement with that of the man who said that horse and elephant were possessed by kings alone.[2]

44. Nearchus says that the skins of gold-mining ants are like those of leopards. But Megasthenes speaks of these ants as follows: that among the Derdae, a large tribe of Indians living towards the east and in the mountains, there is a plateau approximately three thousand stadia in circuit, and that

[1] On this clause see critical note.
[2] § 41 above.

STRABO

δίων· ὑποκειμένων δὲ τούτῳ χρυσωρυχείων, οἱ μεταλλεύοντες εἶεν μύρμηκες, θηρία[1] ἀλωπέκων οὐκ ἐλάττω, τάχος ὑπερφυὲς ἔχοντα καὶ ζῶντα[2] ἀπὸ θήρας· ὀρύττει[3] δὲ χειμῶνι τὴν γῆν, σωρεύει[4] τε πρὸς τοῖς στομίοις, καθάπερ οἱ ἀσφάλακες· ψῆγμα δ᾽ ἐστὶ χρυσοῦ μικρᾶς ἑψήσεως δεόμενον· τοῦθ᾽ ὑποζυγίοις μετίασιν οἱ πλησιόχωροι λάθρα· φανερῶς γὰρ διαμάχονται καὶ διώκουσι φεύγοντας, καταλαβόντες δὲ διαχρῶνται καὶ αὐτοὺς καὶ τὰ ὑποζύγια· πρὸς δὲ τὸ λαθεῖν κρέα θήρεια προτιθέασι κατὰ μέρη, περισπασθέντων δ᾽ ἀναιροῦνται τὸ ψῆγμα καὶ τοῦ τυχόντος τοῖς ἐμπόροις ἀργὸν διατίθενται, χωνεύειν οὐκ εἰδότες.

45. Ἐπεὶ δ᾽ ἐν τῷ περὶ τῶν θηρευτῶν λόγῳ καὶ περὶ τῶν θηρίων ἐμνήσθημεν, ὧν τε Μεγασθένης εἶπε καὶ ἄλλοι, προσθετέον καὶ ταῦτα. ὁ μὲν γὰρ Νέαρχος τὸ τῶν ἑρπετῶν θαυμάζει πλῆθος καὶ τὴν κακίαν· ἀναφεύγειν γὰρ ἐκ τῶν πεδίων εἰς τὰς κατοικίας τὰς διαλανθανούσας ἐν ταῖς ἐπικλύσεσι καὶ πληροῦν τοὺς οἴκους· διὰ δὴ τοῦτο καὶ ὑψηλὰς ποιεῖσθαι τὰς κλίνας, ἔστι δ᾽ ὅτε καὶ ἐξοικίζεσθαι πλεονασάντων· εἰ δὲ μὴ τὸ πολὺ τοῦ πλήθους ὑπὸ τῶν ὑδάτων διεφθείρετο, κἂν ἐρημωθῆναι τὴν χώραν. καὶ τὴν μικρότητα δ᾽ αὐτῶν εἶναι χαλεπὴν καὶ τὴν ὑπερβολὴν τοῦ μεγέθους, τὴν μὲν διὰ τὸ δυσφύλακτον, τὴν δὲ δι᾽

[1] θηρία, Kramer and later editors, for θηρίων.
[2] ἔχοντα καὶ ζῶντα, Kramer and later editors, for ἔχοντες ζῶντες.
[3] ὀρύττουσι Eh.
[4] σωρεύουσι E, ἀσπάλακες Xylander and other editors before Kramer.

76

below it are gold mines, of which the miners are
ants, animals that are no smaller than foxes, are
surpassingly swift, and live on the prey they catch.
They dig holes in winter and heap up the earth at
the mouths of the holes, like moles;[1] and the gold-
dust requires but little smelting. The neighbouring
peoples go after it on beasts of burden by stealth,
for if they go openly the ants fight it out with them
and pursue them when they flee, and then, having
overtaken them, exterminate both them and their
beasts; but to escape being seen by the ants, the
people lay out pieces of flesh of wild beasts at
different places, and when the ants are drawn away
from around the holes, the people take up the gold-
dust and, not knowing how to smelt it, dispose of it
unwrought to traders at any price it will fetch.

45. But since, in my account of the hunters and
of the wild beasts, I have mentioned what both
Megasthenes and others have said, I must go on to
add the following. Nearchus wonders at the number
of the reptiles and their viciousness, for he says that
at the time of the inundations they flee up from the
plains into the settlements that escape the inundations, and fill the houses; and that on this account,
accordingly, the inhabitants not only make their
beds high, but sometimes even move out of their
houses when infested by too many of them; and that
if the greater part of the multitude of reptiles were
not destroyed by the waters, the country would be
depopulated; and that the smallness of some of
them is troublesome as well as the huge size of others,
the small ones because it is difficult to guard against
them, and the huge ones because of their strength,

[1] A species of the *Spalacidae*.

ἰσχύν, ὅπου καὶ ἑκκαιδεκαπήχεις ἐχίδνας ὁρᾶσθαι·
ἐπῳδοὺς δὲ περιφοιτᾶν ἰᾶσθαι πεπιστευμένους,
καὶ εἶναι σχεδόν τι μόνην ταύτην ἰατρικήν· μηδὲ
γὰρ νόσους εἶναι πολλὰς διὰ τὴν λιτότητα τῆς
διαίτης καὶ τὴν ἀοινίαν· εἰ δὲ γένοιντο, ἰᾶσθαι
τοὺς σοφιστάς. Ἀριστόβουλος δὲ τῶν θρυλουμένων μεγεθῶν οὐδὲν ἰδεῖν φησιν, ἔχιοναν δὲ μόνον
ἐννέα πηχῶν καὶ σπιθαμῆς. καὶ ἡμεῖς δ᾽ ἐν
Αἰγύπτῳ κομισθεῖσαν ἐκεῖθεν τηλικαύτην πως
εἴδομεν. ἔχεις δὲ πολλούς φησι πολὺ ἐλάττους
καὶ ἀσπίδας, σκορπίους δὲ μεγάλους, οὐδὲν δὲ
τούτων οὕτως ὀχλεῖν ὡς τὰ λεπτὰ ὀφείδια, οὐ
μείζω σπιθαμιαίων· εὑρίσκεσθαι γὰρ ἐν σκηναῖς,
ἐν σκεύεσιν, ἐν θριγγοῖς[1] ἐγκεκρυμμένα, τοὺς δὲ
πληγέντας αἱμορροεῖν ἐκ παντὸς πόρου μετὰ
ἐπωδυνίας, ἔπειτα ἀποθνήσκειν, εἰ μὴ βοηθήσει
τις εὐθύς· τὴν δὲ βοήθειαν ῥαδίαν εἶναι διὰ τὴν
C 707 ἀρετὴν τῶν Ἰνδικῶν ῥιζῶν καὶ φαρμάκων. κροκοδείλους τε οὔτε πολλοὺς οὔτε βλαπτικοὺς ἀνθρώπων ἐν τῷ Ἰνδῷ φησιν εὑρίσκεσθαι, καὶ τὰ ἄλλα
δὲ ζῷα τὰ πλεῖστα τὰ αὐτά ἅπερ ἐν τῷ Νείλῳ
γεννᾶσθαι πλὴν ἵππου ποταμίου. Ὀνησίκριτος
δὲ καὶ τοῦτόν φησι γεννᾶσθαι. τῶν δ᾽ ἐκ
θαλάττης φησὶν ὁ Ἀριστόβουλος εἰς μὲν τὸν
Νεῖλον ἀνατρέχειν μηδὲν ἔξω θρίσσης καὶ κεσ-
τρέως καὶ δελφῖνος διὰ τοὺς κροκοδείλους, ἐν

[1] Instead of θριγγοῖς, CDEFhisw read θρύοις ("rushes");
x reads θριγγίοις, and Corais θριγκοῖς.

[1] Or "baggage."   [2] See critical note.

inasmuch as vipers even sixteen cubits long are to be seen; and that charmers go around who are believed to cure the wounds; and that this is almost the only art of medicine, for the people do not have many diseases on account of the simplicity of their diet and their abstinence from wine; but that if diseases arise, they are cured by the Wise Men. But Aristobulus says that he saw none of the animals of the huge size that are everywhere talked about, except a viper nine cubits and one span long. And I myself saw one of about the same size in Aegypt that had been brought from India. He says that you have many much smaller vipers, and asps, and large scorpions, but that none of these is so troublesome as the slender little snakes that are no more than a span long, for they are found hidden in tents, in vessels,[1] and in hedges[2]; and that persons bitten by them bleed from every pore with anguish, and then die unless they receive aid immediately; but that aid is easy because of the virtue of the Indian roots and drugs. He says further that crocodiles, neither numerous nor harmful to man, are to be found in the Indus, and also that most of the other animals are the same as those which are found in the Nile except the hippopotamus. Onesicritus, however, says that this animal too is found in India. And Aristobulus says that on account of the crocodiles no sea-fish swim up into the Nile except the *thrissa*,[3] the *cestreus*,[4] and the dolphin,[5] but that there is a

---

[3] Apparently of the genus *Trichiuridae* (cutlass fish), or else *Engraulidae* (small herring-like fish used for pickling and sauces).

[4] Apparently of the genus *Mugilidae* (grey mullets).

[5] The dolphin, however, is a mammal, not a fish.

δὲ τῷ Ἰνδῷ πλῆθος· τῶν δὲ καρίδων τὰς μὲν μικρὰς μέχρι ὄρους[1] ἀναθεῖν, τὰς δὲ μεγάλας μέχρι τῶν συμβολῶν τοῦ τε Ἰνδοῦ καὶ τοῦ Ἀκεσίνου. περὶ μὲν οὖν τῶν θηρίων τοσαῦτα λέγεται· ἐπανιόντες δ' ἐπὶ τὸν Μεγασθένη λέγωμεν τὰ ἑξῆς, ὧν ἀπελίπομεν.

46. Μετὰ γὰρ τοὺς θηρευτὰς καὶ τοὺς ποιμένας τέταρτόν φησιν εἶναι μέρος τοὺς ἐργαζομένους τὰς τέχνας καὶ τοὺς καπηλικοὺς καὶ οἷς ἀπὸ τοῦ σώματος ἡ ἐργασία· ὧν οἱ μὲν φόρον τελοῦσι καὶ λειτουργίας παρέχονται τακτάς, τοῖς δ' ὁπλοποιοῖς καὶ ναυπηγοῖς μισθοὶ καὶ τροφαὶ παρὰ βασιλέως ἔκκεινται· μόνῳ γὰρ ἐργάζονται· παρέχει δὲ τὰ μὲν ὅπλα τοῖς στρατιώταις ὁ στρατοφύλαξ, τὰς δὲ ναῦς μισθοῦ τοῖς πλέουσιν ὁ ναύαρχος καὶ τοῖς ἐμπόροις.

47. Πέμπτον δ'[2] ἐστὶ τὸ τῶν πολεμιστῶν, οἷς τὸν ἄλλον χρόνον ἐν σχολῇ καὶ πότοις ὁ βίος ἐστίν, ἐκ τοῦ βασιλικοῦ διαιτωμένοις, ὥστε τὰς ἐξόδους, ὅταν ᾖ[3] χρεία, ταχέως ποιεῖσθαι, πλὴν τῶν σωμάτων μηδὲν ἄλλο κομίζοντας παρ' ἑαυτῶν.

48. Ἕκτοι δ' εἰσὶν οἱ ἔφοροι· τούτοις δ' ἐποπτεύειν δέδοται τὰ πραττόμενα καὶ ἀναγγέλλειν λάθρα τῷ βασιλεῖ, συνεργοὺς ποιουμένοις τὰς ἑταίρας, τοῖς μὲν ἐν τῇ πόλει τὰς ἐν τῇ πόλει, τοῖς δὲ ἐν στρατοπέδῳ τὰς αὐτόθι· καθίστανται δ' οἱ ἄριστοι καὶ πιστότατοι.

---

[1] For ὄρους, Groskurd conj. τῶν ὀρῶν, Corais Οὔρων.
[2] δ', before ἐστί, Meineke inserts.   [3] ᾖ z, εἴη other MSS.

---

[1] Of the genus Caridea (shrimp, prawns, and the like).

large number of different fish in the Indus. Of the *carides*,[1] the small ones swim up the Indus only as far as a mountain,[2] but the large ones as far as the confluence of the Indus and the Acesines. So much, then, is reported about the wild animals. Let me now return to Megasthenes and continue his account from the point where I left off.

46. After the hunters and the shepherds, he says, follows the fourth caste—the artisans, the tradesmen, and the day-labourers; and of these, some pay tribute to the state and render services prescribed by the state, whereas the armour-makers and ship-builders receive wages and provisions, at a published scale, from the king, for these work for him alone; and arms are furnished the soldiers by the commander-in-chief, whereas the ships are let out for hire to sailors and merchants by the admiral.

47. The fifth caste is that of the warriors, who, when they are not in service, spend their lives in idleness and at drinking-bouts, being maintained at the expense of the royal treasury; so that they make their expeditions quickly when need arises, since they bring nothing else of their own but their bodies.

48. The sixth is that of the inspectors,[3] to whom it is given to inspect what is being done and report secretly to the king, using the courtesans as colleagues, the city inspectors using the city courtesans and the camp inspectors the camp courtesans; but the best and most trustworthy men are appointed to this office.

---

[2] "A mountain" is unintelligible. The only plausible emendations yield "the mountains" or "the Uri" (a people mentioned by Pliny 6. 20, 23). See critical note.

[3] *i.e.* of political and military officials.

49. Ἕβδομοι δ' οἱ σύμβουλοι καὶ σύνεδροι τοῦ βασιλέως, ἐξ ὧν τὰ ἀρχεῖα καὶ δικαστήρια καὶ ἡ διοίκησις τῶν ὅλων. οὐκ ἔστι δ' οὔτε γαμεῖν ἐξ ἄλλου γένους οὔτ' ἐπιτήδευμα οὔτ' ἐργασίαν μεταλαμβάνειν ἄλλην ἐξ ἄλλης, οὐδὲ πλείους μεταχειρίζεσθαι τὸν αὐτόν, πλὴν εἰ τῶν φιλοσόφων τις εἴη· ἐᾶσθαι γὰρ τοῦτον δι' ἀρετήν.

50. Τῶν δ' ἀρχόντων οἱ μέν εἰσιν ἀγορανόμοι, οἱ δ' ἀστυνόμοι, οἱ δ' ἐπὶ τῶν στρατιωτῶν· ὧν οἱ μὲν ποταμοὺς ἐξεργάζονται καὶ ἀναμετροῦσι τὴν γῆν, ὡς ἐν Αἰγύπτῳ, καὶ τὰς κλειστὰς διώρυγας, ἀφ' ὧν εἰς τὰς ὀχετείας ταμιεύεται τὸ ὕδωρ, ἐπισκοποῦσιν, ὅπως ἐξ ἴσης πᾶσιν ἡ τῶν ὑδάτων C 708 παρείη χρῆσις. οἱ δ' αὐτοὶ καὶ τῶν θηρευτῶν ἐπιμελοῦνται καὶ τιμῆς καὶ κολάσεώς εἰσι κύριοι τοῖς ἐπαξίοις· καὶ φορολογοῦσι δὲ καὶ τὰς τέχνας τὰς περὶ τὴν γῆν ἐπιβλέπουσιν, ὑλοτόμων, τεκτόνων, χαλκέων, μεταλλευτῶν· ὁδοποιοῦσι δὲ καὶ κατὰ δέκα στάδια στήλην τιθέασι, τὰς ἐκτροπὰς καὶ τὰ διαστήματα δηλοῦσαν.

51. Οἱ δ' ἀστυνόμοι εἰς ἓξ πεντάδας διήρηνται· καὶ οἱ μὲν τὰ δημιουργικὰ σκοποῦσιν, οἱ δὲ ξενοδοχοῦσιν· καὶ γὰρ καταγωγὰς νέμουσι καὶ τοῖς βίοις παρακολουθοῦσι, παρέδρους δόντες, καὶ προπέμπουσιν ἢ αὐτοὺς ἢ τὰ χρήματα τῶν

---

[1] The " city commissioners " (ἀστύνομοι) at Athens (ten in number) had charge of the police, the streets, and the public works.

[2] i.e. the market commissioners.

[3] i.e. when the inundations destroyed the landmarks.

[4] See § 40 above.

49. The seventh is that of the advisers and councillors of the king, who hold the chief offices of state, the judgeships, and the administration of everything. It is not legal for a man either to marry a wife from another caste or to change one's pursuit or work from one to another; nor yet for the same man to engage in several, except in case he should be one of the philosophers, for, Megasthenes says, the philosopher is permitted to do so on account of his superiority.

50. Of the officials, some are market commissioners, others are city commissioners,[1] and others are in charge of the soldiers. Among these, the first [2] keep the rivers improved and the land remeasured,[3] as in Aegypt, and inspect the closed canals from which the water is distributed into the conduits, in order that all may have an equal use of it. The same men also have charge of the hunters and are authorized to reward or punish those who deserve either. They also collect the taxes [4] and superintend the crafts connected with the land—those of wood-cutters, carpenters, workers in brass, and miners. And they make roads, and at every ten stadia place pillars showing the by-roads and the distances.

51. The city commissioners are divided into six groups of five each. One group looks after the arts of the handicraftsmen. Another group entertains strangers, for they assign them lodgings, follow closely their behaviour, giving them attendants,[5] and either escort them forth or forward the property [6] of those who die; and they take care of

[5] *i.e.* partly as advisers, partly as spies (Tozer, *op. cit.*, p. 320).

[6] *i.e.* to their relatives.

STRABO

ἀποθανόντων, νοσούντων τε ἐπιμελοῦνται καὶ
ἀποθανόντας θάπτουσι. τρίτοι δ᾽ εἰσίν, οἳ τὰς
γενέσεις καὶ θανάτους ἐξετάζουσι, πότε καὶ πῶς,
τῶν τε φόρων χάριν καὶ ὅπως μὴ ἀφανεῖς εἶεν
αἱ κρείττους καὶ χείρους γοναὶ καὶ θάνατοι.
τέταρτοι δ᾽[1] οἱ περὶ τὰς καπηλείας καὶ μετα-
βολάς· οἷς μέτρων μέλει καὶ τῶν ὡραίων, ὅπως
ἀπὸ συσσήμου πωλοῖτο. οὐκ ἔστι δὲ πλείω τὸν
αὐτὸν μεταβάλλεσθαι, πλὴν εἰ διττοὺς ὑποτελοίη
φόρους. πέμπτοι δ᾽ οἱ προεστῶτες τῶν δημιουρ-
γουμένων καὶ πωλοῦντες ταῦτ᾽ ἀπὸ συσσήμου,
χωρὶς μὲν τὰ καινά, χωρὶς δὲ τὰ παλαιά· τῷ
μιγνύντι δὲ ζημία. ἕκτοι δὲ καὶ ὕστατοι οἱ τὰς
δεκάτας ἐκλέγοντες τῶν πωλουμένων· θάνατος δὲ
τῷ κλέψαντι τὸ τέλος. ἰδίᾳ μὲν ἕκαστοι ταῦτα,
κοινῇ δ᾽ ἐπιμελοῦνται τῶν τε ἰδίων καὶ τῶν
πολιτικῶν καὶ τῆς τῶν δημοσίων ἐπισκευῆς,
τιμῶν[2] τε καὶ ἀγορᾶς καὶ λιμένων καὶ ἱερῶν.

52. Μετὰ δὲ τοὺς ἀστυνόμους τρίτη ἐστὶ
συναρχία ἡ περὶ τὰ στρατιωτικά, καὶ αὕτη ταῖς
πεντάσιν ἑξαχῇ διωρισμένη· ὧν τὴν μὲν μετὰ
τοῦ ναυάρχου τάττουσι, τὴν δὲ μετὰ τοῦ ἐπὶ τῶν
βοϊκῶν ζευγῶν, δι᾽ ὧν ὄργανα κομίζεται καὶ
τροφὴ αὐτοῖς τε καὶ κτήνεσι καὶ τὰ ἄλλα τὰ
χρήσιμα τῆς στρατιᾶς. οὗτοι δὲ καὶ τοὺς δια-

[1] δ᾽, before οἱ, Meineke inserts.
[2] τιμῶν, Meineke (following conj. of Kramer), emends to
τειχῶν.

[1] i.e. "the stamp impressed on weights and measures,"
which were "tested every six months" (Tozer, op. cit., p. 320,
quoting Lassen, op. cit., II. p. 572).

84

them when they are sick and bury them when they die. The third group is that of those who scrutinize births and deaths, when and how they take place, both for the sake of taxes and in order that births and deaths, whether better or worse, may not be unknown. The fourth group is that which has to do with sales and barter; and these look after measures and the fruits of the season, that the latter may be sold by stamp.[1] But the same man cannot barter more than one thing without paying double taxes. The fifth group is that of those who have charge of the works made by artisans and sell these by stamp, the new apart from the old; and the man who mixes them is fined. The sixth and last group is that of those who collect a tenth part of the price of the things sold; and death is the penalty for the man who steals.[2] These are the special duties performed by each group, but they all take care jointly of matters both private and public, and of the repairs of public works, of prices,[3] market-places, harbours, and temples.

52. After the city commissioners there is a third joint administration, in charge of military affairs, which is also divided into six groups of five each. Of these groups, one is stationed with the admiral; another with the man in charge of the ox-teams, by which are transported instruments of war and food for both man and beast and all other requisites of the army. These also furnish the menials, I mean

---

[2] *i.e.* the taxpayer who cheats the government.

[3] Meineke emends the Greek word for " prices " to that for " walls " (see critical note), thus making " walls, market-places, harbours, and temples " in apposition with " public works."

κόνους παρέχουσι, τυμπανιστάς, κωδωνοφόρους,
ἔτι δὲ καὶ ἱπποκόμους καὶ μηχανοποιοὺς καὶ τοὺς
τούτων ὑπηρέτας· ἐκπέμπουσί τε πρὸς κώδωνας
τοὺς χορτολόγους, τιμῇ καὶ κολάσει τὸ τάχος
κατασκευαζόμενοι καὶ τὴν ἀσφάλειαν. τρίτοι δέ
εἰσιν οἱ τῶν πεζῶν ἐπιμελούμενοι· τέταρτοι δ᾽ οἱ
τῶν ἵππων· πέμπτοι δ᾽ ἁρμάτων· ἕκτοι δὲ ἐλεφάντων. βασιλικοί τε σταθμοὶ καὶ ἵπποις καὶ
C 709 θηρίοις, βασιλικὸν δὲ καὶ ὁπλοφυλάκιον· παρα-
δίδωσι γὰρ ὁ στρατιώτης τήν τε σκευὴν εἰς τὸ
ὁπλοφυλάκιον καὶ τὸν ἵππον εἰς τὸν ἱππῶνα καὶ
τὸ θηρίον ὁμοίως· χρῶνται δ᾽ ἀχαλινώτοις. τὰ
δ᾽ ἅρματα ἐν ταῖς ὁδοῖς βόες ἕλκουσιν, οἱ δὲ
ἵπποι ἀπὸ φορβειᾶς ἄγονται τοῦ μὴ παρεμπί-
πρασθαι τὰ σκέλη, μηδὲ τὸ πρόθυμον αὐτῶν
τὸ ὑπὸ τοῖς ἅρμασιν ἀμβλύνεσθαι. δύο δ᾽ εἰσὶν
ἐπὶ τῷ ἅρματι παραβάται πρὸς τῷ ἡνιόχῳ· ὁ δὲ
τοῦ ἐλέφαντος ἡνίοχος τέταρτος, τρεῖς δ᾽ οἱ ἀπ᾽
αὐτοῦ τοξεύοντες.

53. Εὐτελεῖς δὲ κατὰ τὴν δίαιταν Ἰνδοὶ πάντες,
μᾶλλον δ᾽ ἐν ταῖς στρατείαις· οὐδ᾽ ὄχλῳ περιττῷ
χαίρουσι· διόπερ εὐκοσμοῦσι. πλείστη δ᾽ ἐκεχει-
ρία περὶ τὰς κλοπάς· γενόμενος [1] γοῦν ἐν τῷ
Σανδροκόττου στρατοπέδῳ φησὶν ὁ Μεγασθένης,
τετταράκοντα μυριάδων πλήθους ἱδρυμένου, μηδεμίαν ἡμέραν ἰδεῖν ἀνηνεγμένα κλέμματα πλειόνων
ἢ διακοσίων δραχμῶν ἄξια, ἀγράφοις καὶ ταῦτα
νόμοις χρωμένοις. οὐδὲ γὰρ γράμματα εἰδέναι

---

[1] γενόμενος, Tzschucke and later editors, for γενομένους.

᾿ i.e. the elephants.   [2] i.e. of royal ownership.
[3] i.e. before they are used in battle.

drum-beaters, gong-carriers, as also grooms and machinists and their assistants; and they send forth the foragers to the sound of bells, and effect speed and safety by means of reward and punishment. The third group consists of those in charge of the infantry; the fourth, of those in charge of the horses; the fifth, of those in charge of the chariots; and the sixth, of those in charge of the elephants. The stalls for both horses and beasts [1] are royal,[2] and the armoury is also royal; for the soldier returns the equipment to the armoury, the horse to the royal horse-stable, and likewise the beast; and they use them without bridles. The chariots are drawn on the march by oxen; but the horses are led by halter, in order that their legs may not be chafed by harness, and also that the spirit they have when drawing chariots may not be dulled.[3] There are two combatants in each chariot in addition to the charioteer; but the elephant carries four persons, the driver and three bowmen, and these three shoot arrows from the elephant's back.

53. All Indians live a simple life, and especially when they are on expeditions; and neither do they enjoy useless disturbances; and on this account they behave in an orderly manner. But their greatest self-restraint pertains to theft; at any rate, Megasthenes says that when he was in the camp of Sandrocottus, although the number in camp was forty thousand, he on no day saw reports of stolen articles that were worth more than two hundred drachmae; and that too among a people who use unwritten laws only. For, he continues, they have no knowledge of written letters,[4] and regulate every

[4] But cf. § 67 (below).

αὐτούς, ἀλλ᾽ ἀπὸ μνήμης ἕκαστα διοικεῖσθαι·
εὐπραγεῖν[1] δ᾽ ὅμως διὰ τὴν ἁπλότητα καὶ τὴν
εὐτέλειαν· οἶνόν τε γὰρ οὐ πίνειν, ἀλλ᾽ ἐν θυσίαις
μόνον, πίνειν δ᾽ ἀπ᾽ ὀρύζης ἀντὶ κριθίνων συντι-
θέντας· καὶ σιτία δὲ τὸ πλέον ὄρυζαν εἶναι
ῥοφητήν. καὶ ἐν τοῖς νόμοις δὲ καὶ συμβολαίοις
τὴν ἁπλότητα ἐλέγχεσθαι ἐκ τοῦ μὴ πολυδίκους
εἶναι· οὔτε γὰρ ὑποθήκης[2] οὔτε παρακαταθήκης
εἶναι δίκας, οὐδὲ μαρτύρων οὐδὲ σφραγίδων αὐτοῖς
δεῖν, ἀλλὰ πιστεύειν παραβαλλομένους· καὶ τὰ
οἴκοι δὲ τὸ πλέον ἀφρουρεῖν. ταῦτα μὲν δὴ
σωφρονικά, τἆλλα δ᾽ οὐδ᾽[3] ἄν τις ἀποδέξαιτο·
τὸ μόνους διαιτᾶσθαι ἀεὶ καὶ τὸ μὴ μίαν εἶναι
πᾶσιν ὥραν κοινὴν δείπνου τε καὶ ἀρίστου, ἀλλ᾽
ὅπως ἑκάστῳ φίλον· πρὸς γὰρ τὸν κοινωνικὸν καὶ
τὸν πολιτικὸν βίον ἐκείνως κρεῖττον.

54. Γυμνασίων[4] δὲ μάλιστα τρῖψιν δοκι-
μάζουσι καὶ ἄλλως καὶ διὰ σκυταλίδων ἐβενίνων
λείων ἐξομαλίζονται τὰ σώματα. λιταὶ δὲ καὶ
αἱ ταφαὶ καὶ μικρὰ χώματα. ὑπεναντίως δὲ τῇ
ἄλλῃ λιτότητι κοσμοῦνται. χρυσοφοροῦσι γὰρ
καὶ διαλίθῳ κόσμῳ χρῶνται σινδόνας τε φοροῦσιν
εὐανθεῖς καὶ σκιάδια αὐτοῖς ἕπεται· τὸ γὰρ
κάλλος τιμῶντες ἀσκοῦσιν ὅσα καλλωπίζει τὴν
ὄψιν. ἀλήθειάν τε ὁμοίως καὶ ἀρετὴν ἀπο-
δέχονται· διόπερ οὐδὲ τῇ ἡλικίᾳ τῶν γερόντων
προνομίαν διδόασιν, ἂν μὴ καὶ τῷ φρονεῖν πλεο-

----

[1] εὐπραγεῖν F, εὖ πράττειν other MSS.
[2] ὑποθήκης, Tyrwhitt and later editors. for ἐπιθήκης.
[3] Instead of οὐδ᾽, mxz and Corais and Meineke read οὐκ.
[4] Γυμνασίων E, Γυμνάσιον other MSS. ; so Corais and
Meineke.

single thing from memory; but still they fare happily, because of their simplicity and their frugality; and indeed they do not drink wine, except at sacrifices, but drink a beverage which they make from rice instead of barley;[1] and also that their food consists for the most part of rice porridge; and their simplicity is also proven in their laws and contracts, which arises from the fact that they are not litigious; for they do not have lawsuits over either pledges or deposits, or have need of witnesses or seals, but trust persons with whom they stake their interests; and further, they generally leave unguarded what they have at their homes. Now these things tend to sobriety; but no man could approve those other habits of theirs—of always eating alone and of not having one common hour for all for dinner and breakfast instead of eating as each one likes; for eating in the other way is more conducive to a social and civic life.

54. For exercise they approve most of all of rubbing; and, among other ways, they smooth out their bodies through means of smooth sticks of ebony. Their funerals are simple and their mounds small. But, contrary to their simplicity in general, they like to adorn themselves; for they wear apparel embroidered with gold, and use ornaments set with precious stones, and wear gay-coloured linen garments, and are accompanied with sun-shades; for, since they esteem beauty, they practise everything that can beautify their appearance. Further, they respect alike virtue and truth; and therefore they give no precedence even to the age of old men, unless these are also superior in wisdom. They

---

[1] " Arrack " is the name of this beverage.

STRABO

νεκτῶσι. πολλὰς δὲ γαμοῦσιν ὠνητὰς παρὰ τῶν
γονέων, λαμβάνουσί τε ἀντιδιδόντες ζεῦγος βοῶν,
ὧν τὰς μὲν εὐπειθείας¹ χάριν, τὰς δ' ἄλλας
ἡδονῆς καὶ πολυτεκνίας· εἰ δὲ μὴ σωφρονεῖν
C 710 ἀναγκάσαιεν, πορνεύειν ἔξεστι. θύει δὲ οὐδεὶς
ἐστεφανωμένος οὐδὲ θυμιᾷ οὐδὲ σπένδει, οὐδὲ
σφάττουσι τὸ ἱερεῖον, ἀλλὰ πνίγουσιν, ἵνα μὴ
λελωβημένον, ἀλλ' ὁλόκληρον διδῶται τῷ θεῷ.
ψευδομαρτυρίας δ' ὁ ἁλοὺς ἀκρωτηριάζεται, ὅ τε
πηρώσας οὐ τὰ αὐτὰ μόνον ἀντιπάσχει, ἀλλὰ
καὶ χειροκοπεῖται· ἐὰν δὲ καὶ τεχνίτου χεῖρα ἢ
ὀφθαλμὸν ἀφέληται, θανατοῦται. δούλοις δὲ
οὗτος μέν φησι μηδένα Ἰνδῶν χρῆσθαι, Ὀνησίκριτος δὲ τῶν ἐν τῇ Μουσικανοῦ τοῦτ' ἴδιον
ἀποφαίνει, καὶ ὡς κατόρθωμά γε· καθάπερ καὶ
ἄλλα πολλὰ λέγει τῆς χώρας ταύτης κατορθώ-
ματα, ὡς εὐνομωτάτης.

55. Τῷ βασιλεῖ δ' ἡ μὲν τοῦ σώματος θεραπεία
διὰ γυναικῶν ἐστιν, ὠνητῶν καὶ αὐτῶν παρὰ τῶν
πατέρων· ἔξω δὲ τῶν θυρῶν οἱ σωματοφύλακες
καὶ τὸ λοιπὸν στρατιωτικόν· μεθύοντα δὲ κτείνασα
γυνὴ βασιλέα γέρας ἔχει συνεῖναι τῷ ἐκείνον
διαδεξαμένῳ· διαδέχονται δ' οἱ παῖδες. οὐδ'
ὑπνοῖ μεθ' ἡμέραν ὁ βασιλεύς, καὶ νύκτωρ δὲ
καθ' ὥραν ἀναγκάζεται τὴν κοίτην ἀλλάττειν διὰ
τὰς ἐπιβουλάς. τῶν τε μὴ² κατὰ πόλεμον ἐξόδων μία μέν ἐστιν ἡ ἐπὶ τὰς κρίσεις, ἐν αἷς

¹ εὐπαθείας i.
² τῶν τε μή, Corais and later editors, for τῶν γε μήν.

90

marry many wives, whom they purchase from their
parents, and they get them in exchange for a yoke
of oxen, marrying some of them for the sake of
prompt obedience and the others for the sake of
pleasure and numerous offspring; but if the husband
does not force them to be chaste, they are permitted
to prostitute themselves. No one wears a garland
when he makes sacrifice or burns incense or pours
out a libation; neither do they cut the throat of
the victim, but strangle it, in order that it may be
given to the god in its entirety and not mutilated.
Anyone caught guilty of false-witness has his hands
and feet cut off, and anyone who maims a person
not only suffers in return the same thing, but also
has his hands cut off; and if he causes the loss of a
hand or an eye of a craftsman, he is put to death.
But although Megasthenes says that no Indian uses
slaves, Onesicritus declares that slavery is peculiar
to the Indians in the country of Musicanus, and tells
what a success it is there, just as he mentions many
other successes of this country, speaking of it as a
country excellently governed.

55. Now the care of the king's person is com-
mitted to women, who also are purchased from their
fathers; and the body-guards and the rest of the
military force are stationed outside the gates. And
a woman who kills a king when he is drunk receives
as her reward the privilege of consorting with his
successor; and their children succeed to the throne.
Again, the king does not sleep in daytime; and
even at night he is forced to change his bed from
time to time because of the plots against him.
Among the non-military departures he makes from
his palace, one is that to the courts, where he spends

διημερεύει διακούων οὐδὲν ἧττον κἂν ὥρα γένηται
τῆς τοῦ σώματος θεραπείας. αὕτη δ' ἐστὶν ἡ διὰ
τῶν σκυταλίδων τρῖψις (ἅμα γὰρ καὶ διακούει
καὶ τρίβεται τεττάρων περιστάντων τριβέων),
ἑτέρα δ' ἐστὶν ἡ ἐπὶ τὰς θυσίας ἔξοδος. τρίτη δ'
ἐπὶ θήραν βακχική τις, κύκλῳ γυναικῶν περι-
κεχυμένων, ἔξωθεν δὲ τῶν δορυφόρων· παρε-
σχοίνισται δ' ἡ ὁδός, τῷ δὲ παρελθόντι ἐντὸς[1]
μέχρι γυναικῶν θάνατος· προηγοῦνται δὲ τυμπα-
νισταὶ καὶ κωδωνοφόροι. κυνηγετεῖ δ' ἐν μὲν
τοῖς περιφράγμασιν ἀπὸ βήματος τοξεύων (παρε-
στᾶσι δ' ἔνοπλοι δύο ἢ τρεῖς γυναῖκες), ἐν δὲ ταῖς
ἀφράκτοις θήραις ἀπ' ἐλέφαντος· αἱ δὲ γυναῖκες
αἱ μὲν ἐφ' ἁρμάτων, αἱ δ' ἐφ' ἵππων, αἱ δὲ καὶ ἐπ'
ἐλεφάντων, ὡς καὶ συστρατεύουσιν, ἠσκημέναι
παντὶ ὅπλῳ.

56. Ἔχει μὲν οὖν καὶ ταῦτα πολλὴν ἀήθειαν
πρὸς τὰ παρ' ἡμῖν, ἔτι μέντοι μᾶλλον τὰ τοιάδε.
φησὶ γὰρ τοὺς Καύκασον οἰκοῦντας ἐν τῷ φανερῷ
γυναιξὶ μίσγεσθαι καὶ σαρκοφαγεῖν τὰ τῶν
συγγενῶν σώματα· πετροκυλιστὰς δ' εἶναι κερκοπιθήκους, οἳ λίθους κατακυλίουσι κρημνοβατ-
οῦντες ἐπὶ τοὺς διώκοντας· τά τε παρ' ἡμῖν
ἥμερα ζῷα τὰ πλεῖστα παρ' ἐκείνοις ἄγρια εἶναι·
ἵππους τε λέγει μονοκέρωτας ἐλαφοκράνους·
καλάμους δέ, μῆκος μὲν τριάκοντα ὀργυιῶν τοὺς
C 711 ὀρθίους, τοὺς δὲ χαμαικλινεῖς πεντήκοντα, πάχος
δέ, ὥστε τὴν διάμετρον τοῖς μὲν εἶναι τρίπηχυν,
τοῖς δὲ διπλασίαν.

---

[1] ἐκτός CDFmosw.

the whole day hearing cases to the end, none the less even if the hour comes for the care of his person. This care of his person consists of his being rubbed with sticks of wood, for while he is hearing the cases through, he is also rubbed by four men who stand around him and rub him. A second departure is that to the sacrifices. A third is that to a kind of Bacchic chase wherein he is surrounded by women, and, outside them, by the spear-bearers. The road is lined with ropes; and death is the penalty for anyone who passes inside the ropes to the women; and they are preceded by drum-beaters and gong-carriers. The king hunts in the fenced enclosures, shooting arrows from a platform in his chariot (two or three armed women stand beside him), and also in the unfenced hunting-grounds from an elephant; and the women ride partly in chariots, partly on horses, and partly on elephants, and they are equipped with all kinds of weapons, as they are when they go on military expeditions with the men.

56. Now these customs are very novel as compared with our own, but the following are still more so. For example, Megasthenes says that the men who inhabit the Caucasus have intercourse with the women in the open and that they eat the bodies of their kinsmen; and that the monkeys are stone-rollers, and, haunting precipices, roll stones down upon their pursuers; and that most of the animals which are tame in our country are wild in theirs. And he mentions horses with one horn and the head of a deer; and reeds, some straight up thirty fathoms in length, and others lying flat on the ground fifty fathoms, and so large that some are three cubits and others six in diameter.

57. Ὑπερεκπίπτων δ᾽ ἐπὶ τὸ μυθῶδες πεντα-
σπιθάμους ἀνθρώπους λέγει καὶ τρισπιθάμους,
ὧν τινας ἀμύκτηρας, ἀναπνοὰς ἔχοντας μόνον δύο
ὑπὲρ τοῦ στόματος· πρὸς δὲ τοὺς τρισπιθάμους
πόλεμον εἶναι ταῖς γεράνοις (ὃν καὶ Ὅμηρον
δηλοῦν) καὶ τοῖς πέρδιξιν, οὓς χηνομεγέθεις εἶναι·
τούτους δ᾽ ἐκλέγειν αὐτῶν τὰ ᾠὰ καὶ φθείρειν,
ἐκεῖ γὰρ ᾠοτοκεῖν τὰς γεράνους· διόπερ μηδαμοῦ
μήτ᾽ [1] ᾠὰ εὑρίσκεσθαι γεράνων, μήτ᾽ οὖν νεόττια·
πλειστάκις δ᾽ ἐκπίπτειν γέρανον χαλκῆν ἔχουσαν
ἀκίδα ἀπὸ τῶν ἐκεῖθεν πληγμάτων. ὅμοια δὲ
καὶ τὰ περὶ τῶν Ἐνωτοκοιτῶν καὶ τῶν ἀγρίων
ἀνθρώπων καὶ ἄλλων τερατωδῶν. τοὺς μὲν οὖν
ἀγρίους μὴ κομισθῆναι παρὰ Σανδρόκοττον,
ἀποκαρτερεῖν γάρ· ἔχειν δὲ τὰς μὲν πτέρνας
πρόσθεν, τοὺς δὲ ταρσοὺς ὄπισθεν καὶ τοὺς δακ-
τύλους. ἀστόμους δέ τινας ἀχθῆναι, ἡμέρους
ἀνθρώπους, οἰκεῖν δὲ περὶ τὰς πηγὰς τοῦ Γάγγου,
τρέφεσθαι δ᾽ ἀτμοῖς ὀπτῶν κρεῶν καὶ καρπῶν
καὶ ἀνθέων ὀσμαῖς, ἀντὶ τῶν στομάτων ἔχοντας
ἀναπνοάς, χαλεπαίνειν δὲ τοῖς δυσώδεσι, καὶ διὰ
τοῦτο περιγίνεσθαι μόλις, καὶ μάλιστα ἐν στρατοπέδῳ. περὶ δὲ τῶν ἄλλων διηγεῖσθαι τοὺς
φιλοσόφους, Ὠκύποδάς τε [2] ἱστοροῦντας, ἵππων
μᾶλλον ἀπιόντας, Ἐνωτοκοίτας τε [3] ποδήρη τὰ
ὦτα ἔχοντας, ὡς ἐγκαθεύδειν, ἰσχυροὺς δ᾽, ὥστ᾽
ἀνασπᾶν δένδρα καὶ ῥήττειν νευράν, Μονομμάτους

---

[1] μήτ᾽, Corais and later editors, for μηδ᾽.
[2] τε, Kramer, for δέ.   [3] τε, Kramer, for δέ.

---

[1] About 22½ inches.   [2] Iliad 3. 6.
[3] Cf. 2. 1. 9.   [4] Swift-footed.
[5] i.e. men that sleep in their ears.

57. But Megasthenes, going beyond all bounds to the realm of myth, speaks of people five spans long and three spans [1] long, some without nostrils, having instead merely two breathing orifices above their mouths; and he says that it is the people three spans long that carry on war with the cranes (the war to which Homer [2] refers) and with the partridges, which are as large as geese; and that these people pick out and destroy the eggs of the cranes, which, he adds, lay eggs there; and that it is on this account that neither eggs nor, of course, young cranes are anywhere to be found; and that very often a crane escapes from the fights there with a bronze arrow-point in its body. Like this, also, are the stories of the people that sleep in their ears,[3] and the wild people, and other monstrosities. Now the wild people, he continues, could not be brought to Sandrocottus, for they would starve themselves to death; and they have their heels in front, with toes and flat of the foot behind; but certain mouthless people were brought to him, a gentle folk; and they live round the sources of the Ganges; and they sustain themselves by means of vapours from roasted meats and odours from fruits and flowers, since instead of mouths they have only breathing orifices; and they suffer pain when they breathe bad odours, and on this account can hardly survive, particularly in a camp. He says that the other peoples were described to him by the philosophers, who reported the Ocypodes,[4] a people who run away faster than horses; and Enotocoetae,[5] who have ears that extend to their feet, so that they can sleep in them, and are strong enough to pluck up trees and to break bowstrings; and another people,

95

τε ἄλλους, ὦτα μὲν ἔχοντας κυνός, ἐν μέσῳ δὲ τῷ
μετώπῳ τὸν ὀφθαλμόν, ὀρθοχαίτας, λασίους τὰ
στήθη· τοὺς δὲ Ἀμύκτηρας εἶναι παμφάγους,
ὠμοφάγους, ὀλιγοχρονίους, πρὸ γήρως θνήσκον-
τας· τοῦ δὲ στόματος τὸ ἄνω προχειλότερον εἶναι
πολύ· περὶ δὲ τῶν χιλιετῶν Ὑπερβορέων τὰ
αὐτὰ λέγει Σιμωνίδῃ καὶ Πινδάρῳ καὶ ἄλλοις
μυθολόγοις. μῦθος δὲ καὶ τὸ ὑπὸ Τιμαγένους
λεχθέν,[1] ὅτι χαλκὸς ὕοιτο σταλαγμοῖς χαλκοῖς
καὶ σύροιτο. ἐγγυτέρω δὲ πίστεώς φησιν ὁ
Μεγασθένης, ὅτι οἱ ποταμοὶ καταφέροιεν ψῆγμα
χρυσοῦ καὶ ἀπ᾽ αὐτοῦ φόρος ἀπάγοιτο τῷ
βασιλεῖ· τοῦτο γὰρ καὶ ἐν Ἰβηρίᾳ συμβαίνει.

58. Περὶ δὲ τῶν φιλοσόφων λέγων τοὺς μὲν
ὀρεινοὺς αὐτῶν φησιν ὑμνητὰς εἶναι τοῦ Διονύσου,
δεικνύντας τεκμήρια τὴν ἀγρίαν ἄμπελον, παρὰ
μόνοις[2] φυομένην, καὶ κιττὸν καὶ δάφνην καὶ
μυρρίνην καὶ πύξον καὶ ἄλλα τῶν ἀειθαλῶν, ὧν
μηδὲν εἶναι πέραν Εὐφράτου, πλὴν ἐν παραδείσοις σπάνια καὶ μετὰ πολλῆς ἐπιμελείας σωζό-
C 712 μενα· Διονυσιακὸν δὲ καὶ τὸ σινδονοφορεῖν καὶ τὸ
μιτροῦσθαι καὶ μυροῦσθαι καὶ βάπτεσθαι ἄνθινα
καὶ τοὺς βασιλέας κωδωνοφορεῖσθαι καὶ τυμπανί-
ζεσθαι κατὰ τὰς ἐξόδους· τοὺς δὲ πεδιασίους τὸν
Ἡρακλέα τιμᾶν. ταῦτα μὲν οὖν μυθώδη καὶ ὑπὸ
πολλῶν ἐλεγχόμενα, καὶ μάλιστα τὰ περὶ τῆς
ἀμπέλου καὶ τοῦ οἴνου· πέραν γὰρ τοῦ Εὐφράτου
καὶ τῆς Ἀρμενίας ἐστὶ πολλὴ καὶ ἡ Μεσοποταμία

---

[1] ὡς, before ὅτι, omitted by mz and the editors.
[2] After μόνοις F reads αὐτοῖς.

---

[1] i.e. one-eyed.   [2] " People without noses."

Monommati,[1] with dog's ears, with the eye in the middle of the forehead, with hair standing erect, and with shaggy breasts; and that the Amycteres [2] eat everything, including raw meat, and live but a short time, dying before old age; and the upper lip protrudes much more than the lower. Concerning the Hyperboreans who live a thousand years he says the same things as Simonides and Pindar and other myth-tellers. The statement of Timagenes is also a myth, that brass rained from the sky in brazen drops and was swept down.[3] But Megasthenes is nearer the truth when he says that the rivers carry down gold-dust and that part of it is paid as a tax to the king; for this is also the case in Iberia.[4]

58. Speaking of the philosophers, Megasthenes says that those who inhabit the mountains hymn the praises of Dionysus and point out as evidences [5] the wild grape-vine, which grows in their country alone, and the ivy, laurel, myrtle, box-tree, and other evergreens, no one of which is found on the far side of the Euphrates except a few in parks, which can be kept alive only with great care; and that the custom of wearing linen garments, mitres, and gay-coloured garments, and for the king to be attended by gong-carriers and drum-beaters on his departures from the palace, are also Dionysiac; but the philosophers in the plains worship Heracles. Now these statements of Megasthenes are mythical and refuted by many writers, and particularly those about the vine and wine; for much of Armenia, and the whole of Mesopotamia, and the part of Media

[3] i.e. by rivers.   [4] See 3. 2. 8.
[5] i.e. evidences of his former presence there (see 11. 5. 5).

STRABO

ὅλη καὶ ἡ Μηδία ἑξῆς μέχρι καὶ Περσίδος καὶ
Καρμανίας· τούτων δὲ τῶν ἐθνῶν ἑκάστου πολὺ
μέρος εὐάμπελον καὶ εὔοινον λέγεται.
59. Ἄλλην δὲ διαίρεσιν ποιεῖται περὶ τῶν
φιλοσόφων, δύο γένη φάσκων, ὧν τοὺς μὲν Βραχμᾶνας καλεῖ, τοὺς δὲ Γαρμᾶνας. τοὺς μὲν οὖν
Βραχμᾶνας εὐδοκιμεῖν μᾶλλον,[1] μᾶλλον γὰρ καὶ
ὁμολογεῖν ἐν τοῖς δόγμασιν· ἤδη δ᾽ εὐθὺς καὶ
κυομένους ἔχειν ἐπιμελητάς, λογίους ἄνδρας, οὓς
προσιόντας λόγῳ[2] μὲν ἐπᾴδειν δοκεῖν καὶ τὴν
μητέρα καὶ τὸν κυόμενον εἰς εὐτεκνίαν, τὸ δ᾽
ἀληθὲς σωφρονικάς τινας παραινέσεις καὶ ὑπο-
θήκας διδόναι· τὰς δ᾽ ἥδιστα ἀκρωμένας μάλιστα
εὐτέκνους εἶναι νομίζεσθαι· μετὰ δὲ τὴν γένεσιν
ἄλλους καὶ ἄλλους διαδέχεσθαι τὴν ἐπιμέλειαν,
ἀεὶ τῆς μείζονος ἡλικίας χαριεστέρων τυγχανού-
σης διδασκάλων· διατρίβειν δὲ τοὺς φιλοσόφους
ἐν ἄλσει πρὸ τῆς πόλεως ὑπὸ περιβόλῳ συμ-
μέτρῳ, λιτῶς ζῶντας ἐν στιβάσι καὶ δοραῖς,
ἀπεχομένους ἐμψύχων καὶ ἀφροδισίων, ἀκρω-
μένους λόγων σπουδαίων, μεταδιδόντας καὶ τοῖς
ἐθέλουσι· τὸν δ᾽ ἀκροώμενον οὔτε λαλῆσαι θέμις
οὔτε χρέμψασθαι, ἀλλ᾽ οὐδὲ πτύσαι· ἢ ἐκβάλ-
λεσθαι τῆς συνουσίας τὴν ἡμέραν ἐκείνην, ὡς
ἀκολασταίνοντα· ἔτη δ᾽ ἑπτὰ καὶ τριάκοντα
οὕτως ζήσαντα ἀναχωρεῖν εἰς τὴν ἑαυτοῦ κτῆσιν
ἕκαστον, καὶ ζῆν ἀδεῶς καὶ ἀνειμένως μᾶλλον,

[1] μᾶλλον, Corais aud later editors insert.
[2] λόγῳ, Tyrwhitt and later editors, for λόγων CDFh, λόγον
other MSS.

[1] Brahmans.   [2] Sramans.

next thereafter, extending as far as Persis and Carmania, are on the far side of the Euphrates; and a large part of the country of each of these tribes is said to have good vines and good wine.

59. Megasthenes makes another division in his discussion of the philosophers, asserting that there are two kinds of them, one kind called Brachmanes [1] and the other Garmanes; [2] that the Brachmanes, however, enjoy fairer repute, for they are more in agreement in their dogmas; and that from conception, while in the womb, the children are under the care of learned men, who are reputed to go to the mother and the unborn child, and, ostensibly, to enchant them to a happy birth, but in truth to give prudent suggestions and advice; and that the women who hear them with the greatest pleasure are believed to be the most fortunate in their offspring; and that after the birth of children different persons, one after another, succeed to the care of them, the children always getting more accomplished teachers as they advance in years; and that the philosophers tarry in a grove in front of the city in an enclosure merely commensurate with their needs, leading a frugal life, lying on straw mattresses and skins, abstaining from animal food and the delights of love, and hearkening only to earnest words, and communicating also with anyone who wishes to hear them; and that the hearer is forbidden either to talk or to cough or even to spit; and if he does, he is banished from association with them for that day as a man who has no control over himself; and that, after having lived in this way for thirty-seven years, they retire, each man to his own possessions, where they live more freely and under less restraint,

99

σινδονοφοροῦντα καὶ χρυσοφοροῦντα μετρίως ἐν
τοῖς ὠσὶ καὶ ταῖς χερσί, προσφερόμενον σάρκας
τῶν μὴ πρὸς τὴν χρείαν συνεργῶν ζῴων, δριμέων
καὶ ἀρτυτῶν ἀπεχόμενον· γαμεῖν δ' ὅτι πλείστας
εἰς πολυτεκνίαν, ἐκ πολλῶν γὰρ καὶ τὰ σπουδαῖα
πλείω γίνεσθαι ἄν· ἀδουλοῦσί τε τὴν ἐκ τέκνων
ὑπηρεσίαν, ἐγγυτάτω οὖσαν, πλείω δεῖν παρα-
σκευάζεσθαι·[1] ταῖς δὲ γυναιξὶ ταῖς γαμεταῖς μὴ
συμφιλοσοφεῖν τοὺς Βραχμᾶνας· εἰ μὲν μοχθηραὶ
γένοιντο, ἵνα μή τι τῶν οὐ θεμιτῶν ἐκφέροιεν εἰς
τοὺς βεβήλους· εἰ δὲ σπουδαῖαι, μὴ καταλείποιεν
αὐτούς· οὐδένα γὰρ ἡδονῆς καὶ πόνου κατα-
φρονοῦντα, ὡς δ' αὕτως ζωῆς καὶ θανάτου, ἐθέλειν
ὑφ' ἑτέρῳ εἶναι· τοιοῦτον δ' εἶναι τὸν σπουδαῖον
C 713 καὶ τὴν σπουδαίαν. πλείστους δ' αὐτοῖς εἶναι
λόγους περὶ τοῦ θανάτου· νομίζειν γὰρ δὴ τὸν
μὲν ἐνθάδε βίον ὡς ἂν ἀκμὴν κυομένων εἶναι,
τὸν δὲ θάνατον γένεσιν εἰς τὸν ὄντως βίον
καὶ τὸν εὐδαίμονα τοῖς φιλοσοφήσασι· διὸ τῇ
ἀσκήσει πλείστῃ χρῆσθαι πρὸς τὸ ἑτοιμο-
θάνατον· ἀγαθὸν δὲ ἢ κακὸν μηδὲν εἶναι τῶν
συμβαινόντων ἀνθρώποις, οὐ γὰρ ἂν τοῖς αὐτοῖς
τοὺς μὲν ἄχθεσθαι, τοὺς δὲ χαίρειν, ἐνυπνιώδεις
ὑπολήψεις ἔχοντας, καὶ τοὺς αὐτοὺς τοῖς αὐτοῖς
τοτὲ μὲν ἄχθεσθαι. τοτὲ δ' αὖ χαίρειν μεταβαλλο-
μένους τὰ δὲ περὶ φύσιν, τὰ μὲν εὐήθειαν ἐμφαίνειν

---

[1] The words ἂν . . . παρασκευάζεσθαι are omitted by moxz;
the other MSS. read ἀναδουλοῦσί τε τὴν ἐκ τέκνων μὴ ἔχουσι
δούλους ὑπηρεσίαν (μὴ ἔχουσι δούλους obviously being a gloss).
The above reading is that of Kramer and later editors.

[1] Tozer (*Selections*, note *ad loc.*) interprets τὰ σπουδαῖα to
mean the number of "their comforts."

wearing linen garments, ornaments of gold in moderation in their ears and on their hands, and partake of meats of animals that are of no help to man in his work, but abstain from pungent and seasoned food; and that they marry as many wives as possible, in order to have numerous children, for from many wives the number of earnest children [1] would be greater; and, since they have no servants, it is necessary for them to provide for more service from children—the service that is nearest at hand; but that the Brachmanes do not share their philosophy with their wedded wives, for fear, in the first place, that they might tell some forbidden secret to the profane if they became corrupt, and, secondly, that they might desert them if they became earnest, for no person who has contempt for pleasure and toil, and likewise for life and death, is willing to be subject to another; and that the earnest man and the earnest woman are such persons; and that they converse more about death than anything else, for they believe that the life here is, as it were, that of a babe still in the womb, and that death, to those who have devoted themselves to philosophy, is birth into the true life, that is, the happy life; and that they therefore discipline themselves most of all to be ready for death; and that they believe that nothing that happens to mankind is good or bad, for otherwise some would not be grieved and others delighted by the same things, both having dream-like notions, and that the same persons cannot at one time be grieved and then in turn change and be delighted by the same things. As for the opinions of the Brachmanes about the natural world, Megasthenes says that some of their opinions indicate mental

φησίν, ἐν ἔργοις γὰρ αὐτοὺς κρείττους ἢ λόγοις
εἶναι, διὰ μύθων τὰ πολλὰ πιστουμένους· περὶ
πολλῶν δὲ τοῖς Ἕλλησιν ὁμοδοξεῖν· ὅτι γὰρ
γενητὸς ὁ κόσμος καὶ φθαρτός, λέγειν κἀκείνους,
καὶ ὅτι σφαιροειδής, ὅ τε διοικῶν αὐτὸν καὶ ποιῶν
θεὸς δι᾽ ὅλου διαπεφοίτηκεν[1] αὐτοῦ· ἀρχαὶ δὲ
τῶν μὲν συμπάντων ἕτεραι, τῆς δὲ κοσμοποιίας
τὸ ὕδωρ· πρὸς δὲ τοῖς τέτταρσι στοιχείοις
πέμπτη τίς ἐστι φύσις, ἐξ ἧς ὁ οὐρανὸς καὶ τὰ
ἄστρα· γῆ δ᾽ ἐν μέσῳ ἵδρυται τοῦ παντός. καὶ
περὶ σπέρματος δὲ καὶ ψυχῆς ὅμοια λέγεται καὶ
ἄλλα πλείω· παραπλέκουσι δὲ καὶ μύθους, ὥσπερ
καὶ Πλάτων περί τε ἀφθαρσίας ψυχῆς καὶ τῶν
καθ᾽ ᾅδου κρίσεων καὶ ἄλλα τοιαῦτα. περὶ μὲν
τῶν Βραχμάνων ταῦτα λέγει.

60. Τοὺς δὲ Γαρμᾶνας,[2] τοὺς μὲν ἐντιμοτάτους
Ὑλοβίους φησὶν ὀνομάζεσθαι, ζῶντας ἐν ταῖς
ὕλαις ἀπὸ φύλλων καὶ καρπῶν ἀγρίων, ἐσθῆτος[3]
φλοιῶν δενδρείων, ἀφροδισίων χωρὶς καὶ οἴνου·
τοῖς δὲ βασιλεῦσι συνεῖναι, δι᾽ ἀγγέλων πυνθανο-
μένοις περὶ τῶν αἰτίων καὶ δι᾽ ἐκείνων θερα-
πεύουσι καὶ λιτανεύουσι τὸ θεῖον· μετὰ δὲ τοὺς
Ὑλοβίους δευτερεύειν κατὰ τιμὴν τοὺς ἰατρικοὺς

[1] διαπεφύτηκεν F.
[2] Γαρμάνας F, Γερμᾶνας other MSS.
[3] ἐσθῆτας δ᾽ ἔχειν ἀπὸ moz, Tzschucke and Corais ; Kramer
thinks that οὔσης has fallen out of the MSS. after ἐσθῆτος ;
Meineke conj. ἐσθητοὺς φλοιῷ δενδρείῳ.

[1] i.e. therefore, not everlasting (see Aristotle, Cael. 1. 11).
[2] See 1. 1. 20 and footnote. [3] Brahma.

simplicity, for the Brachmanes are better in deeds than in words, since they confirm most of their beliefs through the use of myths; and that they are of the same opinion as the Greeks about many things; for example, their opinion that the universe was created [1] and is destructible, as also the Greeks assert, and that it is spherical in shape,[2] and that the god [3] who made it and regulates it pervades the whole of it; and that the primal elements of all things else are different, but that water was the primal element of all creation; and that, in addition to the four elements, there is a fifth natural element of which the heavens and the heavenly bodies are composed; and that the earth is situated in the centre of the universe. And writers mention similar opinions of the Brachmanes about the seed [4] and the soul, as also several other opinions of theirs. And they also weave in myths, like Plato, about the immortality of the soul and the judgments in Hades and other things of this kind. So much for his account of the Brachmanes.

60. As for the Garmanes, he says that the most honourable of them are named Hylobii [5] and that they live in forests, subsisting on leaves and wild fruits, clothed with the bark of trees, and abstaining from wine and the delights of love; and that they communicate with the kings, who through messengers inquire about the causes of things and through the Hylobii worship and supplicate the Divinity; and that, after the Hylobii, the physicians are second in

---

[4] " They supposed the Creator to have dropped into the water a seed, from which the world-egg sprang "(Tozer, p. 327, quoting Larsen).

[5] Forest-dwellers (in 16. 2. 39 called Gymno-sophists).

καὶ ὡς περὶ τὸν ἄνθρωπον φιλοσόφους, λιτοὺς
μέν, μὴ ἀγραύλους [1] δέ, ὀρύζῃ καὶ ἀλφίτοις τρεφο-
μένους, ἃ παρέχειν αὐτοῖς πάντα τὸν αἰτηθέντα
καὶ ὑποδεξάμενον ξενίᾳ· δύνασθαι δὲ καὶ πολυ-
γόνους ποιεῖν καὶ ἀρρενογόνους καὶ θηλυγόνους
διὰ φαρμακευτικῆς· τὴν δὲ ἰατρείαν διὰ σιτίων
τὸ πλέον, οὐ διὰ φαρμάκων ἐπιτελεῖσθαι· τῶν
φαρμάκων δὲ μάλιστα εὐδοκιμεῖν τὰ ἐπίχριστα
καὶ τὰ καταπλάσματα, τἆλλα δὲ κακουργίας
πολὺ μετέχειν· ἀσκεῖν δὲ καὶ τούτους κἀκείνους
καρτερίαν, τήν τε ἐν πόνοις καὶ τὴν ἐν ταῖς
ἐπιμοναῖς, ὥστ᾽ ἐφ᾽ ἑνὸς σχήματος ἀκίνητον
διατελέσαι τὴν ἡμέραν ὅλην· ἄλλους δ᾽ εἶναι
τοὺς μὲν μαντικοὺς καὶ ἐπῳδοὺς καὶ τῶν περὶ
C 714 τοὺς κατοιχομένους λόγων καὶ νομίμων ἐμπείρους,
ἐπαιτοῦντας καὶ κατὰ κώμας καὶ πόλεις, τοὺς
δὲ χαριεστέρους μὲν τούτων καὶ ἀστειοτέρους,
οὐδ᾽ αὐτοὺς δὲ ἀπεχομένους τῶν καθ᾽ ᾅδην [2]
θρυλουμένων, ὅσα δοκεῖ πρὸς εὐσέβειαν καὶ
ὁσιότητα· [3] συμφιλοσοφεῖν δ᾽ ἐνίοις καὶ γυναῖκας,
ἀπεχομένας καὶ αὐτὰς ἀφροδισίων.

61. Ἀριστόβουλος δὲ τῶν ἐν Ταξίλοις σοφιστῶν ἰδεῖν δύο φησί, Βραχμᾶνας ἀμφοτέρους, τὸν
μὲν πρεσβύτερον ἐξυρημένον, τὸν δὲ νεώτερον
κομήτην, ἀμφοτέροις δ᾽ ἀκολουθεῖν μαθητάς· τὸν
μὲν οὖν ἄλλον χρόνον κατ᾽ ἀγορὰν διατρίβειν,
τιμωμένους ἀντὶ συμβούλων, ἐξουσίαν ἔχοντας, ὅ
τι βούλονται τῶν ὠνίων, φέρεσθαι δωρεάν· ὅτῳ δ᾽

---

[1] ἀγραύλους E, ὑγραύλους other MSS.   [2] ᾅδου moz.
[3] After ὁσιότητά Corais inserts τείνειν.

---

[1] Cf. §§ 61, 63 (below).

honour, and that they are, as it were, humanitarian philosophers, men who are of frugal habits but do not live out of doors, and subsist upon rice and barley-groats, which are given to them by everyone of whom they beg or who offers them hospitality; and that through sorcery they can cause people to have numerous offspring, and to have either male or female children; and that they cure diseases mostly through means of cereals, and not through means of medicaments; and that, among their medicaments, their ointments and their poultices are most esteemed, but that the rest of their remedies have much in them that is bad; and that both this class and the other practise such endurance, both in toils and in perseverance, that they stay in one posture all day long without moving;[1] and that there are also diviners and enchanters, who are skilled both in the rites and in the customs pertaining to the deceased, and go about begging alms from village to village and from city to city; and that there are others more accomplished and refined than these, but that even these themselves do not abstain from the common talk about Hades, insofar as it is thought to be conducive to piety and holiness; and that women, as well as men, study philosophy with some of them, and that the women likewise abstain from the delights of love.

61. Aristobulus says that he saw two of the sophists at Taxila, both Brachmanes; and that the elder had had his head shaved but that the younger had long hair, and that both were followed by disciples; and that when not otherwise engaged they spent their time in the market-place, being honoured as counsellors and being authorized to take as a gift any merchandise they wished; and

ἂν προσίωσι, καταχεῖν αὐτῶν τοῦ σησαμίνου λίπους, ὥστε καὶ κατὰ τῶν ὀμμάτων ῥεῖν· τοῦ τε
μέλιτος πολλοῦ προκειμένου καὶ τοῦ σησάμου,
μάζας ποιουμένους τρέφεσθαι δωρεάν· παρερχο-
μένους δὲ καὶ πρὸς τὴν Ἀλεξάνδρου τράπεζαν,
παραστάντας δειπνεῖν καὶ [1] καρτερίαν διδάσκειν,
παραχωροῦντας εἴς τινα τόπον πλησίον, ὅπου
τὸν μὲν πρεσβύτερον, πεσόντα ὕπτιον, ἀνέχεσθαι
τῶν ἡλίων καὶ τῶν ὄμβρων (ἤδη γὰρ ὕειν, ἀρχομένου τοῦ ἔαρος), τὸν δ' ἑστάναι μονοσκελῆ,
ξύλον ἐπηρμένον ἀμφοτέραις ταῖς χερσὶν ὅσον
τρίπηχυ, κάμνοντος δὲ τοῦ σκέλους, ἐπὶ θάτερον
μεταφέρειν τὴν βάσιν καὶ διατελεῖν οὕτως τὴν
ἡμέραν ὅλην· φανῆναι δ' ἐγκρατέστερον μακρῷ
τὸν νεώτερον· συνακολουθήσαντα γὰρ μικρὰ τῷ
βασιλεῖ ταχὺ ἀναστρέψαι πάλιν ἐπ' οἴκου, μετ-
ιόντος τε, αὐτὸν κελεῦσαι ἥκειν, εἴ του βούλεται
τυγχάνειν· τὸν δὲ συναπᾶραι μέχρι τέλους καὶ
μεταμφιάσασθαι καὶ μεταθέσθαι τὴν δίαιταν,
συνόντα τῷ βασιλεῖ· ἐπιτιμώμενον δὲ ὑπό τινων
λέγειν, ὡς ἐκπληρώσειε τὰ τετταράκοντα ἔτη τῆς
ἀσκήσεως, ἃ ὑπέσχετο. Ἀλέξανδρον δὲ τοῖς
παισὶν αὐτοῦ δοῦναι δωρεάν.

62. Τῶν δ' ἐν Ταξίλοις νομίμων καινὰ καὶ ἀήθη
λέγει· τό τε τοὺς μὴ δυναμένους ἐκδιδόναι τὰς
παῖδας ὑπὸ πενίας προάγειν εἰς ἀγορὰν ἐν ἀκμῇ
τῆς ὥρας, κόχλῳ [2] τε καὶ τυμπάνοις (οἷσπερ καὶ
τὸ πολεμικὸν σημαίνουσιν), ὄχλου προσκληθέντος,
τῷ δὲ προσελθόντι τὰ ὀπίσθια πρῶτον ἀνασύ-

---

[1] καί, Corais and later editors insert.
[2] κόχλῳ CFx, ὄχλῳ other MSS.

that anyone whom they accosted poured over them sesame oil, in such profusion that it flowed down over their eyes; and that since quantities of honey and sesame were put out for sale, they made cakes of it and subsisted free of charge; and that they came up to the table of Alexander, ate dinner standing, and taught him a lesson in endurance by retiring to a place near by, where the elder fell to the ground on his back and endured the sun's rays and the rains (for it was now raining, since the spring of the year had begun); and that the younger stood on one leg holding aloft in both hands a log about three cubits in length, and when one leg tired he changed the support to the other and kept this up all day long; and that the younger showed a far greater self-mastery than the elder; for although the younger followed the king a short distance, he soon turned back again towards home, and when the king went after him, the man bade him to come himself if he wanted anything of him; but that the elder accompanied the king to the end, and when he was with him changed his dress and mode of life; and that he said, when reproached by some, that he had completed the forty years of discipline which he had promised to observe; and that Alexander gave his children a present.

62. Aristobulus mentions some novel and unusual customs at Taxila: those who by reason of poverty are unable to marry off their daughters, lead them forth to the market-place in the flower of their age to the sound of both trumpets and drums (precisely the instruments used to signal the call to battle), thus assembling a crowd; and to any man who comes forward they first expose her rear parts up

ρεσθαι μέχρι τῶν ὤμων, εἶτα τὰ πρόσθεν, ἀρέσα-
σαν δὲ καὶ συμπεισθεῖσαν, ἐφ᾽ οἷς ἂν δοκῇ,
συνοικεῖν· καὶ τὸ γυψὶ ῥίπτεσθαι τὸν τετελευτη-
κότα· τὸ δὲ πλείους ἔχειν γυναῖκας κοινὸν καὶ
ἄλλων. παρά τισι δ᾽ ἀκούειν φησὶ καὶ συγκατα-
καιομένας τὰς γυναῖκας τοῖς ἀνδράσιν ἀσμένας,
τὰς δὲ μὴ ὑπομενούσας ἀδοξεῖν· εἴρηται καὶ ἄλλοις
ταῦτα.

63. Ὀνησίκριτος δὲ πεμφθῆναί φησιν αὐτὸς
C 715 διαλεξόμενος τοῖς σοφισταῖς τούτοις· ἀκούειν γὰρ
τὸν Ἀλέξανδρον, ὡς γυμνοὶ διατελοῖεν καὶ καρ-
τερίας ἐπιμελοῖντο οἱ ἄνθρωποι, ἐν τιμῇ τε
ἄγοιντο πλείστῃ, παρ᾽ ἄλλους δὲ μὴ βαδίζοιεν
κληθέντες, ἀλλὰ κελεύοιεν ἐκείνους φοιτᾶν παρ᾽
αὐτούς, εἴ του μετασχεῖν ἐθέλοιεν τῶν πραττο-
μένων ἢ λεγομένων ὑπ᾽ αὐτῶν· τοιούτων δὴ ὄντων,
ἐπειδὴ οὔτε αὐτῷ πρέπειν ἐδόκει παρ᾽ ἐκείνους
φοιτᾶν οὔτε ἐκείνους βιάζεσθαι παρὰ τὰ πάτρια
ποιεῖν τι ἄκοντας, αὐτὸς ἔφη πεμφθῆναι· κατα-
λαβεῖν δὲ ἄνδρας πεντεκαίδεκα ἀπὸ σταδίων εἴκοσι [1] τῆς πόλεως, ἄλλον ἐν ἄλλῳ σχήματι ἑστῶτα ἢ
καθήμενον ἢ κείμενον γυμνόν, ἀκίνητον ἕως ἑσπέρας, εἶτ᾽ ἀπερχόμενον εἰς τὴν πόλιν· χαλεπώ-
τατον δ᾽ εἶναι τὸ τὸν ἥλιον ὑπομεῖναι οὕτω
θερμόν, ὥστε τῶν ἄλλων μηδένα ὑπομένειν
γυμνοῖς ἐπιβῆναι τοῖς ποσὶ τῆς γῆς ῥᾳδίως κατὰ
μεσημβρίαν.

64. Διαλεχθῆναι δ᾽ ἑνὶ τούτων Καλάνῳ, ὃν καὶ
συνακολουθῆσαι τῷ βασιλεῖ μέχρι Περσίδος καὶ

---

[1] ὀκτώ F.

[1] See § 59 (above).

to the shoulders and then her front parts, and if she
pleases him, and at the same time allows herself to
be persuaded, on approved terms, he marries her;
and the dead are thrown out to be devoured by
vultures; and to have several wives is a custom
common also to others.[1]   And he further says that
he heard that among certain tribes wives were glad
to be burned up along with their deceased husbands,
and that those who would not submit to it were
held in disgrace; and this custom is also mentioned
by other writers.[2]

63. Onesicritus says that he himself was sent to
converse with these sophists; for Alexander had
heard that the people always went naked and devoted
themselves to endurance, and that they were held in
very great honour, and that they did not visit other
people when invited, but bade them to visit them
if they wished to participate in anything they did
or said; and that therefore, such being the case,
since to Alexander it did not seem fitting either to
visit them or to force them against their will to do
anything contrary to their ancestral customs, he
himself was sent; and that he found fifteen men at
a distance of twenty stadia from the city, who were
in different postures, standing or sitting or lying
naked and motionless till evening, and that they
then returned to the city; and that it was very hard
to endure the sun, which was so hot that at midday
no one else could easily endure walking on the
ground with bare feet.

64. Onesicritus says that he conversed with one
of these sophists, Calanus, who accompanied the king
as far as Persis and died in accordance with the

[2] See § 30 (above); and cf. Diodorus Siculus 19. 23.

ἀποθανεῖν τῷ πατρίῳ νόμῳ, τεθέντα ἐπὶ πυρ-
καϊάν· τότε δ' ἐπὶ λίθων τυχεῖν κείμενον· προσιὼν οὖν καὶ προσαγορεύσας εἰπεῖν ἔφη, διότι
πεμφθείη παρὰ τοῦ βασιλέως ἀκροασόμενος τῆς
σοφίας αὐτῶν, καὶ ἀπαγγελῶν πρὸς αὐτόν· εἰ
οὖν μηδεὶς εἴη φθόνος, ἕτοιμος εἴη μετασχεῖν τῆς
ἀκροάσεως· ἰδόντα δ' ἐκεῖνον χλαμύδα καὶ καυ-
σίαν φοροῦντα καὶ κρηπῖδα, καταγελάσαντα, Τὸ
παλαιόν, φάναι, πάντ' ἦν ἀλφίτων καὶ ἀλεύρων
πλήρη, καθάπερ νῦν κόνεως· καὶ κρῆναι δ' ἔρρεον,
αἱ μὲν ὕδατος, γάλακτος δ' ἄλλαι, καὶ ὁμοίως
μέλιτος, αἱ δ' οἴνου, τινὲς δ' ἐλαίου· ὑπὸ πλησ-
μονῆς δ' οἱ ἄνθρωποι καὶ τρυφῆς εἰς ὕβριν ἐξέπεσον. Ζεὺς δὲ μισήσας τὴν κατάστασιν ἠφά-
νισε πάντα καὶ διὰ πόνου τὸν βίον ἀπέδειξε.
σωφροσύνης δὲ καὶ τῆς ἄλλης ἀρετῆς παρελθού-
σης εἰς μέσον, πάλιν εὐπορία τῶν ἀγαθῶν
ὑπῆρξεν. ἐγγὺς δ' ἐστὶν ἤδη νυνὶ κόρου καὶ
ὕβρεως τὸ πρᾶγμα, κινδυνεύει τε ἀφανισμὸς τῶν
ὄντων γενέσθαι. ταῦτα εἰπόντα κελεύειν, εἰ βού-
λοιτο ἀκροάσασθαι, καταθέμενον τὴν σκευὴν
γυμνὸν ἐπὶ τῶν αὐτῶν λίθων κείμενον, μετέχειν
τῶν λόγων, ἀπορουμένου δὲ αὐτοῦ, Μάνδανιν,[1]
ὅσπερ ἦν πρεσβύτατος καὶ σοφώτατος αὐτῶν, τὸν
μὲν ἐπιπλῆξαι ὡς ὑβριστήν, καὶ ταῦτα ὕβρεως
κατηγορήσαντα, αὐτὸν δὲ προσκαλέσασθαι καὶ
εἰπεῖν, ὡς τὸν μὲν βασιλέα ἐπαινοίη, διότι ἀρχὴν

---

[1] Instead of Μάνδανιν E reads κάνδανις; and the name
given by Arrian (*Exp.* 7. 2. 2) and Plutarch (*Alex.* 8. 65)
is Δάνδαμις; but in Strabo the MSS. again read Μάνδανιν in
§ 68 (below).

---

[1] See end of this paragraph.

ancestral custom, being placed upon a pyre and burned up.[1] He says that Calanus happened to be lying on stones when he first saw him; that he therefore approached him and greeted him; and told him that he had been sent by the king to learn the wisdom of the sophists and report it to him, and that if there was no objection he was ready to hear his teachings; and that when Calanus saw the mantle and broad-brimmed hat and boots he wore, he laughed at him and said: " In olden times the world was full of barley-meal and wheaten-meal, as now of dust; and fountains then flowed, some with water, others with milk and likewise with honey, and others with wine, and some with olive oil; but, by reason of his gluttony and luxury, man fell into arrogance beyond bounds. But Zeus, hating this state of things, destroyed everything and appointed for man a life of toil. And when self-control and the other virtues in general reappeared, there came again an abundance of blessings. But the condition of man is already close to satiety and arrogance, and there is danger of destruction of everything in existence." And Onesicritus adds that Calanus, after saying this, bade him, if he wished to learn, to take off his clothes, to lie down naked on the same stones, and thus to hear his teachings; and that while he was hesitating what to do, Mandanis,[2] who was the oldest and wisest of the sophists, rebuked Calanus as a man of arrogance, and that too after censuring arrogance himself; and that Mandanis called him [3] and said that he commended the king because, although busied with the government of so great an

[2] By Arrian, *Alexander*, 7. 2., and Plutarch, *Alexander* 8. 65, called " Dandamis."   [3] Onesicritus.

τοσαύτην διοικῶν ἐπιθυμοίη σοφίας· μόνον γὰρ
ἴδοι αὐτὸν ἐν ὅπλοις φιλοσοφοῦντα· ὠφελιμώτα-
τον δ' εἴη τῶν ἁπάντων, εἰ οἱ τοιοῦτοι φρονοῖεν,
C 716 οἷς πάρεστι δύναμις τοὺς μὲν ἑκουσίους πείθειν
σωφρονεῖν, τοὺς δ' ἀκουσίους ἀναγκάζειν· αὐτῷ
δὲ συγγνώμη εἴη, εἰ δι' ἑρμηνέων τριῶν διαλεγό-
μενος, πλὴν φωνῆς μηδὲν συνιέντων πλέον ἢ οἱ
πολλοί, μηδὲν ἰσχύσει τῆς ὠφελείας ἐπίδειξιν
ποιήσασθαι· ὅμοιον γάρ, ὡς ἂν εἰ διὰ βορβόρου
καθαρὸν ἀξιοῖ τις ὕδωρ ῥεῖν.

65. Τὰ γοῦν λεχθέντα εἰς τοῦτ' ἔφη συντείνειν,
ὡς εἴη λόγος ἄριστος, ὃς ἡδονὴν καὶ λύπην
ψυχῆς ἀφαιρήσεται· καὶ ὅτι λύπη καὶ πόνος
διαφέρει· τὸ μὲν γὰρ πολέμιον, τὸ δὲ φίλιον[1]
αὐτοῖς, τά γε σώματα ἀσκοῦσι πρὸς πόνον, ἵν' αἱ
γνῶμαι ῥωννύοιντο, ἀφ' ὧν καὶ στάσεις παύοιεν
καὶ σύμβουλοι πᾶσιν ἀγαθῶν παρεῖεν καὶ κοινῇ
καὶ ἰδίᾳ· καὶ δὴ καὶ Ταξίλη[2] νῦν συμβουλεύ-
σειε[3] δέχεσθαι τὸν Ἀλέξανδρον· κρείττω μὲν γὰρ
αὐτοῦ δεξάμενον εὖ πείσεσθαι, χείρω δὲ εὖ
διαθήσειν. ταῦτ' εἰπόντα ἐξερέσθαι, εἰ καὶ ἐν
τοῖς Ἕλλησι λόγοι τοιοῦτοι λέγοιντο· εἰπόντος
δ', ὅτι καὶ Πυθαγόρας τοιαῦτα λέγοι,[4] κελεύοι[5]
τε ἐμψύχων ἀπέχεσθαι, καὶ Σωκράτης καὶ Διο-
γένης, οὗ καὶ αὐτὸς ἀκροάσαιτο, ἀποκρίνασθαι,
ὅτι τἄλλα μὲν νομίζοι φρονίμως αὐτοῖς δοκεῖν, ἐν
δ' ἁμαρτάνειν, νόμον πρὸ τῆς φύσεως τιθεμένους·

---

[1] φίλιον E, φίλον other MSS.
[2] καὶ Ταξίλη E, τάξει ᾗ other MSS.
[3] συμβασιλεύσαιεν Dhi.
[4] λέγοι DFh, λέγει other MSS.
[5] κελεύοι DFh, κελεύει other MSS.

empire, he was desirous of wisdom; for the king was
the only philosopher in arms that he ever saw, and
that it was the most useful thing in the world if
those men were wise who have the power of per-
suading the willing, and forcing the unwilling, to
learn self-control; but that he might be pardoned
if, conversing through three interpreters, who, with
the exception of language, knew no more than the
masses, he should be unable to set forth anything
in his philosophy that would be useful; for that, he
added, would be like expecting water to flow pure
through mud!

65. At all events, all he said, according to Onesicritus, tended to this, that the best teaching is that
which removes pleasure and pain from the soul; and
that pain and toil differ, for the former is inimical
to man and the latter friendly, since man trains the
body for toil in order that his opinions may be
strengthened, whereby he may put a stop to dis-
sensions and be ready to give good advice to all,
both in public and in private; and that, furthermore,
he had now advised Taxiles to receive Alexander,
for if he received a man better than himself he would
be well treated, but if inferior, he would improve
him.   Onesicritus says that, after saying this, Mandanis inquired whether such doctrines were taught
among the Greeks; and that when he answered that
Pythagoras taught such doctrines, and also bade
people to abstain from meat, as did also Socrates
and Diogenes, and that he himself had been a pupil
of Diogenes, Mandanis replied that he regarded the
Greeks as sound-minded in general, but that they
were wrong in one respect, in that they preferred
custom to nature; for otherwise, Mandanis said,

οὐ γὰρ ἂν¹ αἰσχύνεσθαι γυμνούς, ὥσπερ αὐτόν,
διάγειν, ἀπὸ λιτῶν ζῶντας· καὶ γὰρ οἰκίαν
ἀρίστην εἶναι, ἥτις ἂν ἐπισκευῆς ἐλαχίστης
δέηται· ἔφη δ᾿ αὐτοὺς καὶ τῶν περὶ φύσιν πολλὰ
ἐξετάσαι καὶ προσημασιῶν, ὄμβρων, αὐχμῶν,
νόσων· ἀπιόντας δ᾿ εἰς τὴν πόλιν κατὰ τὰς
ἀγορὰς σκεδάννυσθαι· ὅτῳ δ᾿ ἂν κομίζοντι σῦκα
ἢ βότρυς παρατύχωσι,² λαμβάνειν δωρεὰν παρ-
έχοντος· εἰ δ᾿ ἔλαιον εἴη, καταχεῖσθαι αὐτῶν
καὶ ἀλείφεσθαι· ἅπασαν δὲ πλουσίαν οἰκίαν
ἀνεῖσθαι αὐτοῖς μέχρι γυναικωνίτιδος, εἰσιόντας
δὲ δείπνου κοινωνεῖν καὶ λόγων· αἴσχιστον δ᾿
αὐτοῖς νομίζεσθαι νόσον σωματικήν· τὸν δ᾿ ὑπο-
νοήσαντα καθ᾿ αὑτοῦ τοῦτο, ἐξάγειν ἑαυτὸν διὰ
πυρός, νήσαντα πυράν, ὑπαλειψάμενον δὲ καὶ
καθίσαντα ἐπὶ τὴν πυρὰν ὑφάψαι κελεύειν,
ἀκίνητον δὲ καίεσθαι.

66. Νέαρχος δὲ περὶ τῶν σοφιστῶν οὕτω λέγει·
τοὺς μὲν Βραχμᾶνας πολιτεύεσθαι καὶ παρακο-
λουθεῖν τοῖς βασιλεῦσι συμβούλους, τοὺς δ᾿
ἄλλους σκοπεῖν τὰ περὶ τὴν φύσιν· τούτων δ᾿
εἶναι καὶ Κάλανον· συμφιλοσοφεῖν δ᾿ αὐτοῖς καὶ
γυναῖκας, τὰς δὲ διαίτας ἁπάντων σκληράς. περὶ
δὲ τῶν κατὰ τοὺς ἄλλους νομίμων τοιαῦτα
ἀποφαίνεται· τοὺς μὲν νόμους ἀγράφους εἶναι,
τοὺς μὲν κοινούς, τοὺς δ᾿ ἰδίους, ἀήθειαν ἔχοντας
C 717 πρὸς τοὺς τῶν ἄλλων· οἷον τὸ τὰς παρθένους
ἆθλον παρά τισι προκεῖσθαι τῷ πυγμὴν νική-
σαντι, ὥστ᾿ ἀπροίκους συνεῖναι· παρ᾿ ἄλλοις δὲ

---

¹ ἄν, Corais and later editors insert.
² παρατύχωσι E, περιτύχωσι other MSS.

they would not be ashamed to go naked, like himself, and live on frugal fare; for, he added, the best house is that which requires the least repairs. And Onesicritus goes on to say that they inquire into numerous natural phenomena, including prognostics, rains, droughts, and diseases; and that when they depart for the city they scatter to the different market-places; and whenever they chance upon anyone carrying figs or bunches of grapes, they get fruit from that person as a free offering; but that if it is oil, it is poured down over them and they are anointed with it; and that the whole of a wealthy home is open to them, even to the women's apartments, and that they enter and share in meals and conversation; and that they regard disease of the body as a most disgraceful thing; and that he who suspects disease in his own body commits suicide through means of fire, piling a funeral pyre; and that he anoints himself, sits down on the pyre, orders it to be lighted, and burns without a motion.

66. Nearchus speaks of the sophists as follows: That the Brachmanes engage in affairs of state and attend the kings as counsellors; but that the other sophists investigate natural phenomena; and that Calanus is one of these; and that their wives join them in the study of philosophy; and that the modes of life of all are severe. As for the customs of the rest of the Indians, he declares as follows: That their laws, some public and some private, are unwritten, and that they contain customs that are strange as compared with those of the other tribes; for example, among some tribes the virgins are set before all as a prize for the man who wins the victory in a fist-fight, so that they marry the victor without dowry; and

κατὰ συγγένειαν κοινῇ τοὺς καρποὺς ἐργασα-
μένους, ἐπὰν συγκομίσωσιν, αἴρεσθαι φορτίον
ἕκαστον εἰς διατροφὴν τοῦ ἔτους, τὸν δ' ἄλλον
ἐμπιπράναι τοῦ ἔχειν εἰσαῦθις ἐργάζεσθαι καὶ
μὴ ἀργὸν εἶναι. ὁπλισμὸν δ' εἶναι τόξον καὶ
ὀϊστοὺς τριπήχεις, ἢ σαύνιον, καὶ πέλτην καὶ
μάχαιραν πλατεῖαν τρίπηχυν· ἀντὶ δὲ χαλινῶν
φιμοῖς χρῆσθαι κημῶν μικρὸν διαφέρουσιν· ἥλοις
δὲ τὰ χείλη διαπεπάρθαι.

67. Τὴν δὲ φιλοτεχνίαν τῶν Ἰνδῶν ἐμφανίζων
σπόγγους φησὶν ἰδόντας παρὰ τοῖς Μακεδόσι
μιμήσασθαι, τρίχας καὶ σχοινία λεπτὰ καὶ
ἀρπεδόνος διαρράψαντας εἰς ἔρια, καὶ μετὰ τὸ
πιλῆσαι[1] τὰ μὲν ἐξελκύσαντας, τὰ δὲ βάψαντας
χροιαῖς· στλεγγιδοποιούς τε καὶ ληκυθοποιοὺς
ταχὺ γενέσθαι πολλούς· ἐπιστολὰς δὲ γράφειν
ἐν σινδόσι λίαν κεκροτημέναις, τῶν ἄλλων γράμ-
μασιν αὐτοὺς μὴ χρῆσθαι φαμένων· χαλκῷ δὲ
χρῆσθαι χυτῷ, τῷ δ' ἐλατῷ μή· τὴν δ' αἰτίαν
οὐκ εἶπε, καίτοι τὴν ἀτοπίαν εἰπὼν τὴν παρα-
κολουθοῦσαν, ὅτι θραύεται κεράμου δίκην τὰ
σκεύη πεσόντα. τῶν δὲ περὶ τῆς Ἰνδικῆς λεγομένων καὶ τοῦτ' ἐστίν, ὅτι ἀντὶ τοῦ προσκυνεῖν
προσεύχεσθαι τοῖς βασιλεῦσι καὶ πᾶσι τοῖς ἐν
ἐξουσίᾳ καὶ ὑπεροχῇ νόμος. φέρει δὲ καὶ λιθίαν[2]

---

[1] πιλῆσαι, Casaubon and the later editors, for πλῆσαι.
[2] λιθείαν hoxz and Meineke.

---

[1] i.e. the horses are controlled by the nose with a halter-
like contrivance rather than by the mouth with bridles.

among other tribes different groups cultivate the crops in common on the basis of kinship, and, when they collect the produce, they each carry off a load sufficient for sustenance during the year, but burn the remainder in order to have work to do thereafter and not be idle. Their weapons, he says, consist of bow and arrows, the latter three cubits long, or a javelin, and a small shield and a broad sword three cubits long; and instead of bridles they use nose-bands, which differ but slightly from a muzzle; [1] and the lips of their horses have holes pierced through them by spikes.[2]

67. Nearchus, in explaining the skill of the Indians in handiwork, says that when they saw sponges in use among the Macedonians they made imitations by sewing tufts of wool through and through with hairs and light cords and threads, and that after compressing them into felt they drew out the inserts and dyed the sponge-like felt with colours; and that makers of strigils and of oil-flasks quickly arose in great numbers; and that they write missives on linen cloth that is very closely woven, though the other writers say that they make no use of written characters; and that they use brass that is cast, and not the kind that is forged; and he does not state the reason, although he mentions the strange result that follows the use of the vessels made of cast brass, that when they fall to the ground they break into pieces like pottery. Among the statements made concerning India is also the following, that it is the custom, instead of making obeisance, to offer prayers to the kings and to all who are in authority and of superior rank. The

---

[2] *i.e.* spikes, or raised points, inside the nose-bands.

ἡ χώρα πολυτελὴ κρυστάλλων καὶ ἀνθράκων παντοίων, καθάπερ τῶν μαργαριτῶν.

68. Τῆς δ' ἀνομολογίας τῶν συγγραφέων ἔστω παράδειγμα καὶ ὁ περὶ τοῦ Καλάνου λόγος· ὅτι μὲν γὰρ συνῆλθεν Ἀλεξάνδρῳ καὶ ἀπέθανεν ἑκὼν παρ' αὐτῷ διὰ πυρός, ὁμολογοῦσι· τὸν δὲ τρόπον οὐ τὸν αὐτόν φασιν, οὐδὲ κατὰ τὰς αὐτὰς αἰτίας. ἀλλ' οἱ μὲν οὕτως εἰρήκασι· συνακολουθῆσαι γὰρ ὡς ἐγκωμιαστὴν τοῦ βασιλέως ἔξω τῶν τῆς Ἰνδικῆς ὅρων παρὰ τὸ κοινὸν ἔθος τῶν ἐκεῖ φιλοσόφων· ἐκείνους γὰρ τοῖς αὐτόθι συνεῖναι βασιλεῦσιν, ὑφηγουμένους τὰ περὶ τοὺς θεούς, ὡς τοὺς μάγους τοῖς Πέρσαις· ἐν Πασαργάδαις δὲ νοσήσαντα, τότε πρῶτον αὐτῷ νόσου γενομένης, ἐξαγαγεῖν ἑαυτόν, ἄγοντα ἔτος ἑβδομηκοστὸν καὶ τρίτον, μὴ προσέχοντα ταῖς τοῦ βασιλέως δεήσεσι· γενομένης δὲ πυρᾶς καὶ τεθείσης ἐπ' αὐτῆς χρυσῆς κλίνης, κατακλιθέντα εἰς αὐτήν, ἐγκαλυψάμενον ἐμπρησθῆναι. οἱ δὲ ξύλινον οἶκον γενέσθαι, φυλλάδος δ' ἐμπλησθέντος καὶ ἐπὶ τῆς στέγης πυρᾶς γενομένης, ἐγκλεισθέντα ὥσπερ ἐκέλευσε, μετὰ τὴν πομπὴν μεθ' ἧς ἧκε,[1] ρίψαντα ἑαυτὸν ὡς ἂν δοκὸν συνεμπρησθῆναι τῷ οἴκῳ. Μεγασθένης δ' ἐν τοῖς μὲν φιλοσόφοις οὐκ εἶναι δόγμα φησὶν ἑαυτοὺς ἐξάγειν· τοὺς δὲ ποιοῦντας τοῦτο νεανικοὺς κρίνεσθαι, τοὺς μὲν σκληροὺς τῇ φύσει φερομένους ἐπὶ πληγὴν ἢ κρημνόν, τοὺς δ' ἀπόνους ἐπὶ βυθόν, τοὺς δὲ

C 718

---

[1] ἧκε F, εἶχε other MSS.

---

[1] e.g. carbuncles, rubies, garnets.

country also produces precious stones, I mean crystals and anthraces of all kinds,[1] as also pearls.

68. As an example of the lack of agreement among the historians, let us compare their accounts of Calanus. They all agree that he went with Alexander and that he voluntarily died by fire in Alexander's presence; but their accounts of the manner in which he was burned up are not the same, and neither do they ascribe his act to the same cause. Some state it thus: that he went along as a eulogiser of the king, going outside the boundaries of India, contrary to the common custom of the philosophers there, for the philosophers attend the kings in India only, guiding them in their relations with the gods, as the Magi attend the Persian kings; but that at Pasargadae he fell ill, the first illness of his life, and despatched himself during his seventy-third year, paying no attention to the entreaties of the king; and that a pyre was made and a golden couch placed on it, and that he laid himself upon it, covered himself up, and was burned to death. But others state it thus: that a wooden house was built, and that it was filled with leaves and that a pyre was built on its roof, and that, being shut in as he had bidden, after the procession which he had accompanied, flung himself upon the pyre and, like a beam of timber, was burned up along with the house. But Megasthenes says that suicide is not a dogma among the philosophers, and that those who commit suicide are adjudged guilty of the impetuosity of youth; that some who are by nature hardy rush to meet a blow or over precipices; whereas others, who shrink from suffering, plunge into deep waters;[2]

[2] *i.e.* drown themselves.

STRABO

πολυπόνους ἀπαγχομένους, τοὺς δὲ πυρώδεις εἰς
πῦρ ὠθουμένους· οἷος ἦν καὶ ὁ Κάλανος, ἀκόλα-
στος ἄνθρωπος καὶ ταῖς Ἀλεξάνδρου τραπέζαις
δεδουλωμένος· τοῦτον μὲν οὖν ψέγεσθαι, τὸν δὲ
Μάνδανιν ἐπαινεῖσθαι, ὃς τῶν τοῦ Ἀλεξάνδρου
ἀγγέλων καλούντων πρὸς τὸν Διὸς υἱὸν πειθομένῳ
τε δῶρα ἔσεσθαι ὑπισχνουμένων, ἀπειθοῦντι δὲ
κόλασιν, μήτ᾽ ἐκεῖνον φαίη Διὸς υἱόν, ὅν γε
ἄρχειν μηδὲ πολλοστοῦ μέρους τῆς γῆς· μήτε[1]
αὐτῷ δεῖν τῶν παρ᾽ ἐκείνου δωρεῶν, ὧν[2] οὐδεὶς
κόρος· μήτε δὲ ἀπειλῆς εἶναι φόβον, ᾧ ζῶντι μὲν
ἀρκοῦσα εἴη τροφὸς ἡ Ἰνδική, ἀποθανὼν δὲ ἀπαλ-
λάξαιτο τῆς τετρυχωμένης ἀπὸ γήρως σαρκός,
μεταστὰς εἰς βελτίω καὶ καθαρώτερον βίον· ὥστ᾽
ἐπαινέσαι τὸν Ἀλέξανδρον καὶ συγχωρῆσαι.

69. Λέγεται δὲ καὶ ταῦτα παρὰ τῶν συγγραφέων, ὅτι σέβονται μὲν τὸν ὄμβριον Δία Ἰνδοὶ
καὶ τὸν Γάγγην ποταμὸν καὶ τοὺς ἐγχωρίους δαί-
μονας. ὅταν δὲ βασιλεὺς λούῃ τὴν τρίχα, μεγάλην
ἑορτὴν ἄγουσι καὶ μεγάλα δῶρα πέμπουσι τὸν
ἑαυτοῦ πλοῦτον ἕκαστος ἐπιδεικνύμενος κατὰ
ἅμιλλαν. τῶν τε μυρμήκων τινὰς καὶ πτερωτοὺς
λέγουσι τῶν χρυσωρύχων· ψήγματά τε χρυσοῦ
καταφέρειν τοὺς ποταμούς, καθάπερ τοὺς Ἰβη-
ρικούς· ἐν δὲ ταῖς κατὰ τὰς ἑορτὰς πομπαῖς
πολλοὶ μὲν ἐλέφαντες πέμπονται χρυσῷ κεκο-

[1] μήτε, Corais and later editors, for μηδέ.
[2] ὧν, all MSS. except *moz*, which read ᾧ. Kramer conj.
πόθος for κόρος, citing Arrian 7. 2. 3.

128

and others, who are much suffering, hang them·
selves; and others, who have a fiery temperament,
fling themselves into fire; and that such was Calanus,
a man who was without self-control and a slave to
the table of Alexander; and that therefore Calanus
is censured, whereas Mandanis is commended; for
when Alexander's messengers summoned Mandanis
to visit the son of Zeus and promised that he would
receive gifts if he obeyed, but punishment if
he disobeyed, he replied that, in the first place,
Alexander was not the son of Zeus, inasmuch as he
was not ruler over even a very small part of the
earth, and, secondly, that he had no need of gifts
from Alexander, of which there was no satiety,[1] and,
thirdly, that he had no fear of threats, since India
would supply him with sufficient food while he was
alive, and when he died he would be released from
the flesh wasted by old age and be translated to a
better and purer life; and that the result was that
Alexander commended him and acquiesced.

69. The following statements are also made by
the historians: that the Indians worship Zeus and the
Ganges River and the local deities. And when the
king washes his hair, they celebrate a great festival
and bring big presents, each man making rivalry in
display of his own wealth. And they say that some
of the ants that mine gold[2] have wings; and that
gold-dust is brought down by the rivers, as by the
rivers in Iberia.[3] And in the processions at the time
of festivals many elephants are paraded, all adorned

---

[1] Or perhaps, " for which he had no longing " (see critical
note).

[2] Cp. §§ 37 and 44 (above).

[3] See 3. 2. 8.

σμημένοι καὶ ἀργύρῳ, πολλὰ δὲ τέθριππα καὶ
βοϊκὰ ζεύγη· εἶθ᾽ ἡ στρατιὰ κεκοσμημένη· καὶ
χρυσώματα δὲ τῶν μεγάλων λεβήτων καὶ κρατήρων ὀργυιαίων· καὶ τοῦ Ἰνδικοῦ χαλκοῦ[1]
τράπεζαί τε[2] καὶ θρόνοι καὶ ἐκπώματα καὶ
λουτῆρες, λιθοκόλλητα τὰ πλεῖστα σμαράγδοις
καὶ βηρύλλοις καὶ ἄνθραξιν Ἰνδικοῖς· καὶ ἐσθὴς
δὲ ποικίλη χρυσόπαστος, καὶ βόνασοι[3] καὶ
παρδάλεις καὶ λέοντες τιθασοὶ καὶ τῶν ποικίλων
ὀρνέων καὶ εὐφθόγγων πλῆθος. ὁ δὲ Κλείταρχός
φησιν ἁμάξας τετρακύκλους, δένδρα κομιζούσας
τῶν μεγαλοφύλλων, ἐξ ὧν ἀπήρτηται[4] γένη
τετιθασευμένων ὀρνέων, ὧν εὐφωνότατον μὲν
εἴρηκε τὸν ὠρίωνα, λαμπρότατον δὲ κατὰ τὴν
ὄψιν καὶ πλείστην ἔχοντα ποικιλίαν τὸν καλούμενον κατρέα.[5] τὴν γὰρ ἰδέαν ταῷ μάλιστα
ἐγγίζειν. τὴν δὲ λοιπὴν εἰκονογραφίαν παρ᾽
ἐκείνου ληπτέον.

70. Φιλοσόφους τε τοῖς Βραχμᾶσιν ἀντιδιαι-
C 719 ροῦνται Πράμνας, ἐριστικούς τινας καὶ ἐλεγκ-
τικούς· τοὺς δὲ Βραχμᾶνας φυσιολογίαν καὶ
ἀστρονομίαν ἀσκεῖν, γελωμένους ὑπ᾽ ἐκείνων ὡς
ἀλαζόνας καὶ ἀνοήτους. τούτων δὲ τοὺς μὲν
ὀρεινοὺς καλεῖσθαι, τοὺς δὲ γυμνήτας, τοὺς δὲ
πολιτικοὺς καὶ προσχωρίους· τοὺς μὲν ὀρεινοὺς

---

[1] καί, before τράπεζαι, Corais ejects.
[2] τε, Corais and later editors, for δέ.
[3] καὶ βόνασοι, Meineke ; CDE*gh* have a lacuna of about
six letters ; *vw* read καὶ . . . ασοι, *i* καὶ ἄρκοι, *x* καὶ θηρία ;
Tzschucke καὶ θηρία . . . ασοι ; Corais καὶ θηρία ἄρκοι ;
Groskurd καὶ θηρία βόνασοι.
[4] ἀπήρτηται, Schneider (note on Aelian, *An.* 12. 22), for
ἀπείργηται.

122

with gold and silver, as also many four-horse chariots and ox-teams; and then follows the army, all in military uniform; and then golden vessels consisting of large basins and bowls a fathom in breadth; and tables, high chairs, drinking-cups, and bath-tubs, all of which are made of Indian copper and most of them are set with precious stones—emeralds, beryls, and Indian anthraces;[1] and also variegated garments spangled with gold, and tame bisons,[2] leopards, and lions, and numbers of variegated and sweet-voiced birds. And Cleitarchus speaks of four-wheeled carriages on which large-leaved trees are carried, and of different kinds of tamed birds that cling to these trees, and states that of these birds the orion has the sweetest voice, but that the catreus, as it is called, has the most splendid appearance and the most variegated plumage; for its appearance approaches nearest that of the peacock. But one must get the rest of the description from Cleitarchus.

70. In classifying the philosophers, writers oppose to the Brachmanes the Pramnae, a contentious and disputatious sect; and they say that the Brachmanes study natural philosophy and astronomy, but that they are derided by the Pramnae as quacks and fools; and that, of these, some are called " Mountain " Pramnae, others " Naked " Pramnae, and others " City " Pramnae or " Neighbouring " Pramnae; and that the " Mountain " Pramnae wear deer-

[1] See note on "anthraces," § 68 (above).
[2] Aurochs.

---

[5] καστρέα Dh, κάτρεα F.

δοραῖς ἐλάφων χρῆσθαι, πήρας δ' ἔχειν ῥιζῶν
καὶ φαρμάκων μεστάς, προσποιουμένους ἰατρικὴν
μετὰ γοητείας καὶ ἐπῳδῶν καὶ περιάπτων. τοὺς
δὲ γυμνήτας κατὰ τοὔνομα γυμνοὺς διαζῆν, ὑπαι-
θρίους τὸ πλέον, καρτερίαν ἀσκοῦντας, ἣν ἔφαμεν
πρότερον, μέχρι ἑπτὰ ἐτῶν[1] καὶ τριάκοντα, γυναῖκας δὲ συνεῖαι, μὴ μιγνυμένας αὐτοῖς· τούτους
δὲ θαυμάζεσθαι διαφερόντως.

71. Τοὺς δὲ πολιτικοὺς σινδονίτας κατὰ πόλιν
ζῆν ἢ καὶ κατ' ἀγρούς, καθημμένους[2] νεβρίδας
ἢ δορκάδων δοράς· ὡς δ' εἰπεῖν, Ἰνδοὺς ἐσθῆτι
λευκῇ χρῆσθαι καὶ σινδόσι λευκαῖς καὶ καρπά-
σοις, ὑπεναντίως τοῖς εἰποῦσιν εὐανθέστατα
αὐτοὺς ἀμπέχεσθαι φορήματα· κομᾶν δὲ καὶ
πωγωνοτροφεῖν πάντας, ἀναπλεκομένους δὲ μιτροῦσθαι τὰς κόμας.

72. Ἀρτεμίδωρος δὲ τὸν Γάγγην φησὶν ἐκ
τῶν Ἠμωδῶν ὀρῶν καταφερόμενον πρὸς νότον,
ἐπειδὰν κατὰ τὴν Γάγγην γένηται πόλιν, ἐπι-
στρέφειν πρὸς ἔω μέχρι Παλιβόθρων καὶ τῆς
εἰς τὴν θάλατταν ἐκβολῆς. τῶν δὲ συρρεόντων
εἰς αὐτὸν Οἰδάνην[3] τινὰ καλεῖ·[4] τρέφει δὲ καὶ
κροκοδείλους καὶ δελφῖνας. λέγει δὲ καὶ ἄλλα
τινά, συγκεχυμένως δὲ καὶ ἀργῶς, ὧν οὐ φροντιστέον. προσθείη δ' ἄν τις τούτοις καὶ τὰ παρὰ
τοῦ Δαμασκηνοῦ Νικολάου.

73. Φησὶ γὰρ οὗτος ἐν Ἀντιοχείᾳ τῇ ἐπὶ
Δάφνῃ παρατυχεῖν τοῖς Ἰνδῶν πρέσβεσιν, ἀφιγ-

---

[1] ἐτῶν, omitted by all MSS. except E.
[2] καθειμένους CDEFhix, καθημένους w, ἐνημμένους moz and Corais.
[3] Οἰδάνην is probably corrupt. Corais conj. Οἰμάνην; Kramer, Ἰομάνην; C. Müller Διοιδάνην or Διαρδάνην.

skins, and carry wallets full of roots and drugs, pretending to cure people with these, along with witchery and enchantments and amulets; and that the " Naked " Pramnae, as their name implies, live naked, for the most part in the open air, practising endurance, as I have said before,[1] for thirty-seven years; and that women associate with them but do not have intercourse with them; and that these philosophers are held in exceptional esteem.

71. They say that the " City " Pramnae wear linen garments and live in the city, or else out in the country, and go clad in the skins of fawns or gazelles; but that, in general, the Indians wear white clothing, white linen or cotton garments, contrary to the accounts of those who say that they wear highly coloured garments; and that they all wear long hair and long beards, and that they braid their hair and surround it with a head-band.

72. Artemidorus says that the Ganges River flows down from the Emoda mountains towards the south, and that when it arrives at the city Ganges it turns towards the east to Palibothra and its outlet into the sea. And he calls one of its tributaries Oedanes, saying that it breeds both crocodiles and dolphins. And he goes on to mention certain other things, but in such a confused and careless manner that they are not to be considered. But one might add to the accounts here given that of Nicolaüs Damascenus.

73. He says that at Antioch, near Daphnê, he chanced to meet the Indian ambassadors who had

---

[1] §§ 60 and 61 (above).

---

[4] καλεῖ, Casaubon and later editors, for καλεῖν.

μένοις παρὰ Καίσαρα τὸν Σεβαστόν· οὓς ἐκ
μὲν τῆς ἐπιστολῆς πλείους δηλοῦσθαι, σωθῆναι
δὲ τρεῖς μόνους, οὓς ἰδεῖν φησι, τοὺς δ᾽ ἄλλους
ὑπὸ μήκους τῶν ὁδῶν διαφθαρῆναι τὸ πλέον·
τὴν δ᾽ ἐπιστολὴν ἑλληνίζειν ἐν διφθέρᾳ γεγραμ-
μένην, δηλοῦσαν, ὅτι Πῶρος εἴη ὁ γράψας,
ἑξακοσίων δὲ ἄρχων βασιλέων, ὅμως περὶ πολλοῦ ποιοῖτο φίλος εἶναι Καίσαρι, καὶ ἕτοιμος εἴη
δίοδόν τε παρέχειν, ὅπη βούλεται, καὶ συμπράτ-
τειν, ὅσα καλῶς ἔχει. ταῦτα μὲν ἔφη λέγειν
τὴν ἐπιστολήν, τὰ δὲ κομισθέντα δῶρα προσε-
νεγκεῖν ὀκτὼ οἰκέτας γυμνούς, ἐν περιζώμασι
καταπεπασμένους ἀρώμασιν· εἶναι δὲ τὰ δῶρα
τόν τε Ἑρμᾶν, ἀπὸ τῶν ὤμων ἀφῃρημένον ἐκ
νηπίου τοὺς βραχίονας, ὃν καὶ ἡμεῖς εἴδομεν,
καὶ ἐχίδνας μεγάλας καὶ ὄφιν πηχῶν δέκα καὶ
χελώνην ποταμίαν τρίπηχυν, πέρδικά τε μείζω
γυπός. συνῆν δέ, ὥς φησι,[1] καὶ ὁ Ἀθήνησι
C 720 κατακαύσας ἑαυτόν· ποιεῖν δὲ τοῦτο τοὺς μὲν
ἐπὶ κακοπραγίᾳ[2] ζητοῦντας ἀπαλλαγὴν τῶν
παρόντων, τοὺς δ᾽ ἐπ᾽ εὐπραγίᾳ, καθάπερ τοῦ-
τον· ἅπαντα γὰρ κατὰ γνώμην πράξαντα μέχρι
νῦν ἀπιέναι δεῖν, μή τι τῶν ἀβουλήτων χρονίζοντι
συμπέσοι· καὶ δὴ καὶ γελῶντα ἅλεσθαι γυμνὸν
ἐπαληλιμμένον[3] ἐν περιζώματι ἐπὶ τὴν πυράν·

---

[1] φησι, Corais, for φασι.
[2] After κακοπραγίᾳ *w* adds τοὺς δὲ διὰ ἄλλην τινὰ δυστυχίαν.
[3] For ἐπαλιλειμμένον F, ἐπαληειμμένον other MSS., Meineke
writes λιπ᾽ ἀληλιμμένον (cp. λιπ᾽ ἀληλιμμένοι 14. 1. 44).

---

[1] So called from the fact that Hermes was usually repre-
sented as a small god, and sometimes without hands or feet

126

been despatched to Caesar Augustus; that the letter
plainly indicated more than three ambassadors, but
that only three had survived (whom he says he saw),
but the rest, mostly by reason of the long journeys,
had died; and that the letter was written in Greek
on a skin; and that it plainly showed that Porus
was the writer, and that, although he was ruler of
six hundred kings, still he was anxious to be a friend
to Caesar, and was ready, not only to allow him a
passage through his country, wherever he wished to
go, but also to co-operate with him in anything that
was honourable. Nicolaüs says that this was the
content of the letter to Caesar, and that the gifts
carried to Caesar were presented by eight naked
servants, who were clad only in loin-cloths be-
sprinkled with sweet-smelling odours; and that the
gifts consisted of the Hermes,[1] a man who was born
without arms, whom I myself have seen, and large
vipers, and a serpent ten cubits in length, and a river
tortoise three cubits in length, and a partridge larger
than a vulture; and they were accompanied also,
according to him, by the man who burned himself
up at Athens; and that whereas some commit
suicide when they suffer adversity, seeking release
from the ills at hand, others do so when their lot
is happy, as was the case with that man; for, he
adds, although that man had fared as he wished up
to that time, he thought it necessary then to depart
this life, lest something untoward might happen
to him if he tarried here; and that therefore he
leaped upon the pyre with a laugh, his naked body
anointed, wearing only a loin-cloth; and that the

(see Herodotus 2. 51). At Athens any four-cornered pillar
ending in a head or bust was called " a Hermes."

ἐπιγεγράφθαι δὲ τῷ τάφῳ· Ζαρμανοχηγὰς[1]
Ἰνδὸς ἀπὸ Βαργόσης κατὰ τὰ πάτρια Ἰνδῶν
ἔθη ἑαυτὸν ἀπαθανατίσας κεῖται.

II

1. Μετὰ δὲ τὴν Ἰνδικήν ἐστιν ἡ Ἀριανή, μερὶς
πρώτη τῆς ὑπὸ Πέρσαις τῆς μετὰ τὸν Ἰνδὸν
ποταμὸν καὶ τῶν ἄνω σατραπειῶν τῶν ἐκτὸς
τοῦ Ταύρου, τὰ μὲν νότια καὶ τὰ ἀρκτικὰ μέρη
τῇ αὐτῇ θαλάττῃ καὶ τοῖς αὐτοῖς ὄρεσιν ἀφορι-
ζομένη, οἷσπερ καὶ ἡ Ἰνδική, καὶ τῷ αὐτῷ
ποταμῷ τῷ Ἰνδῷ, μέσον ἔχουσα αὐτὸν ἑαυτῆς
τε καὶ τῆς Ἰνδικῆς, ἐντεῦθεν δὲ πρὸς τὴν ἑσπέραν
ἐκτεινομένη μέχρι τῆς ἀπὸ Κασπίων πυλῶν
εἰς Καρμανίαν γραφομένης γραμμῆς, ὥστε εἶναι
τετράπλευρον τὸ σχῆμα. τὸ μὲν οὖν νότιον
πλευρὸν ἀπὸ τῶν ἐκβολῶν ἄρχεται τοῦ Ἰνδοῦ
καὶ τῆς Παταληνῆς, τελευτᾷ δὲ πρὸς Καρμανίαν
καὶ τοῦ Περσικοῦ κόλπου τὸ στόμα, ἄκραν
ἔχον ἐκκειμένην ἱκανῶς πρὸς νότον· εἶτα εἰς τὸν
κόλπον λαμβάνει καμπὴν ὡς ἐπὶ τὴν Περσίδα.
οἰκοῦσι δὲ Ἄρβιες πρῶτον, ὁμώνυμοι τῷ ποταμῷ
Ἄρβει τῷ ὁρίζοντι αὐτοὺς ἀπὸ τῶν ἑξῆς Ὠρειτῶν,
ὅσον χιλίων σταδίων ἔχοντες παραλίαν, ὥς φησι
Νέαρχος· Ἰνδῶν δ᾿ ἐστὶ μερὶς καὶ αὕτη. εἶτ᾿
Ὠρεῖται ἔθνος αὐτόνομον· τούτων δ᾿ ὁ παράπλους
χιλίων ὀκτακοσίων, ὁ δὲ τῶν ἑξῆς Ἰχθυοφάγων

---

[1] Ζαρμανοχάνης x, Ζάομανος χήγαν w and Corais.

[1] The spelling of the name is doubtful. Dio Cassius (54. 9)
refers to the same man as " Zarmarus " (see critical note).

following words were inscribed on his tomb: "Here lies Zarmanochegas,[1] an Indian from Bargosa, who immortalised himself in accordance with the ancestral customs of Indians."

II

1. After India one comes to Ariana, the first portion of the country subject to the Persians after [2] the Indus River and of the upper satrapies situated outside the Taurus. Ariana is bounded on the south and on the north by the same sea and the same mountains as India, as also by the same river, the Indus, which flows between itself and India; and from this river it extends towards the west as far as the line drawn from the Caspian Gates to Carmania, so that its shape is quadrilateral. Now the southern side begins at the outlets of the Indus and at Patalenê, and ends at Carmania and the mouth of the Persian Gulf, where it has a promontory that projects considerably towards the south; and then it takes a bend into the gulf in the direction of Persis. Ariana is inhabited first by the Arbies, whose name is like that of the River Arbis, which forms the boundary between them and the next tribe, the Oreitae; and the Arbies have a seaboard about one thousand stadia in length, as Nearchus says; but this too is a portion of India. Then one comes to the Oreitae, an autonomous tribe. The coasting voyage along the country of this tribe is one thousand eight hundred stadia in length, and the next, along that of the Ichthyophagi, seven

---

[2] *i.e.* "to the west of."

ἑπτακισχίλιοι τετρακόσιοι, οἱ δὲ τῶν Καρμανίων τρισχίλιοι ἑπτακόσιοι μέχρι Περσίδος· ὥσθ' οἱ σύμπαντες μύριοι δισχίλιοι[1] ἐννακόσιοι.

2. Ἀλιτενὴς δ' ἐστὶν ἡ τῶν Ἰχθυοφάγων καὶ ἄδενδρος ἡ πλείστη πλὴν[2] φοινίκων καὶ ἀκάνθης τινὸς καὶ μυρίκης· καὶ ὑδάτων δὲ καὶ τροφῆς ἡμέρου σπάνις· τοῖς δ' ἰχθύσι χρῶνται καὶ αὐτοὶ καὶ θρέμματα καὶ τοῖς ὀμβρίοις ὕδασι καὶ ὀρυκτοῖς· καὶ τὰ κρέα δὲ τῶν θρεμμάτων ἰχθύων προσβάλλει· οἰκήσεις δὲ ποιοῦνται τοῖς ὀστέοις τῶν κητῶν χρώμενοι καὶ κόγχοις ὀστρέων τὸ πλέον, δοκοῖς μὲν ταῖς πλευραῖς καὶ ὑπερείσμασι, θυρώμασι δὲ ταῖς σιαγόσιν· οἱ σπόνδυλοι δ' αὐτοῖς εἰσιν ὅλμοι, ἐν οἷς πτίσσουσι τοὺς ἰχθύας ἐν ἡλίῳ κατοπτήσαντες· εἶτ' ἀρτοποιοῦνται σίτου
C 721 μικρὰ καταμίξαντες· καὶ γὰρ μύλοι αὐτοῖς εἰσι, σιδήρου μὴ ὄντος. καὶ τοῦτο μὲν ἧττον θαυμαστόν, καὶ γὰρ ἄλλοθεν ἐνέγκασθαι δυνατόν· ἀλλὰ πῶς ἐπικόπτουσιν ἀποτριβέντας;[3] λίθοις μέντοι φασίν, οἷς καὶ τὰ βέλη καὶ τὰ ἀκοντίσματα τὰ πεπυρακτωμένα ἀποξύνουσι. τοὺς δ' ἰχθύας, τοὺς μὲν ἐν κλιβάνοις κατοπτῶσι, τοὺς δὲ πλείστους ὠμοφαγοῦσι· περιβάλλονται δὲ καὶ δικτύοις φλοιοῦ φοινικίνου.

3. Ὑπέρκειται δὲ τούτων ἡ Γεδρωσία, τῆς μὲν

---

[1] δισχίλιοι, Kramer and the later editors emend to τρισχίλιοι; but it is better to accept the reading of the MSS. and assume that Strabo does not include in his sum total the coast of the Arbies in India, "about one thousand stadia" in length.

thousand four hundred, and that along the country of the Carmanians as far as Persis, three thousand seven hundred, so that the total voyage is twelve thousand nine hundred stadia.

2. The country of the Ichthyophagi [1] is on the sea-level; and most of it is without trees, except palms and a kind of thorn and the tamarisk; and there is a scarcity both of water and of foods produced by cultivation; and both the people and their cattle use fish for food and drink waters supplied by rains and wells; and the meat of their cattle smells like fish; and they build their dwellings mostly with the bones of whales and with oyster-shells, using the ribs of whales as beams and supports, and the jawbones as doorposts; and they use the vertebral bones of whales as mortars, in which they pound the fish after roasting them in the sun; and then they make bread of this, mixing a small amount of flour with it, for they have grinding-mills, although they have no iron. And this is indeed not so surprising, for they could import grinding-mills from other places; but how do they cut them anew when worn smooth? Why, with the same stones, they say, with which they sharpen arrows and javelins that have been hardened in fire. As for fish, they bake some in covered earthen vessels, but for the most part eat them raw; and they catch them, among other ways, with nets made of palm-bark.

3. Above the country of the Ichthyophagi is

[2] Fish-eaters.

---

[2] πλήν, omitted by all MSS. except Ez.
[3] ἀποτριβέντας, Corais, for ἐπιτριβέντα C, ἀποτριβέντα other MSS.

Ἰνδικῆς ἧττον ἔμπυρος, τῆς δ' ἄλλης Ἀσίας μᾶλλον, καὶ τοῖς καρποῖς καὶ τοῖς ὕδασιν ἐνδεὴς πλὴν θέρους, οὐ πολὺ ἀμείνων τῆς τῶν Ἰχθυοφάγων· ἀρωματοφόρος δὲ νάρδου μάλιστα καὶ σμύρνης, ὥστε τὴν Ἀλεξάνδρου στρατιὰν ὁδεύουσαν ἀντὶ ὀρόφου καὶ στρωμάτων τούτοις χρῆσθαι, εὐωδιαζομένην ἅμα καὶ ὑγιεινότερον τὸν ἀέρα ἔχουσαν παρὰ τοῦτο· γενέσθαι δ' αὐτοῖς θέρους τὴν ἐκ τῆς Ἰνδικῆς ἄφοδον ἐπίτηδες συνέβη· τότε γὰρ ὄμβρους ἔχειν τὴν Γεδρωσίαν καὶ τοὺς ποταμοὺς πληροῦσθαι καὶ τὰ ὑδρεῖα, χειμῶνος δ' ἐπιλείπειν· πίπτειν δὲ τοὺς ὄμβρους ἐν τοῖς ἄνω μέρεσι τοῖς προσαρκτίοις καὶ ἐγγὺς τῶν ὀρῶν· πληρουμένων δὲ τῶν ποταμῶν, καὶ τὰ πεδία τὰ πλησιάζοντα[1] τῇ θαλάττῃ ποτίζεσθαι καὶ ὑδρείων εὐπορεῖν. προέπεμψε δ' εἰς τὴν ἔρημον μεταλλευτὰς τῶν ὑδρείων ὁ βασιλεὺς καὶ τοὺς ναύσταθμα αὐτῷ καὶ τῷ στόλῳ κατασκευάσοντας.

4. Τριχῇ γὰρ διελὼν τὰς δυνάμεις, τῇ μὲν αὐτὸς ὥρμησε διὰ τῆς Γεδρωσίας, ἀφιστάμενος τῆς θαλάττης τὸ πλεῖστον πεντακοσίους σταδίους, ἵν' ἅμα καὶ τῷ ναυτικῷ τὴν παραλίαν ἐπιτηδείαν παρασκευάζοι, πολλάκις δὲ καὶ συνάπτων τῇ θαλάττῃ, καίπερ ἀπόρους καὶ τραχείας ἐχούσῃ[2] τὰς ἀκτάς· τὴν δὲ προέπεμψε μετὰ Κρατεροῦ διὰ τῆς μεσογαίας, ἅμα χειρουμένου[3] τε τὴν Ἀριανὴν καὶ προϊόντος ἐπὶ τοὺς αὐτοὺς τόπους, ἐφ' οὓς Ἀλέξανδρος τὴν πορείαν εἶχε. τὸ δὲ ναυτικὸν Νεάρχῳ καὶ Ὀνησικρίτῳ τῷ

[1] Dhi read λιμνάζοντα.

situated Gedrosia, a country less torrid than India, but more torrid than the rest of Asia; and since it is in lack of fruits and water, except in summer, it is not much better than the country of the Ichthyophagi. But it produces spices, in particular nard plants and myrrh trees, so that Alexander's army on their march used these for tent-coverings and bedding, at the same time enjoying thereby sweet odours and a more salubrious atmosphere; and they made their return from India in the summer on purpose, for at that time Gedrosia has rains, and the rivers and the wells are filled, though in winter they fail, and the rains fall in the upper regions towards the north and near the mountains; and when the rivers are filled the plains near the sea are watered and the wells are full. And the king sent persons before him into the desert country to dig wells and to prepare stations for himself and his fleet.

4. For he divided his forces into three parts, and himself set out with one division through Gedrosia. He kept away from the sea no more than five hundred stadia at most, in order that he might at the same time equip the seaboard for the reception of his fleet ; and he often closely approached the sea, although its shores were hard to traverse and rugged. The second division he sent forward through the interior under the command of Craterus, who at the same time was to subdue Ariana and also to advance to the same region whither Alexander was directing his march. The fleet he gave over to Nearchus and

---

² ἐχούσῃ, Tzschucke and the later editors, for ἐχούσης.

³ χειρουμένου, Groskurd and later editors, for χειρούμενοι.

ἀρχικυβερνήτῃ παραδοὺς ἐκέλευσεν, οἰκείας στά-
σεως ἐπιλαμβανομένους ἐπακολουθεῖν καὶ ἀντι-
παραπλεῖν αὐτοῦ τῇ πορείᾳ.

5. Καὶ δὴ καὶ φησιν ὁ Νέαρχος, ἤδη τοῦ
βασιλέως τελοῦντος τὴν ὁδόν, αὐτὸς μετοπώρου
κατὰ πλειάδος ἐπιτολὴν ἑσπερίαν ἄρξασθαι τοῦ
πλοῦ, μήπω μὲν τῶν πνευμάτων οἰκείων ὄντων,
τῶν δὲ βαρβάρων ἐπιχειρούντων αὐτοῖς καὶ
ἐξελαυνόντων· καταθαρρῆσαι γάρ, ἀπελθόντος
τοῦ βασιλέως, καὶ ἐλευθεριάσαι. Κρατερὸς δ᾽
ἀπὸ τοῦ Ὑδάσπου ἀρξάμενος δι᾽ Ἀραχωτῶν ᾔει
καὶ Δραγγῶν εἰς Καρμανίαν. Πολλὰ δ᾽ ἐταλαι-
C 722 πώρει ὁ Ἀλέξανδρος καθ᾽ ὅλην τὴν ὁδὸν διὰ
λυπρᾶς ἰών· πόρρωθεν δ᾽ ὁμοίως[1] ἐπεχορηγεῖτο
μικρὰ καὶ σπάνια, ὥστε λιμώττειν τὸ στράτευμα·
καὶ τὰ ὑποζύγια ἐπέλιπε, καὶ τὰ σκεύη κατε-
λείπετο ἐν ταῖς ὁδοῖς καὶ τοῖς στρατοπέδοις·
ἀπὸ δὲ τῶν φοινίκων ἦν ἡ σωτηρία, τοῦ τε καρποῦ
καὶ τοῦ ἐγκεφάλου. φασὶ δὲ φιλονεικῆσαι τὸν
Ἀλέξανδρον, καίπερ εἰδότα τὰς ἀπορίας, πρὸς
τὴν κατέχουσαν δόξαν, ὡς Σεμίραμις μὲν ἐξ Ἰνδῶν
φεύγουσα σώθειη μετὰ ἀνδρῶν ὡς εἴκοσι, Κῦρος
δὲ ἑπτά, εἰ δύναιτο αὐτὸς τοσοῦτο στράτευμα
διασῶσαι διὰ τῆς αὐτῆς χώρας, νικῶν καὶ ταῦτα.

6. Πρὸς δὲ τῇ ἀπορίᾳ χαλεπὸν ἦν καὶ τὸ
καῦμα καὶ τὸ βάθος τῆς ψάμμου καὶ ἡ θερμότης,
ἔστι δ᾽ ὅπου καὶ θῖνες ὑψηλοί, ὥστε πρὸς τῷ[2]
δυσχερῶς ἀναφέρειν τὰ σκέλη, καθάπερ ἐκ βυθοῦ,

[1] ὁμοίως, Corais, for ὅμως.
[2] πρὸς τῷ (omitted by *moz*), Corais, for πρὸς τό, other MSS.

[1] See 15. 1. 5.

Onesicritus, the latter his master pilot, giving them orders to take an appropriate position, and to follow, and sail alongside, his line of march.

5. Moreover, Nearchus says that when now the king was completing his journey he himself began the voyage, in the autumn, at the time of the rising of the Pleiad in the west; and that the winds were not yet favourable, and that the barbarians attacked them and tried to drive them out; for, he adds, the barbarians took courage when the king departed and acted like freemen. Craterus set out from the Hydaspes and went through the country of the Arachoti and of the Drangae into Carmania. But Alexander was in great distress throughout the whole journey, since he was marching through a wretched country; and from a distance, likewise, he could procure additional supplies only in small quantities and at rare intervals, so that his army was famished; and the beasts of burden fagged out, and the baggage was left behind on the roads and in the camps; but they were saved by the date palms, eating not only the fruit but also the cabbage at the top. They say that Alexander, although aware of the difficulties, conceived an ambition, in view of the prevailing opinion that Semiramis escaped in flight from India with only about twenty men and Cyrus with seven, to see whether he himself could safely lead that large army of his through the same country and win this victory too.[1]

6. In addition to the resourcelessness of the country, the heat of the sun was grievous, as also the depth and the heat of the sand; and in some places there were sand-hills so high that, in addition to the difficulty of lifting one's legs, as out of a pit,

καὶ ἀναβάσεις εἶναι καὶ καταβάσεις· ἀνάγκη
δ᾽ ἦν καὶ σταθμοὺς ποιεῖσθαι μακρούς, διὰ τὰ
ὑδρεῖα, διακοσίων καὶ τετρακοσίων σταδίων, ἔστι
δ᾽ ὅτε καὶ ἑξακοσίων, νυκτοπορούντας τὸ πλέον.
πόρρω δὲ τῶν ὑδρείων ἐστρατοπεδεύοντο ἐν τριάκοντα σταδίοις πολλάκις τοῦ μὴ ἐμφορεῖσθαι
κατὰ δίψος· πολλοὶ γὰρ ἐμπίπτοντες σὺν ὅπλοις
ἔπινον ὡς ἂν ὑποβρύχιοι, φυσώμενοι δ᾽ ἐπέπλεον
ἐκπεπνευκότες καὶ τὰ ὑδρεῖα βραχέα ὄντα διέ-
φθειρον· οἱ δ᾽ ἐν τῷ ἡλίῳ κατὰ μέσην τὴν ὁδὸν
ἀπηγορευκότες ἔκειντο ὑπὸ δίψους· ἔπειτα τρο-
μώδεις μετὰ παλμοῦ χειρῶν καὶ σκελῶν ἔθνησκον
παραπλησίως, ὡς ἂν ὑπὸ[1] ῥίγους καὶ φρίκης
ἐχόμενοι. συνέβαινε δέ τισι καὶ ἐκτραπομένοις
τὴν ὁδὸν καταδαρθεῖν κρατουμένοις ὑπὸ ὕπνου
καὶ κόπου· ὑστερήσαντες δ᾽ οἱ μὲν ἀπώλοντο
πλάνῃ τῶν ὁδῶν καὶ ὑπὸ ἀπορίας ἁπάντων καὶ
καύματος, οἱ δ᾽ ἐσώθησαν, πολλὰ ταλαιπωρή-
σαντες· πολλὰ δὲ κατέκλυσε καὶ τῶν σωμάτων
καὶ τῶν χρηστηρίων ἐπιπεσὼν χειμάρρους νύκ-
τωρ· καὶ τῆς βασιλικῆς δὲ κατασκευῆς ἐξηλείφθη
πολλή· καὶ τῶν καθοδηγῶν δὲ[2] κατ᾽ ἄγνοιαν
πολὺ εἰς τὴν μεσόγαιαν ἐκτραπομένων, ὥστε
μηκέτι ὁρᾶν τὴν θάλατταν, συνεὶς ὁ βασιλεύς, ἐξαυτῆς ὥρμησε, ζητήσων τὴν ἠιόνα, καὶ
ἐπειδὴ εὗρε καὶ ὀρύξας εἶδεν ὕδωρ πότιμον,
μεταπέμπεται τὸ στρατόπεδον, καὶ λοιπὸν μέχρι
ἡμερῶν ἑπτὰ πλησίον ᾔει τῆς ἠιόνος, εὐπορῶν
ὑδρείας· ἔπειτ᾽ αὖθις εἰς τὴν μεσόγαιαν ἀνεχώ-
ρησεν.

[1] ὑπό, omitted by MSS. except *moxz*.
[2] δέ, omitted by *moxz*, τε other MSS. ; emended by Corais.

there were also ascents and descents to be made. And it was necessary also, on account of the wells, to make long marches of two hundred or three hundred stadia, and sometimes even six hundred, travelling mostly by night. But they would encamp at a distance from the wells, often at a distance of thirty stadia, in order that the soldiers might not, to satisfy their thirst, drink too much water; for many would plunge into the wells, armour and all, and drink as submerged men would; and then, after expiring, would swell up and float on the surface and corrupt the wells, which were shallow; and others, exhausted by reason of thirst, would lie down in the middle of the road in the open sun, and then trembling, along with a jerking of hands and legs, they would die like persons seized with chills or ague. And in some cases soldiers would turn aside from the main road and fall asleep, being overcome by sleep and fatigue. And some, falling behind the army, perished by wandering from the roads and by reason of heat and lack of everything, though others arrived safely, but only after suffering many hardships; and a torrential stream, coming on by night, overwhelmed both a large number of persons and numerous articles; and much of the royal equipment was also swept away; and when the guides ignorantly turned aside so far into the interior that the sea was no longer visible, the king, perceiving their error, set out at once to seek for the shore; and when he found it, and by digging discovered potable water, he sent for the army, and thereafter kept close to shore for seven days, with a good supply of water; and then he withdrew again into the interior.

7. Ἦν δέ τι ὅμοιον τῇ δάφνῃ φυτόν, οὗ τὸ γευσάμενον τῶν ὑποζυγίων ἀπέθνησκε μετὰ ἐπιληψίας καὶ ἀφροῦ· ἄκανθα δὲ τοὺς καρποὺς ἐπὶ C 723 γῆς κεχυμένη, καθάπερ οἱ σίκυοι, πλήρης ἦν ὀποῦ· τούτου δὲ ῥανίδες, εἰς ὀφθαλμὸν ἐμπεσοῦσαι, πᾶν ἀπετύφλουν ζῷον. οἵ τε ὠμοὶ φοίνικες ἔπνιγον πολλούς. ἦν δὲ κίνδυνος καὶ ἀπὸ τῶν ὄφεων· ἐν γὰρ τοῖς θισὶν ἐπεφύκει βοτάνη, ταύτῃ δ' ὑποδεδυκότες ἐλάνθανον, τοὺς δὲ πληγέντας ἀπέκτεινον. ἐν δὲ τοῖς Ὠρείταις τὰ τοξεύματα χρίεσθαι θανασίμοις φαρμάκοις ἔφασαν, ξύλινα ὄντα καὶ πεπυρακτωμένα· τρωθέντα δὲ Πτολεμαῖον κινδυνεύειν· ἐν ὕπνῳ δὲ παραστάντα τινὰ τῷ Ἀλεξάνδρῳ δεῖξαι ῥίζαν αὐτόπρεμνον, ἣν κελεῦσαι τρίβοντα ἐπιτιθέναι τῷ τρωθέντι· ἐκ δὲ τοῦ ὕπνου γενόμενον, μεμνημένον τῆς ὄψεως εὑρεῖν ζητοῦντα τὴν ῥίζαν πολλὴν πεφυκυῖαν καὶ χρήσασθαι καὶ αὐτὸν καὶ τοὺς ἄλλους· ἰδόντας δὲ τοὺς βαρβάρους εὑρημένον τὸ ἀλέξημα ὑπηκόους γενέσθαι τῷ βασιλεῖ. εἰκὸς δέ τινα μηνῦσαι τῶν εἰδότων· τὸ δὲ μυθῶδες προσετέθη κολακείας χάριν. ἐλθὼν δ' εἰς τὸ βασίλειον τῶν Γεδρωσίων ἑξηκοσταῖος ἀπὸ Ὤρων, διαναπαύσας τὰ πλήθη μικρόν, ἀπῆρεν εἰς τὴν Καρμανίαν.

8. Τὸ μὲν δὴ νότιον τῆς Ἀριανῆς πλευρὸν τοιαύτην τινὰ ἔχει τὴν τῆς παραλίας διάθεσιν

---

[1] "Orae" seems surely to be a variant spelling of "Oreitae," as Groskurd points out.

7. There was a kind of plant like the laurel which caused any beast of burden which tasted of it to die with epilepsy, along with foaming at the mouth. And there was a prickly plant, the fruit of which strewed the ground, like cucumbers, and was full of juice; and if drops of this juice struck an eye of any creature, they always blinded it. Further, many were choked by eating unripe dates. And there was also danger from the snakes; for herbs grew on the sand-hills, and beneath these herbs the snakes had crept unnoticed; and they killed every person they struck. It was said that among the Oreitae the arrows, which were made of wood and hardened in fire, were besmeared with deadly poisons; and that Ptolemaeus was wounded and in danger of losing his life; and that when Alexander was asleep someone stood beside him and showed him a root, branch and all, which he bade Alexander to crush and apply to the wound; and that when Alexander awoke from his sleep he remembered the vision, sought for, and found, the root, which grew in abundance; and that he made use of it, both he himself and the others; and that when the barbarians saw that the antidote had been discovered they surrendered to the king. But it is reasonable to suppose that someone who knew of the antidote informed the king, and that the fabulous element was added for the sake of flattery. Having arrived at the royal seat of the Gedrosii on the sixtieth day after leaving the Orae,[1] Alexander gave his multitudinous army only a short rest and then set out for Carmania.

8. Such, then, on the southern side of Ariana, is about the geographical position of the seaboard and

καὶ τῆς ὑπερκειμένης πλησίον γῆς τῆς τῶν
Γεδρωσίων καὶ Ὠρειτῶν. πολλὴ δ' ἐστὶ καὶ
εἰς τὴν μεσόγαιαν ἀνέχουσα καὶ ἡ Γεδρωσία
μέχρι τοῦ συνάψαι Δράγγαις τε καὶ Ἀραχωτοῖς
καὶ Παροπαμισάδαις, περὶ ὧν Ἐρατοσθένης οὕτως
εἴρηκεν (οὐ γὰρ ἔχομέν τι λέγειν βέλτιον περὶ
αὐτῶν)· ὁρίζεσθαι μὲν γάρ φησι τὴν Ἀριανὴν
ἐκ μὲν τῶν πρὸς ἔω τῷ Ἰνδῷ, πρὸς νότον δὲ τῇ
μεγάλη θαλάττη, πρὸς ἄρκτον δὲ τῷ Παροπαμισῷ
καὶ τοῖς ἑξῆς ὄρεσι μέχρι Κασπίων πυλῶν, τὰ
δὲ πρὸς ἑσπέραν τοῖς αὐτοῖς ὅροις, οἷς ἡ μὲν
Παρθυηνὴ πρὸς Μηδίαν, ἡ δὲ Καρμανία πρὸς τὴν
Παραιτακηνὴν καὶ Περσίδα διώρισται· πλάτος
δὲ τῆς χώρας τὸ τοῦ Ἰνδοῦ μῆκος τὸ ἀπὸ τοῦ
Παροπαμισοῦ μέχρι τῶν ἐκβολῶν, μύριοι καὶ
δισχίλιοι στάδιοι (οἱ δὲ τρισχιλίους φασί)· μῆκος
δὲ ἀπὸ Κασπίων πυλῶν, ὡς ἐν τοῖς Ἀσιατικοῖς
σταθμοῖς ἀναγέγραπται, διττόν. μέχρι μὲν
Ἀλεξανδρείας τῆς ἐν Ἀρίοις ἀπὸ Κασπίων
πυλῶν διὰ τῆς Παρθυαίας μία καὶ ἡ αὐτὴ ὁδός·
εἶθ' ἡ μὲν ἐπ' εὐθείας διὰ τῆς Βακτριανῆς καὶ
τῆς ὑπερβάσεως τοῦ ὄρους εἰς Ὀρτόσπανα[1] ἐπὶ[2]
τὴν ἐκ Βάκτρων τρίοδον, ἥτις ἐστὶν ἐν τοῖς Παρο-
παμισάδαις· ἡ δ' ἐκτρέπεται μικρὸν ἀπὸ τῆς
Ἀρίας πρὸς νότον εἰς Προφθασίαν τῆς Δραγ-
γιανῆς· εἶτα πάλιν ἡ λοιπὴ μέχρι τῶν ὅρων τῆς

---

[1] Ὀρτόσπανα. Casaubon and later editors, for Ὀρόσπανα.
[2] ἐπί, Groskurd, for διά.

---

[1] Strabo refers to his description in §§ 1–3 (above).
[2] Ariana, not Gedrosia, as some think.
[3] Merely a portion of Ariana.

of the lands of the Gedrosii and Oreitae, which lands are situated next above the seaboard.[1] It[2] is a large country, and even Gedrosia[3] reaches up into the interior as far as the Drangae, the Arachoti, and the Paropamisadae, concerning whom Eratosthenes has spoken as follows (for I am unable to give any better description). He says that Ariana is bounded on the east by the Indus River, on the south by the great sea, on the north by the Paropamisus mountain and the mountains that follow it as far as the Caspian Gates, and that its parts on the west are marked by the same boundaries by which Parthia is separated from Media and Carmania from Paraetacenê and Persis. He says that the breadth of the country is the length of the Indus from the Paropamisus mountain to the outlets, a distance of twelve thousand stadia (though some say thirteen thousand); and that its length from the Caspian Gates, as recorded in the work entitled *Asiatic Stathmi*,[4] is stated in two ways: that is, as far as Alexandreia in the country of the Arii, from the Caspian Gates through the country of the Parthians, there is one and the same road; and then, from there, one road leads in a straight line through Bactriana and over the mountain pass into Ortospana to the meeting of the three roads from Bactra, which city is in the country of the Paropamisadae; whereas the other turns off slightly from Aria towards the south to Prophthasia in Drangiana, and the remainder of it leads back to the boundaries of India and to the

[4] *i.e.* the various *Halting-places* in Asia. The same records have already been referred to in 15. 1. 11. The author of this work appears to have been a certain Amyntas, who accompanied Alexander on his expedition (see Athenaeus 11. 500 D, 12. 529 E, 2. 67 A, and Aelian 17. 17).

Ἰνδικῆς καὶ τοῦ Ἰνδοῦ· ὥστε μακροτέρα ἐστὶν
αὕτη ἡ διὰ τῶν Δραγγῶν καὶ Ἀραχωτῶν, σταδίων
μυρίων πεντακισχιλίων τριακοσίων ἡ πᾶσα. εἰ
C 724 δή τις ἀφέλοι τοὺς χιλίους[1] τριακοσίους, ἔχοι
ἂν τὸ λοιπὸν τὸ ἐπ' εὐθείας· μῆκος τῆς χώρας,
μυρίων καὶ τετρακισχιλίων· οὐ πολὺ γὰρ ἔλαττον
τὸ[2] τῆς παραλίας, κἂν παραύξωσί τινες αὐτό,[3]
πρὸς τοῖς μυρίοις τὴν Καρμανίαν ἑξακισχιλίων
τιθέντες· ἢ γὰρ σὺν[4] τοῖς κόλποις φανοῦνται
τιθέντες ἢ σὺν τῇ ἐντὸς τοῦ Περσικοῦ κόλπου
παραλίᾳ τῇ Καρμανικῇ. ἐπεκτείνεται δὲ τοῦ-
νομα τῆς Ἀριανῆς μέχρι μέρους τινὸς καὶ Περσῶν
καὶ Μήδων καὶ ἔτι τῶν πρὸς ἄρκτον Βακτρίων
καὶ Σογδιανῶν· εἰσὶ γάρ πως καὶ ὁμόγλωττοι
παρὰ μικρόν.

9. Ἡ δὲ τάξις τῶν ἐθνῶν τοιαύτη· παρὰ μὲν
τὸν Ἰνδὸν οἱ Παροπαμισάδαι, ὧν ὑπέρκειται ὁ
Παροπαμισὸς ὄρος, εἶτ' Ἀραχωτοὶ πρὸς νότον,
εἶτ' ἐφεξῆς πρὸς νότον Γεδρωσηνοὶ σὺν τοῖς
ἄλλοις τοῖς τὴν παραλίαν ἔχουσιν· ἅπασι δὲ
παρὰ τὰ πλάτη τῶν χωρίων παράκειται ὁ Ἰνδός.
τούτων δ' ἐκ μερους τῶν παρὰ τὸν Ἰνδὸν ἔχουσί
τινα Ἰνδοί, πρότερον ὄντα Περσῶν· ἃ ἀφείλετο
μὲν ὁ Ἀλέξανδρος τῶν Ἀριανῶν καὶ κατοικίας
ἰδίας συνεστήσατο, ἔδωκε δὲ Σέλευκος ὁ Νικάτωρ
Σανδροκόττῳ, συνθέμενος ἐπιγαμίαν καὶ ἀντι-
λαβὼν ἐλέφαντας πεντακοσίους. τοῖς Παροπαμισάδαις δὲ παράκεινται πρὸς τὴν ἑσπέραν Ἄριοι,
τοῖς δὲ Ἀραχωτοῖς Δράγγαι καὶ τοῖς Γεδρωσίοις·

---

[1] Instead of χιλίους Di read τρισχιλίους.
[2] τό, Groskurd inserts.   [3] αὐτό x, αὐτῶν other MSS.
[4] γὰρ σύν Fz, γὰρ ἂν σύν other MSS.

Indus; so that this road which leads through the country of the Drangae and Arachoti is longer, its entire length being fifteen thousand three hundred stadia. But if one should subtract one thousand three hundred, one would have as the remainder the length of the country in a straight line, fourteen thousand stadia; for the length of the seacoast is not much less,[1] although some writers increase the total, putting down, in addition to the ten thousand stadia, Carmania with six thousand more; for they obviously reckon the length either along with the gulfs or along with the part of the Carmanian seacoast that is inside the Persian Gulf; and the name of Ariana is further extended to a part of Persia and of Media, as also to the Bactrians and Sogdians on the north; for these speak approximately the same language, with but slight variations.

9. The geographical position of the tribes is as follows: along the Indus are the Paropamisadae, above whom lies the Paropamisus mountain: then, towards the south, the Arachoti: then next, towards the south, the Gedroseni, with the other tribes that occupy the seaboard; and the Indus lies, latitudinally, alongside all these places; and of these places, in part, some that lie along the Indus are held by Indians, although they formerly belonged to the Persians. Alexander took these away from the Arians and established settlements of his own, but Seleucus Nicator gave them to Sandrocottus, upon terms of intermarriage and of receiving in exchange five hundred elephants. Alongside the Paromisadae, on the west, are situated the Arii, and alongside the Arochoti and Gedrosii the Drangae; but the Arii

---

[1] The length given in § 1 (above) is 12,900.

οἱ δ' Ἄριοι τοῖς Δράγγαις ἅμα καὶ πρὸς ἄρκτον
παράκεινται καὶ πρὸς ἑσπέραν, ἐγκυκλούμενοι
μικρά πως. ἡ δὲ Βακτριανὴ τῇ τε Ἀρίᾳ πρὸς
ἄρκτον¹ παράκειται καὶ τοῖς Παροπαμισάδαις,
δι' ὧνπερ Ἀλέξανδρος ὑπερέβαλε τὸν Καύκασον,
ἐλαύνων τὴν ἐπὶ Βάκτρων· πρὸς ἑσπέραν δὲ
ἐφεξῆς εἰσι τοῖς Ἀρίοις Παρθυαῖοι καὶ τὰ περὶ
τὰς Κασπίους πύλας· πρὸς νότον δὲ τούτοις ἡ
ἔρημος τῆς Καρμανίας, εἶθ' ἡ λοιπὴ Καρμανία
καὶ Γεδρωσία.

10. Γνοίη δ' ἄν τις τὰ περὶ τὴν λεχθεῖσαν
ὀρεινὴν ἔτι μᾶλλον, προσιστορήσας τὴν ὁδόν, ᾗ
ἐχρήσατο διώκων τοὺς περὶ Βῆσσον ὡς ἐπὶ
Βάκτρων Ἀλέξανδρος ἐκ τῆς Παρθυηνῆς. εἰς
γὰρ τὴν Ἀριανὴν ἧκεν· εἶτ' εἰς Δράγγας, ὅπου
Φιλώταν ἀνεῖλε τὸν Παρμενίωνος υἱόν, φωράσας
ἐπιβουλήν· ἔπεμψε δὲ καὶ εἰς Ἐκβάτανα τοὺς
καὶ τὸν πατέρα αὐτοῦ ἀνελοῦντας, ὡς κοινωνὸν
τῆς ἐπιβουλῆς. φασὶ δ' αὐτοὺς ἐπὶ δρομάδων
καμήλων ὁδὸν ἡμερῶν τριάκοντα ἢ καὶ τετταράκοντα ἑνδεκαταίους διανύσαι καὶ τελευτῆσαι
τὴν πρᾶξιν. οἱ δὲ Δράγγαι περσίζοντες τἆλλα
κατὰ τὸν βίον οἴνου σπανίζουσι, γίνεται δὲ παρ'
αὐτοῖς καττίτερος. εἶτ' ἐκ Δραγγῶν ἐπί τε τοὺς
Εὐεργέτας ἧκεν, οὓς ὁ Κῦρος οὕτως ὠνόμασε, καὶ
τοὺς Ἀραχωτούς, εἶτα διὰ τῶν Παροπαμισαδῶν
C 725 ὑπὸ Πλειάδος δύσιν· ἔστι δ' ὀρεινὴ καὶ κεχιονο-
βόλητο τότε, ὥστε χαλεπῶς ὡδεύετο· πυκναὶ
μέντοι κῶμαι δεχόμεναι πάντων εὔποροι πλὴν

---

¹ ἄρκτον, Kramer and later editors, for ἀριστερόν.

¹ i.e. Philotas.   ² i.e. "Benefactors."

are situated alongside the Drangae on the north as
well as on the west, almost surrounding a small part
of their country. Bactriana lies to the north alongside both Aria and the Paropamisadae, through
whose country Alexander passed over the Caucasus
on his march to Bactra. Towards the west, next to
the Arii, are situated the Parthians and the region
round the Caspian Gates; and to the south of these
lies the desert of Carmania; and then follows the
rest of Carmania and Gedrosia.

10. One would understand still better the accounts
of the aforesaid mountainous country if one inquired
further into the route which Alexander took in his
pursuit of Bessus from the Parthian territory towards
Bactriana; for he came into Ariana, and then
amongst the Drangae, where he put to death the
son of Parmenio,[1] whom he caught in a plot; and he
also sent persons to Ecbatana to put to death the
father of Philotas, as an accomplice in the plot. It
is said that these persons, riding on dromedaries,
completed in eleven days a journey of thirty days,
or even forty, and accomplished their undertaking.
The Drangae, who otherwise are imitators of the
Persians in their mode of life, have only scanty
supplies of wine, but they have tin in their country.
Then, from the Drangae, Alexander went to the
Evergetae,[2] who were so named by Cyrus,[3] and to
the Arachoti; and then, at the setting of the Pleiad,
through the country of the Paropamisadae, a country
which is mountainous, and at that time was covered
with snow, so that it was hard to travel. However,
numerous villages, well supplied with everything

[3] Cyrus the Elder—in return for their kindly services when
he marched through the desert of Carmania (Arrian 3. 27, 37).

STRABO

ἐλαίου παρεμυθοῦντο τὰς δυσκολίας· εἶχόν τε ἐν
ἀριστερᾷ τὰς ἀκρωρείας. ἔστι δὲ τὰ μεσημβρινὰ
μὲν τοῦ ὄρους τοῦ Παροπαμισοῦ Ἰνδικά τε καὶ
Ἀριανά· τὰ δὲ προσάρκτια τὰ μὲν πρὸς ἑσπέραν
Βάκτρια, τὰ δὲ πρὸς ἕω τῶν ὁμόρων[1] τοῖς
Βακτρίοις βαρβάρων. διαχειμάσας δ᾽ αὐτόθι,
ὑπερδέξιον ἔχων τὴν Ἰνδικήν, καὶ πόλιν κτίσας
ὑπερήκρισεν εἰς τὴν Βακτριανὴν διὰ ψιλῶν ὁδῶν
πλὴν τερμίνθου θαμνώδους ὀλίγης, ἀπορούμενος
καὶ τροφῆς, ὥστε ταῖς τῶν κτηνῶν σαρξὶ χρῆσθαι,
καὶ ταύταις ὠμαῖς διὰ τὴν ἀξυλίαν· πρὸς δὲ τὴν
ὠμοσιτίαν πεπτικὸν ἦν αὐτοῖς τὸ σίλφιον, πολὺ
πεφυκός. πεντεκαιδεκαταῖος δὲ ἀπὸ τῆς κτισ-
θείσης πόλεως καὶ τῶν χειμαδίων ἧκεν εἰς
Ἄδραψα, πόλιν τῆς Βακτριανῆς.

11. Περὶ ταῦτα δέ που τὰ μέρη τῆς ὁμόρου τῇ
Ἰνδικῇ καὶ τὴν Χααρηνὴν εἶναι συμβαίνει· ἔστι
δὲ τῶν ὑπὸ τοῖς Παρθυαίοις αὕτη προσεχεστάτη
τῇ Ἰνδικῇ· διέχει δὲ τῆς Ἀριανῆς δι᾽ Ἀραχωτῶν
καὶ τῆς λεχθείσης ὀρεινῆς σταδίους μυρίους ἐννα-
κισχιλίους. ταύτην δὲ τὴν χώραν διεξιὼν Κρα-
τερός, καταστρεφόμενος ἅμα τοὺς ἀπειθοῦντας, ᾔει
συμμῖξαι τὴν ταχίστην σπεύδων τῷ βασιλεῖ. καὶ

---

[1] τὰ δὲ πρὸς ἕω τῶν ὁμόρων, lacuna supplied by Jones. τοῖς
Βακτρίοις βαρβάρων omitted by E (this MS., however, leaves
a space of about three words) and by *moz*; τοῖς Βακτρίοις
βαρβάροις *iwx*, Casaubon and Corais (who, however, place an
asterisk before the words); Kramer conj. τὰ δὲ πρὸς ἕω
Σογδιανά (citing 11. 8. 8, 11. 11. 2, 3); Müller-Dübner and
Meineke merely indicate a lacuna before τοῖς Βακτρίοις
βαρβάρων.

[1] Strabo seems to refer to the juice of the "terebinth"
above-mentioned.

except oil, received them and alleviated their troubles; and they had the mountain summits on their left. Now the southern parts of the Paropamisus mountain belong to India and Ariana; but as for the parts on the north, those towards the west belong to the Bactrians, whereas those towards the east belong to the barbarians who border on the Bactrians. He spent the winter here, with India above him to the right, and founded a city, and then passed over the top of the mountain into Bactriana, through roads that were bare of everything except a few terebinth trees of the shrub kind; and was so in lack of food that it was necessary to eat the flesh of the beasts of burden, and, for lack of wood, even to eat it raw. But the silphium, which grew in abundance there,[1] was helpful in the digestion of the raw food. On the fifteenth day after founding the city and leaving his winter quarters, he came to Adrapsa,[2] a city in Bactriana.

11. Somewhere in the neighbourhood of these parts of the country that borders on India lies Chaarenê; and this, of all the countries subject to the Parthians, lies closest to India. It is distant from Ariana,[3] through the land of the Arachoti and the above-mentioned mountainous country, nineteen thousand stadia.[4] Craterus traversed this country, at the same time subduing all who refused to submit, and went by the quickest route, being eager to join

---

[2] " Adrapsa " is probably an error for " Gadrapsa " (see Vol. V, p. 280, note 3).

[3] An error, apparently, for Aria.

[4] This figure, as given in the MSS., is preposterous. But a slight emendation yields " ten, or nine, thousand stadia," which is more nearly correct.

STRABO

δὴ περὶ τοὺς αὐτοὺς χρόνους σχεδόν τι συνέδραμον
εἰς τὴν Καρμανίαν αἱ πεζαὶ δυνάμεις ἀμφότεραι.
καὶ μικρὸν ὕστερον οἱ περὶ Νέαρχον εἰσέπλεον
εἰς τὸν Περσικὸν κόλπον, πολλὰ ταλαιπωρήσαντες
διὰ τὴν ἄλην καὶ τὴν ταλαιπωρίαν καὶ τὰ μεγέθη
τῶν κητῶν.

12. Εἰκὸς μὲν οὖν πρὸς ὑπερβολὴν ἠδολεσχη-
κέναι πολλὰ τοὺς πλεύσαντας, ὅμως δ᾽ οὖν εἰρήκασι παραδηλοῦντες ἅμα καὶ τὸ παραστὰν αὐτοῖς
πάθος, διότι προσδοκία μᾶλλον ἢ κίνδυνος ὑπῆρχε
τοῖς ἀληθέσι. τὸ δὲ μάλιστα ταράττον φυσητήρων
μεγέθη, ῥοῦν ἀπεργαζομένων μέγαν ἀθρόον καὶ
ἀχλὺν ἐκ τῶν ἀναφυσημάτων, ὥστε τὰ πρὸ ποδῶν
μέρη μὴ ὁρᾶσθαι· ἐπεὶ δ᾽ οἱ καθηγεμόνες τοῦ
πλοῦ, δεδιότων ταῦτα τῶν ἀνθρώπων, τὴν δ᾽
αἰτίαν οὐχ ὁρώντων, ἐμήνυσαν, ὅτι θηρία εἴη,
τάχα δ᾽ ἀπαλλάττοιτο σάλπιγγος ἀκούσαντα
καὶ κρότου, ἐκ τούτου Νέαρχος ταῖς ναυσὶν ἐπῆγε
μὲν τὸ ῥόθιον, καθ᾽ ἅπερ ἐκώλυον, καὶ ἅμα ταῖς
σάλπιγξιν ἐφόβει· τὰ δὲ θηρία ἔδυνεν, εἶτ᾽ ἀνε-
φαίνετο κατὰ πρύμναν, ὥστε ναυμαχίας ἀγωνίαν
παρεῖχεν· ἀλλ᾽ αὐτίκα ἀφίστατο.

13. Λέγουσι μὲν οὖν καὶ οἱ νῦν πλέοντες εἰς
Ἰνδοὺς μεγέθη θηρίων καὶ ἐπιφανείας, ἀλλ᾽ οὔτε
ἀθρόων οὔτ᾽ ἐπιφερομένων πολλάκις, ἀλλ᾽ ἀποσο-
βηθέντα τῇ κραυγῇ καὶ τῇ σάλπιγγι ἀπαλλάτ-

148

the king; and indeed both forces of infantry gathered together in Carmania at about the same time. And a little later Nearchus sailed with his fleet into the Persian Gulf, having often suffered distress because of his wanderings and hardships and the huge whales.

12. Now it is reasonable to suppose that those who made the journey by sea have prated in many cases to the point of exaggeration; but nevertheless their statements show indirectly at the same time the trouble with which they were afflicted—that underlying their real hardships there was apprehension rather than peril. But what disturbed them most was the spouting whales, which, by their spoutings, would emit such massive streams of water and mist all at once that the sailors could not see a thing that lay before them. But the pilots of the voyage informed the sailors, who were frightened at this and did not see the cause of it, that it was caused by creatures in the sea, and that one could get rid of them by sounding trumpets and making loud noises; and consequently Nearchus led his fleet towards the tumultuous spoutings of the whales, where they impeded his progress, and at the same time frightened them with trumpets; and the whales first dived, and then showed up at the sterns of the ships, thus affording the spectacle of a naval combat, but immediately made off.

13. Those who now sail to India, however, also speak of the size of these creatures and of their manner of appearance, but do not speak of them either as appearing in large groups or as often making attacks, though they do speak of them as being scared away and got rid of by shouts and

STRABO

C 726 τεσθαι. φασὶ δ' αὐτὰ μὲν μὴ πλησιάζειν τῇ
γῇ, τὰ δ' ὀστᾶ διαλυθέντων ψιλωθέντα ἐκκυ-
μαίνεσθαι ῥᾳδίως καὶ χορηγεῖν τὴν λεχθεῖσαν
ὕλην τοῖς Ἰχθυοφάγοις περὶ τὰς καλυβοποιίας.
μέγεθος δὲ τῶν κητῶν φησιν ὁ Νέαρχος τριῶν
καὶ εἴκοσιν ὀργυιῶν. πιστευθέν τι δὲ ἱκανῶς
ὑπὸ τῶν ἐν τῷ στόλῳ φησὶν ὁ Νέαρχος ἐξελέγξαι
ψεῦδος ὄν· ὡς εἴη τις ἐν τῷ πόρῳ νῆσος, ἣ
ἀφανίζοι τοὺς προσορμισθέντας· κέρκουρον γάρ
τινα πλέοντα, ἐπειδὴ κατὰ τὴν νῆσον ταύτην
ἐγεγόνει, μηκέτι ὁραθῆναι· πεμφθέντας δέ τινας
ἐπὶ τὴν ζήτησιν ἐκβῆναι μὲν μὴ θαρρεῖν εἰς τὴν
νῆσον ἐκπλέοντας, ἀνακαλεῖν δὲ κραυγῇ τοὺς
ἀνθρώπους, μηδενὸς δ' ὑπακούοντος, ἐπανελθεῖν.
ἁπάντων δ' αἰτιωμένων τὴν νῆσον, αὐτὸς ἔφη
πλεῦσαι καὶ προσορμισθεὶς ἐκβῆναι μετὰ μέρους
τῶν συμπλευσάντων καὶ περιελθεῖν τὴν νῆσον·
ὡς δ' οὐδὲν εὕρισκεν ἴχνος τῶν ζητουμένων,
ἀπογνόντα ἐπανελθεῖν καὶ διδάξαι τοὺς ἀνθρώπους, ὡς ἡ μὲν νῆσος ψευδῆ τὴν αἰτίαν ἔχοι
(καὶ γὰρ αὐτῷ καὶ τοῖς συνεκβᾶσιν ὁ αὐτὸς
ὑπάρξαι ἂν [1] φθόρος), ἄλλος δέ τις τῷ κερκούρῳ
τρόπος τοῦ ἀφανισμοῦ συμβαίη, μυρίων ὄντων
δυνατῶν.

14. Ἡ δὲ Καρμανία τελευταία μέν ἐστι τῆς
ἀπὸ τοῦ Ἰνδοῦ [2] παραλίας, ἀρκτικωτέρα δ' ἐστὶ
πολὺ τῆς τοῦ Ἰνδοῦ ἐκβολῆς· τὸ μέντοι πρῶτον
αὐτῆς ἄκρον ἔκκειται πρὸς νότον εἰς τὴν μεγάλην

[1] ἄν, added by *moz* and the editors.
[2] The words παραλίας . . . Ἰνδοῦ are omitted by all MSS.
except EF.

[1] 15. 2. 2.

trumpets. They say that these creatures do not
approach the land, but that the bones of those that
have died, when bared of flesh, are readily thrown
ashore by the waves, and supply the Ichthyophagi
with the above-mentioned material for the construction of their huts.[1] According to Nearchus, the size
of the whales is twenty-three fathoms.[2] Nearchus
says that he found to be false a thing confidently
believed by the sailors in the fleet—I mean their
belief that there was an island in the passage which
caused the disappearance of all who moored near it;
for he says that, although a certain light boat on a
voyage was no longer to be seen after it approached
this island, and although certain men sent in quest
of the lost people sailed out past the island and
would not venture to disembark upon it, but called
the people with loud outcry, and, when no one
answered their cry, came on back, yet he himself,
though one and all charged their disappearance to
the island, sailed thither, moored there, disembarked
with a part of those who sailed with him, and went
all over it; but that he found no trace of the people
sought, gave up his search, came on back, and informed his people that the charge against the island
was false (for otherwise both he himself and those
who disembarked with him would have met with
the same destruction), but that the disappearance of
the light boat took place in some other way, since
countless other ways were possible.

14. Carmania is last on the seaboard that begins
at the Indus, though it is much more to the north
than the outlet of the Indus. The first promontory
of Carmania, however, extends out towards the

[2] *i.e.* about 140 feet in length.

STRABO

θάλατταν, ποιήσασα[1] δὲ τὸ στόμα τοῦ Περσικοῦ
κόλπου πρὸς τὴν ἀπὸ τῆς εὐδαίμονος Ἀραβίας
ἄκραν, ἐν ἀπόψει οὖσαν, κάμπτεται πρὸς τὸν
Περσικὸν κόλπον, ἕως ἂν συνάψῃ τῇ Περσίδι·
πολλὴ δὲ καὶ ἐν[2] τῇ μεσογαίᾳ ἐστὶν ἐκτεινομένη
μεταξὺ τῆς Γεδρωσίας καὶ τῆς Περσίδος, παραλ-
λάττουσα πλέον τῆς Γεδρωσίας πρὸς τὴν ἄρκτον.
δηλοῖ δ᾽ ἡ εὐκαρπία· καὶ γὰρ πάμφορος καὶ
μεγαλόδενδρος πλὴν ἐλαίας καὶ ποταμοῖς κατάρρυτος. ἡ δὲ Γεδρωσία διαφέρει μικρὸν τῆς τῶν
Ἰχθυοφάγων, ὥστ᾽ ἀκαρπία κατέχει πολλάκις·
διὸ φυλάττουσι τὸν ἐνιαύσιον καρπὸν εἰς ἔτη
πλείω ταμιευόμενοι. Ὀνησίκριτος δὲ λέγει ποταμὸν ἐν τῇ Καρμανίᾳ καταφέροντα ψήγματα
χρυσοῦ· καὶ ὀρυκτοῦ δὲ εἶναι μέταλλον καὶ
ἀργύρου καὶ χαλκοῦ καὶ μίλτου· ὄρη τε εἶναι
δύο, τὸ μὲν ἀρσενικοῦ, τὸ δὲ ἁλός. ἔχει δέ
τινα καὶ ἔρημον συνάπτουσαν ἤδη τῇ Παρθυαίᾳ
καὶ τῇ Παραιτακηνῇ. γεώργια δ᾽ ἔχει παραπλήσια τοῖς Περσικοῖς, τά τε ἄλλα καὶ ἄμπελον·
ταύτης δ᾽ ἡ Καρμανία λεγομένη παρ᾽ ἡμῖν καὶ
δίπηχυν ἔχει πολλάκις τὸν βότρυν, πυκνόρρωγά
C 727 τε ὄντα καὶ μεγαλόρρωγα, ἣν εἰκὸς ἐκεῖ εὐερνεστέ-
ραν εἶναι. χρῶνται δ᾽ ὄνοις οἱ πολλοὶ καὶ πρὸς
πόλεμον σπάνει τῶν ἵππων· ὄνον τε θύουσι τῷ
Ἄρει, ὅνπερ καὶ[3] σέβονται θεῶν μόνον, καί εἰσι
πολεμισταί. γαμεῖ δ᾽ οὐδείς, πρὶν ἂν πολεμίου

[1] ποιήσασα, Kramer, for ποιήσας. [2] ἐν, E inserts.
[3] ὅνπερ καί, Corais, from conj. of Bertram, for ὅν πέρσαι.

[1] So the Greek word, but of course Strabo means yellow
orpiment (arsenic trisulphide).

152

south into the great sea; and Carmania, after forming, along with the cape that extends from Arabia Felix, which is in full view, the mouth of the Persian Gulf, bends towards the Persian Gulf until it borders on Persis. Carmania is a large country and, in the interior, extends between Gedrosia and Persis, although it deviates more towards the north than Gedrosia. This is plainly indicated by its fruitfulness; for it produces all manner of fruits, is full of large trees except the olive, and is also watered by rivers. Gedrosia differs but little from the country of the Ichthyophagi, and therefore often suffers crop failures; and on this account they keep the annual crop in storage, dealing it out for several years. Onesicritus speaks of a river in Carmania that brings down gold-dust; and he says that there are also mines of silver and copper and ruddle, and also that there are two mountains, one consisting of arsenic [1] and the other of salt. Carmania also has a desert which borders at once [2] upon Parthia and Paraetacenê. And it has farm crops similar to those of the Persians, the vine among all the rest. It is from this vine that " the Carmanian," as we here call it, originated—a vine which often has clusters of even two cubits,[3] these clusters being thick with large grapes; and it is reasonable to suppose that this vine is more flourishing there than here. Because of scarcity of horses most of the Carmanians use asses, even for war; and they sacrifice an ass to Ares, the only god they worship, and they are a warlike people. No one marries before he has cut

[2] *i.e.* at its north-western corner.
[3] In circumference, surely.

κεφαλὴν ἀποτεμὼν ἀνενέγκῃ ἐπὶ τὸν βασιλέα·
ὁ δὲ τὸ κρανίον μὲν ἐπὶ τῶν βασιλείων ἀνατίθησι,
τὴν δὲ γλῶτταν λεπτοτομήσας καὶ¹ καταμίξας
ἀλεύρῳ, γευσάμενος αὐτὸς δίδωσι τῷ ἀνενέγκαντι
καὶ τοῖς οἰκείοις κατασιτήσασθαι· ἐνδοξότατος δ᾿
ἐστίν, ᾧ πλεῖσται κεφαλαὶ ἀνηνέχθησαν. Νέαρχος
δὲ τὰ πλεῖστα ἔθη καὶ τὴν διάλεκτον τῶν Καρ-
μανιτῶν Περσικά τε καὶ Μηδικὰ εἴρηκε. τὸ δὲ
στόμα τοῦ Περσικοῦ κόλπου οὐ² μεῖζον διάρματος
ἡμερησίου.

III

1. Μετὰ δὲ Καρμανίαν ἡ Περσίς ἐστι, πολλὴ
μὲν ἐν τῇ παραλίᾳ τοῦ ἀπ᾿ αὐτῆς ὀνομαζομένου
κόλπου, πολὺ δὲ μείζων ἐν τῇ μεσογαίᾳ, καὶ
μάλιστα ἐπὶ μῆκος τὸ ἀπὸ τοῦ νότου καὶ τῆς
Καρμανίας ἐπὶ τὰς ἄρκτους καὶ τὰ περὶ Μηδίαν
ἔθνη. τριττὴ³ δ᾿ ἐστὶ καὶ τῇ φύσει καὶ τῇ τῶν
ἀέρων κράσει. ἡ μὲν γὰρ παραλία καυματηρά
τε καὶ ἀμμώδης⁴ καὶ σπανιστὴ καρποῖς ἐστι
πλὴν φοινίκων (ὅσον ἐν τετρακισχιλίοις καὶ
τετρακοσίοις ἢ τριακοσίοις ἐξεταζομένη σταδίοις,
καταστρέφουσα εἰς ποταμὸν μέγιστον τῶν ταύτῃ,
καλούμενον Ὀρόατιν)· ἡ δ᾿ ὑπὲρ ταύτης ἐστὶ
πάμφορος καὶ πεδινὴ καὶ θρεμμάτων ἀρίστη
τροφός, ποταμοῖς τε καὶ λίμναις πληθύει. τρίτη
δ᾿ ἐστὶν ἡ πρὸς βορρᾶν χειμέριος καὶ ὀρεινή· πρὸς
δὲ ταῖς ἐσχατιαῖς εἰσιν οἱ καμηλοβοσκοί. μῆκος

¹ καί, added by vz and the editors.
² οὐ, inserted by Corais.
³ τριττή Ex, τρίτη other MSS.

off the head of an enemy and brought it to the king;
and the king stores the skull in the royal palace;
and he then minces the tongue, mixes it with flour,
tastes it himself, and gives it to the man who brought
it to him, to be eaten by himself and family; and
that king is held in the highest repute to whom the
most heads have been brought. Nearchus states
that the language and most of the customs of the
Carmanians are like those of the Medes and Persians.
The voyage across the mouth of the Persian Gulf
requires no more than one day.

III

1. After Carmania one comes to Persis. A large
portion of this country lies on the seaboard of the
gulf which is named after it, but a much larger
portion of it lies in the interior, particularly in the
direction of its length, that is, from the south and
Carmania towards the north and the tribes of Media.
Persis is of a threefold character, both in its nature
and in the temperature of its air. For, in the first
place, its seaboard is burning hot, sandy, and stinted
of fruits except dates (its length is reckoned at about
forty-four, or forty-three, hundred stadia, and it
terminates at the largest of the rivers in that part
of the world, the Oroatis, as it is called); secondly,
the portion above the seaboard produces everything,
is level, and is excellent for the rearing of cattle,
and also abounds with rivers and lakes; the third
portion, that on the north, is wintry and mountainous; and it is on the borders of this portion that
the camel-breeders live. Now, according to Eratos-

---

4 ἀμμώδης, Tyrwhitt, for ἀνεμώδης; so the later editors.

μὲν οὖν ἐστι κατ' Ἐρατοσθένη τὸ ἐπὶ τὰς
ἄρκτους καὶ τὰς Κασπίους πύλας περὶ ὀκτακισχιλίων, κατά τινας προπιπτούσας ἄκρας, λοιπὴ
δ' ἐστὶν ἐπὶ Κασπίους πύλας οὐ πλεῖον ἢ τῶν
δισχιλίων· πλάτος δὲ τὸ ἐν τῇ μεσογαίᾳ τὸ ἀπὸ
Σούσων εἰς Περσέπολιν[1] στάδιοι τετρακισχίλιοι
διακόσιοι, κἀντεῦθεν ἐπὶ τοὺς τῆς Καρμανίας ὅρους
ἄλλοι χίλιοι ἑξακόσιοι. φῦλα δὲ[2] οἰκεῖ τὴν
χώραν οἵ τε Πατεισχορεῖς λεγόμενοι καὶ οἱ
Ἀχαιμενίδαι καὶ οἱ Μάγοι· οὗτοι μὲν οὖν σεμνοῦ
τινός εἰσι βίου ζηλωταί, Κύρτιοι δὲ καὶ Μάρδοι[3]
ληστρικοί, ἄλλοι δὲ γεωργικοί.

2. Σχεδὸν δέ τι καὶ ἡ Σουσὶς μέρος γεγένηται
τῆς Περσίδος, μεταξὺ αὐτῆς κειμένη καὶ τῆς Βαβυλωνίας, ἔχουσα πόλιν ἀξιολογωτάτην τὰ Σοῦσα.
οἱ γὰρ Πέρσαι κρατήσαντες Μήδων καὶ ὁ Κῦρος,
ὁρῶντες τὴν μὲν οἰκείαν γῆν ἐπ' ἐσχάτοις που
ταττομένην, τὴν δὲ Σουσίδα ἐνδοτέρω καὶ πλη-
σιαιτέραν τῇ Βαβυλωνίᾳ καὶ τοῖς ἄλλοις ἔθνεσιν
ἐνταῦθα ἔθεντο τὸ τῆς ἡγεμονίας βασίλειον· ἅμα
καὶ τὸ ὅμορον τῆς χώρας ἀποδεξάμενοι καὶ τὸ
C 728 ἀξίωμα τῆς πόλεως καὶ κρεῖττον τὸ μηδέποτε
καθ' ἑαυτὴν τὴν Σουσίδα πραγμάτων μεγάλων
ἐπίβολον γεγονέναι, ἀλλ' ἀεὶ ὑφ' ἑτέροις ὑπάρξαι
καὶ ἐν μέρει τετάχθαι[4] συστήματος μείζονος,
πλὴν εἰ ἄρα τὸ παλαιὸν τὸ κατὰ τοὺς ἥρωας.
λέγεται γὰρ δὴ καὶ κτίσμα Τιθωνοῦ Μέμνονος
πατρός, κύκλον ἔχουσα ἑκατὸν καὶ εἴκοσι σταδίων,

---

[1] Περσέπολις E, Περσαίπολις other MSS.
[2] δέ, the editors, for τε.
[3] Μάρδοι, Casaubon, for Μαραοί.
[4] τετάχθαι, Corais, for τέτακται.

thenes, the length of the country towards the north
and the Caspian Gates is about eight thousand stadia,
if reckoned from certain promontories,[1] and the
remainder to the Caspian Gates is not more than
two thousand stadia;[2] and the breadth, in the
interior, from Susa to Persepolis, is four thousand
two hundred stadia, and thence to the borders of
Carmania sixteen hundred more. The tribes which
inhabit the country are the Pateischoreis, as they
are called, and the Achaemenidae and the Magi.
Now the Magi follow with zeal a kind of august life,
whereas the Cyrtii and the Mardi are brigands and
others are farmers.

2. I might almost say that Susis also is a part of
Persis; it lies between Persis and Babylonia and has
a most notable city, Susa. For the Persians and
Cyrus, after mastering the Medes, saw that their
native land was situated rather on the extremities
of their empire, and that Susa was farther in and
nearer to Babylonia and the other tribes, and therefore established the royal seat of their empire at
Susa. At the same time, also, they were pleased
with the high standing of the city and with the fact
that its territory bordered on Persis, and, better still,
with the fact that it had never of itself achieved anything of importance, but always had been subject to
others and accounted merely a part of a larger
political organisation, except, perhaps, in ancient
times, in the times of the heroes. For Susa too is
said to have been founded by Tithonus the father
of Memnon, with a circuit of one hundred and

[1] The text seems to be corrupt. A clearer statement of
this same dimension, as quoted from Eratosthenes, is given in
2. 1. 26.
[2] In 2. 1. 26 the text reads "about *three* thousand stadia."

παραμήκης τῷ σχήματι· ἡ δ' ἀκρόπολις ἐκαλεῖτο
Μεμνόνιον· λέγονται δὲ καὶ Κίσσιοι οἱ Σούσιοι·
φησὶ δὲ καὶ Αἰσχύλος τὴν μητέρα Μέμνονος
Κισσίαν. ταφῆναι δὲ λέγεται Μέμνων περὶ
Πάλτον τῆς Συρίας παρὰ Βαδᾶν ποταμόν, ὡς
εἴρηκε Σιμωνίδης ἐν Μέμνονι διθυράμβῳ τῶν
Δηλιακῶν. τὸ δὲ τεῖχος ᾠκοδόμητο τῆς πόλεως
καὶ ἱερὰ καὶ βασίλεια παραπλησίως, ὥσπερ τὰ
τῶν Βαβυλωνίων ἐξ ὀπτῆς πλίνθου καὶ ἀσφάλτου, καθάπερ εἰρήκασί τινες. Πολύκλειτός τε
διακοσίων φησὶ τὸν κύκλον καὶ ἀτείχιστον.

3. Κοσμήσαντες δὲ τὰ ἐν Σούσοις βασίλεια
μάλιστα τῶν ἄλλων, οὐδὲν ἧττον καὶ τὰ ἐν
Περσεπόλει καὶ τὰ ἐν Πασαργάδαις ἐξετίμησαν·
καὶ ἥ γε γάζα καὶ οἱ θησαυροὶ καὶ τὰ μνήματα
ἐνταῦθα ἦν τοῖς Πέρσαις, ὡς ἐν τόποις ἐρυμνοτέ-
ροις καὶ ἅμα προγονικοῖς. ἦν δὲ καὶ ἄλλα
βασίλεια τὰ ἐν Γάβαις ἐν τοῖς ἀνωτέρω που
μέρεσι τῆς Περσίδος καὶ τὰ ἐν τῇ παραλίᾳ τὰ
κατὰ τὴν Ταόκην[1] λεγομένην. ταῦτα μὲν τὰ
κατὰ τὴν τῶν Περσῶν ἀρχήν, οἱ δ' ὕστερον
ἄλλοις ἐχρήσαντο, ὡς εἰκός, εὐτελεστέροις τισίν,
ἅτε καὶ τῆς Περσίδος ἠλαττωμένης ὑπό τε τῶν
Μακεδόνων καὶ ἔτι μᾶλλον ὑπὸ τῶν Παρθυαίων.
καὶ γὰρ εἰ βασιλεύονται μέχρι νῦν ἴδιον βασιλέα
ἔχοντες οἱ Πέρσαι, τῇ γε δυνάμει πλεῖστον
ἀπολείπονται καὶ τῷ Παρθυαίων προσέχουσι
βασιλεῖ.

4. Τὰ μὲν οὖν Σοῦσα ἐν μεσογαίοις κεῖται ἐπὶ
τῷ Χοάσπῃ ποταμῷ περαιτέρω κατὰ τὸ ζεῦγμα,

---

[1] Ταόκην, Casaubon, for Ὤκην Dh, Ὄκην (Ὀκήν F), other
MSS.

twenty stadia, and oblong in shape; and its acropolis was called Memnonium; and the Susians are also called Cissians; and Aeschylus [1] calls the mother of Memnon Cissia. Memnon is said to have been buried in the neighbourhood of Paltus in Syria, by the river Badas, as Simonides states in his dithyramb entitled *Memnon*, one of his Delian poems. The wall and the temples and the royal palace were built like those of the Babylonians, of baked brick and asphalt, as some writers state. Polycleitus says that the city is two hundred stadia in circuit and that it has no walls.

3. Although they adorned the palace at Susa more than any other, they esteemed no less highly the palaces at Persepolis and Pasargadae; at any rate, the treasure and the riches and the tombs of the Persians were there, since they were on sites that were at the same time hereditary and more strongly fortified by nature. And there were also other palaces—that at Gabae, somewhere in the upper parts of Persis, and that on the coast near Taocê, as it is called. These were the palaces in the time of the empire of the Persians, but the kings of later times used others, naturally less sumptuous, since Persis had been weakened, not only by the Macedonians, but still more so by the Parthians. For although the Persians are still under the rule of a king, having a king of their own, yet they are most deficient in power and are subject to the king of the Parthians.

4. Now Susa is situated in the interior on the Choaspes River at the far end of the bridge, but its

---

[1] *Persae* 17. 118.

ἡ δὲ χώρα μέχρι τῆς θαλάττης καθήκει· καί ἐστιν
αὐτῆς ἡ παραλία μέχρι τῶν ἐκβολῶν σχεδόν τι
τοῦ Τίγριος ἀπὸ τῶν ὅρων τῆς Περσικῆς παραλίας
σταδίων ὡς τρισχιλίων. ῥεῖ δὲ διὰ τῆς χώρας ὁ
Χοάσπης εἰς τὴν αὐτὴν τελευτῶν παραλίαν,
ἀπὸ τῶν Οὐξίων τὰς ἀρχὰς ἔχων. παρεμ-
πίπτει γάρ τις ὀρεινὴ τραχεῖα καὶ ἀπότομος
μεταξὺ τῶν Σουσίων καὶ τῆς Περσίδος, στενὰ
ἔχουσα δυσπάροδα καὶ ἀνθρώπους λῃστάς, οἳ
μισθοὺς ἐπράττοντο καὶ αὐτοὺς τοὺς βασιλέας
κατὰ τὴν ἐκ Σούσων εἰς Πέρσας εἰσβολήν.
φησὶ δὲ Πολύκλειτος εἰς λίμνην τινὰ συμβάλλειν
τόν τε Χοάσπην καὶ τὸν Εὔλαιον[1] καὶ ἔτι τὸν
Τίγριν, εἶτ' ἐκεῖθεν εἰς τὴν θάλατταν ἐκδιδόναι·
πρὸς δὲ τῇ λίμνῃ καὶ ἐμπόριον εἶναι, τῶν ποτα-
C 729   μῶν μὲν οὐ δεχομένων τὰ ἐκ τῆς θαλάττης, οὐδὲ
καταπεμπόντων διὰ τοὺς καταράκτας ἐπίτηδες
γενομένους, πεζῇ δ' ἐμπορευομένων· ὀκτακοσίους
γὰρ εἶναι σταδίους εἰς Σοῦσα λέγουσιν.[2] ἄλλοι
δέ φασι τοὺς διὰ Σουσίων ποταμοὺς εἰς ἓν ῥεῦμα
τὸ τοῦ Τίγριος συμπίπτειν κατὰ[3] τὰς μεταξὺ
διώρυγας τοῦ Εὐφράτου· διὰ δὲ τοῦτο κατὰ τὰς
ἐκβολὰς ὀνομάζεσθαι Πασίτιγριν.

5. Νέαρχος δὲ τὸν παράπλουν τῆς Σουσίδος
τεναγώδη φήσας πέρας αὐτοῦ λέγει τὸν Εὐφράτην
ποταμόν· πρὸς δὲ τῷ στόματι κώμην οἰκεῖσθαι
τὴν ὑποδεχομένην τὰ ἐκ τῆς Ἀραβίας φορτία·
συνάπτειν γὰρ ἐφεξῆς τὴν τῶν Ἀράβων παραλίαν
τῷ στόματι τοῦ Εὐφράτου καὶ τοῦ Πασιτίγριος,

---

[1] CDohxz read Εὔλεον.
[2] ἄλλοι, after λέγουσιν, Corais omits.
[3] κατά, Corais and Meineke, for καί.

territory extends down to the sea; and its seaboard is about three thousand stadia in length, extending from the boundaries of the Persian seaboard approximately to the outlets of the Tigris. The Choaspes River flows through Susis, terminating at the same seaboard, and has its sources in the territory of the Uxii; for a kind of mountainous country intrudes between the Susians and Persis; it is rugged and sheer, and has narrow defiles that are hard to pass, and was inhabited by brigands, who would exact payments even from the kings themselves when they passed from Susis into Persis. Polycleitus says that the Choaspes, the Eulaeus, and also the Tigris meet in a kind of lake, and then empty from that lake into the sea; and that there is an emporium near the lake, since, on account of the cataracts, purposely constructed, the rivers cannot receive the merchandise that comes in from the sea nor bring down any either, and that all traffic is carried on by land; for the distance to Susa is said to be eight hundred[1] stadia. Others, however, say that the rivers which flow through Susis meet in one stream, that of the Tigris, opposite the intermediate canals of the Euphrates; and that on this account the Tigris, at its outlets, has the name of Pasitigris.[2]

5. Nearchus says that the coast of Persis is covered with shoal-waters and that it ends at the Euphrates River; and that at the mouth of this river there is an inhabited village which receives the merchandise from Arabia; for the seaboard of the Arabians borders next on the mouth of the Euphrates and the Pasiti-

[1] Apparently an error for eighteen hundred.
[2] The Pasitigris, properly so called, is one of the rivers which flow from Susis (see Arrian, *Anab.* 3. 17. 1, *Ind.* 42. 4, and Pliny, 6. 129 and 145).

τὸ δὲ μεταξὺ πᾶν ἐπέχειν λίμνην, τὴν ὑποδεχομένην τὸν Τίγριν. ἀναπλεύσαντι δὲ τῷ Πασι-
τίγρει σταδίους πεντήκοντα καὶ ἑκατόν, τὴν
σχεδίαν εἶναι τὴν ἄγουσαν ἐπὶ Σούσων ἐκ τῆς
Περσίδος, ἀπέχουσαν Σούσων σταδίους ἑξήκοντα·
τὸν δὲ Πασίτιγριν ἀπὸ τοῦ Ὀροάτιδος διέχειν περὶ
δισχιλίους σταδίους· διὰ δὲ τῆς λίμνης ἐπὶ τὸ
στόμα τοῦ Τίγριος τὸν ἀνάπλουν εἶναι σταδίων
ἑξακοσίων· πλησίον δὲ τοῦ στόματος κώμην
οἰκεῖσθαι τὴν Σουσιανήν, διέχουσαν τῶν Σούσων
σταδίους πεντακοσίους· ἀπὸ δὲ τοῦ στόματος τοῦ
Εὐφράτου καὶ μέχρι Βαβυλῶνος τὸν ἀνάπλουν
εἶναι διὰ γῆς[1] οἰκουμένης καλῶς σταδίων πλειόνων
ἢ τρισχιλίων. Ὀνησίκριτος δὲ πάντας φησὶν
ἐκβάλλειν εἰς τὴν λίμνην, τόν τε Εὐφράτην καὶ
τὸν Τίγριν· ἐκπεσόντα δὲ πάλιν τὸν Εὐφράτην
ἐκ τῆς λίμνης ἰδίῳ στόματι πρὸς τὴν θάλατταν
συνάπτειν.

6. Ἔστι δὲ καὶ ἄλλα πλείω στενὰ διεκβάλ-
λοντι τὰ ἐν τοῖς Οὐξίοις κατ' αὐτὴν τὴν Περσίδα,
ἃ καὶ αὐτὰ βίᾳ διῆλθεν Ἀλέξανδρος, κατά τε τὰς
Περσικὰς πύλας καὶ κατ' ἄλλους τόπους διεξιὼν
τὴν χώραν, καὶ κατοπτεῦσαι σπεύδων τὰ κυριώτατα μέρη καὶ τὰ γαζοφυλάκια, ἃ τοσούτοις
χρόνοις ἐξεπεπλήρωτο, οἷς ἐδασμολόγησαν Πέρσαι
τὴν Ἀσίαν· ποταμοὺς δὲ διέβη πλείους τοὺς
διαρρέοντας τὴν χώραν καὶ καταφερομένους εἰς
τὸν Περσικὸν κόλπον. μετὰ γὰρ τὸν Χοάσπην ὁ
Κοπράτας ἐστὶ καὶ ὁ Πασίτιγρις, ὃς ἐκ τῆς

---

[1] γῆς, Tzschucke, from conj. of Casaubon, for τῆς.

[1] Apparently an error for six hundred.

gris, the whole of the intervening space being occupied by a lake, that is, the lake that receives the Tigris; and that on sailing up the Pasitigris one hundred and fifty stadia one comes to the raft-bridge that leads from Persis to Susa, being sixty [1] stadia distant from Susa; and that the Pasitigris is about two thousand stadia distant from the Oroatis; and that the inland voyage on the lake to the mouth of the Tigris is six hundred stadia; and that near the mouth there is an inhabited Susian village, [2] which is five hundred stadia distant from Susa; and that the voyage inland from the mouth of the Euphrates to Babylon, through a very prosperous land, is more than three thousand stadia. Onesicritus says that all the rivers empty into the lake, both the Euphrates and the Tigris; but that the Euphrates, again issuing from the lake, joins with the sea by its own separate mouth.

6. There are also several other narrow defiles as one passes out through the territory of the Uxii in the neighbourhood of Persis itself; and Alexander forced his way through these passes too, both at the Persian Gates and at other places, when he was passing through the country and was eager to spy out the most important parts of the country, and the treasure-holds, which had become filled with treasures in those long periods of time in which the Persians had collected tribute from Asia; and he crossed several rivers that flowed through the country and down into the Persian Gulf. For after the Choaspes, one comes to the Copratas River and the Pasitigris, which latter also flows from the

[2] The name of this village, according to Arrian (*Indica* 42), was Aginis.

Οὐξίας καὶ αὐτὸς ῥεῖ· ἔστι δὲ καὶ Κῦρος ποταμός,
διὰ τῆς κοίλης καλουμένης Περσίδος ῥέων περὶ
Πασαργάδας, οὗ μετέλαβε τὸ ὄνομα βασιλεύς,
ἀντὶ Ἀγραδάτου μετονομασθεὶς Κῦρος. πρὸς
αὐτῇ δὲ τῇ Περσεπόλει τὸν Ἀράξην διέβη. ἦν
δὲ ἡ Περσέπολις[1] μετὰ Σοῦσα κάλλιστα κατεσκευασμένη μεγίστη πόλις,[2] ἔχουσα βασίλεια
ἐκπρεπῆ, καὶ μάλιστα τῇ πολυτελείᾳ τῶν κειμένων. ῥεῖ δ᾽ ὁ Ἀράξης ἐκ τῶν Παραιτακῶν·[3]
συμβάλλει δ᾽ εἰς αὐτὸν ὁ Μῆδος, ἐκ Μηδίας
ὁρμηθείς. φέρονται δὲ δι᾽ αὐλῶνος παμφόρου
συνάπτοντος τῇ Καρμανίᾳ καὶ τοῖς ἑωθινοῖς
μέρεσι τῆς χώρας, καθάπερ καὶ αὐτὴ ἡ Περσέπολις. ἐνέπλησε δὲ ὁ Ἀλέξανδρος τὰ ἐν
C 730 Περσεπόλει[4] βασίλεια, τιμωρῶν τοῖς Ἕλλησιν,
ὅτι κἀκείνων ἱερὰ καὶ πόλεις οἱ Πέρσαι πυρὶ καὶ
σιδήρῳ διεπόρθησαν.

7. Εἶτ᾽ εἰς Πασαργάδας ἧκε· καὶ τοῦτο δ᾽ ἦν
βασίλειον ἀρχαῖον. ἐνταῦθα δὲ καὶ τὸν Κύρου
τάφον εἶδεν ἐν παραδείσῳ, πύργον οὐ μέγαν, τῷ
δασεῖ τῶν δένδρων ἐναποκεκρυμμένον, κάτω μὲν
στερεόν, ἄνω δὲ στέγην ἔχοντα καὶ σηκόν, στενὴν
τελέως ἔχοντα τὴν εἴσοδον· δι᾽ ἧς παρελθεῖν
εἴσω φησὶν Ἀριστόβουλος, κελεύσαντος τοῦ
βασιλέως, καὶ κοσμῆσαι τὸν τάφον· ἰδεῖν δὲ
κλίνην τε χρυσῆν καὶ τράπεζαν σὺν ἐκπώμασι
καὶ πύελον χρυσῆν καὶ ἐσθῆτα πολλὴν κόσμον τε
λιθοκόλλητον· κατὰ μὲν οὖν τὴν πρώτην ἐπιδη-
μίαν ταῦτ᾽ ἰδεῖν, ὕστερον δὲ συληθῆναι καὶ τὰ

---

[1] Περσέπολις DE*i*, Περσαίπολις other MSS.
[2] The words μετὰ . . . πόλις are found only in F.
[3] CDF*h* read Παρετάκων.

country of the Uxii. There is also a river Cyrus, which flows through Coelê [1] Persis, as it is called, in the neighbourhood of Pasargadae; and the king assumed the name of this river, changing his name from Agradatus to Cyrus. Alexander crossed the Araxes near Persepolis itself. Persepolis, next to Susa, was the most beautifully constructed city, and the largest, having a palace that was remarkable, particularly in respect to the high value of its treasures. The Araxes flows from the country of the Paraetaci; and this river is joined by the Medus, which has its source in Media. These rivers run through a very productive valley which borders on Carmania and the eastern parts of the country, as does also Persepolis itself. Alexander burnt up the palace at Persepolis, to avenge the Greeks, because the Persians had destroyed both temples and cities of the Greeks by fire and sword.

7. Alexander then went to Pasargadae; and this too was an ancient royal residence. Here he saw also, in a park, the tomb of Cyrus; it was a small tower and was concealed within the dense growth of trees. The tomb was solid below, but had a roof and sepulchre above, which latter had an extremely narrow entrance. Aristobulus says that at the behest of the king he passed through this entrance and decorated the tomb; and that he saw a golden couch, a table with cups, a golden coffin, and numerous garments and ornaments set with precious stones; and that he saw all these things on his first visit, but that on a later visit the place had been robbed

[1] Hollow.

μὲν ἄλλα ἐκκομισθῆναι, τὴν δὲ κλίνην θραυσθῆναι
μόνον καὶ τὴν πύελον, μεταθέντων τὸν νεκρόν, δι'
οὗ¹ δῆλον γενέσθαι, διότι προνομευτῶν ἔργον ἦν,
οὐχὶ τοῦ σατράπου, καταλιπόντων ἃ μὴ δυνατὸν
ἦν ῥᾳδίως ἐκκομίσαι· συμβῆναι δὲ ταῦτα, καίπερ
φυλακῆς περικειμένης Μάγων, σίτισιν λαμβανόν-
των καθ' ἡμέραν πρόβατον, διὰ μηνὸς δ' ἵππον.
ἀλλ' ὁ ἐκτοπισμὸς τῆς Ἀλεξάνδρου στρατιᾶς εἰς
Βάκτρα καὶ Ἰνδοὺς πολλά τε ἄλλα νεωτερισθῆναι
παρεσκεύασε, καὶ δὴ καὶ τοῦθ' ἓν τῶν νεωτερισ-
θέντων ὑπῆρξεν. οὕτω μὲν οὖν Ἀριστόβουλος
εἴρηκε, καὶ τὸ ἐπίγραμμα δὲ ἀπομνημονεύει τοῦτο·
ὦ ἄνθρωπε, ἐγὼ Κῦρός εἰμι, ὁ τὴν ἀρχὴν τοῖς
Πέρσαις κτησάμενος καὶ τῆς Ἀσίας βασιλεύς·
μὴ οὖν φθονήσῃς μοι τοῦ μνήματος. Ὀνησίκριτος δὲ τὸν μὲν πύργον δεκάστεγον εἴρηκε, καὶ
ἐν μὲν τῇ ἀνωτάτω στέγῃ κεῖσθαι τὸν Κῦρον,
ἐπίγραμμα δ' εἶναι Ἑλληνικόν, Περσικοῖς κε-
χαραγμένον γράμμασιν· ἐνθάδ' ἐγὼ κεῖμαι Κῦρος
βασιλεὺς βασιλήων· καὶ ἄλλο περσίζον πρὸς τὸν
αὐτὸν νοῦν.

8. Μέμνηται δ' Ὀνησίκριτος καὶ τὸ ἐπὶ τῷ²
Δαρείου τάφῳ γράμμα τόδε. φίλος ἦν τοῖς φίλοις·
ἱππεὺς καὶ τοξότης ἄριστος ἐγενόμην·³ κυνηγῶν
ἐκράτουν· πάντα ποιεῖν ἠδυνάμην. Ἄριστος δ'
ὁ Σαλαμίνιος πολὺ μέν ἐστι νεώτερος τούτων,
λέγει δὲ δίστεγον τὸν πύργον καὶ μέγαν, ἐν δὲ τῇ

¹ δι' οὗ, Tyrwhitt, for δ' οὐ ; so the later editors.
² τῷ moxz, τοῦ other MSS.

and everything had been carried off except the couch
and the coffin, which had only been broken to pieces,
and that the robbers had removed the corpse to
another place, a fact which plainly proved that it
was an act of plunderers, not of the satrap, since they
left behind only what could not easily be carried off;
and that the robbery took place even though the
tomb was surrounded by a guard of Magi, who
received for their maintenance a sheep every day
and a horse every month.[1] But just as the remoteness of the countries to which Alexander's army
advanced, Bactra and India, had led to numerous
other revolutionary acts, so too this was one of the
revolutionary acts. Now Aristobulus so states it,
and he goes on to record the following inscription on
the tomb: " O man, I am Cyrus, who acquired the
empire for the Persians and was king of Asia; grudge
me not, therefore, my monument." Onesicritus,
however, states that the tower had ten stories and
that Cyrus lay in the uppermost story, and that
there was one inscription in Greek, carved in Persian
letters, " Here I lie, Cyrus, king of kings," and
another written in the Persian language with the
same meaning.

8. Onesicritus records also the following inscription
on the tomb of Dareius: " I was friend to my
friends; as horseman and bowman I proved myself
superior to all others; as hunter I prevailed; I
could do everything." Aristus of Salamis is indeed
a much later writer than these, but he says that the
tower has only two stories and is large; that it was

[1] The horse, of course, was sacrificed to Cyrus (cf. Arrian
6. 29).

---

[3] ἐγενόμην, Xylander, for γενόμην.

Περσῶν διαδοχῇ ἱδρῦσθαι, φυλάττεσθαι δὲ τὸν
τάφον· ἐπίγραμμα δὲ τὸ λεχθὲν Ἑλληνικὸν καὶ
ἄλλο Περσικὸν πρὸς τὸν αὐτὸν νοῦν. τοὺς δὲ
Πασαργάδας ἐτίμησε Κῦρος, ὅτι τὴν ὑστάτην
μάχην ἐνίκησεν Ἀστυάγην ἐνταῦθα τὸν Μῆδον,
καὶ τὴν ἀρχὴν τῆς Ἀσίας μετήνεγκεν εἰς ἑαυτὸν
καὶ πόλιν ἔκτισε καὶ βασίλειον κατεσκεύασε τῆς
νίκης μνημεῖον.

C 731 9. Πάντα δὲ τὰ ἐν τῇ Περσίδι χρήματα ἐξε-
σκευάσατο εἰς τὰ Σοῦσα, καὶ αὐτὰ θησαυρῶν καὶ
κατασκευῆς μεστά· οὐδὲ τοῦθ᾽ ἡγεῖτο τὸ βασίλειον, ἀλλὰ τὴν Βαβυλῶνα, καὶ διενοεῖτο ταύτην
προσκατασκευάζειν· κἀνταῦθα δ᾽ ἔκειντο θησαυροί.
φασὶ δέ, χωρὶς τῶν ἐν Βαβυλῶνι καὶ τῶν ἐν τῷ
στρατοπέδῳ τῶν παρὰ[1] ταῦτα μὴ ληφθέντων
αὐτὰ τὰ ἐν Σούσοις καὶ τὰ ἐν Περσίδι τέτταρας
μυριάδας ταλάντων ἐξετασθῆναι· τινὲς δὲ καὶ
πέντε λέγουσιν· ἄλλοι δὲ πάντα πάντοθεν συναχ-
θῆναι παραδεδώκασιν εἰς Ἐκβάτανα ὀκτωκαίδεκα
μυριάδας ταλάντων· τὰ δὲ Δαρείῳ φυγόντι ἐκ τῆς
Μηδίας συνεκκομισθέντα τάλαντα ὀκτακισχίλια
διήρπασαν οἱ δολοφονήσαντες αὐτόν.

10. Τὴν γοῦν Βαβυλῶνα ὁ Ἀλέξανδρος προέ-
κρινεν, ὁρῶν καὶ τῷ μεγέθει πολὺ ὑπερβάλλουσαν
καὶ τοῖς ἄλλοις. εὐδαίμων δ᾽ οὖσα ἡ Σουσίς,
ἔκπυρον τὸν ἀέρα ἔχει καὶ[2] καυματηρόν, καὶ
μάλιστα τὸν περὶ τὴν πόλιν, ὥς φησιν ἐκεῖνος·

---

[1] παρά, Corais, for περί.
[2] καί, added by Eiw and the editors.

---

[1] i.e. when the empire passed from the Medes to the Persians.

built at the time of the succession of the Persians,[1] and that the tomb was kept under guard; and that there was one inscription written in Greek, that quoted above, and another written in the Persian language with the same meaning. Cyrus held Pasargadae in honour, because he there conquered Astyages the Mede in his last battle, transferred to himself the empire of Asia, founded a city, and constructed a palace as a memorial of his victory.

9. Alexander carried off with him all the wealth in Persis to Susa, which was also full of treasures and equipment; and neither did he regard Susa as the royal residence, but rather Babylon, which he intended to build up still further; and there too treasures lay stored. They say that, apart from the treasures in Babylon and in the camp, which were not included in the total, the value of those in Susa and Persis alone was reckoned at forty thousand talents, though some say fifty; and others have reported that all treasures from all sources were brought together at Ecbatana and that they were valued at one hundred and eighty thousand talents; and the treasures which were carried along with Dareius in his flight from Media, eight thousand talents in value, were taken as booty by those who slew him.

10. At all events, Alexander preferred Babylon, since he saw that it far surpassed the others, not only in its size, but also in all other respects. Although Susis is fertile, it has a hot and scorching atmosphere, and particularly in the neighbourhood of the city, according to that writer.[2] At any rate, he says that

[2] Whether Aristobulus or Nearchus or Onesicritus, the translator does not know.

τὰς γοῦν σαύρας καὶ τοὺς ὄφεις, θέρους ἀκμάζοντος
τοῦ ἡλίου κατὰ μεσημβρίαν, διαβῆναι μὴ φθάνειν
τὰς ὁδοὺς τὰς ἐν τῇ πόλει, ἀλλ᾽ ἐν μέσαις περι-
φλέγεσθαι· ὅπερ τῆς Περσίδος μηδαμοῦ συμβαίνειν, καίπερ νοτιωτέρας οὔσης· λουτρὰ δὲ
ψυχρὰ προτεθέντα ἐκθερμαίνεσθαι παραχρῆμα,
τὰς δὲ κριθὰς διασπαρείσας εἰς τὸν ἥλιον ἄλλεσθαι,[1] καθάπερ ἐν τοῖς ἰπνοῖς τὰς κάχρυς·[2] διὸ
καὶ ταῖς στέγαις ἐπὶ δύο πήχεις τὴν γῆν ἐπιτίθεσθαι, ὑπὸ δὲ τοῦ βάρους ἀναγκάζεσθαι στενοὺς
μὲν μακροὺς[3] δὲ ποιεῖσθαι τοὺς οἴκους, ἀπορου-
μένους μακρῶν μὲν δοκῶν, δεομένους δὲ μεγάλων οἴκων διὰ τὸ πνῖγος. ἴδιον δέ τι πάσχειν
τὴν φοινικίνην δοκόν· στερεὰν γὰρ οὖσαν, πα-
λαιουμένην οὐκ εἰς τὸ κάτω τὴν ἔνδοσιν λαμβάνειν, ἀλλ᾽ εἰς τὸ ἄνω μέρος κυρτοῦσθαι τῷ
βάρει καὶ βέλτιον ἀνέχειν τὴν ὀροφήν. αἴτιον
δὲ τῶν καυμάτων λέγεται τὸ ὑπερκεῖσθαι πρὸς
ἄρκτον ὄρη ὑψηλὰ τὰ προεκδεχόμενα ἅπαντας τοὺς βορείους ἀνέμους· ὑπερπετεῖς δὴ
πνέοντες ἀπὸ τῶν ἀκρωτηρίων μετέωροί τε τῶν
πεδίων οὐ προσάπτονται, ἀλλὰ παρελαύνουσιν[4]
εἰς τὰ νοτιώτερα τῆς Σουσίδος· αὕτη δὲ νηνεμίαις
κατέχεται, καὶ μάλιστα τότε, ἡνίκα ἐτησίαι τὴν
ἄλλην γῆν καταψύχουσιν ἐκκαομένην ὑπὸ τῶν
καυμάτων.

11. Πολύσιτος δ᾽ ἄγαν ἐστίν, ὥστε ἑκατον-
τάχουν δι᾽ ὁμαλοῦ καὶ κριθὴν καὶ πυρὸν ἐκτρέ-
φειν, ἔστι δ᾽ ὅτε καὶ διακοσιοντάχουν· διόπερ

[1] ἄλλεσθαι, Corais and Meineke, who cite Plutarch (Al. x.
35) and Theophrastus (Hist. Plant. 8. 11), for ἀλήθεσθαι moz,
ἀλεαίνεσθαι other MSS.

when the sun is hottest, at noon, the lizards and the snakes could not cross the streets in the city quickly enough to prevent their being burnt to death in the middle of the streets. He says that this is the case nowhere in Persis, although Persis lies more to the south; and that cold water for baths is put out in the sun and immediately heated, and that barley spread out in the sun bounces like parched barley in ovens; and that on this account earth is put on the roofs of the houses to the depth of two cubits, and that by reason of this weight the inhabitants are forced to build their houses both narrow and long; and that, although they are in want of long beams, yet they need large houses on account of the suffocating heat; and that the palm-tree beam has a peculiar property, for, although it is rigid, it does not, when aged, give way downwards, but curves upwards because of the weight and better supports the roof. It is said that the cause of the heat is the fact that lofty mountains lie above the country on the north and that these mountains intercept all the northern winds. Accordingly, these winds, blowing aloft from the tops of the mountains and high above the plains, do not touch the plains, although they blow on the more southerly parts of Susis. But calm prevails here, particularly at the time when the Etesian winds cool the rest of the land that is scorched by heat.

11. Susis abounds so exceedingly in grain that both barley and wheat regularly produce one hundred-fold, and sometimes even two hundred; on this

<hr>

2 κάχρυς, F Epit., κάγχρυς E, κέγκρυς CD*h*, κέγχρους *moxz*.

3 Xylander and Tzschucke emend μακρούς to μικρούς.

4 E reads προσελαύνουσι.

οὐδὲ πημ̣ ὺς τὰς αὔλακας τέμνουσι· πυκνού-
μεν̣αι γὰρ κωλύουσιν αἱ ῥίζαι τὴν βλάστην. τὴν
δ᾽ ἄμπελον οὐ φυομένην πρότερον Μακεδόνες
κατεφύτευσαν κἀκεῖ καὶ ἐν Βαβυλῶνι, οὐ
ταφρεύοντες, ἀλλὰ παττάλους κατασεσιδηρω-
C 732 μένους [1] ἐξ ἄκρων πήττοντες, εἶτ᾽ ἐξαιροῦντες,
ἀντὶ δ᾽ αὐτῶν τὰ κλήματα καθιέντες εὐθέως. ἡ
μὲν δὴ μεσόγαια [2] τοιαύτη· ἡ δὲ παραλία τενα-
γώδης ἐστὶ καὶ ἀλίμενος· διὰ τοῦτο γοῦν καί
φησιν ὁ Νέαρχος μηδὲ καθοδηγῶν ἐπιχωρίων
τυγχάνειν, ἡνίκα τῷ στόλῳ παρέπλει πρὸς τὴν
Βαβυλωνίαν ἐκ τῆς Ἰνδικῆς, ὅτι προσόρμους οὐκ
εἶχεν,[3] οὐδ᾽ ἀνθρώπων εὐπορεῖν οἷός τ᾽ ἦν τῶν
ἡγησομένων κατ᾽ ἐμπειρίαν.

12. Γειτνιᾷ δὲ τῇ Σουσίδι τῆς Βαβυλωνίας ἡ
Σιτακηνὴ μὲν πρότερον, Ἀπολλωνιᾶτις δὲ ὕστερον προσαγορευθεῖσα. ἀπὸ τῶν ἄρκτων δ᾽
ὑπέρκεινται ἀμφοῖν πρὸς ἕω Ἐλυμαῖοί τε καὶ
Παραιτακηνοί, λῃστρικοὶ ἄνδρες καὶ ὀρεινῇ
τραχείᾳ πεποιθότες· μᾶλλον δ᾽ οἱ Παραιτακηνοὶ
τοῖς Ἀπολλωνιάταις ἐπίκεινται, ὥστε καὶ χεῖρον
ἐκείνους διατιθέασιν. οἱ δὲ Ἐλυμαῖοι κἀκείνοις
καὶ τοῖς Σουσίοις, τούτοις δὲ καὶ οἱ Οὔξιοι
προσπολεμοῦσιν· ἧττον δὲ νῦν, ὡς εἰκός, διὰ
τὴν τῶν Παρθυαίων ἰσχύν, ὑφ᾽ οἷς εἰσιν ἅπαντες
οἱ ταύτῃ. εὖ μὲν οὖν πραττόντων ἐκείνων, εὖ

---

[1] κατασεσιδηρωμένους, Kramer, from conj. of Corais, for
ἅτε σεσιδηρωμένους CDF*hi* (*moz* omits ἅτε), κατεσεσιδηρω-
μένους other MSS.

[2] The words τοιαύτη . . . γοῦν are transferred to this
position by Corais, Groskurd and Meineke (Kramer approving) from their position in the MSS. after τοιαύτη at
end of § 12. Instead of these words the MSS. read (after

account, also, the people do not cut the furrows close together, for the crowding of the roots hinders the sprouting. The vine did not grow there until the Macedonians planted it, both there and at Babylon; however, they did not dig trenches, but only thrust into the ground iron-pointed stakes, and then pulled them out and replaced them at once with the plants. Such, then, is the interior; but the seaboard is full of shallows and without harbours. On this account, at any rate, Nearchus goes on to say that he met with no native guides when he was sailing along the coast with his fleet from India to Babylonia; that the coast had no mooring-places, and that he was also unable to find any experienced people to guide him.

12. Neighbouring Susis is the part of Babylonia which was formerly called Sitacenê, but is now called Apolloniatis. Above both, on the north and towards the east, lie the countries of the Elymaei and the Paraetaceni, who are predatory peoples and rely on the ruggedness of their mountains. But the Paraetaceni are situated closer to the Apollioniatae, and therefore treat them worse. The Elymaei carry on war against both that people and the Susians, whereas the Uxii too carry on war against the Elymaei; but less so at the present time, in all probability, because of the might of the Parthians, to whom all the peoples in that part of the world are subject. Now when the Parthians fare well, all their subjects fare well too,

---

μεσόγαια) the words πολλάκις, καὶ δὴ καὶ ἐφ᾽ ἡμῶν ἄλλοτ᾽ ἄλλως συνέβη, which except for the form of the verb συνέβη, are repeated by the M.M towards the end of § 12 and rightly omitted by the editors.

[3] εἶχεν, Kramer and later editors, Iul ἔγειν.

πράττουσιν ἅπαντες καὶ οἱ ὑπήκοοι αὐτῶν· στασιαζόντων δέ, ὅπερ συμβαίνει πολλάκις, καὶ δὴ καὶ ἐφ' ἡμῶν, ἄλλοτ' ἄλλως συμβαίνει καὶ οὐ τὰ αὐτὰ πᾶσι· τοῖς μὲν γὰρ συνήνεγκεν ἡ ταραχή, τοῖς δὲ παρὰ γνώμην ἀπήντησεν. ἡ μὲν δὴ χώρα ἥ τε Περσὶς καὶ ἡ Σουσιανὴ τοιαύτη.

13. Τὰ δ'[1] ἔθη τὰ Περσικὰ καὶ τούτοις καὶ Μήδοις τὰ αὐτὰ καὶ ἄλλοις πλείοσι, περὶ ὧν εἰρήκασι μὲν πλείους, τὰ δὲ καίρια καὶ ἡμῖν λεκτέον. Πέρσαι τοίνυν ἀγάλματα μὲν καὶ βωμοὺς οὐχ ἱδρύονται, θύουσι δ' ἐν ὑψηλῷ τόπῳ, τὸν οὐρανὸν ἡγούμενοι Δία· τιμῶσι δὲ καὶ Ἥλιον,[1] ὃν καλοῦσι Μίθρην, καὶ Σελήνην καὶ Ἀφροδίτην καὶ πῦρ καὶ γῆν καὶ ἀνέμους καὶ ὕδωρ· θύουσι δ' ἐν καθαρῷ τόπῳ κατευξάμενοι, παραστησάμενοι τὸ ἱερεῖον ἐστεμμένον· μελίσαντος δὲ τοῦ Μάγου τὰ κρέα τοῦ ὑφηγουμένου τὴν ἱερουργίαν ἀπίασι διελόμενοι, τοῖς θεοῖς οὐδὲν ἀπονείμαντες μέρος· τῆς γὰρ ψυχῆς φασι τοῦ ἱερείου δεῖσθαι τὸν θεόν, ἄλλου δὲ οὐδενός· ὅμως δὲ τοῦ ἐπίπλου τι μικρὸν τιθέασιν, ὥς λέγουσί τινες, ἐπὶ τὸ πῦρ.

14. Διαφερόντως δὲ τῷ πυρὶ καὶ τῷ ὕδατι θύουσι, τῷ μὲν πυρί, προστιθέντες ξηρὰ ξύλα τοῦ λέπους χωρίς, πιμελὴν ἐπιτιθέντες ἄνωθεν· εἶθ' ὑφάπτουσιν, ἔλαιον καταχέοντες, οὐ φυσῶντες, ἀλλὰ ῥιπίζοντες· τοὺς δὲ φυσήσαντας ἢ νεκρὸν ἐπὶ πῦρ θέντας[2] ἢ βόλβιτον θανατοῦσι· τῷ δ'

---

[1] δ', Corais and later editors insert.
[2] Dhi read ἐπιθέντας.

---

[1] The Sun.

but when there is an insurrection, as is often the
case, even indeed in our own times, the results are
different at different times and not the same for all;
for some have benefited by disturbances, whereas
others have been disappointed in their expectations.
Such, then, are the countries of Persis and Susis.

13. But the Persion customs are the same as those
of these peoples and the Medes and several other
peoples; and while several writers have made statements about all these peoples, I too must tell what
is suitable to my purpose. Now the Persians do not
erect statues or altars, but offer sacrifice on a high
place, regarding the heavens as Zeus; and they also
worship Helius,[1] whom they call Mithras, and
Selenê [2] and Aphroditê, and fire and earth and winds
and water;[3] and with earnest prayer they offer
sacrifice in a purified place, presenting the victim
crowned;[4] and when the Magus, who directs the
sacrifice, has divided the meat the people go away
with their shares, without setting apart a portion
for the gods, for they say that the god requires
only the soul of the victim and nothing else; but
still, according to some writers, they place a small
portion of the caul upon the fire.

14. But it is especially to fire and water that they
offer sacrifice. To fire they offer sacrifice by adding
dry wood without the bark and by placing fat on
top of it; and then they pour oil upon it and light
it below, not blowing with their breath, but fanning
it; and those who blow the fire with their breath
or put anything dead or filthy upon it are put to

[2] The Moon.　　　　[3] So Herodotus 1. 131.
[4] Herodotus (1. 132) says that he who offers the sacrifice
wears a crown.

ὕδατι, ἐπὶ λίμνην ἢ ποταμὸν ἢ κρήνην ἐλθόντες,
βόθρον ὀρύξαντες εἰς τοῦτον σφαγιάζονται,
C 733 φυλαττόμενοι, μή τι τοῦ πλησίον ὕδατος αἱ-
μαχθείη, ὡς μιανοῦντες· εἶτ' ἐπὶ μυρρίνην ἢ
δάφνην διαθέντες τὰ κρέα, ῥάβδοις λεπτοῖς
ἐφάπτονται οἱ Μάγοι καὶ ἐπάδουσιν, ἀποσπέν-
δοντες ἔλαιον ὁμοῦ γάλακτι καὶ μέλιτι κεκρα-
μένον οὐκ εἰς πῦρ, οὐδ' ¹ ὕδωρ, ἀλλ' εἰς τοὔδαφος·
τὰς δ' ἐπῳδὰς ποιοῦνται πολὺν χρόνον ῥάβδων
μυρικίνων λεπτῶν δέσμην κατέχοντες.

15. Ἐν δὲ τῇ Καππαδοκίᾳ (πολὺ γὰρ ² ἐκεῖ ³ ἐστι
τὸ τῶν Μάγων φῦλον, οἳ καὶ Πύραιθοι καλοῦνται·
πολλὰ δὲ καὶ τῶν Περσικῶν θεῶν ἱερά) οὐδὲ
μαχαίρᾳ θύουσιν, ἀλλὰ κορμῷ τινι, ὡς ἂν
ὑπέρῳ τύπτοντες. ἔστι δὲ καὶ Πυραιθεῖα, σηκοί
τινες ἀξιόλογοι· ἐν δὲ τούτοις μέσοις βωμός, ἐν
ᾧ πολλή τε σποδός, καὶ πῦρ ἄσβεστον φυλάτ-
τουσιν οἱ Μάγοι· καὶ καθ' ἡμέραν δὲ εἰσιόντες,
ἐπάδουσιν ὥραν σχεδόν τι, πρὸ τοῦ πυρὸς τὴν
δέσμην τῶν ῥάβδων ἔχοντες, τιάρας περικεί-
μενοι πιλωτάς, καθεικυίας ἑκατέρωθεν μέχρι τοῦ
καλύπτειν τὰ χείλη τὰς παραγναθίδας. ταὐτὰ ⁴
δ' ἐν τοῖς τῆς Ἀναΐτιδος ⁵ καὶ τοῦ Ὠμάνου ἱεροῖς
νενόμισται· τούτων δὲ καὶ σηκοί εἰσι, καὶ ξόανον
τοῦ Ὠμάνου πομπεύει. ταῦτα μὲν οὖν ἡμεῖς
ἑωράκαμεν, ἐκεῖνα δ' ἐν ταῖς ἱστορίαις λέγεται καὶ
τὰ ἐφεξῆς.

¹ οὐδ' x, οὐχ other MSS.
² Instead of γάρ, Dh read μᾶλλον.
³ ἐκεῖ, Meineke inserts, omitting ἐστι; Jones, however,
retains the ἐστι, following Groskurd and Kramer.
⁴ ταὐτά, Corais, for ταῦτα.
⁵ Ἀναΐτιδος, Xylander, ναΐτιδος.

death. And to water they offer sacrifice by going to a lake or river or spring, where, having dug a trench leading thereto, they slaughter a victim, being on their guard lest any of the water near by should be made bloody, believing that the blood would pollute the water; and then, placing pieces of meat on myrtle or laurel branches, the Magi touch them with slender wands and make incantations, pouring oil mixed with both milk and honey, though not into fire or water, but upon the ground; and they carry on their incantations for a long time, holding in their hands a bundle of slender myrtle wands.

15. In Cappadocia (for there the sect of the Magi, who are also called Pyraethi,[1] is large, and in that country are also many temples of the Persian gods), the people do not sacrifice victims with a sword either, but with a kind of tree-trunk, beating them to death as with a cudgel. They also have Pyraetheia, noteworthy enclosures; and in the midst of these there is an altar, on which there is a large quantity of ashes and where the Magi keep the fire ever burning. And there, entering daily, they make incantations for about an hour, holding before the fire their bundle of rods and wearing round their heads high turbans of felt, which reach down over their cheeks far enough to cover their lips. The same customs are observed in the temples of Anaïtis and Omanus; and these temples also have sacred enclosures; and the people carry in procession a wooden statue of Omanus. Now I have seen this myself; but those other things, as also what follows, are recorded in the histories.

---

[1] Fire-kindlers.

16. Εἰς γὰρ ποταμὸν οὔτ' οὐροῦσιν οὔτε νίπτονται Πέρσαι, οὐδὲ λούονται οὐδὲ νεκρὸν ἐμβάλλουσιν[1] οὐδ' ἄλλα τῶν δοκούντων εἶναι μυσαρῶν. ὅτῳ δ' ἂν θύσωσι θεῷ, πρώτῳ τῷ πυρὶ εὔχονται.

17. Βασιλεύονται δ' ὑπὸ τῶν ἀπὸ γένους· ὁ δ' ἀπειθῶν ἀποτμηθεὶς κεφαλὴν καὶ βραχίονα ῥίπτεται. γαμοῦσι δὲ πολλὰς καὶ ἅμα παλλακὰς τρέφουσι πλείους πολυτεκνίας χάριν. τιθέασι δὲ καὶ οἱ βασιλεῖς ἆθλα πολυτεκνίας κατ' ἔτος· τὰ δὲ τρεφόμενα μέχρι ἐτῶν τεττάρων οὐκ ἄγεται τοῖς γονεῦσιν εἰς ὄψιν. οἱ δὲ γάμοι κατὰ τὰς ἀρχὰς τῆς ἐαρινῆς ἰσημερίας ἐπιτελοῦνται· παρέρχεται δ' ἐπὶ τὸν θάλαμον, προφαγὼν μῆλον ἢ καμήλου μυελόν, ἄλλο δ' οὐδὲν τὴν ἡμέραν ἐκείνην.

18. Ἀπὸ δὲ πέντε ἐτῶν ἕως τετάρτου καὶ εἰκοστοῦ παιδεύονται τοξεύειν καὶ ἀκοντίζειν καὶ ἱππάζεσθαι καὶ ἀληθεύειν, διδασκάλοις τε λόγων τοῖς σωφρονεστάτοις χρῶνται, οἳ καὶ τὸ μυθῶδες πρὸς τὸ συμφέρον ἀνάγοντες παραπλέκουσι, καὶ μέλους χωρὶς καὶ μετ' ᾠδῆς ἔργα θεῶν τε καὶ ἀνδρῶν τῶν ἀρίστων ἀναδιδόντες. συνάγουσι δ' εἰς ἕνα τόπον, ψόφῳ χαλκοῦ πρὸ ὄρθρου διεγείροντες ὡς ἐπὶ ἐξοπλισίαν ἢ θήραν· τάξαντες δ' ἀνὰ πεντήκοντα ἡγεμόνα τῶν βασιλέως τινὰ C 734 παίδων αὐτοῖς ἢ σατράπου τρέχοντι κελεύουσιν ἕπεσθαι, χωρίον ἀφορίσαντες τριάκοντα ἢ τετταράκοντα σταδίων. ἀπαιτοῦσι δὲ καὶ λόγον ἑκά-

---

[1] CDmoxz read ἐκβάλλουσιν.

16. For the Persians neither urinate, nor wash themselves, in a river; nor yet bathe therein or cast therein anything dead or any other thing that is considered unclean. And to whatever god they offer sacrifice, to him they first offer prayer with fire.

17. They are governed by hereditary kings. And he who is disobedient has his head and arms cut off and his body cast forth. The men marry many wives, and at the same time maintain several concubines, for the sake of having many children. The kings set forth prizes annually for those who have the most children; but the children are not brought into the presence of their parents until they are four years old. Marriages are consummated at the beginning of the vernal equinox; and the bridegroom passes to the bridal chamber, having first eaten an apple or a camel's marrow, but nothing else during that day.

18. From five years of age to twenty-four they are trained to use the bow, to throw the javelin, to ride horseback, and to speak the truth; and they use as teachers of science their wisest men, who also interweave their teachings with the mythical element, thus reducing that element to a useful purpose, and rehearse both with song and without song the deeds both of the gods and of the noblest men. And these teachers wake the boys up before dawn by the sound of brazen instruments, and assemble them in one place, as though for arming themselves or for a hunt; and then they divide the boys into companies of fifty, appoint one of the sons of the king or of a satrap as leader of each company, and order them to follow their leader in a race, having marked off a distance of thirty or forty stadia. They require

179

στου μαθήματος, ἅμα καὶ μεγαλοφωνίαν καὶ
πνεῦμα καὶ πλευρὰν ἀσκοῦντες, καὶ πρὸς καῦμα
δὲ καὶ πρὸς ψῦχος καὶ ὄμβρους καὶ χειμάρρων
διαβάσεις, ὥστ᾿ ἄβροχα φυλάττειν καὶ ὅπλα καὶ
ἐσθῆτα, καὶ ποιμαίνειν δὲ καὶ ἀγραυλεῖν καὶ
καρποῖς ἀγρίοις χρῆσθαι, τερμίνθῳ, δρυοβαλά-
νοις, ἀχράδι. καλοῦνται[1] δ᾿ οὗτοι Κάρδακες, ἀπὸ
κλοπείας τρεφόμενοι· κάρδα γὰρ τὸ ἀνδρῶδες καὶ
πολεμικὸν λέγεται. ἡ δὲ καθ᾿ ἡμέραν δίαιτα
ἄρτος μετὰ τὸ γυμνάσιον καὶ μᾶζα καὶ κάρδαμον
καὶ ἁλῶν χόνδρος καὶ κρέα ὀπτὰ ἢ ἑφθὰ ἐξ
ὕδατος, ποτὸν δ᾿ ὕδωρ. θηρεύουσι δὲ σαύνια ἀφ᾿
ἵππων βάλλοντες καὶ τοξεύματα καὶ σφενδονοῦντες.[2] δείλης δὲ φυτουργεῖν καὶ ῥιζοτομεῖν
ἀσκοῦσι καὶ ὁπλοποιεῖν καὶ λίνα καὶ ἄρκυς
φιλοτεχνεῖν. οὐχ ἅπτονται δὲ τῶν θηρευμάτων
οἱ παῖδες, ἀλλὰ κομίζειν οἴκαδε ἔθος. τίθεται
δ᾿ ὑπὸ τοῦ βασιλέως ἆθλα δρόμου καὶ τῶν
ἄλλων τῶν[3] ἐν τοῖς πεντάθλοις. κοσμοῦνται δ᾿
οἱ παῖδες χρυσῷ, τὸ πυρωπὸν τιθεμένων ἐν τιμῇ·
διὸ οὐδὲ νεκρῷ προσφέρουσι, καθάπερ οὐδὲ τὸ
πῦρ, κατὰ τιμήν.

---

[1] Meineke, following conj. of Corais, Groskurd and Kramer,
ejects the words καλοῦντοι . . . λέγεται.
[2] σφενδονοῦντες, Meineke emends to σφενδονῶντες.
[3] ἄλλων τῶν, Meineke, following Groskurd, inserts.

---

[1] The tree is the *Pistacia terebinthus*.
[2] This statement appears to be an interpolation (see critical
note).

them also to give an account of each lesson, at the same time training them in loud speaking and in breathing, and in the use of their lungs, and also training them to endure heat and cold and rains, and to cross torrential streams in such a way as to keep both armour and clothing dry, and also to tend flocks and live outdoors all night and eat wild fruits, such as pistachio nuts,[1] acorns, and wild pears. These are called Cardaces, since they live on thievery, for " carda " means the manly and warlike spirit.[2] Their daily food after their gymnastic exercises consists of bread, barley-cake, cardamum,[3] grains of salt, and roasted or boiled meat; but their drink is water. They hunt by throwing spears from horseback, and with bows and slings; and late in the afternoon they are trained in the planting of trees and in the cutting and gathering of roots [4] and in making weapons and in the art of making linen cloths and hunters' nets. The boys do not touch the meat of wild animals, though it is the custom to bring them home. Prizes are offered by the king for victory in running and in the four other contests of the pentathla.[5] The boys are adorned with gold, since the people hold in honour the fiery appearance of that metal; and on this account, in honour of its fiery appearance, they do not apply gold, just as they do not apply fire, to a dead body.

[3] The *Nasturtium orientale*, also called *Tropaeolum majus*. The plant, a kind of cress, contains a pungent juice; and its seeds are prepared and eaten like our mustard.

[4] *i.e.* for medicinal purposes.

[5] The pentathla were (1) jumping, (2) discus-throwing, (3) running, (4) wrestling, and (5) javelin-throwing (if not boxing).

19. Στρατεύονται δὲ καὶ ἄρχουσιν ἀπὸ εἴκοσιν
ἐτῶν ἕως πεντήκοντα, πεζοί τε καὶ ἱππεῖς·
ἀγορᾶς δὲ οὐχ ἅπτονται, οὔτε γὰρ πωλοῦσιν οὔτ᾽
ὠνοῦνται. ὁπλίζονται δὲ γέρρῳ ῥομβοειδεῖ, παρὰ[1]
δὲ τὰς φαρέτρας σαγάρεις ἔχουσι καὶ κοπίδας,
περὶ δὲ τῇ κεφαλῇ πίλημα πυργωτόν, θώραξ δ᾽
ἐστὶν αὐτοῖς φολιδωτός. ἐσθὴς δὲ τοῖς ἡγεμόσι
μὲν ἀναξυρὶς τριπλῆ, χιτὼν δὲ χειριδωτὸς διπλοῦς
ἕως γόνατος, ὁ ὑπενδύτης μὲν λευκός, ἀνθινὸς δ᾽
ὁ ἐπάνω· ἱμάτιον δὲ θέρους μὲν πορφυροῦν ἢ
ἀνθινόν, χειμῶνος δ᾽ ἀνθινόν, τιᾶραι παραπλή-
σιαι ταῖς τῶν Μάγων, ὑπόδημα κοῖλον διπλοῦν.
τοῖς δὲ πολλοῖς χιτὼν ἕως μεσοκνημίου καὶ
διπλοῦς, ῥάκος δὲ σινδόνιόν τι περὶ τῇ κεφαλῇ·
ἔχει δ᾽ ἕκαστος τόξον καὶ σφενδόνην. δειπνοῦσι
δὲ[2] πολυτελῶς Πέρσαι, τιθέντες καὶ ὁλομελῆ καὶ
πολλὰ καὶ ποικίλα· κόσμος τε λαμπρὸς στρω-
μνῆς ἐκπωμάτων τε καὶ τῶν ἄλλων, ὥστε χρυσῷ
καὶ ἀργύρῳ καταλάμπεσθαι.

20. Ἐν οἴνῳ τὰ μέγιστα βουλεύονται, καὶ
βεβαιότερα τῶν ἐν νήψει τίθενται. τῶν κατὰ
τὰς ὁδοὺς συναντώντων τοὺς μὲν γνωρίμους καὶ
ἰσοτίμους φιλοῦσι προσιόντες,[3] τοῖς δὲ ταπεινο-
τέροις παραβάλλουσι τὴν γνάθον καὶ δέχονται
ταύτῃ τὸ φίλημα· οἱ δ᾽ ἔτι ταπεινότεροι προσκυ-
C 735 νοῦσι μόνον. θάπτουσι δὲ κηρῷ περιπλάσαντες
τὰ σώματα, τοὺς δὲ Μάγους οὐ θάπτουσιν, ἀλλ᾽

---

[1] E reads περί. [2] δέ, omitted by all MSS. except Eiz.
[3] προσίοντες D, προσίοντας other MSS.

19. They serve in the army and hold commands from twenty to fifty years of age, both as foot-soldiers and as horsemen; and they do not approach a market-place, for they neither sell nor buy. They arm themselves with a rhomboidal wicker-shield; and besides quivers they have swords and knives; and on their heads they wear a tower-like hat; and their breastplates are made of scales of iron. The garb of the commanders consists of three-ply trousers, and of a double tunic, with sleeves, that reaches to the knees, the under garment being white and the upper vari-coloured. In summer they wear a purple or vari-coloured cloak, in winter a vari-coloured one only; and their turbans are similar to those of the Magi; and they wear a deep double shoe. Most of the people wear a double tunic that reaches to the middle of the shin, and a piece of linen cloth round the head; and each man has a bow and a sling. Persians dine in an extravagant manner, serving whole animals in great numbers and of various kinds; and their couches, as also their drinking-cups and everything else, are so brilliantly ornamented that they gleam with gold and silver.

20. They carry on their most important deliberations when drinking wine; and they regard decisions then made as more lasting than those made when they are sober. When they meet people on the streets, they approach and kiss those with whom they are acquainted and who are of equal rank, and to those of lower rank they offer the cheek and in that way receive the kiss; but those of still lower rank merely make obeisance. They smear the bodies of the dead with wax before they bury them, though they do not bury the Magi but leave their

οἰωνοβρώτους[1] ἐῶσι· τούτοις δὲ καὶ μητράσι συνέρχεσθαι πάτριον νενόμισται. τοιαῦτα μὲν τὰ ἔθη.

21. Ἔστι δ᾽ ἴσως καὶ ταῦτα τῶν ἐθίμων, ἅ φησι Πολύκριτος.[2] ἐν γὰρ Σούσοις ἑκάστῳ τῶν βασιλέων ἐπὶ τῆς ἄκρας ἰδίᾳ πεποιῆσθαι οἴκησιν καὶ θησαυροὺς καὶ παραθέσεις ὧν ἐπράττοντο φόρων, ὑπομνήματα τῆς οἰκονομίας· πράττεσθαι δ᾽ ἐκ μὲν τῆς παραλίας ἀργύριον, ἐκ δὲ τῆς μεσογαίας ἃ φέρει ἑκάστη χώρα, ὥστε καὶ χρώματα καὶ φάρμακα καὶ τρίχα ἢ[3] ἐρέαν ἤ τι τοιοῦθ᾽ ἕτερον καὶ θρέμματα ὁμοίως. τὸν δὲ διατάξαντα τοὺς φόρους Δαρεῖον εἶναι, τὸν[4] Μακρόχειρα, καὶ κάλλιστον ἀνθρώπων, πλὴν τοῦ μήκους τῶν βραχιόνων καὶ τῶν πήχεων· ἅπτεσθαι γὰρ καὶ τῶν γονάτων· τὸν δὲ πλεῖστον χρυσὸν καὶ ἄργυρον ἐν κατασκευαῖς εἶναι, νομίσματι δὲ οὐ πολλῷ· πρός τε τὰς δωρεὰς ἐκεῖνα κεχαρισμένα νομίζειν μᾶλλον καὶ πρὸς κειμηλίων ἀπόθεσιν· τὸ δὲ νόμισμα τὸ πρὸς τὰς χρείας ἀρκοῦν ἱκανὸν εἶναι, κόπτειν δὲ πάλιν τὸ τοῖς ἀναλώμασι σύμμετρον.

22. Τὰ γὰρ οὖν ἔθη σωφρονικὰ τὰ πλείω· διὰ δὲ τὸν πλοῦτον εἰς τρυφὴν ἐξέπεσον οἱ βασιλεῖς, ὥστε πυρὸν μὲν ἐξ Ἄσσου τῆς Αἰολίδος μετήεσαν, οἶνον δ᾽ ἐκ Συρίας τὸν Χαλυβώνιον, ὕδωρ δὲ

---

[1] οἰωνοβρώτους C, οἰωνοβότους w, οἰωνοβρότους other MSS.

[2] C. Müller (Ind. Var. Lect., p. 1035) would emend Πολύκριτος to Πολύκλειτος (cp. reference to him in 15. 3. 2).

[3] ἤ, Kramer inserts (καί, Corais).

[4] τὸν Μακρόχειρα . . . γονάτων, Meineke, following conj. of Kramer, ejects.

bodies to be eaten by birds; and these Magi, by ancestral custom, consort even with their mothers. Such are the customs of the Persians.

21. Perhaps also the following, mentioned by Polycritus,[1] is one of their customs. He says that in Susa each one of the kings built for himself on the acropolis a separate habitation, treasure-houses, and storage places for what tributes they each exacted, as memorials of his administration; and that they exacted silver from the people on the sea-board, and from the people in the interior such things as each country produced, so that they also received dyes, drugs, hair, or wool, or something else of the kind, and likewise cattle; and that the king who arranged the separate tributes was Dareius, called the Long-armed, and the most handsome of men, except for the length of his arms, for they reached even to his knees;[2] and that most of the gold and silver is used in articles of equipment, but not much in money; and that they consider those metals as better adapted for presents and for depositing in storehouses; and that so much coined money as suffices their needs is enough; and that they coin only what money is commensurate with their expenditures.

22. For their customs are in general temperate; but on account of their wealth the kings fell into such luxury that they sent for wheat from Assus in Aeolis, for Chalymonian wine from Syria, and for

[1] An error, apparently, for Polycleitus (see critical note).
[2] This is thought by various editors to be an interpolation (see critical note). Plutarch (*Artaxerxes* 1) refers to Artaxerxes as having been surnamed " Long-armed " because his right arm was longer than his left; but the above statement in regard to Dareius lacks corroboration.

ἐκ τοῦ Εὐλαίου πάντων ἐλαφρότατον, ὥστ᾽ ἐν
Ἀττικῇ κοτύλῃ δραχμῇ ἀφολκότερον εἶναι.

23. Συνέβη δὲ τοῖς Πέρσαις ἐνδοξοτάτοις γενέσθαι τῶν βαρβάρων παρὰ τοῖς Ἕλλησιν, ὅτι
τῶν μὲν ἄλλων οὐδένες τῶν τῆς Ἀσίας ἀρξάντων
Ἑλλήνων ἦρξαν, οὐδ᾽ ᾔδεισαν οὐδ᾽ ἐκεῖνοι τούτους, οὐδ᾽ οἱ Ἕλληνες τοὺς βαρβάρους, ἀλλ᾽ ἐπὶ
μικρὸν μόνον ἐκ τῆς πόρρωθεν ἀκοῆς. Ὅμηρος
γοῦν οὔτε τὴν τῶν Συρῶν οὔτε τὴν τῶν Μήδων
ἀρχὴν οἶδεν· οὐδὲ γὰρ ἄν, Θήβας Αἰγυπτίας
ὀνομάζων καὶ τὸν ἐκεῖ καὶ τὸν ἐν Φοινίκῃ πλοῦτον, τὸν ἐν Βαβυλῶνι καὶ Νίνῳ[1] καὶ Ἐκβατάνοις
παρεσιώπησε. πρῶτοι δὲ Πέρσαι καὶ Ἑλλήνων
ἐπῆρξαν, Λυδοὶ δὲ ἐπῆρξαν μέν, ἀλλ᾽ οὔτε τῆς
Ἀσίας ὅλης ἐπάρξαντες,[2] ἀλλὰ μέρους τινὸς
μικροῦ, τοῦ ἐντὸς Ἅλυος μόνον, καὶ ταῦτ᾽ ἐπ᾽
ὀλίγον χρόνον τὸν κατὰ Κροῖσον καὶ Ἀλυάττην.
κρατηθέντες δ᾽ ὑπὸ Περσῶν, εἰ καί τι τῆς δόξης
ἦν αὐτοῖς, ἀφῃρέθησαν τοῦθ᾽ ὑπ᾽ ἐκείνων. Πέρσαι
δ᾽, ἀφ᾽ οὗ κατέλυσαν τὰ Μήδων, εὐθὺς καὶ Λυ-
δῶν ἐκράτησαν καὶ τοὺς κατὰ τὴν Ἀσίαν Ἕλληνας ὑπηκόους ἔσχον· ὕστερον δὲ καὶ διέβησαν
C 736 εἰς τὴν Ἑλλάδα, καὶ ἡττηθέντες πολλοῖς καὶ
πολλάκις ἀγῶσιν,[3] ὅμως διετέλεσαν τὴν Ἀσίαν
μέχρι τῶν ἐπὶ θαλάττῃ τόπων κατέχοντες, ἕως ὑπὸ
Μακεδόνων κατεπολεμήθησαν.

---

[1] καὶ Νίνῳ, omitted by moz, Νείλῳ CDFhvwx, Σούσοις i.
[2] ἐπάρξαντες, omitted by moxz, Corais and Meineke.

water from the Eulaeus, which is so far the lightest of all waters that an Attic cotyle [1] of it weighs a drachm less than other waters.

23. The Persians, of all the barbarians, became the most famous among the Greeks, because none of the other barbarians who ruled Asia ruled Greeks; neither were these people acquainted with the Greeks nor yet the Greeks with the barbarians, except for a short time by distant hearsay. Homer, at any rate, knows neither of the empire of the Syrians nor of that of the Medes; for otherwise, since he names Aegyptian Thebes and mentions the wealth there and the wealth in Phoenicia, he would not have passed by in silence that in Babylon and Ninus and Ecbatana. The Persians were the first people to rule over Greeks. The Lydians had indeed ruled over Greeks, but not also over the whole of Asia—only over a small part of it, that inside the Halys River, and that too for only a short time, in the time of Croesus and Alyattes. But the Lydians were mastered by the Persians and deprived by them of whatever glory they had. The Persians, as soon as they broke up the power of the Medes, immediately mastered the Lydians and also got as their subjects the Greeks in Asia; and later they even crossed over into Greece; and, though often defeated in many battles, still they continued to hold Asia as far as the places on the sea until they were subdued by the Macedonians.

---

[1] Nearly half a pint.

---

[3] F reads πολλοῖς καὶ πολλάκοις (sic) ἀγῶσιν καὶ πολλάκις; *moz* πολλοῖς ἀγῶσιν καὶ πολλάκις. Kramer and C. Müller would read πολλοῖς καὶ μεγάλοις ἀγῶσιν.

24. Ὁ μὲν οὖν εἰς τὴν ἡγεμονίαν καταστήσας αὐτοὺς Κῦρος ἦν· διαδεξάμενος δὲ τοῦτον Καμβύσης υἱὸς ὑπὸ τῶν Μάγων κατελύθη· τούτους δ' ἀνελόντες οἱ ἑπτὰ Πέρσαι Δαρείῳ τῷ Ὑστάσπεως παρέδοσαν τὴν ἀρχήν· εἶθ' οἱ ἀπὸ τούτου διαδεχόμενοι κατέληξαν εἰς Ἄρσην, ὃν ἀποκτείνας Βαγῶος ὁ εὐνοῦχος κατέστησε Δαρεῖον, οὐκ ὄντα τοῦ γένους τῶν βασιλέων. τοῦτον δὲ καταλύσας Ἀλέξανδρος αὐτὸς ἦρξε[1] δέκα ἢ ἕνδεκα ἔτη· εἶτ' εἰς πλείους τοὺς διαδεξαμένους καὶ τοὺς ἐπιγόνους τούτων μερισθεῖσα ἡ ἡγεμονία τῆς Ἀσίας διελύθη· συνέμεινε δ' ὅσον πεντήκοντα ἐπὶ τοῖς διακοσίοις ἔτη. νῦν δ' ἤδη καθ' αὑτοὺς συνεστῶτες οἱ Πέρσαι βασιλέας ἔχουσιν ὑπηκόους ἑτέροις βασιλεῦσι, πρότερον μὲν Μακεδόσι, νῦν δὲ Παρθυαίοις.

[1] Instead of δέκα, Dh and Corais read δώδεκα.

24. Now the man who established the Persians in their hegemony was Cyrus.[1] Cyrus was succeeded by his son Cambyses, who was deposed by the Magi. The Magi were slain by the Seven Persians, who then gave over the empire to Dareius, the son of Hystaspes. And then the successors of Dareius came to an end with Arses. Arses was slain by Bagoüs the eunuch, who set up as king another Dareius, who was not of the royal family. Him Alexander deposed, and reigned himself for ten or eleven years. And then the hegemony of Asia was divided amongst his several successors and their descendants, and then dissolved. The hegemony of the Persians over Asia lasted about two hundred and fifty years. But now, though again organised into a state of their own, the Persians have kings that are subject to other kings, formerly to the kings of Macedonia, but now to those of the Parthians.

[1] Cyrus the Elder.

BOOK XVI

1. Τῇ δὲ Περσίδι καὶ τῇ Σουσιανῇ συνάπτουσιν
οἱ Ἀσσύριοι· καλοῦσι δ' οὕτω τὴν Βαβυλωνίαν
καὶ πολλὴν τῆς κύκλῳ γῆς, ἧς ἐν μέρει καὶ ἡ
Ἀτουρία ἐστίν, ἐν ᾗπερ ἡ Νίνος καὶ ἡ Ἀπολλωνιᾶτις καὶ Ἐλυμαῖοι καὶ Παραιτάκαι καὶ ἡ περὶ τὸ
Ζάγρον[1] ὄρος Χαλωνῖτις[2] καὶ τὰ περὶ τὴν Νίνον
πεδία, Δολομηνή τε καὶ Καλαχηνὴ καὶ Χαζηνὴ
καὶ Ἀδιαβηνή, καὶ τὰ τῆς Μεσοποταμίας ἔθνη
τὰ περὶ Γοροδυαίους καὶ τοὺς περὶ Νίσιβιν
Μυγδόνας μέχρι τοῦ Ζεύγματος τοῦ κατὰ τὸν
Εὐφράτην καὶ τῆς πέραν τοῦ Εὐφράτου πολλή,[3]
ἣν Ἄραβες κατέχουσι, καὶ οἱ ἰδίως ὑπὸ τῶν νῦν
C 737 λεγόμενοι Σύροι μέχρι Κιλίκων καὶ Φοινίκων καὶ
Ἰουδαίων[4] καὶ τῆς θαλάττης τῆς κατὰ τὸ
Αἰγύπτιον πέλαγος καὶ τὸν Ἰσσικὸν κόλπον.

2. Δοκεῖ δὲ τὸ τῶν Σύρων ὄνομα διατεῖναι ἀπὸ
μὲν τῆς Βαβυλωνίας μέχρι τοῦ Ἰσσικοῦ κόλπου,
ἀπὸ δὲ τούτου μέχρι τοῦ Εὐξείνου τὸ παλαιόν.
οἱ γοῦν Καππάδοκες ἀμφότεροι, οἵ τε πρὸς τῷ
Ταύρῳ καὶ οἱ πρὸς τῷ Πόντῳ, μέχρι νῦν Λευκό-

---

[1] Ζάδρον E, Ζάγριον Dhix Tzschucke, Corais.
[2] Χαλωνῖτις Casaubon, for Χαλωνίτης D, Χαωνῖτις other MSS.
[3] πολλή, Kramer, for πολλῆς.
[4] Ἰουδαίων, in marg. FCz, for Λιβύων. Corais writes καὶ
Ἰουδαίων καὶ Λιβύων.

BOOK XVI

I

1. THE country of the Assyrians borders on Persis and Susiana. This name [1] is given to Babylonia and to much of the country all round, which latter, in part, is also called Aturia, in which are Ninus, Apolloniatis, the Elymaei, the Paraetacae, the Chalonitis in the neighbourhood of Mt. Zagrus, the plains in the neighbourhood of Ninus, and also Dolomenê and Calachenê and Chazenê and Adiabenê, and the tribes of Mesopotamia in the neighbourhood of the Gordyaeans, and the Mygdonians in the neighbourhood of Nisibis, as far as the Zeugma [2] of the Euphrates, as also much of the country on the far side of the Euphrates, which is occupied by Arabians, and those people who in a special sense of the term are called by the men of to-day Syrians, who extend as far as the Cilicians and the Phoenicians and the Judaeans and the sea that is opposite the Aegyptian Sea and the Gulf of Issus.

2. It seems that the name of the Syrians extended not only from Babylonia to the Gulf of Issus, but also in ancient times from this gulf to the Euxine. At any rate, both tribes of the Cappadocians, both those near the Taurus and those near the Pontus, have to the present time been called " White

---

[1] *i.e.* " Assyria."   [2] Bridge.

συροι καλοῦνται, ὡς ἂν ὄντων τινῶν Σύρων καὶ
μελάνων· οὗτοι δ' εἰσὶν οἱ ἐκτὸς τοῦ Ταύρου·
λέγω δὲ Ταῦρον, μέχρι τοῦ Ἀμανοῦ διατείνων
τοὔνομα. οἱ δ' ἱστοροῦντες τὴν Σύρων ἀρχὴν
ὅταν φῶσι Μήδους μὲν ὑπὸ Περσῶν καταλυθῆναι,
Σύρους δὲ ὑπὸ Μήδων, οὐκ ἄλλους τινὰς τοὺς
Σύρους λέγουσιν, ἀλλὰ τοὺς ἐν Βαβυλῶνι καὶ
Νίνῳ κατεσκευασμένους τὸ βασίλειον· ὧν ὁ μὲν
Νίνος ἦν ὁ τὴν Νίνον ἐν τῇ Ἀτουρίᾳ κτίσας, ἡ δὲ
τούτου γυνή, ἥπερ καὶ διεδέξατο τὸν ἄνδρα,
Σεμίραμις· ἧς ἐστι κτίσμα ἡ Βαβυλών. οὗτοι
δὲ ἐκράτησαν τῆς Ἀσίας, καὶ τῆς Σεμιράμιδος,
χωρὶς τῶν ἐν Βαβυλῶνι ἔργων, πολλὰ [1] καὶ ἄλλα
κατὰ πᾶσαν γῆν σχεδὸν δείκνυται, ὅση τῆς
ἠπείρου ταύτης ἐστί, τά τε χώματα, ἃ δὴ καλοῦσι
Σεμιράμιδος, καὶ τείχη καὶ ἐρυμάτων κατασκευαὶ
καὶ συρίγγων τῶν ἐν αὐτοῖς καὶ ὑδρείων καὶ
κλιμάκων καὶ διωρύγων ἐν ποταμοῖς καὶ λίμναις
καὶ ὁδῶν καὶ γεφυρῶν. ἀπέλιπον δὲ τοῖς μεθ'
ἑαυτοὺς τὴν ἀρχὴν μέχρι τῆς Σαρδαναπάλου καὶ
Ἀρβάκου· [2] μετέστη δ' εἰς Μήδους ὕστερον.[3]

3. Ἡ μὲν οὖν Νίνος [4] πόλις ἠφανίσθη παραχρῆμα μετὰ [5] τὴν τῶν Σύρων κατάλυσιν. πολὺ
δὲ μείζων ἦν τῆς Βαβυλῶνος, ἐν πεδίῳ κειμένη
τῆς Ἀτουρίας· ἡ δ' Ἀτουρία τοῖς περὶ Ἄρβηλα
τόποις ὅμορός [6] ἐστι, μεταξὺ ἔχουσα τὸν Λύκον
ποταμόν. τὰ μὲν οὖν Ἄρβηλα τῆς Βαβυλωνίας
ὑπάρχει, ἃ κατ' αὐτήν ἐστιν· ἐν δὲ τῇ περαίᾳ τοῦ

---

[1] All MSS. except E read δέ after πολλά.
[2] Ἀρβάκου, Casaubon, for Ὀρβάκου.
[3] Dhi read σήμερον.   [4] Νίνων CDFhiw.
[5] κατά Es.

Syrians," [1] as though some Syrians were black, these being the Syrians who live outside the Taurus; and when I say "Taurus," I am extending the name as far as the Amanus. When those who have written histories of the Syrian empire say that the Medes were overthrown by the Persians and the Syrians by the Medes, they mean by the Syrians no other people than those who built the royal palaces in Babylon and Ninus; and, of these Syrians, Ninus was the man who founded Ninus in Aturia, and his wife, Semiramis, was the woman who succeeded her husband and founded Babylon. These two gained the mastery of Asia; and as for Semiramis, apart from her works at Babylon, many others are also to be seen throughout almost the whole of that continent, I mean the mounds called the Mounds of Semiramis, and walls, and the construction of fortifications with aqueducts therein, and of reservoirs for drinking-water, and of ladder-like ascents of mountains, and of channels in rivers and lakes, and of roads and bridges. And they left to their successors their empire until the time of the empires of Sardanapalus and Arbaces. But later the empire passed over to the Medes.

3. Now the city Ninus [2] was wiped out immediately after the overthrow of the Syrians. [3] It was much greater than Babylon, and was situated in the plain of Aturia. Aturia borders on the region of Arbela, with the Lycus River lying between them. Now Arbela, which lies opposite to Babylonia, belongs to that country; and in the country on the

---

[1] Cf. 12. 3. 9.   [2] Nineveh.   [3] 608 B.C.

---

[6] ὅμορος Exz, ὅμοιος other MSS.

Λύκου τὰ τῆς Ἀτουρίας πεδία τῇ Νίνῳ περίκειται. ἐν δὲ τῇ Ἀτουρίᾳ ἐστὶ Γαυγάμηλα κώμη,
ἐν ᾗ συνέβη νικηθῆναι καὶ ἀποβαλεῖν τὴν ἀρχὴν
Δαρεῖον. ἔστι μὲν οὖν τόπος ἐπίσημος οὗτος καὶ
τοὔνομα, μεθερμηνευθὲν γάρ ἐστι καμήλου οἶκος·
ὠνόμασε δ' οὕτω Δαρεῖος ὁ Ὑστάσπεω, κτῆμα
δοὺς εἰς διατροφὴν τῇ καμήλῳ τῇ συνεκπεπονη-
κυίᾳ μάλιστα τὴν ὁδὸν τὴν διὰ τῆς ἐρήμου
Σκυθίας μετὰ τῶν φορτίων, ἐν οἷς ἦν καὶ ἡ
διατροφὴ τῷ βασιλεῖ. οἱ μέντοι Μακεδόνες, τοῦτο
μὲν ὁρῶντες κώμιον εὐτελές, τὰ δὲ Ἄρβηλα
κατοικίαν ἀξιόλογον (κτίσμα, ὥς φασιν, Ἀρβήλου
τοῦ Ἀθμονέως), περὶ Ἄρβηλα τὴν μάχην καὶ
νίκην κατεφήμισαν καὶ τοῖς συγγραφεῦσιν οὕτω
παρέδωκαν.

4. Μετὰ δὲ Ἄρβηλα καὶ τὸ Νικατόριον ὄρος
(ὃ προσωνόμασεν Ἀλέξανδρος, νικήσας τὴν περὶ
Ἄρβηλα μάχην) ὁ Κάπρος ἐστὶ ποταμὸς ἐν ἴσῳ
C 738 διαστήματι, ὅσῳ καὶ ὁ Λύκος· ἡ δὲ χώρα Ἀρτα-
κηνὴ[1] λέγεται. περὶ Ἄρβηλα δέ ἐστι καὶ
Δημητριὰς πόλις· εἶθ' ἡ τοῦ νάφθα πηγὴ καὶ τὰ
πυρὰ καὶ τὸ τῆς Ἀνέας[2] ἱερὸν καὶ Σαδράκαι, τὸ
Δαρείου τοῦ Ὑστάσπεω βασίλειον, καὶ ὁ
Κυπαρισσὼν καὶ ἡ τοῦ Κάπρου διάβασις, συνάπ-
τουσα ἤδη Σελευκείᾳ καὶ Βαβυλῶνι.

5. Ἡ δὲ Βαβυλὼν καὶ αὐτὴ μέν ἐστιν ἐν
πεδίῳ, τὸν δὲ κύκλον ἔχει τοῦ τείχους τριακοσίων
ὀγδοήκοντα πέντε σταδίων, πάχος δὲ τοῦ τείχους

---

[1] Ἀρτακηνή is otherwise unknown. Groskurd conj. Ἀρβη-
ληνή (noting Ἀρβηλῖτις in Ptolemaeus 6. 1 and Pliny 6. 13.
16); Kramer prefers Ἀδιαβηνή; C. Müller conj. Γαραμηνή.
[2] Ἀνέας, Xylander and Kramer emend to Ἀκαίας; Corais
conj. Ἀναΐτιδος.

196

far side of the Lycus River lie the plains of Aturia, which surround Ninus. In Aturia is a village Gaugamela, where Dareius was conquered and lost his empire. Now this is a famous place, as is also its name, which, being interpreted, means " Camel's House." Dareius, the son of Hystaspes, so named it, having given it as an estate for the maintenance of the camel which helped most on the toilsome journey through the deserts of Scythia with the burdens containing sustenance and support for the king. However, the Macedonians, seeing that this was a cheap village, but that Arbela was a notable settlement (founded, as it is said, by Arbelus, the son of Athmoneus), announced that the battle and victory took place near Arbela and so transmitted their account to the historians.

4. After Arbela and Mt. Nicatorium [1] (a name applied to it by Alexander after his victory in the neighbourhood of Arbela), one comes to the Caprus River, which lies at the same distance from Arbela as the Lycus. The country is called Artacenê.[2] Near Arbela lies the city Demetrias; and then one comes to the fountain of naphtha, and to the fires, and to the temple of Anea,[3] and to Sandracae, and to the royal palace of Dareius the son of Hystaspes, and to Cyparisson, and to the crossing of the Caprus River, where, at last, one is close to Seleuceia and Babylon.

5. Babylon, too, lies in a plain; and the circuit of its wall is three hundred and eighty-five stadia. The thickness of its wall is thirty-two feet; the

[1] " Mount of Victory."

[2] Probably an error for Adiabenê (see 16. 1. 8 and 16. 1. 18).

[3] Apparently the same as the goddess Anaïtis (cf. 11. 8. 4 and 15. 3. 15).

STRABO

ποδῶν δύο καὶ τριάκοντα, ὕψος δὲ τῶν μὲν μεσοπυρ-
γίων πήχεις πεντήκοντα, τῶν δὲ πύργων ἑξήκοντα,
ἡ δὲ πάροδος τοῖς ἐπὶ τοῦ τείχους, ὥστε¹ τέθριππα
ἐναντιοδρομεῖν ἀλλήλοις ῥᾳδίως· διόπερ τῶν
ἑπτὰ θεαμάτων λέγεται καὶ τοῦτο καὶ ὁ κρεμασ-
τὸς κῆπος, ἔχων ἐν τετραγώνῳ σχήματι ἑκάστην
πλευρὰν τεττάρων πλέθρων· συνέχεται δὲ ψα-
λιδώμασι καμαρωτοῖς, ἐπὶ πεττῶν ἱδρυμένοις
κυβοειδῶν ἄλλοις ἐπ' ἄλλοις· οἱ δὲ πεττοὶ κοῖλοι
πλήρεις γῆς, ὥστε δέξασθαι φυτὰ δένδρων τῶν
μεγίστων, ἐξ ὀπτῆς πλίνθου καὶ ἀσφάλτου
κατεσκευασμένοι καὶ αὐτοὶ καὶ αἱ ψαλίδες καὶ
τὰ καμαρώματα. ἡ δ' ἀνωτάτω στέγη προσ-
βάσεις κλιμακωτὰς ἔχει, παρακειμένους δ' αὐταῖς
καὶ κοχλίας, δι' ὧν τὸ ὕδωρ ἀνῆγον εἰς τὸν κῆπον
ἀπὸ τοῦ Εὐφράτου συνεχῶς οἱ πρὸς τοῦτο τεταγ-
μένοι. ὁ γὰρ ποταμὸς διὰ μέσης ῥεῖ τῆς πόλεως
σταδιαῖος τὸ πλάτος· ἐπὶ δὲ τῷ ποταμῷ ὁ κῆπος.
ἔστι δὲ καὶ ὁ τοῦ Βήλου τάφος αὐτόθι, νῦν μὲν
κατεσκαμμένος Ξέρξης δ' αὐτὸν κατέσπασεν, ὥς
φασιν· ἦν δὲ πυραμὶς τετράγωνος ἐξ ὀπτῆς
πλίνθου, καὶ αὐτὴ σταδιαία τὸ ὕψος, σταδιαία
δὲ καὶ ἑκάστη τῶν πλευρῶν· ἣν Ἀλέξανδρος
ἐβούλετο ἀνασκευάσαι, πολὺ δ' ἦν ἔργον καὶ
πολλοῦ χρόνου (αὐτὴ γὰρ ἡ χοῦς εἰς ἀνακάθαρσιν
μυρίοις ἀνδράσι δυεῖν μηνῶν ἔργον ἦν), ὥστ' οὐκ
ἔφθη τὸ ἐγχειρηθὲν ἐπιτελέσαι· παραχρῆμα γὰρ
ἡ νόσος καὶ ἡ τελευτὴ συνέπεσε τῷ βασιλεῖ.

¹ ὥστε Dhi, Corais, and Meineke, for ὡς.

height thereof between the towers is fifty cubits [1];
that of the towers is sixty cubits; and the passage
on top of the wall is such that four-horse chariots
can easily pass one another; and it is on this account
that this and the hanging garden are called one of
the Seven Wonders of the World. The garden is
quadrangular in shape, and each side is four plethra
in length. It consists of arched vaults, which are
situated, one after another, on checkered, cube-like
foundations. The checkered foundations, which are
hollowed out, are covered so deep with earth that
they admit of the largest of trees, having been
constructed of baked brick and asphalt——the foundations themselves and the vaults and the arches.
The ascent to the uppermost terrace-roofs is made
by a stairway; and alongside these stairs there were
screws, through which the water was continually
conducted up into the garden from the Euphrates
by those appointed for this purpose. For the river,
a stadium in width, flows through the middle of the
city; and the garden is on the bank of the river.
Here too is the tomb of Belus, now in ruins, having
been demolished by Xerxes, as it is said. It was a
quadrangular pyramid of baked brick, not only being
a stadium in height, but also having sides a stadium
in length. Alexander intended to repair this pyramid; but it would have been a large task and would
have required a long time (for merely the clearing
away of the mound was a task for ten thousand men
for two months), so that he could not finish what he
had attempted; for immediately the king was overtaken by disease and death. None of his successors

[1] Cp. the account of Herodotus (1. 178), who gives much
larger dimensions.

τῶν δ' ὕστερον οὐδεὶς ἐφρόντισεν· ἀλλὰ καὶ τὰ
λοιπὰ ὠλιγωρήθη καὶ κατήρειψαν τῆς πόλεως τὰ
μὲν οἱ Πέρσαι, τὰ δ' ὁ χρόνος καὶ ἡ τῶν Μακεδόνων ὀλιγωρία περὶ τὰ τοιαῦτα, καὶ μάλιστα
ἐπειδὴ τὴν Σελεύκειαν ἐπὶ τῷ Τίγρει πλησίον τῆς
Βαβυλῶνος ἐν τριακοσίοις που σταδίοις ἐτείχισε
Σέλευκος ὁ Νικάτωρ. καὶ γὰρ ἐκεῖνος καὶ οἱ μετ'
αὐτὸν ἅπαντες περὶ ταύτην ἐσπούδασαν τὴν
πόλιν καὶ τὸ βασίλειον ἐνταῦθα μετήνεγκαν·
καὶ δὴ καὶ νῦν ἡ μὲν γέγονε Βαβυλῶνος
μείζων, ἡ δ' ἔρημος ἡ πολλή, ὥστ' ἐπ' αὐτῆς μὴ
ἂν ὀκνῆσαί τινα εἰπεῖν, ὅπερ ἔφη τις τῶν
κωμικῶν ἐπὶ τῶν Μεγαλοπολιτῶν τῶν ἐν
Ἀρκαδίᾳ·

ἐρημία μεγάλη 'στὶν ἡ Μεγάλη πόλις.

C 739 διὰ δὲ τὴν τῆς ὕλης σπάνιν ἐκ φοινικίνων ξύλων αἱ
οἰκοδομαὶ συντελοῦνται καὶ δοκοῖς καὶ στύλοις·
περὶ δὲ τοὺς στύλους στρέφοντες ἐκ τῆς καλάμης
σχοινία περιτιθέασιν, εἶτ' ἐπαλείφοντες χρώμασι
καταγράφουσι, τὰς δὲ θύρας ἀσφάλτῳ· ὑψηλαὶ
δὲ καὶ αὗται καὶ οἱ οἶκοι, καμαρωτοὶ πάντες διὰ
τὴν ἀξυλίαν. ψιλὴ γὰρ ἡ χώρα καὶ θαμνώδης ἡ
πολλὴ πλὴν φοίνικος· οὗτος δὲ πλεῖστος ἐν τῇ
Βαβυλωνίᾳ, πολὺς δὲ καὶ ἐν Σούσοις καὶ ἐν τῇ
παραλίᾳ τῇ [1] Περσίδι καὶ ἐν τῇ Καρμανίᾳ.
κεράμῳ δ' οὐ χρῶνται· οὐδὲ γὰρ κατομβροῦνται.
παραπλήσια δὲ καὶ τὰ ἐν Σούσοις καὶ τῇ
Σιτακηνῇ.

6. Ἀφώριστο δ' ἐν τῇ Βαβυλωνίᾳ [2] κατοικία

---

[1] τῇ, Meineke inserts.

cared for this matter; and even what was left of the
city was neglected and thrown into ruins, partly by
the Persians and partly by time and by the indiffer-
ence of the Macedonians to things of this kind, and
in particular after Seleucus Nicator had fortified
Seleuceia on the Tigris near Babylon, at a distance
of about three hundred stadia therefrom. For not
only he, but also all his successors, were strongly
interested in Seleuceia and transferred the royal
residence to it. What is more, Seleuceia at the
present time has become larger than Babylon,
whereas the greater part of Babylon is so deserted
that one would not hesitate to say what one of the
comic poets said in reference to the Megalopolitans
in Arcadia: " The Great City [1] is a great desert." [2]
On account of the scarcity of timber their buildings
are finished with beams and pillars of palm-wood.
They wind ropes of twisted reed round the pillars;
and then they plaster them and paint them with
colours, though they coat the doors with asphalt.
Both these and the private homes are built high,
all being vaulted on account of the lack of timber;
for, with the exception of the palm tree, most of
the country is bare of trees and bears shrubs only.
The palm is most abundant in Babylonia, and is
found in abundance in Susa and on the coast of
Persis and in Carmania. They do not use tiles
much on their houses, for they get no rain; and
this is likewise the case both in Susa and Sitacenê.

6. In Babylonia a settlement is set apart for the

[1] " Megalopolis " means " Great City."
[2] Strabo makes the same quotation in 8. 8. 1.

---

[2] Βαβυλωνί, Groskurd and Meineke emend to Βαβυλωνία.

τοῖς ἐπιχωρίοις φιλοσόφοις, τοῖς Χαλδαίοις προσαγορευομένοις, οἳ περὶ ἀστρονομίαν εἰσὶ τὸ πλέον· προσποιοῦνται δέ τινες καὶ γενεθλιαλογεῖν, οὓς οὐ καταδέχονται οἱ ἕτεροι. ἔστι δὲ καὶ φῦλόν τι τὸ τῶν Χαλδαίων καὶ χώρα τῆς Βαβυλωνίας ὑπ' ἐκείνων οἰκομένη, πλησιάζουσα καὶ τοῖς Ἄραψι καὶ τῇ κατὰ Πέρσας λεγομένῃ θαλάττῃ. ἔστι δὲ καὶ τῶν Χαλδαίων τῶν ἀστρονομικῶν γένη πλείω· καὶ γὰρ Ὀρχηνοί τινες προσαγορεύονται καὶ Βορσιππηνοὶ καὶ ἄλλοι πλείους, ὡς ἂν κατὰ αἱρέσεις, ἄλλα καὶ ἄλλα νέμοντες περὶ τῶν αὐτῶν δόγματα. μέμνηνται δὲ καὶ τῶν ἀνδρῶν ἐνίων οἱ μαθηματικοί, καθάπερ Κιδήνα τε καὶ Ναβουριανοῦ καὶ Σουδίνου. καὶ Σέλευκος δ' ὁ ἀπὸ τῆς Σελευκείας Χαλδαῖός ἐστι καὶ ἄλλοι πλείους ἀξιόλογοι ἄνδρες.

7. Τὰ δὲ Βόρσιππα ἱερὰ πόλις ἐστὶν Ἀρτέμιδος καὶ Ἀπόλλωνος, λινουργεῖον μέγα. πληθύουσι δὲ ἐν αὐτῇ νυκτερίδες μείζους πολὺ τῶν ἐν ἄλλοις τόποις· ἁλίσκονται δ' εἰς βρῶσιν καὶ ταριχεύονται.

8. Περιέχεται δ' ἡ χώρα τῶν Βαβυλωνίων ἀπὸ μὲν τῆς ἠοῦς ὑπό τε Σουσίων καὶ Ἐλυμαίων καὶ Παραιτακηνῶν, ἀπὸ δὲ τῆς μεσημβρίας ὑπὸ τοῦ Περσικοῦ κόλπου καὶ τῶν Χαλδαίων μέχρι Ἀράβων τῶν Μεσηνῶν,[1] ἀπὸ δὲ τῆς ἑσπέρας ὑπό τε Ἀράβων τῶν Σκηνιτῶν μέχρι τῆς Ἀδιαβηνῆς καὶ τῆς Γορδυαίας, ἀπὸ δὲ τῶν ἄρκτων ὑπό τε Ἀρμενίων καὶ Μήδων μέχρι τοῦ Ζάγρου καὶ τῶν περὶ αὐτὸν[2] ἐθνῶν.

[1] Μεσηνῶν, Letronne, for Ἐλεσηνῶν F, Ἀλεσηνῶν other MSS.; so later editors.   [2] αὐτόν, Jones, for αὐτό.

local philosophers, the Chaldaeans, as they are called, who are concerned mostly with astronomy; but some of these, who are not approved of by the others, profess to be genethlialogists.[1] There is also a tribe of the Chaldaeans, and a territory inhabited by them, in the neighbourhood of the Arabians and of the Persian Sea, as it is called. There are also several tribes of the Chaldaean astronomers. For example, some are called Orcheni, others Borsippeni, and several others by different names, as though divided into different sects which hold to various different dogmas about the same subjects. And the mathematicians make mention of some of these men; as, for example, Cidenas and Naburianus and Sudinus. Seleucus of Seleuceia is also a Chaldaean, as are also several other noteworthy men.

7. Borsippa is a city sacred to Artemis and Apollo; and it manufactures linen in great quantities. It abounds in bats, much larger in size than those in other places; and these bats are caught and salted for food.

8. The country of the Babylonians is surrounded on the east by the Susians and Elymaeans and Paraetacenians, and on the south by the Persian Gulf and the Chaldaeans as far as the Mesenian [2] Arabians, and on the west by the Arabians called Scenitae,[3] as far as Adiabenê and Gordyaea, and on the north by the Armenians and the Medes as far as the Zagrus and the tribes about that river.

---

[1] i.e. to be astrologers, or to know how to cast nativities.
[2] Cf. "Mesenê" in 2. 1. 31.
[3] "Tent-dwellers."

STRABO

9. Διαρρεῖται δ' ὑπὸ πλειόνων μὲν ποταμῶν ἡ
χώρα, μεγίστων δὲ τοῦ τε Εὐφράτου καὶ τοῦ
Τίγριος· μετὰ γὰρ τοὺς Ἰνδικοὺς οὗτοι λέγονται
δευτερεύειν κατὰ τὰ νότια μέρη τῆς Ἀσίας οἱ
ποταμοί· ἔχουσι δ' ἀνάπλους, ὁ μὲν ἐπὶ τὴν
Ὦπιν καὶ[1] τὴν νῦν Σελεύκειαν (ἡ δὲ Ὦπις κώμη
ἐμπόριον τῶν κύκλῳ τόπων), ὁ δ' ἐπὶ Βαβυλῶνα,
C 740 πλειόνων ἢ τρισχιλίων σταδίων. οἱ μὲν οὖν
Πέρσαι τοὺς ἀνάπλους ἐπίτηδες κωλύειν θέλοντες,
φόβῳ τῶν ἔξωθεν ἐφόδων, καταράκτας χειροποιή-
τους κατεσκευάκεισαν· ὁ δὲ Ἀλέξανδρος ἐπιών,
ὅσους οἷός τε ἦν, ἀνεσκεύασε, καὶ μάλιστα τοὺς
ἐπὶ τὴν Ὦπιν. ἐπεμελήθη δὲ καὶ τῶν διωρύγων·
πλημμυρεῖ γὰρ ὁ Εὐφράτης κατὰ τὴν ἀρχὴν τοῦ
θέρους, ἀπὸ τοῦ ἔαρος ἀρξάμενος, ἡνίκα τήκονται
αἱ χιόνες αἱ ἀπὸ τῆς Ἀρμενίας, ὥστ' ἀνάγκη
λιμνάζειν[2] καὶ κατακλύζεσθαι τὰς ἀρούρας, εἰ
μὴ διοχετεύει τις ταφρείαις καὶ διώρυξι τὸ ἐκπῖπ-
τον τοῦ ῥοῦ καὶ ἐπιπολάζον ὕδωρ, καθάπερ καὶ
ἐν Αἰγύπτῳ τὸ τοῦ Νείλου· ἐντεῦθεν μὲν οὖν
αἱ διώρυγες γεγένηνται· χρεία δέ ἐστιν ὑπουρ-
γίας μεγάλης· βαθεῖα γὰρ ἡ γῆ καὶ μαλακὴ
καὶ εὐένδοτος, ὥστε καὶ ἐκσύρεται ῥᾳδίως
ὑπὸ τῶν ῥευμάτων καὶ γυμνοῖ τὰ πεδία, πληροῖ
δὲ τὰς διώρυγας καὶ τὰ στόματα αὐτῶν ἐμφράττει
ῥᾳδίως ἡ χοῦς· οὕτω δὲ συμβαίνει πάλιν τὴν
ὑπέρχυσιν τῶν ὑδάτων εἰς τὰ πρὸς τῇ θαλάττῃ
πεδία ἐκπίπτουσαν λίμνας ἀποτελεῖν καὶ ἕλη καὶ

[1] Meissner would omit καί. But according to Strabo's
usage Σελεύκειαν might be appositional with Ὦπιν with the
καί quite as well as without it.
[2] λιμνάζεσθαι Dhi.

204

9. The country is traversed by several rivers, though the largest are the Euphrates and the Tigris. Next to the Indian rivers these two, among those in the southern parts of Asia, are said to hold the second place. And they are navigable inland: the Tigris to Opis and the present Seleuceia [1] (the village Opis is an emporium of the places situated round it) and the Euphrates to Babylon, a distance of more than three thousand stadia. Now the Persians, wishing on purpose to prevent voyaging up these rivers, for fear of attacks from without, had constructed artificial cataracts, but Alexander, when he went against them, destroyed as many of them as he could, and in particular those to Opis. He also paid careful attention to the canals; for the Euphrates rises to flood-tide at the beginning of summer, beginning first to rise in the spring when the snows in Armenia melt; so that of necessity it forms lakes and deluges the ploughed lands, unless the excess of the stream, or the surface water, is distributed by means of trenches and canals, as is the case with the Nile in Aegypt. Now this is the origin of the canals; but there is need of much labour to keep them up, for the soil is so deep and soft and yielding that it is easily swept out by the streams, and the plains are laid bare, and the canals are easily filled, and their mouths choked, by the silt; and thus it results again that the overflow of the waters, emptying into the plains near the sea, forms lakes and marshes and reed-beds, which last supply reeds from

[1] Bruno Meissner (*Klio, Beiträge zur Alten Geschichte,* XIX. 1925, p. 103), comparing 2. 1. 26, understands Strabo to mean that Opis and "the present Seleuceia" are identical (see critical note).

STRABO

καλαμῶνας, ἐξ ὧν καλάμινα πλέκεται παντοῖα
σκεύη, τὰ μὲν ὑγροῦ δεκτικὰ τῇ ἀσφάλτῳ περι-
αλειφόντων, τοῖς δ' ἄλλοις ψιλῶς χρωμένων· καὶ
ἱστία δὲ ποιοῦνται καλάμινα, ψιάθοις ἢ ῥιψὶ
παραπλήσια.
10. Τὸ μὲν οὖν παντάπασι κωλύειν τὴν τοιαύτην
πλήμμυραν οὐχ οἷόν τε ἴσως, τὸ δὲ τὴν δυνατὴν
προσφέρειν βοήθειαν ἡγεμόνων ἀγαθῶν ἐστιν.
ἡ δὲ βοήθεια αὕτη· τὴν μὲν πολλὴν παρέκχυσιν
ἐμφράξει κωλύειν, τὴν δὲ πλήρωσιν, ἣν ἡ χοῦς
ἐργάζεται, τοὐναντίον ἀνακαθάρσει τῶν διωρύγων
καὶ ἐξανοίξει τῶν στομάτων. ἡ μὲν οὖν ἀνακά-
θαρσις ῥᾳδία, ἡ δὲ ἔμφραξις πολυχειρίας δεῖται·
εὐένδοτος γὰρ οὖσα ἡ γῆ καὶ μαλακὴ τὴν ἐπιφορη-
θεῖσαν οὐχ ὑπομένει χοῦν, ἀλλ' εἴκουσα συνεφέλ-
κεται κἀκείνην καὶ ποιεῖ δυσέγχωστον[1] τὸ στόμα.
καὶ γὰρ καὶ τάχους δεῖ πρὸς τὸ ταχέως κλεισθῆναι
τὰς διώρυγας καὶ μὴ πᾶν ἐκπεσεῖν ἐξ αὐτῶν τὸ
ὕδωρ. ξηρανθεῖσαι γὰρ τοῦ θέρους ξηραίνουσι
καὶ τὸν ποταμόν· ταπεινωθεὶς δὲ τὰς ἐποχετείας
οὐ δύναται παρέχεσθαι κατὰ καιρὸν ὧν δεῖται
πλεῖστον τοῦ θέρους ἔμπυρος οὖσα ἡ χώρα καὶ
καυματηρά· διαφέρει δ' οὐδὲν ἢ τῷ πλήθει τῶν
ὑδάτων κατακλύζεσθαι τοὺς καρπούς, ἢ τῇ λει-
ψυδρίᾳ τῷ δίψει διαφθείρεσθαι· ἅμα δὲ καὶ τοὺς
ἀνάπλους, πολὺ τὸ χρήσιμον ἔχοντας, ἀεὶ λυμαινομένους[2] ὑπ' ἀμφοτέρων τῶν λεχθέντων παθῶν,
οὐχ οἷόν τε ἐπανορθοῦν, εἰ μὴ ταχὺ μὲν ἐξανοίγοιτο[3] τὰ στόμια τῶν διωρύγων, ταχὺ δὲ κλείοιτο

[1] δυσέγχωστον, Schneider, for δυσένχωστον F, δυσεύχωστον
other MSS.
[2] After λυμαινομένους all MSS. except F read γάρ; before
that word Meineke, from conj. of Corais, inserts δέ.
206

which all kinds of reed-vessels are woven. Some of these vessels, when smeared all over with asphalt, can hold water, whereas the others are used in their bare state. They also make reed-sails, which are similar to rush-mats or wicker-work.

10. Now it is impossible, perhaps, altogether to prevent overflows of this kind, but it is the part of good rulers to afford all possible aid. The aid required is this: to prevent most of the overflowing by means of dams, and to prevent the filling up effected by the silt, on the contrary, by keeping the canals cleared and the mouths opened up. Now the clearing of the canals is easy, but the building of dams requires the work of many hands; for, since the earth readily gives in and is soft, it does not support the silt that is brought upon it, but yields to the silt, and draws it on, along with itself, and makes the mouth hard to dam. And indeed there is also need of quick work in order to close the canals quickly and to prevent all the water from emptying out of them. For when they dry up in the summer, they dry up the river too; and when the river is lowered it cannot supply the sluices with water at the time needed, since the water is needed most in summer, when the country is fiery hot and scorched; and it makes no difference whether the crops are submerged by the abundance of water, or are destroyed by thirst for water. At the same time, also, the voyages inland, with their many advantages, were always being thwarted by the two above-mentioned causes, and it was impossible to correct the trouble unless the mouths of the canals were quickly opened up and quickly closed, and

---

[3] ἐξανοίγοιτο, Kramer, for κλείοιντο ; so the later editors.

καὶ αἱ διώρυγες ἀεὶ μετριάζοιεν, ὥστε μήτε[1] πλεονάζειν ἐν αὐταῖς τὸ ὕδωρ μήτ' ἐλλείπειν.

C 741　11. Φησὶ δ' Ἀριστόβουλος τὸν Ἀλέξανδρον αὐτόν, ἀναπλέοντα καὶ κυβερνῶντα τὸ σκάφος, ἐπισκοπεῖν καὶ ἀνακαθαίρειν τὰς διώρυγας μετὰ τοῦ πλήθους τῶν συνακολουθησάντων· ὡς δ' αὔτως καὶ τὰ στόμια ἐμφράττειν, τὰ δ' ἀνοίγειν· κατανοήσαντα δὲ μίαν τὴν μάλιστα τείνουσαν[2] ἐπὶ τὰ ἕλη καὶ τὰς λίμνας τὰς πρὸ τῆς Ἀραβίας, δυσμεταχείριστον ἔχουσαν τὸ στόμα καὶ μὴ ῥᾳδίως ἐμφράττεσθαι δυναμένην διὰ τὸ εὐένδοτον καὶ μαλακόγειον, ἄλλο ἀνοῖξαι καινὸν στόμα, ἀπὸ σταδίων τριάκοντα ὑπόπετρον λαβόντα χωρίον, κἀκεῖ μεταγαγεῖν τὸ ῥεῖθρον· ταῦτα δὲ ποιεῖν, προνοοῦντα ἅμα καὶ τοῦ μὴ τὴν Ἀραβίαν δυσείσβολον τελέως ὑπὸ τῶν λιμνῶν ἢ καὶ τῶν ἑλῶν ἀποτελεσθῆναι, νησίζουσαν ἤδη διὰ τὸ πλῆθος τοῦ ὕδατος· διανοεῖσθαι γὰρ δὴ κατακτᾶσθαι τὴν χώραν ταύτην καὶ στόλους καὶ ὁρμητήρια ἤδη κατεσκευάσθαι, τὰ πλοῖα τὰ μὲν ἐν Φοινίκῃ τε καὶ Κύπρῳ ναυπηγησάμενον διάλυτά τε καὶ γομφωτά, ἃ κομισθέντα εἰς Θάψακον σταθμοῖς[3] ἑπτὰ εἶτα τῷ ποταμῷ κατακομισθῆναι μέχρι Βαβυλῶνος, τὰ δ' ἐν τῇ Βαβυλωνίᾳ συμπηξάμενον τῶν ἐν τοῖς ἄλσεσι καὶ τοῖς παραδείσοις κυπαρίττων· σπάνις γὰρ ὕλης ἐνταῦθα· ἐν δὲ Κοσσαίοις καὶ ἄλλοις τισὶ μετρία τίς ἐστιν εὐπορία. σκέψασθαι μὲν οὖν αἰτίαν

---

[1] μήτε, Corais, for μηδέ.
[2] τείνουσαν, the editors, for συντείνουσαν.
[3] σταθμοῖς F, σταδίοις other MSS. and editors before Kramer.

unless the canals were regulated so that the water in them neither was excessive nor failed.

11. Aristobulus says that Alexander himself, when he was sailing up the river and piloting the boat, inspected the canals and with his multitude of followers cleared them; and that he likewise stopped up some of the mouths and opened others; and when he noticed that one canal, the one which stretched most directly towards the marshes and lakes that lay in front of Arabia, had a mouth most difficult to deal with and could not easily be stopped up because of the yielding and soft nature of the soil, he opened up another mouth, a new one, at a distance of thirty stadia from it, having selected a place with a rocky bottom, and that he diverted the stream to that place; and that in doing this he was taking forethought at the same time that Arabia should not be made utterly difficult to enter by the lakes or even by the marshes, since, on account of the abundance of water, that country was already taking the form of an island. For of course Alexander, he says, intended to acquire possession of that country, and had already prepared fleets and bases of operations, having built some of his boats in Phoenicia and Cypros, boats that were constructed with bolts and could be taken to pieces, which were conveyed by a seven days' journey to Thapsacus and then down the river to Babylon, and having built others in Babylonia, from the cypress trees in the groves and the parks; for there is a scarcity of timber in Babylonia, although there is a moderately good supply of timber in the countries of the Cossaei and certain other tribes. Now Alexander alleged

STRABO

τοῦ πολέμου φησίν, ἐπειδὴ μόνοι τῶν ἁπάντων
οὐ πρεσβεύσαιντο οἱ Ἄραβες ὡς αὐτόν, τὸ δ'
ἀληθὲς ὀρεγόμενον πάντων εἶναι κύριον· καὶ
ἐπεὶ δύο θεοὺς ἐπυνθάνετο τιμᾶσθαι μόνους ὑπ'
αὐτῶν, τόν τε Δία καὶ τὸν Διόνυσον, τοὺς τὰ
κυριώτατα πρὸς τὸ ζῆν παρέχοντας, τρίτον ὑπολαβεῖν ἑαυτὸν τιμήσεσθαι, κρατήσαντα καὶ ἐπι-
τρέψαντα τὴν πάτριον αὐτονομίαν ἔχειν, ἣν εἶχον
πρότερον. ταῦτά τε δὴ πραγματεύεσθαι περὶ
τὰς διώρυγας τὸν Ἀλέξανδρον, καὶ τοὺς τάφους
σκευωρεῖσθαι τοὺς τῶν βασιλέων καὶ δυναστῶν·
τοὺς γὰρ πλείστους ἐν ταῖς λίμναις εἶναι.

12. Ἐρατοσθένης δέ, τῶν λιμνῶν μνησθεὶς τῶν
πρὸς τῇ Ἀραβίᾳ, φησὶ τὸ ὕδωρ ὑπορούμενον
διεξόδων ἀνοῖξαι πόρους ὑπὸ γῆς καὶ δι' ἐκείνων
ὑποφέρεσθαι μέχρι Κοιλοσύρων· ἀναθλίβεσθαι
δὲ εἰς τοὺς περὶ Ῥινοκόλουρα[1] καὶ τὸ Κάσιον
ὄρος τόπους[2] καὶ ποιεῖν τὰς ἐκεῖ λίμνας καὶ τὰ
βάραθρα. οὐκ οἶδα δ', εἰ πιθανῶς εἴρηκεν· αἱ
γὰρ τοῦ Εὐφράτου παρεκχύσεις αἱ ποιοῦσαι τὰς
πρὸς τῇ Ἀραβίᾳ λίμνας καὶ τὰ ἕλη πλησίον
εἰσὶ τῆς κατὰ Πέρσας θαλάττης, ὁ δὲ διείργων
ἰσθμὸς οὔτε πολύς ἐστιν οὔτε πετρώδης, ὥστε
C 742 ταύτῃ μᾶλλον εἰκὸς ἦν βιάσασθαι τὸ ὕδωρ εἰς τὴν
θάλατταν, εἴτ' ὑπὸ γῆς[3] εἴτ' ἐπιπολῆς, ἢ πλείους
τῶν ἑξακισχιλίων σταδίων διανύειν, ἄνυδρον καὶ
ξηρὰν οὕτω, καὶ ταῦτα ὁρῶν ἐν μέσῳ κειμένων,

[1] Ῥινοκόλουρα, Tzschucke and Corais, for Ῥινοκορούρα (see readings in 16. 2. 31 and 16. 4. 24).

as cause of the war, Aristobulus says, that the Arabians were the only people on earth who did not send ambassadors to him, but in truth was reaching out to be lord of all; and when he learned that they worshipped two gods only, Zeus and Dionysus, the gods who supply the most requisite needs of life, he took it for granted that they would worship him as a third if he mastered them and allowed them to keep the ancestral independence which they had had before. Accordingly, he adds, Alexander busied himself thus with the canals, and also inspected thoroughly the tombs of the kings and potentates, most of which are situated among the lakes.

12. Eratosthenes, when he mentions the lakes near Arabia, says that when the water is deprived of exits it opens up underground passages and through these flows underground as far as the country of Coelê-Syria, and that it is pressed up into the region of Rhinocolura and Mt. Casius and forms the lakes and the pits there; but I do not know whether or not his statement is plausible; for the side-outflows of the Euphrates which form the lakes near Arabia and the marshes are near the Persian Sea, but the isthmus which separates them is neither large nor rocky, so that it was more likely that the water forced its way into the sea in this region, whether underground or on the surface, than that it traversed a distance of more than six thousand stadia, through a country so waterless and dry, and that too when mountains intervene, I mean Mt.

---

[2] τόπους, Corais, for ποταμούς.
[3] γῆν *mrw*, Tschucke, and Corais.

211

STRABO

τοῦ τε Λιβάνου καὶ τοῦ Ἀντιλιβανου καὶ τοῦ
Κασίου.[1] οἱ μὲν δὴ τοιαῦτα λέγουσι.

13. Πολύκλειτος δέ φησι μὴ πλημμυρεῖν τὸν
Εὐφράτην· διὰ γὰρ πεδίων φέρεσθαι μεγάλων,
τὰ δ᾽ ὄρη τὰ μὲν δισχιλίους ἀφεστάναι σταδίους,
τὰ δὲ Κοσσαῖα μόλις χιλίους, οὐ πάνυ ὑψηλά,
οὐδὲ νιφόμενα σφοδρῶς, οὐδ᾽ ἀθρόαν ἐπιφέροντα
τῇ χιόνι τὴν τῆξιν· εἶναι γὰρ καὶ τὰ ὕψη τῶν
ὀρῶν ἐν[2] τοῖς ὑπὲρ Ἐκβατάνων μέρεσι τοῖς
προσβορείοις· ἐν δὲ τοῖς πρὸς νότον σχιζόμενα
καὶ πλατυνόμενα πολὺ ταπεινοῦσθαι· ἅμα δὲ καὶ
τὸ πολὺ τοῦ ὕδατος ἐκδέχεσθαι τὸν Τίγριν καὶ
οὕτως πλημμυρεῖν.[3] τὸ μὲν οὖν ὕστατον ῥηθὲν
φανερῶς ἄτοπον· εἰς γὰρ τὰ αὐτὰ κατέρχεται
πεδία. τὰ δὲ[4] λεχθέντα ὕψη τῶν ὀρῶν ἀνωμα-
λίαν ἔχει, πῇ μὲν ἐξηρμένα μᾶλλον τὰ βόρεια,
πῇ δὲ πλατυνόμενα τὰ μεσημβρινά· ἡ δὲ χιὼν
οὐ τοῖς ὕψεσι κρίνεται μόνον, ἀλλὰ καὶ τοῖς
κλίμασι· τό τε αὐτὸ ὄρος τὰ βόρεια μέρη νίφεται
μᾶλλον ἢ τὰ νότια. καὶ τὴν χιόνα συμμένουσαν
ἔχει μᾶλλον ἐκεῖνα ἢ ταῦτα. ὁ μὲν οὖν Τίγρις
ἐκ τῶν νοτιωτάτων μερῶν τῆς Ἀρμενίας, ἃ

[1] Κασίου, Tzschucke, for Μασσύου CDF, Μασσίου hisw, Κασσίου Ald.
[2] ἐν, Corais, for ἀεί.
[3] καὶ οὕτως πλημμυρεῖν (omitting τά after οὕτως) transferred by Meineke, from conj. of Kramer, from position after κατέρχεται πεδία (below).
[4] δέ, Meineke inserts, following conj. of Kramer.

[1] Eratosthenes' reference to "Rhinocolura" in connection with "Mt. Casius," shows that he meant the Mt. Casius
near Aegypt and not the Syrian Mt. Casius. Eratosthenes,
like other writers (Polybius 5. 80, Diodorus Siculus 1. 30,

Libanus and Mt. Antilibanus and Mt. Casius.[1]
Such, then, are the accounts of Aristobulus and
Eratosthenes.

13. Polycleitus, however, says that the Euphrates
does not overflow; for, he says, it flows through
large plains; and as for the mountains, some stand
at a distance of two thousand stadia from it, but
the Cossaean mountains at a distance of scarcely
one thousand, which latter are not very high, are
not covered very deeply with snow, and do not
cause the snow to melt quickly in great quantities;
for, he says, the heights of the mountains lie
in the region above Ecbatana towards the north,
but, in the region towards the south, they split,
broaden out, and become much lower, and at the
same time most of their waters are received by the
Tigris and thus overflow the plains. Now this last
assertion is obviously absurd, for the Tigris flows
down into the same plains as the Euphrates, and the
above-mentioned heights of the mountains have
different altitudes, the northern heights being more
elevated in some places, whereas the southern
broaden out in some places; but the quantity of
snow is not determined merely by the heights, but
also by their latitudes; and the same mountain
has more snow in its northern parts than in its
southern, and the snow continues longer in the
former than in the latter. Now the Tigris receives
from the southernmost parts of Armenia, which are

and Josephus 13. 13), extended the name " Coelê-Syria,"
which was properly applied only to the country between
Mts. Libanus and Antilibanus, to include that part of Syria
which borders on Aegypt and Arabia. Hence, quite apart
from the truth or falsity of Eratosthenes' statement, he was
clearly misinterpreted by Strabo.

πλησίον ἐστὶ τῆς Βαβυλωνίας, δεχόμενος τὸ ἐκ
τῶν χιόνων ὕδωρ οὐ πολὺ ὄν, ἅτε ἐκ τῆς νοτίου
πλευρᾶς, ἧττον ἂν πλημμύροι· ὁ δὲ Εὐφράτης
τὸ ἐξ ἀμφοτέρων δέχεται τῶν μερῶν, καὶ οὐκ
ἐξ ἑνὸς ὄρους, ἀλλὰ πολλῶν, ὡς ἐδηλοῦμεν [1] ἐν
τῇ περιηγήσει τῆς Ἀρμενίας, προστιθεὶς τὸ μῆκος
τοῦ ποταμοῦ, ὅσον μὲν τὸ ἐν τῇ μεγάλῃ Ἀρμενίᾳ
διέξεισι καὶ τῇ μικρᾷ, ὅσον δὲ τὸ ἐκ τῆς μικρᾶς
Ἀρμενίας καὶ τῆς Καππαδοκίας διὰ τοῦ Ταύρου
διεκβαλὼν ἕως Θαψάκου φέρεται, τὴν κάτω
Συρίαν καὶ τὴν Μεσοποταμίαν ἀφορίζων, ὅσον
δὲ τὸ λοιπὸν μέχρι Βαβυλῶνος καὶ τῆς ἐκβολῆς
ὁμοῦ τρισμυρίων καὶ ἑξακισχιλίων σταδίων. τὰ
μὲν οὖν περὶ τὰς διώρυγας τοιαῦτα.

14. Ἡ δὲ χώρα φέρει κριθὰς μέν, ὅσας οὐκ
ἄλλη (καὶ γὰρ τριακοσιοντάχουν [2] λέγουσι), τὰ
δὲ ἄλλα ἐκ τοῦ φοίνικος παρέχεται· καὶ γὰρ
ἄρτον καὶ οἶνον καὶ ὄξος καὶ μέλι καὶ ἄλφιτα·
τά τε πλεκτὰ παντοῖα ἐκ τούτου· τοῖς δὲ πυρῆσιν
ἀντ᾽ ἀνθράκων οἱ χαλκεῖς χρῶνται, βρεχόμενοι
δὲ τοῖς σιτιζομένοις εἰσὶ τροφὴ βουσὶ καὶ προ-
βάτοις. φασὶ δ᾽ εἶναι Περσικὴν ᾠδήν, ἐν ᾗ τὰς
ὠφελείας τριακοσίας καὶ ἑξήκοντα διαριθμοῦνται·
C 743 ἐλαίῳ δὲ χρῶνται τῷ σησαμίνῳ τὸ πλέον· οἱ δ᾽
ἄλλοι τόποι σπανίζουσι τούτου τοῦ φυτοῦ.

15. Γίνεται δ᾽ ἐν τῇ Βαβυλωνίᾳ καὶ ἄσφαλτος
πολλή, περὶ ἧς Ἐρατοσθένης μὲν οὕτως εἴρηκεν,
ὅτι ἡ μὲν ὑγρά, ἣν καλοῦσι νάφθαν, γίνεται ἐν τῇ
Σουσίδι, ἡ δὲ ξηρά, δυναμένη πήττεσθαι, ἐν τῇ

---

[1] ἐδηλοῦμεν, Corais unnecessarily emends to ἐδήλουν.
[2] τριακοσιοντάχουν, Meineke, for τριακοσιάχια Ald., τρια-
κισιόχοα conj. of Lobeck.

near Babylonia, the water of the melted snows, which is not much, since it comes from the southern side, and this river would therefore be flooded less than the Euphrates; but the Euphrates receives the water from both parts, and not merely from one mountain, but from many, as I made clear in my description of Armenia,[1] where I added the length of that river, giving first the length of its course in Greater Armenia and Lesser Armenia, and secondly its length from Lesser Armenia and Cappadocia through the Taurus as far as Thapsacus, where it forms the boundary between Lower Syria and Mesopotamia, and, thirdly, the rest of its length as far as Babylon and the outlet, a length, all told, of thirty-six thousand stadia. So much, then, for the canals.

14. The country produces larger crops of barley than any other country[2] (bearing three hundredfold, they say), and its other needs are supplied by the palm tree; for this tree yields bread, wine, vinegar, honey, and meal; and all kinds of woven articles are supplied by that tree; and the bronze-smiths use the stones of the fruit instead of charcoal; and when soaked in water these stones are used as food for oxen and sheep which are being fattened. There is said to be a Persian song wherein are enumerated three hundred and sixty uses of the palm tree; and, as for oil, the people use mostly that of sesame, but this plant is rare in all other places.

15. Babylonia produces also great quantities of asphalt, concerning which Eratosthenes states that the liquid kind, which is called naphtha, is found in Susis, but the dry kind, which can be solidified, in

[1] See 11. 12. 3 and 11. 14. 2.
[2] Cf. 11. 4. 3, 15. 3. 11, and Herodotus 1. 193.

STRABO

Βαβυλωνία· ταύτης δ' ἐστὶν ἡ πηγὴ τοῦ Εὐφράτου πλησίον· πλημμύροντος δὲ τούτου κατὰ
τὰς τῶν χιόνων τήξεις καὶ αὐτὴ πληροῦται καὶ
ὑπέρχυσιν εἰς τὸν ποταμὸν λαμβάνει· ἐνταῦθα
δὲ συνίστανται βῶλοι μεγάλαι πρὸς τὰς οἰκο-
δομὰς ἐπιτήδειαι τὰς διὰ τῆς ὀπτῆς πλίνθου.
ἄλλοι δὲ καὶ τὴν ὑγρὰν ἐν τῇ Βαβυλωνίᾳ γίνεσθαί
φασι. περὶ μὲν οὖν τῆς ξηρᾶς εἴρηται, πόσον
τὸ χρήσιμον τὸ ἐκ τῶν οἰκοδομιῶν μάλιστα·
φασὶ δὲ καὶ πλοῖα πλέκεσθαι, ἐμπλασθέντα δ'
ἀσφάλτῳ πυκνοῦσθαι. τὴν δὲ ὑγράν, ἣν νάφθαν
καλοῦσι, παράδοξον ἔχειν συμβαίνει τὴν φύσιν·
προσαχθεὶς[1] γὰρ ὁ νάφθας πυρὶ πλησίον ἀναρ-
πάζει τὸ πῦρ, κἂν ἐπιχρίσας αὐτῷ σῶμα προσα-
γάγῃς, φλέγεται· σβέσαι δ' ὕδατι οὐχ οἷόν τε
(ἐκκαίεται γὰρ μᾶλλον), πλὴν εἰ πάνυ πολλῷ,
ἀλλὰ πηλῷ καὶ ὄξει καὶ στυπτηρίᾳ καὶ ἰξῷ
πνιγεὶς[2] σβέννυται. πείρας δὲ χάριν φασὶν
Ἀλέξανδρον ἐν λουτρῷ προσχέαι παιδὶ τοῦ νάφθα
καὶ προσαγαγεῖν λύχνον· φλεγόμενον δὲ τὸν
παῖδα ἐγγὺς ἐλθεῖν τοῦ ἀπολέσθαι, πλὴν πολλῷ
σφόδρα καταντλοῦντες τῷ ὕδατι ἐξίσχυσαν καὶ
διέσωσαν οἱ περιεστῶτες. Ποσειδώνιος δέ φησι
τοῦ ἐν τῇ Βαβυλωνίᾳ νάφθα τὰς πηγάς, τὰς μὲν
εἶναι λευκοῦ, τὰς δὲ μέλανος· τούτων δὲ[3] τὰς
μὲν εἶναι θείου ὑγροῦ, λέγω δὲ τὰς τοῦ λευκοῦ
(ταύτας δ' εἶναι τὰς ἐπισπώσας τὰς φλόγας),
τὰς δὲ τοῦ μέλανος, ἀσφάλτου ὑγρᾶς, ᾧ ἀντ'
ἐλαίου τοὺς λύχνους κάουσι.[4]

---

[1] προσαχθείς D, προσαφθείς other MSS.
[2] πνιγείς Epit., for πνιγέντα ; so Meineke.
[3] δή Dh. [4] καίουσι CFmoxz.

216

Babylonia; and that there is a fountain of this
latter asphalt near the Euphrates River; and that
when this river is at its flood at the time of the
melting of the snows, the fountain of asphalt is also
filled and overflows into the river; and that there
large clods of asphalt are formed which are suitable
for buildings constructed of baked bricks. Other
writers say that the liquid kind also is found in
Babylonia. Now writers state in particular the
great usefulness of the dry kind in the construction
of buildings, but they say also that boats are woven
with reeds and, when plastered with asphalt, are
impervious to water. The liquid kind, which they
call naphtha, is of a singular nature; for if the
naphtha is brought near fire it catches the fire;
and if you smear a body with it and bring it near
to the fire, the body bursts into flames; and it is
impossible to quench these flames with water (for
they burn more violently), unless a great amount is
used, though they can be smothered and quenched
with mud, vinegar, alum, and bird-lime. It is said
that Alexander, for an experiment, poured some
naphtha on a boy in a bath and brought a lamp
near him; and that the boy, enveloped in flames,
would have been nearly burned to death if the
bystanders had not, by pouring on him a very great
quantity of water, prevailed over the fire and saved
his life. Poseidonius says of the springs of naphtha
in Babylonia, that some send forth white naphtha
and others black; and that some of these, I mean
those that send forth white naphtha, consist of
liquid sulphur (and it is these that attract the
flames), whereas the others send forth black naphtha,
liquid asphalt, which is burnt in lamps instead of oil.

16. Πάλαι μὲν οὖν ἡ Βαβυλὼν ἦν μητρόπολις τῆς Ἀσσυρίας, νῦν δὲ Σελεύκεια, ἡ ἐπὶ τῷ Τίγρει λεγομένη. πλησίον δ' ἐστὶ κώμη, Κτησιφῶν λεγομένη, μεγάλη· ταύτην δ' ἐποιοῦντο χειμάδιον οἱ τῶν Παρθυαίων βασιλεῖς, φειδόμενοι τῶν Σελευκέων, ἵνα μὴ κατασταθμεύοιντο ὑπὸ τοῦ Σκυθικοῦ φύλου καὶ στρατωτικοῦ. δυνάμει οὖν Παρθικῇ[1] πόλις ἀντὶ κώμης ἐστί, καὶ τὸ μέγεθος τοσοῦτόν γε πλῆθος δεχομένη καὶ τὴν κατασκευὴν ὑπ' ἐκείνων αὐτῶν κατεσκευασμένη καὶ τὰ ὤνια καὶ τὰς τέχνας προσφόρους ἐκείνοις πεπορισμένη. εἰώθασι γὰρ ἐνταῦθα τοῦ χειμῶνος διάγειν οἱ βασιλεῖς διὰ τὸ εὐάερον· θέρους δὲ ἐν Ἐκβατάνοις καὶ τῇ Ὑρκανίᾳ διὰ τὴν ἐπικράτειαν τῆς παλαιᾶς δόξης. ὥσπερ δὲ Βαβυλωνίαν τὴν χώραν καλοῦμεν, οὕτω καὶ τοὺς ἄνδρας τοὺς ἐκεῖθεν Βαβυλωνίους καλοῦμεν, οὐκ C 744 ἀπὸ τῆς πόλεως, ἀλλ' ἀπὸ τῆς χώρας· ἀπὸ δὲ τῆς Σελευκείας ἧττον, κἂν ἐκεῖθεν ὦσι, καθάπερ Διογένη τὸν Στωικὸν φιλόσοφον.

17. Ἔστι δὲ καὶ Ἀρτεμίτα, πόλις ἀξιόλογος, διέχουσα πεντακοσίους τῆς Σελευκείας σταδίους, πρὸς ἕω τὸ πλέον, καθάπερ καὶ ἡ Σιτακηνή. καὶ γὰρ αὕτη, πολλή τε καὶ ἀγαθή, μέση[2] Βαβυλῶνος τέτακται καὶ τῆς Σουσίδος, ὥστε τοῖς ἐκ Βαβυλῶνος εἰς Σοῦσα βαδίζουσι διὰ τῆς Σιτα-

---

[1] Παρθικῇ, Kramer, for Παρθική.
[2] For μέση E reads μέχρι.

16. And in ancient times Babylon was the metropolis of Assyria; but now Seleuceia is the metropolis, I mean the Seleuceia on the Tigris, as it is called. Near by is situated a village called Ctesiphon, a large village. This village the kings of the Parthians were wont to make their winter residence, thus sparing the Seleuceians, in order that the Seleuceians might not be oppressed by having the Scythian folk or soldiery quartered amongst them. Because of the Parthian power, therefore, Ctesiphon is a city rather than a village; its size is such that it lodges a great number of people, and it has been equipped with buildings by the Parthians themselves; and it has been provided by the Parthians with wares for sale and with the arts that are pleasing to the Parthians; for the Parthian kings are accustomed to spend the winter there because of the salubrity of the air, but the summer at Ecbatana and in Hyrcania because of the prevalence of their ancient renown. And as we call the country Babylonia, so also we call the men from there Babylonians, that is, not after the city, but after the country; but we do not call men after Seleuceia, if they are from there, as, for example, Diogenes the Stoic philosopher.[1]

17. And there is also Artemita, a noteworthy city, which is five hundred stadia distant from Seleuceia, being situated almost directly towards the east, as is also Sitacenê. For Sitacenê too, both extensive and fertile, lies between Babylon and Susis, so that the whole of the journey for people travelling from Babylon to Susa is through Sitacenê towards the

[1] *i.e.* Diogenes was known as " Diogenes the Babylonian " (as in Cicero, *de Nat. Deorum* 1. 5), not as " Diogenes the Seleuceian."

κηνῆς ἡ ὁδὸς ἅπασα πρὸς ἔω· πρὸς ἔω δ ἐστὶ
καὶ τοῖς ἐκ Σούσων εἰς τὴν μεσόγαιαν τῆς
Περσίδος διὰ τῆς Οὐξίας καὶ τοῖς ἐκ τῆς
Περσίδος εἰς τὰ μέσα τῆς Καρμανίας. τὴν μὲν
οὖν Καρμανίαν ἐγκυκλοῦται πρὸς[1] ἄρκτον ἡ
Περσίς, πολλὴ οὖσα· ταύτῃ δὲ συνάπτει ἡ
Παραιτακηνὴ καὶ ἡ Κοσσαία μέχρι Κασπίων
πυλῶν, ὀρεινὰ καὶ λῃστρικὰ ἔθνη· τῇ δὲ Σουσίᾳ
ἡ Ἐλυμαΐς,[2] καὶ αὐτὴ τραχεῖα ἡ πολλὴ καὶ
λῃστρική· τῇ δὲ Ἐλυμαΐδι[3] τὰ περὶ τὸν Ζάγρον
καὶ ἡ Μηδία.

18. Κοσσαῖοι μὲν οὖν εἰσι τοξόται τὸ πλέον,
καθάπερ καὶ οἱ συνεχεῖς ὀρεινοί, προνομεύοντες
ἀεί· χώραν γὰρ ἔχουσιν ὀλίγην τε καὶ λυπράν,
ὥστ᾽ ἐκ τῶν ἀλλοτρίων ἀνάγκη ζῆν· ἀνάγκη δὲ
καὶ ἰσχύειν· ἅπαντες γάρ εἰσι μάχιμοι· τοῖς γοῦν
Ἐλυμαίοις συνεμάχουν μύριοι καὶ τρισχίλιοι,
πολεμοῦσι πρός τε Βαβυλωνίους καὶ Σουσίους.
οἱ δὲ Παραιτακηνοὶ μᾶλλον μὲν τῶν Κοσσαίων
ἐπιμελοῦνται γῆς· ὅμως δὲ καὶ αὐτοὶ λῃστηρίων
οὐκ ἀπέχονται. Ἐλυμαῖοι δὲ καὶ μείζω τούτων
κέκτηνται χώραν καὶ ποικιλωτέραν. ὅση μὲν
οὖν ἀγαθὴ γεωργοὺς ἔχει τοὺς ἐνοικοῦντας,
ἡ δ᾽ ὀρεινὴ στρατιώτας τρέφει, τοξότας τοὺς
πλείστους· πολλὴ δὲ οὖσα πολὺ καὶ τὸ
στρατιωτικὸν παρέχεται, ὥστε καὶ ὁ βασιλεὺς
αὐτῶν δύναμιν κεκτημένος μεγάλην οὐκ ἀξιοῖ
τῷ τῶν Παρθυαίων βασιλεῖ παραπλησίως τοῖς

---

[1] Before ἄρκτον Meineke, from conj. of Groskurd, inserts
ἑσπέραν καί.
[2] Ἐλυμαῖς, the editors, for Ελυμάντις F, Ἐλυμάτις other
MSS.

east; and the journey for people travelling from Susa into the interior of Persis through Uxia, and for people travelling from Persis into the middle of Carmania, is also towards the east. Now Carmania is encircled on the north by Persis, which is a large country; and bordering on this country are Paraetacenê and Cossaea as far as the Caspian Gates, which is inhabited by mountainous and predatory tribes. And bordering on Susis is Elymaïs, most of which is rugged and inhabited by brigands; and bordering Elymaïs are Media and the region of the Zagrus.

18. Now the Cossaeans, like the neighbouring mountaineers, are for the most part bowmen, and are always out on foraging expeditions; for they have a country that is small and barren, so that they must needs live at the expense of the other tribes. And they are of necessity a powerful people, for they are all fighters; at any rate, thirteen thousand Cossaeans joined the Elymaeans in battle, when the latter were warring against both the Babylonians and the Susians. But the Paraetaceni are more interested in agriculture than the Cossaeans; but still even they themselves do not abstain from brigandage. The Elymaeans possess a larger and more diversified country than the Paraetaceni. Now all of it that is fertile is inhabited by farmers, whereas the mountainous part of it is a nursery of soldiers, mostly bowmen; and since the latter part is extensive, it can furnish so large a military force that their king, since he possesses great power, refuses to be subject to the king of

---

[2] 'Ελυμαΐδι, the editors, for 'Ελυμάτιδι.

ἄλλοις ὑπήκοος εἶται· ὁμοίως δὲ¹ καὶ πρὸς τοὺς
Μακεδόνας ὕστερον τοὺς τῆς Συρίας ἄρχοντας
διέκειτο. Ἀντίοχον μὲν οὖν τὸν Μέγαν τὸ τοῦ βήλου συλᾶν ἱερὸν ἐπιχειρήσαντα ἀνεῖλον ἐπιθέ-
μενοι καθ' αὑτοὺς οἱ πλησίον βάρβαροι. ἐκ δὲ τῶν
ἐκείνῳ συμβάντων παιδευθεὶς ὁ Παρθυαῖος χρόνοις ὕστερον ἀκούων τὰ ἱερὰ πλούσια παρ' αὐτοῖς,
ὁρῶν δ' ἀπειθοῦντας, ἐμβάλλει μετὰ δυνάμεως
μεγάλης, καὶ τό τε τῆς Ἀθηνᾶς ἱερὸν εἷλε καὶ
τὸ τῆς Ἀρτέμιδος, τὰ Ἄζαρα,² καὶ ἦρε ταλάντων
μυρίων γάζαν· ᾑρέθη δὲ καὶ πρὸς τῷ Ἡδυφῶντι
ποταμῷ Σελεύκεια, μεγάλη πόλις· Σολόκη δ' ἐκαλεῖτο πρότερον, τρεῖς δ' εἰσὶν εἰς τὴν χώραν εὐ-
φυεῖς εἰσβολαί· ἐκ μὲν τῆς Μηδίας καὶ τῶν περὶ
τὸν Ζάγρον τόπων διὰ τῆς Μασσαβατικῆς, ἐκ δὲ
τῆς Σουσίδος διὰ τῆς Γαβιανῆς (ἐπαρχίαι δ'
C 745 εἰσὶν αὗται τῆς Ἐλυμαίας ἥ τε Γαβιανὴ καὶ ἡ
Μασσαβατική), τρίτη δ' ἐστὶν ἡ ἐκ τῆς Περσίδος. ἔστι δὲ καὶ Κορβιανὴ³ ἐπαρχία τῆς Ἐλυ-
μαΐδος. ὅμοροι δ' εἰσὶ τούτοις Σαγαπηνοί τε καὶ
Σιλακηνοί, δυναστεῖαι μικραί. τοσαῦτα μὲν καὶ
τοιαῦτα ἔθνη πρὸς ἔω τὰ ὑπερκείμενα τῆς Βαβυλωνίας. πρὸς ἄρκτον δὲ τὴν Μηδίαν ἔφαμεν καὶ
τὴν Ἀρμενίαν· ἀπὸ δὲ δύσεώς ἐστιν ἡ Ἀδιαβηνὴ
καὶ ἡ Μεσοποταμία.

¹ Kramer conj. that the words καὶ πρὸς τοὺς Πέρσας have
fallen out after ὁμοίως δέ.
² For τὰ Ἄζαρα F reads τὰ Ἄξαρα; Tzschucke and Corais,
from conj. of Casaubon, read τὰ Ζάρα. But see τὰ Ἄζαρα in
11. 14. 3.

the Parthians like the other tribes; and their king was likewise disposed towards [1] the Macedonians, who ruled Syria in later times. Now when Antiochus the Great attempted to rob the temple of Belus, the neighbouring barbarians, all by themselves, attacked him and slew him. In later times the king of Parthia, though warned by what had happened to Antiochus, hearing that the temples in that country contained great wealth, and seeing that the inhabitants were disobedient subjects, made an invasion with a great force, and took both the temple of Athena and that of Artemis, the latter called Azara, and carried off treasures valued at ten thousand talents. And Seleuceia near the Hedyphon River, a large city, was also taken. In earlier times Seleuceia was called Solocê. There are three entrances into the country that have been supplied by nature: one from Media and the region of the Zagrus through Massabaticê; another from Susis through Gabianê (these, both Gabianê and Massabaticê, are provinces of Elymaea), and the third from Persis. And Corbianê is also a province of Elymaïs. And the countries of the Sagapeni and the Silaceni, small domains, border on that of these people. Such is the size and such is the nature of the tribes situated above Babylonia towards the east. But, as I have said, Media and Armenia are situated on the north; and Adiabenê and Mesopotamia are situated on the west.

---

[1] Kramer suggests that the Greek for " the Persians and " has fallen out of the MSS. here (see critical note).

---

[3] Κορβιανή, Kramer, for Κορβίανα F, Κυρβιανά moz, Κορβιανά other MSS.; so Meineke and Müller-Dübner.

19. Τῆς μὲν οὖν Ἀδιαβηνῆς ἡ πλείστη πεδίας ἐστί, καὶ αὐτὴ τῆς Βαβυλωνίας μέρος οὖσα, ἔχουσα δ᾽ ὅμως ἄρχοντα ἴδιον, ἔστιν ὅπη καὶ τῇ Ἀρμενίᾳ προσχωροῦσα· οἱ γὰρ Μῆδοι καὶ οἱ Ἀρμένιοι, τρίτοι δὲ Βαβυλώνιοι τὰ μέγιστα τῶν ἐθνῶν τῶν ταύτῃ διετέλουν οὕτως ἐξ ἀρχῆς συνεστῶτες, ὥστ᾽ ἀλλήλοις ἐπιτίθεσθαι κατὰ καιροὺς τοὺς οἰκείους ἕκαστοι καὶ πάλιν διαλύεσθαι· καὶ τοῦτο καὶ μέχρι τῆς τῶν Παρθυαίων ἐπικρατείας διέμεινε. τῶν μὲν οὖν Μήδων καὶ τῶν Βαβυλωνίων ἐπάρχουσι Παρθυαῖοι, τῶν δ᾽ Ἀρμενίων οὐδ᾽ ἅπαξ· ἀλλ᾽ ἔφοδοι μὲν γεγόνασι πολλάκις, ἀνὰ κράτος δ᾽ οὐχ ἑάλωσαν, ἀλλ᾽ ὅ γε Τιγράνης καὶ ἐρρωμένως ἀντεπεκράτησεν, ὡς ἐν τοῖς Ἀρμενιακοῖς εἴρηται. ἡ μὲν οὖν Ἀδιαβηνὴ τοιαύτη· καλοῦνται δ᾽ οἱ Ἀδιαβηνοὶ καὶ Σακκόποδες·[1] περὶ δὲ τῆς Μεσοποταμίας ἐροῦμεν ἐφεξῆς καὶ τῶν πρὸς μεσημβρίαν ἐθνῶν, ἐπιόντες ἐπὶ μικρὸν πρότερον τὰ λεγόμενα περὶ τῶν ἐθῶν τῶν παρὰ τοῖς Ἀσσυρίοις.

20. Τἆλλα μὲν οὖν ἔοικε τοῖς Περσικοῖς, ἴδιον δὲ τὸ καθεστάναι τρεῖς ἄνδρας σώφρονας ἑκάστης ἄρχοντας φυλῆς, οἳ τὰς ἐπιγάμους κόρας προσάγοντες εἰς τὸ πλῆθος ἀποκηρύττουσι τοῖς νυμφίοις ἀεὶ τὰς ἐντιμοτέρας πρώτας. οὕτω μὲν αἱ συζυγίαι τελοῦνται· ὁσάκις δ᾽ ἂν μιχθῶσιν ἀλλήλοις, ἐπιθυμιάσοντες[2] ἐξανίστανται ἑκάτερος χωρίς· ὄρθρου δὲ λούονται πρὶν ἀγγείου τινὸς

---

[1] The words καλοῦνται . . . Σακκόποδες (Σακόποδες F) are suspected by Kramer and ejected by Meineke.

[2] ἐπιθυμιάσοντες, Groskurd, for ἐπιθυμιάσαντες.

19. Now as for Adiabenê, the most of it consists of plains; and though it too is a part of Babylonia, still it has a ruler of its own; and in some places it borders also on Armenia. For the Medes and the Armenians, and third the Babylonians, the three greatest of the tribes in that part of the world, were so constituted from the beginning, and continued to be, that at times opportune for each they would attack one another and in turn become reconciled. And this continued down to the supremacy of the Parthians. Now the Parthians rule over the Medes and the Babylonians, but they have never once ruled over the Armenians; indeed, the Armenians have been attacked many times, but they could not be overcome by force, since Tigranes opposed all attacks mightily, as I have stated in my description of Armenia.[1] Such, then, is Adiabenê; and the Adiabeni are also called Saccopodes;[2] but I shall next describe Mesopotamia and the tribes on the south, after briefly going over the accounts given of the customs of Assyria.

20. Now in general their customs are like those of the Persians, but it is a custom peculiar to them to appoint three wise men as rulers of each tribe, who present in public the marriageable girls, and sell them by auction to the bridegrooms, always selling first those who are the more highly prized. Thus marriages are contracted; and every time they have intercourse with one another, they arise and go out, each apart from the other, to offer incense; and in the morning they bathe themselves before

[1] See 11. 14. 15.
[2] *i.e.* "Sack-feet." But the name is suspected (see critical note).

ἅψασθαι· παραπλησίως γάρ, ὥσπερ ἀπὸ νεκροῦ
τὸ λουτρὸν ἐν ἔθει ἐστίν, οὕτω καὶ ἀπὸ συνουσίας. πάσαις δὲ ταῖς Βαβυλωνίαις ἔθος κατά
τι λόγιον ξένῳ μίγνυσθαι, πρός τι Ἀφροδίσιον
ἀφικομέναις μετὰ πολλῆς θεραπείας καὶ ὄχλου·
θώμιγγι δ' ἔστεπται ἑκάστη· ὁ δὲ προσιὼν
καταθεὶς ἐπὶ τὰ γόνατα, ὅσον καλῶς ἔχει ἀργύριον, συγγίνεται, ἄπωθεν τοῦ τεμένους ἀπα-
γαγών· τὸ δ' ἀργύριον ἱερὸν τῆς Ἀφροδίτης
νομίζεται. ἀρχεῖα δ' ἐστὶ τρία, τὸ τῶν ἀφει-
μένων ἤδη τῆς στρατείας καὶ τὸ τῶν ἐνδοξοτάτων
C 746 καὶ τὸ τῶν γερόντων, χωρὶς τοῦ ὑπὸ τοῦ βασιλέως καθισταμένου. τούτου δ' ἐστὶ τὸ τὰς παρθένους ἐκδιδόναι καὶ τὸ τὰς περὶ τῆς μοιχείας
δικάζειν δίκας, ἄλλου[1] δὲ τὸ τὰς τῆς κλοπῆς,
τρίτου[2] τὸ περὶ τῶν βιαίων. τοὺς δ' ἀρρώστους
εἰς τὰς τριόδους ἐκτιθέντες πυνθάνονται τῶν
παριόντων, εἴ τίς τι ἔχοι λέγειν τοῦ πάθους ἄκος·
οὐδείς τέ ἐστιν οὕτω κακὸς τῶν παριόντων, ὃς
οὐκ ἐντυχών, εἴ τι φρονεῖ σωτήριον, ὑποτίθεται.
ἐσθὴς δ' αὐτοῖς ἐστι χιτὼν λινοῦς ποδήρης καὶ
ἐπενδύτης ἐρεοῦς, ἱμάτιον λευκόν, κόμη μακρά,[3]
ὑπόδημα ἐμβάδι ὅμοιον. φοροῦσι δὲ καὶ σφρα-
γῖδα καὶ σκῆπτρον οὐ λιτόν, ἀλλ' ἐπίσημον, ἔχον
ἐπάνω μῆλον ἢ ῥόδον ἢ κρίνον ἤ τι τοιοῦτον·
ἀλείφονται δ' ἐκ τοῦ σησάμου· θρηνοῦσι δὲ τοὺς
ἀποθανόντας, ὡς Αἰγύπτιοι καὶ πολλοὶ τῶν
ἄλλων· θάπτουσι δ' ἐν μέλιτι, κηρῷ περιπλά-

---

[1] ἄλλῳ CDF*hmoz*.
[2] τρίτου, Tzschucke, for τρίτον.
[3] μακρά, Corais, for μικρά.

they touch any vessel; for just as ablution is customary after touching a corpse, so also it is customary after intercourse. And in accordance with a certain oracle all the Babylonian women have a custom of having intercourse with a foreigner, the women going to a temple of Aphrodite with a great retinue and crowd; and each woman is wreathed with a cord round her head. The man who approaches a woman takes her far away from the sacred precinct, places a fair amount of money upon her lap, and then has intercourse with her; and the money is considered sacred to Aphrodite. They have three tribunals: that of those who are already freed from military service, and that of the most famous, and that of the old men, apart from that appointed by the king. It is the duty of this last to give girls in marriage and to pass judgment in cases of adultery; and the duty of another to pass judgment in cases of theft, and of a third to pass judgment in cases of assault. They place the sick where three roads meet and question those who pass by, on the chance that some one has a cure for the malady; and no one of those who pass by is so base as not to suggest some cure when he falls in with them if he has any in mind. Their clothing consists of a linen tunic reaching to the feet, an upper garment made of wool, and a white cloak; and they wear their hair long, and use a shoe that is like a buskin. They wear also a seal, and carry a staff that is not plain but has a design on it, having on top an apple or rose or lily or something of the kind; and they anoint themselves with sesame; and they bewail the dead, like the Egyptians and many other nations; and they bury their dead in honey, first besmearing

σαντες. τρεῖς δ' εἰσὶ φρατρίαι τῶν ἀπόρων
σίτου· ἕλειοι δ' εἰσὶν οὗτοι καὶ ἰχθυοφάγοι, διαι-
τώμενοι παραπλησίως τοῖς κατὰ τὴν Γεδρωσίαν.

21. Μεσοποταμία δ' ἀπὸ τοῦ συμβεβηκότος
ὠνόμασται· εἴρηται δ', ὅτι κεῖται μεταξὺ τοῦ
Εὐφράτου καὶ τοῦ Τίγριος καὶ διότι ὁ μὲν Τίγρις
τὸ ἑωθινὸν αὐτῆς μόνον κλύζει πλευρόν, τὸ δ'
ἑσπέριον καὶ νότιον ὁ Εὐφράτης· πρὸς ἄρκτον
δὲ ὁ Ταῦρος ὁ τοὺς Ἀρμενίους διορίζων ἀπὸ τῆς
Μεσοποταμίας. τὸ μὲν οὖν μέγιστον ὃ ἀφίστανται
διάστημα ἀπ' ἀλλήλων τὸ πρὸς τοῖς ὄρεσίν ἐστι·
τοῦτο δ' ἂν εἴη τὸ αὐτό, ὅπερ εἴρηκεν Ἐρατοσθένης,
τὸ ἀπὸ Θαψάκου, καθ' ὃ ἦν τὸ ζεῦγμα τοῦ Εὐφράτου τὸ παλαιόν, ἐπὶ τὴν τοῦ Τίγριος διάβασιν,
καθ' ἣν διέβη Ἀλέξανδρος αὐτόν, δισχιλίων τετρα-
κοσίων· τὸ δ' ἐλάχιστον μικρῷ πλέον τῶν διακοσίων κατὰ Σελεύκειάν που καὶ Βαβυλῶνα.
διαρρεῖ δ' ὁ Τίγρις τὴν Θωπῖτιν καλουμένην
λίμνην κατὰ πλάτος μέσην· περαιωθεὶς δ' ἐπὶ
θάτερον χεῖλος κατὰ γῆς δύεται μετὰ πολλοῦ
ψόφου καὶ ἀναφυσημάτων· ἐπὶ πολὺ δ' ἐνεχθεὶς
ἀφανής, ἀνίσχει πάλιν οὐ πολὺ ἄπωθεν τῆς
Γορδυαίας· οὕτω δὲ σφοδρῶς διεκβάλλει τὴν
λίμνην, ὥς φησιν Ἐρατοσθένης, ὥστε ἁλμυρὰν
αὐτὴν οὖσαν καὶ ἄνιχθυν γλυκεῖαν κατὰ τοῦτ'
εἶναι τὸ μέρος καὶ ῥοώδη καὶ ἰχθύων πλήρη.

22. Ἐπὶ μῆκος δὲ συχνὸν προπέπτωκεν ἡ συνα-
γωγὴ τῆς Μεσοποταμίας, καὶ πλοίῳ πως ἔοικε·[1]
ποιεῖ δὲ τὸ πλεῖστον τῆς περιφερείας ὁ Εὐφράτης·

---

[1] ἔοικε, Corais, for ἐῴκει.

---

[1] i.e. "a country between rivers."   [2] 11.14. 2.

them with wax. But three of their tribes have no grain; and these live in marshes and are fish-eaters, living a life similar to that of the inhabitants of Gedrosia.

21. Mesopotamia[1] has its name from what is the fact in the case. As I have said,[2] it lies between the Euphrates and the Tigris; and the Tigris washes its eastern side only, whereas the Euphrates washes its western and southern sides; and on the north is the Taurus, which separates Armenia from Mesopotamia. Now the greatest distance by which the two rivers are separated is that towards the mountains; and this distance might be the same as that stated by Eratosthenes—I mean that from Thapsacus, where was the old bridge of the Euphrates, to the crossing of the Tigris, where Alexander crossed it—two thousand four hundred stadia; but the shortest distance between the two rivers is somewhere in the neighbourhood of Seleuceia and Babylon, slightly more than two hundred stadia. The Tigris flows through the middle of Lake Thopitis, as it is called, in the direction of its breadth; and, after traversing it to the opposite shore, it sinks underground with upward blasts and a loud noise; and having flowed for a considerable distance invisible, it rises again not far away from Gordyaea; and it traverses the lake so impetuously, as Eratosthenes says, that, although the lake elsewhere is briny and without fish, yet in this part it is fresh, runs like a river, and is full of fish.

22. Mesopotamia contracts in shape, projecting to a considerable length; and the shape of it somewhat resembles that of a boat; and the greatest part of its periphery is formed by the Euphrates. The

καί ἐστι τὸ μὲν ἀπὸ τῆς Θαψάκου μέχρι Βαβυλῶνος, ὡς εἴρηκεν Ἐρατοσθένης, τετρακισχίλιοι
καὶ ὀκτακόσιοι στάδιοι· τὸ δ᾽ ἀπὸ τοῦ κατὰ
Κομμαγηνὴν Ζεύγματος, ἥπερ ἐστὶν ἀρχὴ τῆς
C 747 Μεσοποταμίας, οὐκ ἔλαττον τῶν δισχιλίων σταδίων ἕως ἐπὶ Θάψακον.

23. Ἔστι δ᾽ ἡ μὲν παρόρειος εὐδαίμων ἱκανῶς·
ἔχουσι δ᾽ αὐτῆς τὰ μὲν πρὸς τῷ Εὐφράτῃ καὶ τῷ
Ζεύγματι, τῷ τε νῦν τῷ κατὰ τὴν Κομμαγηνὴν
καὶ τῷ πάλαι τῷ κατὰ τὴν Θάψακον, οἱ[1] Μυγδόνες
κατονομασθέντες ὑπὸ τῶν Μακεδόνων· ἐν οἷς
ἐστιν ἡ Νίσιβις, ἣν καὶ αὐτὴν Ἀντιόχειαν τὴν
ἐν τῇ Μυγδονίᾳ προσηγόρευσαν, ὑπὸ τῷ Μασίῳ
ὄρει κειμένην, καὶ Τιγρανόκερτα καὶ περὶ Κάρρας
καὶ Νικηφόριον χωρία καὶ Χορδίραζα καὶ Σίννακα,
ἐν ᾗ Κράσσος διεφθάρη, δόλῳ ληφθεὶς ὑπὸ Σου-
ρήνα, τοῦ τῶν Παρθυαίων στρατηγοῦ.

24. Πρὸς δὲ τῷ Τίγρει τὰ τῶν Γορδυαίων[2]
χωρία, οὓς οἱ πάλαι Καρδούχους ἔλεγον, καὶ αἱ
πόλεις αὐτῶν[3] Σάρεισά τε καὶ Σάταλκα καὶ
Πίνακα, κράτιστον ἔρυμα, τρεῖς ἄκρας ἔχουσα,
ἑκάστην ἰδίῳ τείχει τετειχισμένην, ὥστε οἷον
τρίπολιν εἶναι. ἀλλ᾽ ὅμως καὶ ὁ Ἀρμένιος εἶχεν
ὑπήκοον καὶ οἱ Ῥωμαῖοι βίᾳ παρέλαβον, καίπερ
ἔδοξαν οἱ Γορδυαῖοι διαφερόντως ἀρχιτεκτονικοί
τινες εἶναι καὶ πολιορκητικῶν ὀργάνων ἔμπειροι·
διόπερ αὐτοῖς εἰς ταῦτα ὁ Τιγράνης ἐχρῆτο. ἐγένετο δὲ καὶ ἡ λοιπὴ Μεσοποταμία ὑπὸ Ῥωμαίοις.
Πομπήιος δ᾽ αὐτῆς τὰ πολλὰ τῷ Τιγράνῃ προσέ-

[1] τε, after οἵ, Groskurd omits; so the later editors.
[2] Γορδυαίων, Tzschucke, from conj. of Wesseling (on *Diodorus*
14. 27), for Παρθυαίων; so the later editors.

distance from Thapsacus to Babylon, as Eratosthenes states, is four thousand eight hundred stadia; and that from the Zeugma[1] at Commagenê, where Mesopotamia begins, to Thapsacus, is not less than two thousand stadia.

23. The country alongside the mountains is quite fertile; the parts of it near the Euphrates and the Zeugma, both the present Zeugma at Commagenê and the old Zeugma at Thapsacus, are occupied by the Mygdones, who were so named by the Macedonians. In their country lies Nisibis, which is also called Mygdonian Antiocheia; it lies at the foot of Mt. Masius, and so do Tigranocerta and the regions of Carrhae and Nicephorium, and Chordiraza and Sinnaca, in which last Crassus was slain, being treacherously captured by Surena, the Parthian general.[2]

24. Near the Tigris lie the places belonging to the Gordyaeans, whom the ancients called Carduchians; and their cities are named Sareisa and Satalca and Pinaca, a very powerful fortress, with three citadels, each enclosed by a separate fortification of its own, so that they constitute, as it were, a triple city. But still it not only was held in subjection by the king of the Armenians, but the Romans took it by force, although the Gordyaeans had an exceptional repute as master-builders and as experts in the construction of siege engines; and it was for this reason that Tigranes used them in such work. But also the rest of Mesopotamia became subject to the Romans. Pompey assigned to Tigranes

---

[1] Bridge.   [2] 51 B.C.

---

[3] αὐτῶν, Groskurd, for ὧν; so the later editors.

νειμεν, ὅσα ἦν ἀξιόλογα· ἔστι γὰρ εὔβοτος ἡ
χώρα καὶ εὐερνής, ὥστε καὶ τὰ ἀειθαλῆ τρέφειν
καὶ ἄρωμα τὸ ἄμωμον· καὶ λεοντοβότος ἐστί·
φέρει δὲ καὶ τὸν νάφθαν καὶ τὴν γαγγῖτιν λίθον,[1]
ἣν φεύγει τὰ ἑρπετά.

25. Λέγεται δὲ Γόρδυς ὁ Τριπτολέμου τὴν
Γορδυηνὴν οἰκῆσαι, ὕστερον δὲ καὶ Ἐρετριεῖς
οἱ ἀναρπασθέντες ὑπὸ Περσῶν. περὶ μὲν οὖν
Τριπτολέμου δηλώσομεν ἐν τοῖς Συριακοῖς αὐτίκα.

26. Τὰ δὲ πρὸς μεσημβρίαν κεκλιμένα τῆς
Μεσοποταμίας καὶ ἀπωτέρω τῶν ὀρῶν, ἄνυδρα
καὶ λυπρὰ ὄντα, ἔχουσιν οἱ Σκηνῖται Ἄραβες,
λῃστρικοί τινες καὶ ποιμενικοί, μεθιστάμενοι
ῥᾳδίως εἰς ἄλλους τόπους, ὅταν ἐπιλείπωσιν αἱ
νομαὶ καὶ αἱ λεηλασίαι. τοῖς οὖν παρορείοις
ὑπό τε τούτων κακοῦσθαι συμβαίνει καὶ ὑπὸ
τῶν Ἀρμενίων· ὑπέρκεινται δὲ καὶ καταδυναστεύ-
ουσι διὰ τὴν ἰσχύν· τέλος δ' ὑπ' ἐκείνοις εἰσὶ τὸ
πλέον ἢ τοῖς Παρθυαίοις· ἐν πλευραῖς γάρ εἰσι
κἀκεῖνοι, τήν τε Μηδίαν ἔχοντες καὶ τὴν
Βαβυλωνίαν.

27. Μεταξὺ δὲ τοῦ Εὐφράτου καὶ τοῦ Τίγριος
ῥεῖ καὶ ἄλλος ποταμός, Βασίλειος καλούμενος,
C 748 καὶ περὶ τὴν Ἀνθεμουσίαν ἄλλος, Ἀβόρρας·
διὰ δὲ τῶν Σκηνιτῶν, ὑπὸ ἐνίων[1] Μαλίων νυνὶ
λεγομένων, καὶ τῆς κείνων ἐρημίας ἡ ὁδὸς τοῖς
ἐκ τῆς Συρίας εἰς Σελεύκειαν καὶ Βαβυλῶνα
ἐμπορευομένοις ἐστίν. ἡ μὲν οὖν διάβασις[2] τοῦ

[1] ἐνίων, Groskurd, for τῶν.
[2] διάβασις F, ἀνάβασις other MSS.

[1] This stone is called *gagetes* (i.e. *jet*) by Pliny (10. 9 and 36. 19).

most of the places in this country, I mean all that are worth mentioning; for the country is rich in pasturage, and so rich in plants that it also produces the evergreens and a spice-plant called amomum; and it is a feeding-ground for lions; and it also produces naphtha and the stone called gangitis,[1] which is avoided by reptiles.

25. Gordys, the son of Triptolemus, is said to have taken up his abode in Gordyenê, and later also the Eretrians, who were carried off by the Persians. Of Triptolemus, however, I shall soon give a clear account in my description of the Syrians.[2]

26. The parts of Mesopotamia which incline towards the south and are farther from the mountains, which are waterless and barren, are occupied by the Arabian Scenitae, a tribe of brigands and shepherds, who readily move from one place to another when pasture and booty fail them. Accordingly, the people who live alongside the mountains are harassed not only by the Scenitae, but also by the Armenians, who are situated above them and, through their might, oppress them; and at last they are subject for the most part to the Armenians or else to the Parthians, for the Parthians too are situated on the sides of the country and possess both Media and Babylonia.

27. Between the Euphrates and the Tigris there flows another river, called Basileius; and in the neighbourhood of Anthemusia still another, called Aborras. The road for people travelling from Syria to Seleuceia and Babylon runs through the country of the Scenitae,[3] now called Malians by some writers, and through their desert. Such travellers cross the

---

[2] 16. 2. 5.   [3] Tent-dwellers.

Εὐφράτου κατὰ τὴν Ἀνθεμουσίαν ἐστὶν αὐτοῖς, τόπον τῆς Μεσοποταμίας· ὑπέρκειται δὲ τοῦ ποταμοῦ, σχοίνους τέτταρας διέχουσα, ἡ Βαμβύκη, ἣν καὶ Ἔδεσσαν καὶ Ἱερὰν πόλιν καλοῦσιν, ἐν ᾗ τιμῶσι τὴν Συρίαν θεὸν τὴν Ἀταργάτιν. διαβάντων γὰρ ἡ ὁδός ἐστι διὰ τῆς ἐρήμου μέχρι Σκηνῶν, ἀξιολόγου πόλεως ἐπὶ τοὺς τῆς Βαβυλωνίας ὅρους ἐπί τινος διώρυγος ἱδρυμένης. ἔστι δ' ἀπὸ τῆς διαβάσεως μέχρι Σκηνῶν ἡμερῶν πέντε καὶ εἴκοσιν ὁδός. καμηλῖται δ' εἰσί, καταγωγὰς ἔχοντες τοτὲ μὲν ὑδρείων εὐπόρους, τῶν λακκαίων τὸ πλέον, τοτὲ δ' ἐπακτοῖς χρώμενοι τοῖς ὕδασι. παρέχουσι δ' αὐτοῖς οἱ Σκηνῖται τήν τε εἰρήνην καὶ τὴν μετριότητα τῆς τῶν τελῶν πράξεως, ἧς χάριν φεύγοντες τὴν παραποταμίαν διὰ τῆς ἐρήμου παραβάλλονται, καταλιπόντες ἐν δεξιᾷ τὸν ποταμὸν ἡμερῶν σχεδόν τι τριῶν ὁδόν. οἱ γὰρ παροικοῦντες ἑκατέρωθεν τὸν ποταμὸν φύλαρχοι, χώραν οὐκ εὔπορον ἔχοντες, ἧττον δὲ ἄπορον νεμόμενοι, δυναστείαν ἕκαστος ἰδίᾳ περιβεβλημένος [1] ἴδιον καὶ τελώνιον ἔχει, καὶ τοῦτ' οὐ μέτριον. χαλεπὸν γὰρ ἐν τοῖς τοσούτοις καὶ τούτοις [2] αὐθάδεσι κοινὸν ἀφορισθῆναι μέτρον τὸ τῷ ἐμπόρῳ λυσιτελές. διέχουσι δὲ τῆς Σελευκείας αἱ Σκηναὶ σχοίνους ὀκτωκαίδεκα.

28. Ὅριον δ' ἐστὶ τῆς Παρθυαίων ἀρχῆς ὁ Εὐφράτης καὶ ἡ περαία· τὰ δ' ἐντὸς ἔχουσι Ῥωμαῖοι καὶ τῶν Ἀράβων οἱ φύλαρχοι μέχρι Βαβυλωνίας, οἱ μὲν μᾶλλον ἐκείνοις, οἱ δὲ τοῖς

[1] περιβεβλημένος DFh, παραβεβλημενος other MSS.
[2] τούτοις, Corais, for τοῖς.

Euphrates near Anthemusia, a place in Mesopotamia; and above the river, at a distance of four schoeni, lies Bambycê, which is also called Edessa and Hierapolis,[1] where the Syrian goddess Atargatis is worshipped; for after they cross the river, the road runs through the desert to Scenae, a noteworthy city situated on a canal towards the borders of Babylonia. The journey from the crossing of the river to Scenae requires twenty-five days. And on that road are camel-drivers who keep halting-places, which sometimes are well supplied with reservoirs, generally cisterns, though sometimes the camel-drivers use waters brought in from other places. The Scenitae are peaceful, and moderate towards travellers in the exaction of tribute, and on this account merchants avoid the land along the river and risk a journey through the desert, leaving the river on the right for approximately a three days' journey. For the chieftains who live along the river on both sides occupy country which, though not rich in resources, is less resourceless than that of others, and are each invested with their own particular domains and exact a tribute of no moderate amount. For it is hard among so many peoples, and that too among peoples that are self-willed, for a common standard of tribute to be set that is advantageous to the merchant. Scenae is eighteen schoeni distant from Seleuceia.

28. The Euphrates and the land beyond it constitute the boundary of the Parthian empire. But the parts this side the river are held by the Romans and the chieftains of the Arabians as far as Babylonia, some of these chieftains preferring to give ear to the

[1] Holy City.

Ῥωμαίοις προσέχοντες, οἷσπερ καὶ πλησιόχωροί
εἰσιν· ἧττον μὲν Σκηνῖται οἱ νομάδες οἱ τῷ
ποταμῷ πλησίον, μᾶλλον δ᾽ οἱ ἄπωθεν καὶ πρὸς
τῇ εὐδαίμονι Ἀραβίᾳ. οἱ δὲ Παρθυαῖοι καὶ
πρότερον μὲν ἐφρόντιζον τῆς πρὸς Ῥωμαίους
φιλίας, τὸν δὲ ἄρξαντα πολέμου Κράσσον ἠμύ-
ναντο· καὶ αὐτοὶ ἄρξαντες τῆς μάχης τῶν
ἴσων ἔτυχον, ἡνίκα ἔπεμψαν ἐπὶ τὴν Ἀσίαν
Πάκορον.[1] Ἀντώνιος δέ, συμβούλῳ τῷ Ἀρμενίῳ
χρώμενος, προὐδόθη καὶ κακῶς ἐπολέμησεν· ὁ
δ᾽ ἐκεῖνον διαδεξάμενος Φραάτης, τοσοῦτον ἐσπού-
δασε περὶ τὴν φιλίαν τὴν πρὸς Καίσαρα τὸν
Σεβατόν, ὥστε καὶ τὰ τρόπαια ἔπεμψεν, ἃ κατὰ
Ῥωμαίων ἀνέστησαν Παρθυαῖοι· καὶ καλέσας εἰς
σύλλογον Τίτιον τὸν ἐπιστατοῦντα τότε τῆς
Συρίας, τέτταρας παῖδας γνησίους ἐνεχείρισεν
ὅμηρα αὐτῷ, Σερασπαδάνην[2] καὶ Ῥωδάσπην[3] καὶ
Φραάτην[4] καὶ Βονώνην, καὶ γυναῖκας τούτων δυο
καὶ υἱεῖς τέτταρας, δεδιὼς τὰς στάσεις καὶ τοὺς
ἐπιτιθεμένους αὐτῷ· ᾔδει γὰρ μηδένα ἰσχύσοντα
C 749 καθ᾽ ἑαυτόν, ἂν μή τινα ὑπολάβῃ[5] τοῦ Ἀρσακίου
γένους διὰ τὸ εἶναι σφόδρα φιλαρσάκας τοὺς
Παρθυαίους· ἐκποδὼν οὖν ἐποίησε τοὺς παῖδας,

---

[1] Something like the words τὸν τοῦ Ὠρώδου παῖδα appears
to have fallen out after Πάκορον.

[2] Σερασπαδάνην, Tzschucke, for Σατραπάδην D, Σαρασπάδην
other MSS.

[3] Ῥωδάσπην, Tzschucke, for Κεροσπάδην D, Κεροπάσδην other
MSS.

[4] Φραάτην x, Φραάνην other MSS.

[5] ὑπολάβῃ, all MSS. except moz, which read προσλάβῃ,
Jones restores to the text. Corais reads προσλάβῃ; Meineke
following Kramer, ἐπιλάβῃ; and Casaubon conj. ὑποβάλῃ.

Parthians and others to the Romans, to whom they
are neighbours; less so[1] the nomad Scenitae who
are near the river, but more so those that are far
away and near Arabia Felix. The Parthians were
also in former times eager for friendship with the
Romans, but they defended themselves against
Crassus, who began war with them;[2] and then,
having begun the battle themselves, met with
equal reverses when they sent Pacorus against
Asia.[3] But Antony, using the Armenian[4] as counsellor, was betrayed and fared badly in his war.
Phraates,[5] his successor, was so eager for friendship
with Caesar Augustus that he even sent him the
trophies which the Parthians had set up as memorials
of their defeat of the Romans. And, having called
Titius to a conference, who was at that time praefect
of Syria, he put in his hands as hostages four of his
legitimate sons, Seraspadanes and Rhodaspes and
Phraates and Bonones, and two wives and four sons
of these,[6] for fear of seditions and attempts upon
his life; for he knew that no person could prevail
against him unless that person supported some
member of the house of Arsaces, because of the
fact that the Parthians were extremely fond of the
house. Accordingly, he got rid of his children,

[1] *i.e.* less inclined to give ear to the Romans.   [2] 54 B.C.
[3] Pacorus (son of King Orodes) and Labienus overran
Syria and part of Asia Minor, but were defeated (39 B.C.) by
Ventidius, a legate of Antony. Pacorus again invaded Syria
(38 B.C.), but was again defeated and fell in battle (see
16. 2. 8).
[4] Artavasdes, king of the Armenians (see 11. 13. 4).
[5] Phraates IV, who succeeded his father Orodes as king
and commenced his reign by murdering his father, his thirty
brothers, and his own son.
[6] Cf. 6. 4. 2.

STRABO

ἀφελέσθαι ζητῶν τὴν ἐλπίδα ταύτην τοὺς κακουρ-
γοῦντας. τῶν μὲν οὖν παίδων ὅσοι περίεισιν ἐν
Ῥώμῃ δημοσίᾳ βασιλικῶς τημελοῦνται· καὶ οἱ
λοιποὶ δὲ βασιλεῖς πρεσβευόμενοι καὶ εἰς συλ-
λόγους ἀφικνούμενοι διατετελέκασιν.

II

1. Ἡ δὲ Συρία πρὸς ἄρκτον μὲν ἀφώρισται τῇ
Κιλικίᾳ καὶ τῷ Ἀμανῷ· ἀπὸ θαλάττης δ' ἐπὶ
τὸ ζεῦγμα τοῦ Εὐφράτου στάδιοί εἰσιν (ἀπὸ τοῦ
Ἰσσικοῦ κόλπου μέχρι τοῦ ζεύγματος τοῦ κατὰ
Κομμαγηνὴν)[1] οἱ τὸ λεχθὲν πλευρὸν ἀφορίζοντες
οὐκ ἐλάττους τῶν χιλίων καὶ[2] τετρακοσίων· πρὸς
ἔω δὲ τῷ Εὐφράτῃ καὶ τοῖς ἐντὸς τοῦ Εὐφράτου
Σκηνίταις Ἄραψι· πρὸς δὲ νότον τῇ εὐδαίμονι
Ἀραβίᾳ καὶ τῇ Αἰγύπτῳ· πρὸς δύσιν δὲ τῷ
Αἰγυπτίῳ τε καὶ Συριακῷ πελάγει μέχρι Ἰσσοῦ.
2. Μέρη δ' αὐτῆς τίθεμεν ἀπὸ τῆς Κιλικίας
ἀρξάμενοι καὶ τοῦ Ἀμανοῦ τήν τε Κομμαγηνὴν
καὶ τὴν Σελευκίδα καλουμένην τῆς Συρίας, ἔπειτα
τὴν Κοίλην Συρίαν, τελευταίαν δ' ἐν μὲν τῇ παραλίᾳ τὴν Φοινίκην, ἐν δὲ τῇ μεσογαίᾳ τὴν Ἰουδαίαν.
ἔνιοι δὲ τὴν Συρίαν ὅλην εἴς τε Κοιλοσύρους καὶ
Σύρους[3] καὶ Φοίνικας διελόντες τούτοις ἀναμε-
μίχθαί φασι τέτταρα ἔθνη, Ἰουδαίους, Ἰδουμαίους,
Γαζαίους, Ἀζωτίους, γεωργικοὺς μέν, ὡς τοὺς
Σύρους καὶ Κοιλοσύρους, ἐμπορικοὺς δέ, ὡς τοὺς
Φοίνικας.
3. Καθόλου μὲν οὕτω, καθ' ἕκαστα δὲ ἡ Κομ-

[1] The words in parenthesis are suspected by Kramer and
ejected by Meineke.

seeking thus to deprive evil-doers of that hope. Now all his surviving children are cared for in royal style, at public expense, in Rome, and the remaining kings [1] have also continued to send ambassadors and to go into conferences.[2]

II

1. Syria is bounded on the north by Cilicia and Mt. Amanus; and the distance from the sea to the bridge of the Euphrates (from the Gulf of Issus to the bridge at Commagenê), which forms the boundary of that side, is not less than fourteen hundred stadia. It is bounded on the east by the Euphrates and by the Arabian Scenitae this side the Euphrates; and on the south by Arabia Felix and Aegypt; and on the west by the Aegyptian and Syrian Seas as far as Issus.

2. We set down as parts of Syria, beginning at Cilicia and Mt. Amanus, both Commagenê and the Seleucis of Syria, as the latter is called; and then Coelê-Syria, and last, on the seaboard, Phoenicia, and, in the interior, Judaea. Some writers divide Syria as a whole into Coelo-Syrians and Syrians and Phoenicians, and say that four other tribes are mixed up with these, namely, Judaeans, Idumaeans, Gazaeans, and Azotians, and that they are partly farmers, as the Syrians and Coelo-Syrians, and partly merchants, as the Phoenicians.

3. So much for Syria in general. But in detail:

---

[1] *i.e.* his successors.   [2] *i.e.* with Roman praefects.

---

[2] χιλίων καί, Tzschucke inserts, citing Pliny 5. 12. 13; so the later editors.

[3] καὶ Σύρους, omitted by all MSS. except D.

μαγηνὴ μικρά τίς ἐστιν· ἔχει δ' ἐρυμνὴν πόλιν
Σαμόσατα, ἐν ᾗ τὸ βασίλειον ὑπῆρχε· νῦν δ'
ἐπαρχία γέγονε· χώρα δὲ περίκειται σφόδρα
εὐδαίμων, ὀλίγη δέ. ἐνταῦθα δὲ νῦν ἐστι τὸ
ζεῦγμα τοῦ Εὐφράτου· κατὰ τοῦτο δὲ Σελεύκεια
ἵδρυται, φρούριον τῆς Μεσοποταμίας, προσωρισ-
μένον ὑπὸ Πομπηίου τῇ Κομμαγηνῇ·[1] ἐν ᾧ τὴν
Σελήνην ἐπικληθεῖσαν Κλεοπάτραν Τιγράνης
ἀνεῖλε, καθείρξας χρόνον τινά, ἡνίκα τῆς Συρίας
ἐξέπεσεν.

4. Ἡ δὲ Σελευκὶς ἀρίστη μέν ἐστι τῶν λεχθει-
σῶν μερίδων, καλεῖται δὲ Τετράπολις καί ἐστι
κατὰ τὰς ἐξεχούσας ἐν αὐτῇ πόλεις, ἐπεὶ πλείους
γέ εἰσι· μέγισται δὲ τέτταρες, Ἀντιόχεια ἡ ἐπὶ
Δάφνῃ καὶ Σελεύκεια ἡ ἐν Πιερίᾳ καὶ Ἀπάμεια
δὲ καὶ Λαοδίκεια, αἵπερ καὶ ἐλέγοντο ἀλλήλων
ἀδελφαὶ διὰ τὴν ὁμόνοιαν, Σελεύκου τοῦ Νικάτορος κτίσματα· ἡ μὲν οὖν μεγίστη τοῦ πατρὸς
αὐτοῦ ἐπώνυμος, ἡ δ' ἐρυμνοτάτη αὐτοῦ· αἱ δ'
C 750 ἄλλαι, ἡ μὲν Ἀπάμεια τῆς γυναικὸς αὐτοῦ
Ἀπάμας, ἡ δὲ Λαοδίκεια τῆς μητρός. οἰκείως
δὲ τῇ τετραπόλει καὶ εἰς σατραπείας διῄρητο[2]
τέτταρας ἡ Σελευκίς, ὥς φησι Ποσειδώνιος, εἰς
ὅσας καὶ ἡ Κοίλη Συρία, εἰς μίαν δ' ἡ Μεσοποταμία.[3] ἔστι δ' ἡ μὲν Ἀντιόχεια καὶ αὐτὴ[4]

---

[1] τῇ Κομμαγηνῇ moz, for τῷ Κομμαγηνῷ other MSS.; so
Tzschucke, Corais, and Meineke.
[2] διῄρητο, first hand in D, for διηρεῖτο; so the editors.
[3] The editors suspect this clause. Groskurd conj. that
Strabo wrote either εἰς μίαν δ' ἡ Κομμαγηνὴ καθάπερ καὶ ἡ
Μεσοποταμία or εἰς μίαν δ' ἡ Κομμαγηνὴ καὶ ὁ οἴως ἡ Παρα-
ποταμία. Perhaps, too, some verb like ἐτέτακτο has fallen
out after Μεσοποταμίαν.
[4] αὐτή, Jones, for αὕτη.

Commagenê is rather a small country; and it has a
city fortified by nature, Samosata, where the royal
residence used to be; but it has now become a
province;[1] and the city is surrounded by an exceedingly fertile, though small, territory. Here is now
the bridge of the Euphrates; and near the bridge
is situated Seleuceia, a fortress of Mesopotamia,
which was included within the boundaries of Commagenê by Pompey; and it was here that Tigranes
slew Selenê, surnamed Cleopatra, after imprisoning
her for a time, when she had been banished from
Syria.
4. Seleucis is not only the best of the above-
mentioned portions of Syria, but also is called, and
is, a Tetrapolis, owing to the outstanding cities in
it, for it has several. But the largest are four:
Antiocheia near Daphnê, Seleuceia in Pieria, and
also Apameia and Laodiceia; and these cities, all
founded by Seleucus Nicator, used to be called
sisters, because of their concord with one another.
Now the largest of these cities[2] was named after his
father and the one most strongly fortified by nature
after himself, and one of the other two, Apameia,
after his wife Apama, and the other, Laodiceia,
after his mother. Appropriately to the Tetrapolis,
Seleucis was also divided into four satrapies, as
Poseidonius says, the same number into which
Coelê-Syria was divided, though Mesopotamia
formed only one satrapy.[3] Antiocheia is likewise

[1] *i.e.* a *Roman* province.
[2] Antiocheia.
[3] The text seems to be corrupt. Groskurd conjectures
that Strabo wrote either " Commagenê, like Mesopotamia,
formed one satrapy," or " Commagenê, and likewise Parapo-
tamia, formed one satrapy " (see critical note).

STRABO

τετράπολις, ἐκ τεττάρων συνεστῶσα μερῶν· τε-
τείχισται δὲ καὶ κοινῷ τείχει καὶ ἰδίῳ καθ᾿
ἕκαστον τὸ κτίσμα· τὸ μὲν οὖν πρῶτον αὐτῶν ὁ
Νικάτωρ συνῴκισε, μεταγαγὼν ἐκ τῆς Ἀντιγονίας
τοὺς οἰκήτορας, ἣν πλησίον ἐτείχισεν Ἀντίγονος
ὁ Φιλίππου μικρὸν πρότερον, τὸ δὲ δεύτερον τοῦ
πλήθους τῶν οἰκητόρων ἐστὶ κτίσμα, τὸ δὲ
τρίτον Σελεύκου τοῦ Καλλινίκου, τὸ δὲ τέταρτον
Ἀντιόχου τοῦ Ἐπιφανοῦς.

5. Καὶ δὴ καὶ μητρόπολίς ἐστιν αὕτη τῆς
Συρίας, καὶ τὸ βασίλειον ἐνταῦθα ἵδρυτο τοῖς
ἄρχουσι τῆς χώρας· οὐ πολύ τε λείπεται καὶ
δυνάμει καὶ μεγέθει Σελευκείας τῆς ἐπὶ τῷ Τίγρει
καὶ Ἀλεξανδρείας τῆς πρὸς Αἰγύπτῳ. συνῴκισε
δ᾿ ὁ Νικάτωρ ἐνταῦθα καὶ τοὺς ἀπογόνους[1]
Τριπτολέμου, περὶ οὗ μικρῷ[2] πρόσθεν ἐμνήσθη-
μεν· διόπερ Ἀντιοχεῖς ὡς ἥρωα τιμῶσι καὶ ἄγου-
σιν ἑορτὴν ἐν τῷ Κασίῳ ὄρει τῷ περὶ Σελεύκειαν.
φασὶ δ᾿ αὐτὸν ὑπ᾿ Ἀργείων πεμφθέντα ἐπὶ τὴν
Ἰοῦς ζήτησιν, ἐν Τύρῳ πρῶτον ἀφανοῦς γενη-
θείσης, πλανᾶσθαι κατὰ τὴν Κιλικίαν· ἐνταῦθα
δὲ τῶν σὺν αὐτῷ τινας Ἀργείων κτίσαι τὴν
Ταρσὸν ἀπελθόντας παρ᾿ αὐτοῦ· τοὺς δ᾿ ἄλλους
συνακολουθήσαντας εἰς τὴν ἐξῆς παραλίαν, ἀπο-
γνόντας τῆς ζητήσεως, ἐν τῇ ποταμίᾳ τοῦ Ὀρόντου
καταμεῖναι σὺν αὐτῷ· τὸν μὲν οὖν υἱὸν τοῦ
Τριπτολέμου Γόρδυν, ἔχοντά τινας τῶν σὺν τῷ
πατρὶ λαῶν, εἰς τὴν Γορδυαίαν ἀποικῆσαι· τῶν
δ᾿ ἄλλων τοὺς ἀπογόνους συνοίκους γενέσθαι τοῖς
Ἀντιοχεῦσιν.

[1] ἀπογόνους Ei, ἀπογόνος w, ἀπὸ γένους other MSS.

a Tetrapolis, since it consists of four parts; and each of the four settlements is fortified both by a common wall and by a wall of its own. Now Nicator founded the first of the settlements, transferring thither the settlers from Antigonia, which had been built near it a short time before by Antigonus; the second was founded by the multitude of settlers; the third by Seleucus Callinicus; and the fourth by Antiochus Epiphanes.

5. Furthermore, Antiocheia is the metropolis of Syria; and here was established the royal residence for the rulers of the country. And it does not fall much short, either in power or in size, of Seleuceia on the Tigris or Alexandria in Aegypt. Nicator also settled here the descendants of Triptolemus, whom I mentioned a little before.[1] And it is on this account that the Antiocheians worship him as a hero and celebrate a festival in his honour on Mt. Casius in the neighbourhood of Seleuceia. It is said that he was sent by the Argives in search of Io, who disappeared first in Tyre, and that he wandered through Cilicia; and that there some of his Argive companions left him and founded Tarsus, but the others accompanied him into the next stretch of sea-board, gave up the search in despair, and remained with him in the river-country of the Orontes; and that Gordys, the son of Triptolemus, along with some of the peoples who had accompanied his father, emigrated to Gordyaea, whereas the descendants of the rest became fellow-inhabitants with the Antiocheians.

[1] 16. 1. 25.

[2] μικρόν F ; so Meineke.

6. Ὑπέρκειται δὲ τετταράκοντα σταδίοις ἡ Δάφνη, κατοικία μετρία μέγα δὲ καὶ συνηρεφὲς ἄλσος, διαρρεόμενον πηγαίοις ὕδασιν, ἐν μέσῳ δὲ ἄσυλον τέμενος καὶ νεὼς Ἀπόλλωνος καὶ Ἀρτέμιδος. ἐνταῦθα δὲ πανηγυρίζειν ἔθος τοῖς Ἀντιοχεῦσι καὶ τοῖς ἀστυγείτοσι· κύκλος δὲ τοῦ ἄλσους ὀγδοήκοντα στάδιοι.

7. Ῥεῖ δὲ τῆς πόλεως πλησίον Ὀρόντης ποταμός· οὗτος δ' ἐκ τῆς Κοίλης Συρίας τὰς ἀρχὰς ἔχων, εἶθ' ὑπὸ γῆν ἐνεχθείς, ἀναδίδωσι πάλιν τὸ ῥεῦμα, καὶ διὰ τῆς Ἀπαμέων εἰς τὴν Ἀντιόχειαν προελθών, πλησιάσας τῇ πόλει πρὸς τὴν θάλατταν καταφέρεται τὴν κατὰ Σελεύκειαν· τὸ δ' ὄνομα τοῦ γεφυρώσαντος αὐτὸν Ὀρόντου μετέλαβε, καλούμενος πρότερον Τυφών. μυθεύουσι δ' ἐνταῦθά που τὰ περὶ τὴν κεραύνωσιν τοῦ Τυφῶνος καὶ τοὺς Ἀρίμους, περὶ ὧν εἴπομεν καὶ
C 751 πρότερον· φασὶ δὲ τυπτόμενον τοῖς κεραυνοῖς (εἶναι δὲ δράκοντα) φεύγειν κατάδυσιν ζητοῦντα· τοῖς μὲν οὖν ὁλκοῖς ἐντεμεῖν τὴν γῆν καὶ ποιῆσαι τὸ ῥεῖθρον τοῦ ποταμοῦ, καταδύντα δ' εἰς γῆν ἀναρρῆξαι τὴν πηγήν· ἐκ δὲ τούτου γενέσθαι τοὔνομα τῷ ποταμῷ. πρὸς δύσιν μὲν οὖν θάλαττα ὑπόκειται τῇ Ἀντιοχείᾳ κατὰ Σελεύκειαν, πρὸς ᾗ καὶ τὰς ἐκβολὰς ὁ Ὀρόντης ποιεῖται, διεχούσῃ τῶν μὲν ἐκβολῶν σταδίους τετταράκοντα, τῆς δ' Ἀντιοχείας ἑκατὸν εἴκοσι. ἀνάπλους δ' ἐκ θαλάττης ἐστὶν εἰς τὴν Ἀντιόχειαν αὐθημερόν. πρὸς ἔω δ' ὁ Εὐφράτης ἐστὶ καὶ ἡ Βαμβύκη καὶ ἡ Βέροια καὶ ἡ Ἡράκλεια

---

[1] 12. 8. 19, 13. 4. 6.

6. Lying above Antiocheia, at a distance of forty stadia, is Daphnê, a settlement of moderate size; and also a large, thickly-shaded grove intersected by fountain-streams, in the midst of which there is an asylum-precinct and a temple of Apollo and Artemis. Here it is the custom for the Antiocheians and the neighbouring peoples to hold a general festival. The grove is eighty stadia in circuit.

7. The Orontes River flows near the city. This river has its sources in Coelê-Syria; and then, after flowing underground, issues forth again; and then, proceeding through the territory of the Apameians into that of Antiocheia, closely approaches the latter city and flows down to the sea near Seleuceia. Though formerly called Typhon, its name was changed to that of Orontes, the man who built a bridge across it. Here, somewhere, is the setting of the mythical story of Typhon's stroke by lightning and of the mythical story of the Arimi, of whom I have already spoken.[1] They say that Typhon (who, they add, was a dragon), when struck by the bolts of lightning, fled in search of a descent underground; that he not only cut the earth with furrows and formed the bed of the river, but also descended underground and caused the fountain to break forth to the surface; and that the river got its name from this fact. Now on the west, below Antiocheia and Seleuceia, lies the sea; and it is near Seleuceia that the Orontes forms its outlets, this city being forty stadia distant from the outlets, and one hundred and twenty from Antiocheia. Inland voyages from the sea to Antiocheia are made on the same day one starts. To the east of Antiocheia are the Euphrates, as also Bambycê and Beroea and Hera-

STRABO

τῇ Ἀντιοχείᾳ, πολίχνια τυραννούμενά ποτε
ὑπὸ Διονυσίου τοῦ Ἡρακλέωνος. διέχει δ' ἡ
Ἡράκλεια σταδίους εἴκοσι τοῦ τῆς Ἀθηνᾶς ἱεροῦ
τῆς Κυρρηστίδος.[1]

8. Εἶτα ἡ Κυρρηστική[2] μέχρι τῆς Ἀντιοχίδος·
ἀπὸ δὲ τῶν ἄρκτων ἐστὶ τό τε Ἀμανὸν πλησίον
καὶ ἡ Κομμαγηνή· συνάπτει δὲ τούτοις ἡ Κυρρη-
στικὴ μέχρι δεῦρο παρατείνουσα. ἐνταῦθα δ'
ἐστὶ πόλις Γίνδαρος, ἀκρόπολις τῆς Κυρρηστικῆς
καὶ λῃστήριον εὐφυές, καὶ Ἡράκλειόν τι καλούμενον[3] πλησίον· περὶ οὓς τόπους ὑπὸ Οὐεντιδίου
Πάκορος διεφθάρη, ὁ πρεσβύτατος τῶν τοῦ
Παρθυαίου παίδων, ἐπιστρατεύσας τῇ Συρίᾳ.
τῇ δὲ Γινδάρῳ[4] συνάπτουσιν[5] αἱ Πάγραι τῆς
Ἀντιοχίδος, χωρίον ἐρυμνὸν κατὰ τὴν ὑπέρθεσιν
τοῦ Ἀμανοῦ τὴν ἐκ τῶν Ἀμανίδων πυλῶν εἰς τὴν
Συρίαν κείμενον. ὑποπίπτει μὲν οὖν ταῖς Πάγραις
τὸ τῶν Ἀντιοχέων πεδίον, δι' οὗ ῥεῖ ὁ Ἄρκευθος
ποταμὸς καὶ ὁ Ὀρόντης καὶ ὁ Λαβώτας. ἐν δὲ τούτῳ ἐστὶ τῷ πεδίῳ καὶ ὁ Μελεάγρου χάραξ καὶ ὁ
Οἰνοπάρας ποταμός· ἐφ' ᾧ τὸν Βάλαν Ἀλέξανδρον
μάχῃ νικήσας ὁ Φιλομήτωρ Πτολεμαῖος ἐτελεύτη-
σεν ἐκ τραύματος. ὑπέρκειται δ' αὐτῶν λόφος
Τραπεζὼν ἀπὸ τῆς ὁμοιότητος καλούμενος, ἐφ' ᾧ
Οὐεντίδιος πρὸς Φρανικάτην,[6] τὸν Παρθυαίων

[1] Κυρρηστίδος, Xylander, for Καριστίδος *wr*, Κυριστίδος other MSS.
[2] Κυρρηστική, Xylander, for Κυρριστική ; and so in subse-quent uses of the word.
[3] Dh read ἱερόν after καλούμενον ; so Corais and Meineke.
[4] Γινδάρῳ, the editors, for τὴν δάρον D, Τηνδάρῳ C, Τινδάρῳ other MSS.
[5] E inserts ᾧ before συνάπτουσιν.

cleia, small towns once ruled by the tyrant Dionysius, the son of Heracleon. Heracleia is twenty stadia distant from the temple of Athena Cyrrhestis.

8. Then one comes to Cyrrhesticê, which extends as far as the territory of Antiocheia. On the north, near it, lie both Mt. Amanus and Commagenê. Cyrrhesticê borders on these, extending as far as that. Here is Gindarus, a city, which is the acropolis of Cyrrhesticê and a natural stronghold for robbers; and near it is a place called Heracleium.[1] It was in the neighbourhood of these places that Pacorus, the eldest of the sons of the Parthian king, was killed by Ventidius, when he made an expedition against Syria.[2] On the borders of Gindarus lies Pagrae, which is in the territory of Antiocheia and is a natural stronghold situated near the top of the pass over Mt. Amanus, which leads from the Gates of Amanus into Syria. Now below Pagrae lies the plain of the Antiocheians, through which flow the Arceuthus and Orontes and Labotas Rivers; and in this plain is the palisade of Meleagrer, as also the Oenoparas River, on the banks of which Ptolemy Philometor conquered Alexander Balas but died from a wound.[3] Above these places lies a hill which, from its similarity,[4] is called Trapezon, whereon Ventidius had the fight with Phranicates,[5]

[1] "Heracleium" implies a temple of Heracles.
[2] See 16. 1. 28.
[3] In 146 B.C. He fell from his horse.
[4] i.e. from its table-like shape.
[5] The correct spelling is probably "Pharnapates," as in Dio Cassius (48. 41) and Plutarch (*Antony* 33).

[6] Φρανικάτην, emended to Φαρναπάτης by Tzschucke and Corais.

στρατηγόν, ἔσχε τὸν ἀγῶνα. πρὸς θαλάττῃ δὲ
τούτων ἐστὶν ἡ Σελεύκεια καὶ ἡ Πιερία, ὅρος
συνεχὲς τῷ Ἀμανῷ, καὶ ἡ Ῥωσός, μεταξὺ Ἰσσοῦ
καὶ Σελευκείας ἱδρυμένη. ἐκαλεῖτο δ᾽ ἡ Σελεύκεια
πρότερον Ὕδατος Ποταμοί· ἔρυμα δέ ἐστιν ἀξιόλογον καὶ κρείττων[1] βίας ἡ πόλις. διόπερ καὶ
ἐλευθέραν αὐτὴν ἔκρινε Πομπήιος, ἀποκλείσας
Τιγράνην. πρὸς νότον δ᾽ ἐστὶ τοῖς μὲν Ἀντιοχεῦσιν Ἀπάμεια, ἐν μεσογαίᾳ κειμένη, τοῖς δὲ
Σελευκεῦσι τὸ Κάσιον ὅρος καὶ τὸ Ἀντικάσιον·
ἔτι δὲ πρότερον μετὰ τὴν Σελεύκειαν αἱ ἐκβολαὶ
τοῦ Ὀρόντου· εἶτα τὸ Νυμφαῖον, σπήλαιόν τι
ἱερόν· εἶτα τὸ Κάσιον· ἐφεξῆς δὲ Ποσείδιον
πολίχνη καὶ Ἡράκλεια.

9. Εἶτα Λαοδίκεια, ἐπὶ τῇ θαλάττῃ κάλλιστα
ἐκτισμένη καὶ εὐλίμενος πόλις, χώραν[2] τε ἔχουσα
C 752 πολύοινον πρὸς τῇ ἄλλῃ εὐκαρπίᾳ· τοῖς μὲν οὖν
Ἀλεξανδρεῦσιν αὕτη παρέχει τὸ πλεῖστον τοῦ
οἴνου, τὸ ὑπερκείμενον τῆς πόλεως ὅρος πᾶν κατάμ-
πελον ἔχουσα μέχρι σχεδόν τι τῶν κορυφῶν· αἱ δὲ
κορυφαὶ τῆς μὲν Λαοδικείας πολὺ ἄπωθέν εἰσι,
ἠρέμα ἀπ᾽ αὐτῆς καὶ κατ᾽ ὀλίγον ἀνακλινόμεναι·
τῆς Ἀπαμείας δ᾽ ὑπερκύπτουσιν ἐπ᾽ ὄρθιον ὕψος
ἀνατεταμέναι. ἐλύπησε δ᾽ οὐ μετρίως Δολαβέλ-
λας καταφυγὼν εἰς αὐτὴν καὶ ἐμπολιορκηθεὶς ὑπὸ
Κασσίου μέχρι θανάτου, συνδιαφθείρας ἑαυτῷ
καὶ τῆς πόλεως πολλὰ μέρη.

---

[1] κρείττων CDhimoxz, κ. εἶττον other MSS.
[2] χώραν, Corais, for χῶρον.

---

[1] Rivers-of-Water.

the Parthian general. Near the sea in this region
lie Seleuceia, and Pieria, a mountain continuous
with Mt. Amanus, and Rhosus, which is situated
between Issus and Seleuceia. Seleuceia was in
earlier times called Hydatos-Potamoi.[1] The city
is a notable fortress and is too strong to be taken
by force; and for this reason Pompey, after shutting
Tigranes off from it,[2] adjudged it a free city. To
the south of the Antiocheians is Apameia, which is
situated in the interior; and to the south of the
Seleuceians are Mts. Casius and Anticasius; and
still further after Seleuceia one comes to the outlets
of the Orontes; and then to the Nymphaeum, a
kind of sacred cave; and then to Casium; and next
to Poseidium, a small town, and to Heracleia.

9. Then one comes to Laodiceia, situated on the
sea. It is a city most beautifully built, has a good
harbour, and has territory which, besides its other
good crops, abounds in wine. Now this city furnishes
the most of the wine to the Alexandreians, since
the whole of the mountain that lies above the city
and is possessed by it is covered with vines almost
as far as the summits. And while the summits are
at a considerable distance from Laodiceia, sloping
up gently and gradually from it, they tower above
Apameia, extending up to a perpendicular height.
Laodiceia was afflicted in no moderate degree by
Dolabella, when he fled to it for refuge, was besieged
in it by Cassius till death, and destroyed, along with
himself, many parts of the city.[3]

[2] Tigranes had tried for fourteen years (84–70 B.C.) to
capture the city.
[3] To avoid being captured by Cassius, Dolabella ordered
one of his soldiers to kill him (43 B.C.).

10. Ἡ δ᾽ Ἀπάμεια καὶ πόλιν[1] ἔχει τὸ πλέον εὐερκῆ· λόφος γάρ ἐστιν ἐν πεδίῳ κοίλῳ τετειχισμένος καλῶς, ὃν ποιεῖ χερρονησίζοντα ὁ Ὀρόντης καὶ λίμνη περικειμένη μεγάλη καὶ εἰς ἔλη πλατέα λειμῶνάς τε βούβοτους καὶ ἱπποβότους διαχεομένη[2] ὑπερβάλλοντας τὸ μέγεθος· ἥ τε δὴ πόλις οὕτως ἀσφαλῶς κεῖται, καὶ δὴ καὶ Χερρόνησος ἐκλήθη διὰ τὸ συμβεβηκός, καὶ χώρας εὐπορεῖ παμπόλλης εὐδαίμονος, δι᾽ ἧς ὁ Ὀρόντης ῥεῖ· καὶ περιπόλια[3] συχνὰ ἐν ταύτῃ. ἐνταῦθα δὲ καὶ ὁ Νικάτωρ Σέλευκος τοὺς πεντακοσίους ἐλέφαντας ἔτρεφε καὶ τὸ πλέον τῆς στρατιᾶς, καὶ οἱ ὕστερον βασιλεῖς. ἐκαλεῖτο δὲ καὶ Πέλλα ποτὲ ὑπὸ τῶν πρώτων Μακεδόνων διὰ τὸ τοὺς πλείους τῶν Μακεδόνων ἐνταῦθα οἰκῆσαι τῶν στρατευομένων, τὴν δὲ Πέλλαν ὥσπερ μητρόπολιν γεγονέναι τῶν Μακεδόνων, τὴν Φιλίππου καὶ Ἀλεξάνδρου πατρίδα. ἐνταῦθα δὲ καὶ τὸ λογιστήριον τὸ στρατιωτικὸν καὶ τὸ ἱπποτρόφιον· θήλειαι μὲν ἵπποι βασιλικαὶ πλείους τῶν τρισμυρίων, ὀχεῖα δὲ τούτων τριακόσια· ἐνταῦθα δὲ καὶ πωλοδάμναι καὶ ὁπλομάχοι καὶ ὅσοι παιδευταὶ τῶν πολεμικῶν ἐμισθοδοτοῦντο. δηλοῖ δὲ τὴν δύναμιν ταύτην ἥ τε τοῦ Τρύφωνος ἐπικληθέντος Διοδότου παραύξησις καὶ ἐπίθεσις τῇ βασιλείᾳ τῶν Σύρων, ἐντεῦθεν ὁρμη-

[1] Corais emends πόλιν to ἀκρόπολιν.
[2] The MSS. read λίμνη . . . καὶ ἔλη . . . διαχεομένους. Corais alters as above. Letronne conj. εἰς λίμνην; Kramer κατὰ λίμνην. B. Niese (*Emend. Str.* 14) would parenthesise λόφος . . . Ὀρόντης and emend λίμνη περικειμένη to λίμνην παρακειμένην: and so A. Vogel (*Philologus* 41, p. 32).

10. Apameia also has a city [1] that is in general well fortified; for it is a beautifully fortified hill in a hollow plain, and this hill is formed into a peninsula by the Orontes and by a large lake which lies near by and spreads into broad marshes and exceedingly large cattle-pasturing and horse-pasturing meadows.[2] So the city is thus securely situated; and so, too, it was called Cherronesus,[3] because of the fact in the case; and it is well supplied with a very large and fertile territory, through which the Orontes flows; and in this territory there are numerous dependent towns. Here, too, Seleucus Nicator kept the five hundred elephants and the greater part of the army, as did also the later kings. It was also called Pella at one time, by the first Macedonians, because the majority of the Macedonians who made the expedition took up their abode there, and because Pella, the native city of Philip and Alexander, had become, as it were, the metropolis of the Macedonians. Here, too, were the war-office and the royal stud. The royal stud consisted of more than thirty thousand mares and three hundred stallions. Here, too, were colt-breakers and instructors in heavy-armed warfare, and all instructors who were paid to teach the arts of war. The power of this city is clearly shown by the ascendency of Tryphon,[4] surnamed Diodotus, and by his attack upon the kingdom of the Syrians, when he made this city the base of his operations.

---

[1] For " city " Groskurd conjectures " acropolis."
[2] The text is corrupt (see critical note).
[3] Peninsula.
[4] Usurper of the throne of Syria, reigning 142–139 B.C.

---

[3] περιπόλια, Corais, for περιπολεῖ.

θέντος. ἐγεγένητο μὲν γὰρ ἐν Κασιανοῖς,[1] φρουρίῳ τινὶ τῆς Ἀπαμέων γῆς, τραφεὶς δ᾽ ἐν τῇ Ἀπαμείᾳ καὶ συσταθεὶς τῷ βασιλεῖ καὶ τοῖς περὶ αὐτόν, ἐπειδὴ νεωτερίζειν ὥρμησεν, ἐκ τῆς πόλεως ταύτης ἔσχε τὰς ἀφορμὰς καὶ τῶν περιοικίδων, Λαρίσης τε καὶ τῶν Κασιανῶν[2] καὶ Μεγάρων καὶ Ἀπολλωνίας καὶ ἄλλων τοιούτων, αἳ συνετέλουν εἰς τὴν Ἀπάμειαν ἅπασαι· ἐκεῖνός τε δὴ βασιλεὺς τῆσδε τῆς χώρας ἀνεδείχθη καὶ ἀντέσχε πολὺν χρόνον· Βάσσος τε Κεκίλιος μετὰ δυεῖν ταγμάτων ἀποστήσας τὴν Ἀπάμειαν διεκαρτέρησε τοσοῦτον χρόνον πολιορκούμενος ὑπὸ δυεῖν στρατοπέδων μεγάλων Ῥωμαϊκῶν, ὥστ᾽ οὐ πρότερον εἰς τὴν
C 753 ἐξουσίαν ἧκε, πρὶν ἑκὼν ἐνεχείρισεν ἑαυτόν, ἐφ᾽ οἷς ἐβεβούλητο· καὶ γὰρ τὴν στρατιὰν ἀπέτρεφεν ἡ χώρα καὶ συμμάχων εὐπόρει[3] τῶν πλησίον φυλάρχων, ἐχόντων εὐερκῆ χωρία· ὧν ἐστι καὶ ἡ Λυσίας, ὑπὲρ τῆς λίμνης κειμένη τῆς πρὸς Ἀπαμείᾳ, καὶ Ἀρέθουσα ἡ Σαμψικεράμου καὶ Ἰαμβλίχου, τοῦ ἐκείνου παιδός, φυλάρχων τοῦ Ἐμισηνῶν ἔθνους· οὐ πόρρω δ᾽ οὐδ᾽ Ἡλιούπολις καὶ Χαλκὶς ἡ ὑπὸ Πτολεμαίῳ τῷ Μενναίου, τῷ τὸν Μασσύαν[4] κατέχοντι καὶ τὴν Ἰτουραίων ὀρεινήν. τῶν δὲ συμμαχούντων τῷ Βάσσῳ ἦν καὶ Ἀλχαίδαμνος,[5] ὁ τῶν Ῥαμβαίων βασιλεὺς τῶν ἐντὸς τοῦ Εὐφράτου νομάδων· ἦν δὲ φίλος Ῥωμαίων, ἀδικεῖσθαι δὲ νομίσας ὑπὸ τῶν ἡγεμόνων, ἐκπεσὼν

---

[1] Κασιανοῖς, Groskurd, for Κοσιανοῖς.
[2] Κασιανῶν orz, Κασσιανῶν other MSS.
[3] ηὐπόρει Cmoxz.
[4] Μασσύαν Di, Μασίαν r, Μαρσύαν moxz (Polybius 5. 45. 61) and editors before Kramer.

For he was born at Casiana, a fortress of the Apameian country, and, having been reared at Apameia and closely associated with the king and the king's court, when he set out to effect a revolution, he got his resources from this city and also from its dependencies, I mean Larisa and Casiana and Megara and Apollonia and other places like them, all of which were tributary to Apameia. So Tryphon was proclaimed king of this country and held out for a long time. Cecilius [1] Bassus, with two cohorts, caused Apameia to revolt and, though besieged by two large Roman armies, strongly resisted them for so long a time that he did not come under their power until he voluntarily put himself in their hands upon his own terms; for the country supplied his army with provisions, and he had plenty of allies, I mean the neighbouring chieftains, who possessed strongholds; and among these places was Lysias, which is situated above the lake that lies near Apameia, as also Arethusa, belonging to Sampsiceramus and his son Iamblichus, chieftains of the tribe of the Emeseni; and at no great distance, also, were Heliupolis and Chalcis, which latter was subject to Ptolemaeus the son of Mennaeus, who possessed Massyas and the mountainous country of the Ituraeans. Among the allies of Bassus was also Alchaedamnus, king of the Rhambaeans, who were nomads this side the Euphrates River; and he was a friend of the Romans, but upon the belief that he was being treated unjustly by the Roman governors

---

[1] Apparently an error for " Caecilius."

---

[5] Ἀλχαίδαμνος Dmoz Ἀλχαυδόνιος Dio Cassius (47. 27).

εἰς τὴν Μεσοποταμίαν ἐμισθοφόρει τότε τῷ
Βάσσῳ. ἐντεῦθεν δ' ἐστὶ Ποσειδώνιος ὁ Στωικός,
ἀνὴρ τῶν καθ' ἡμᾶς φιλοσόφων πολυμαθέστατος.
11. Ὅμορος δ' ἐστὶ τῇ Ἀπαμέων πρὸς ἔω μὲν
ἡ τῶν φυλάρχων Ἀράβων καλουμένη Παραπο-
ταμία καὶ ἡ Χαλκιδικὴ ἀπὸ τοῦ Μασσύου[1]
καθήκουσα καὶ πᾶσα ἡ πρὸς νότον τοῖς Ἀπαμεῦ-
σιν, ἀνδρῶν Σκηνιτῶν τὸ πλέον· παραπλήσιοι
δ' εἰσὶ τοῖς ἐν τῇ Μεσοποταμίᾳ νομάσιν· ἀεὶ δ'
οἱ πλησιαίτεροι τοῖς Σύροις ἡμερώτεροι καὶ ἧττον
Ἄραβες καὶ Σκηνῖται, ἡγεμονίας ἔχοντες συν-
τεταγμένας μᾶλλον, καθάπερ ἡ Σαμψικεράμου[2]
Ἀρέθουσα καὶ ἡ Γαμβάρου καὶ ἡ[3] Θέμελλα καὶ
ἄλλων τοιούτων.
12. Τοιαύτη μὲν ἡ μεσόγαια τῆς Σελευκίδος,
ὁ δὲ παράπλους ὁ λοιπὸς ἀπὸ τῆς Λαοδικείας
ἐστὶ τοιοῦτος· τῇ γὰρ Λαοδικείᾳ πλησιάζει
πολίχνια, τό τε Ποσείδιον καὶ τὸ Ἡράκλειον καὶ
τὰ Γάβαλα· εἶτ' ἤδη ἡ τῶν Ἀραδίων παραλία,
Πάλτος καὶ Βαλαναία καὶ Κάρνος, τὸ ἐπίνειον τῆς
Ἀράδου λιμένιον ἔχον· εἶτ' Ἔνυδρα καὶ Μάραθος,
πόλις Φοινίκων ἀρχαία κατεσπασμένη. τὴν δὲ
χώραν Ἀράδιοι κατεκληρούχησαν καὶ τὰ Σίμυρα
τὸ ἐφεξῆς χωρίον· τούτοις δ' ἡ Ὀρθωσία συνεχής
ἐστι καὶ ὁ Ἐλεύθερος ὁ πλησίον ποταμός, ὅνπερ

---

[1] Μασσίου F, Μασίου i, Κοσσύου x, Μαρσύου moz.
[2] Σαμσικεράμου CD.
[3] καὶ ἡ, Casaubon, Corais, and Groskurd would delete,
making "Themella" the abode of Gambarus. C. Müller
conj. that Θέμελλα is an error for Θέλεδα, a place about 25
miles east of Arethusa.

---

[1] See critical note.

he retired to Mesopotamia and then went into the service of Bassus as a mercenary. Poseidonius, the Stoic, the most learned of all philosophers of my time, was a native of Apameia.

11. Bordering on the country of the Apameians, on the east, is the Paropotamia, as it is called, of the Arabian chieftains, as also Chalcidicê, which extends down from Massyas, and all the country to the south of the Apameians, which belongs for the most part to Scenitae. These Scenitae are similar to the nomads in Mesopotamia. And it is always the case that the peoples are more civilised in proportion to their proximity to the Syrians, and that the Arabians and Scenitae are less so, the former having governments that are better organised, as, for example, that of Arethusa under Sampsiceramus, and that of Gambarus, and that of Themellas,[1] and those of other chieftains like them.

12. Such is the interior of the territory of Seleuceia. But the remainder of the coast from Laodiceia is as follows: near Laodiceia are three towns, Poseidium and Heracleium and Gabala; and then forthwith one comes to the seaboard of the Aradians,[2] where are Paltus and Balanaea and Carnus, this last being the naval station of Aradus and having a harbour; and then to Enydra and Marathus, the latter an ancient city of the Phoenicians, now in ruins. Aradians divided up this country among themselves, as also Simyra, the place that comes next thereafter; and continuous with these places is Orthosia, as also Eleutherus, the river near by, which some writers make the boundary of the

[2] *i.e.* the seaboard on the *mainland* belonging to the Aradians, who inhabited the island called Aradus.

ὅριον ποιοῦνταί τινες Σελευκίδος πρὸς τὴν Φοινίκην καὶ τὴν Κοίλην Συρίαν.

13. Πρόκειται δ' ἡ Ἄραδος ῥαχιώδους τινὸς καὶ
ἀλιμένου παραλίας, μεταξὺ τοῦ τε ἐπινείου αὐτῆς
μάλιστα καὶ τῆς Μαράθου, διέχουσα τῆς γῆς σταδίους εἴκοσιν. ἔστι δὲ πέτρα περίκλυστος, ὅσον
ἑπτὰ τὸν κύκλον σταδίων, πλήρης κατοικίας·
τοσαύτῃ δ' εὐανδρίᾳ κέχρηται μέχρι καὶ νῦν, ὥστε
πολυορόφους οἰκοῦσι τὰς οἰκίας. ἔκτισαν δ'
αὐτὴν φυγάδες, ὥς φασιν, ἐκ Σιδόνος. τὴν δ'
ὑδρείαν τὴν μὲν ἐκ τῶν ὀμβρίων καὶ λακκαίων
C 754 ὑδάτων ἔχουσι, τὴν δ' ἐκ τῆς περαίας. ἐν δὲ τοῖς
πολέμοις ἐκ τοῦ πόρου μικρὸν πρὸ τῆς πόλεως
ὑδρεύονται, πηγὴν ἔχοντος ἀφθόνου ὕδατος· εἰς
ἣν περικαταστρέφεται κλίβανος, καθεθεὶς ἀπὸ
τοῦ ὑδρευομένου σκάφους, μολιβοῦς, εὐρύστομος,
εἰς πυθμένα συνηγμένος στενόν, ἔχοντα τρῆμα
μέτριον· τῷ δὲ πυθμένι περιέσφιγκται σωλὴν
σκύτινος, εἴτε ἄσκωμα δεῖ λέγειν, ὁ δεχόμενος
τὸ ἀναθλιβόμενον ἐκ τῆς πηγῆς διὰ τοῦ κλιβάνου
ὕδωρ. τὸ μὲν οὖν πρῶτον ἀναθλιβὲν τὸ τῆς
θαλάττης ἐστί· περιμείναντες δὲ τὴν τοῦ καθαροῦ
καὶ ποτίμου ὕδατος ῥύσιν, ὑπολαμβάνουσιν εἰς
ἀγγεῖα παρεσκευασμένα, ὅσον ἂν δέῃ, καὶ πορθ-
μεύουσιν εἰς τὴν πόλιν.

14. Τὸ παλαιὸν μὲν οὖν οἱ Ἀράδιοι καθ' αὑτοὺς
ἐβασιλεύοντο παραπλησίως ὥσπερ καὶ τῶν
ἄλλων ἑκάστη πόλεων τῶν Φοινικίδων· ἔπειτα
τὰ μὲν οἱ Πέρσαι, τὰ δ' οἱ Μακεδόνες, τὰ δὲ νῦν
Ῥωμαῖοι μετέθηκαν εἰς τὴν παροῦσαν τάξιν. οἱ
δ' οὖν Ἀράδιοι μετὰ τῶν ἄλλων Φοινίκων ὑπή-

territory of Seleuceia on the side towards Phoenicia and Coelê-Syria.

13. Aradus lies off a surfy and harbourless seaboard; it lies approximately between its naval station and Marathus, and is twenty stadia distant from the mainland. It consists of a rock washed all round by the sea, is about seven stadia in circuit, and is full of dwellings; and it has had such a large population, even down to the present time, that the people live in houses with many stories. It was founded, as they say, by exiles from Sidon. They get their water-supply partly from the rains and cisterns and partly from their territory on the mainland. In war-times they get water from the channel at a short distance in front of the city. This channel has an abundant spring; and into this spring the people let down from the water-fetching boat an inverted, wide-mouthed funnel made of lead, the upper part of which contracts into a stem with a moderate-sized hole through it; and round this stem they fasten a leathern tube (unless I should call it bellows), which receives the water that is forced up from the spring through the funnel. Now the first water that is forced up is sea-water, but the boatmen wait for the flow of pure and potable water and catch all that is needed in vessels prepared for the purpose and carry it to the city.

14. Now in ancient times the Aradians were governed independently by kings, as was also the case with each of the other Phoenician cities; but afterwards the Persians, and then the Macedonians, and to-day the Romans, have reduced them to their present order of government. The Aradians, however, together with the other Phoenicians, subjected

κουον τῶν Συριακῶν βασιλέων, ἅτε φίλων·
ἔπειτα στασιασάντων ἀδελφῶν δυεῖν, τοῦ τε
Καλλινίκου Σελεύκου καὶ 'Αντιόχου τοῦ 'Ιέρακος
προσαγορευθέντος, προσθέμενοι τῷ Καλλινίκῳ
ποιοῦνται συμβάσεις, ὥστ' ἐξεῖναι δέχεσθαι τοὺς
καταφεύγοντας ἐκ τῆς βασιλείας παρ' αὐτούς, καὶ
μὴ ἐκδιδόναι ἄκοντας· μὴ μέντοι μηδ' ἐκπλεῖν ἐᾶν
ἄνευ τοῦ ἐπιτρέψαι βασιλέα. συνέβη δὲ ἐκ τούτου μεγάλα αὐτοῖς πλεονεκτήματα· οἱ γὰρ κατα-
φεύγοντες ἐπ' αὐτοὺς οὐχ οἱ τυχόντες ἦσαν, ἀλλ'
οἱ τὰ μέγιστα πεπιστευμένοι καὶ περὶ τῶν μεγίστων δεδιότες· ἐπιξενούμενοι δ' αὐτοῖς εὐεργέτας
ἡγοῦντο καὶ σωτῆρας τοὺς ὑποδεξαμένους, ἀπε-
μνημόνευόν τε τὴν χάριν, καὶ μάλιστα ἐπανελ-
θόντες εἰς τὴν οἰκείαν· ὥστ' ἐκ τούτου χώραν τε
ἐκτήσαντο τῆς περαίας πολλήν, ἧς τὴν πλείστην
ἔχουσι καὶ νῦν, καὶ τἆλλα εὐθήνουν. προσέθεσαν
δὲ τῇ εὐτυχίᾳ ταύτῃ καὶ πρόνοιαν καὶ φιλο-
πονίαν πρὸς τὴν θαλαττουργίαν· ὁρῶντές τε τοὺς
γειτονεύοντας Κίλικας τὰ πειρατήρια συνιστα-
μένους οὐδ' ἅπαξ ἐκοινώνουν αὐτοῖς τῆς τοιαύτης
ἐπιτηδεύσεως.

15. Μετὰ δὲ 'Ορθωσίαν ἐστὶ καὶ τὸν 'Ελεύθερον
Τρίπολις, ἀπὸ τοῦ συμβεβηκότος τὴν ἐπίκλησιν
εἰληφυῖα· τριῶν γάρ ἐστι πόλεων κτίσμα, Τύρου,
Σιδόνος, 'Αράδου· τῇ δὲ Τριπόλει συνεχές ἐστι τὸ
τοῦ Θεοῦ πρόσωπον, εἰς ὃ τελευτᾷ ὁ Λίβανος τὸ
ὄρος· μεταξὺ δὲ Τριήρης, χωρίον τι.

16. Δύο δὲ ταῦτ' ἐστὶν ὄρη τὰ ποιοῦντα τὴν

---

[1] "Tri-city."
[2] "Face-of-God."

themselves to the Syrian kings as friends of theirs; and then, when a quarrel broke out between two brothers, Callinicus Seleucus and Antiochus Hierax, as he was called, the Aradians joined with Callinicus and made an agreement with him whereby they were to be permitted to receive refugees from the kingdom and not to give them up against their will; they were not, however, to permit refugees to sail from the island without permission from the king. From this agreement they got great advantages; for those who fled for refuge to their country were not ordinary people, but men who had held the highest trusts and were in fear of the direst consequences; and, being received as guests, they regarded their hosts as their benefactors and saviours, and requited the favour, in particular when they went back to their homeland; and it is from this fact, therefore, that the Aradians got possession of a considerable territory on the mainland, most of which they hold even at present, and otherwise have prospered. To this good fortune they added both prudence and industry in their maritime affairs; and when they saw that the neighbouring Cilicians were organising piratical adventures they would not even once take part with them in a business of that kind.

15. After Orthosia and the Eleutherus River one comes to Tripolis,[1] which has taken its name from what is the fact in the case, for it is a foundation consisting of three cities, Tyre and Sidon and Aradus. Contiguous to Tripolis is Theuprosopon,[2] where Mt. Libanus terminates; and between the two lies Trieres, a kind of stronghold.

16. Here are two mountains, Libanus and Antili-

Κοίλην καλουμένην Συρίαν,[1] ὡς ἂν παράλληλα, ὅ
τε Λίβανος καὶ ὁ Ἀντιλίβανος, μικρὸν ὕπερθεν
C 755 τῆς θαλάττης ἀρχόμενα ἄμφω· ὁ μὲν Λίβανος τῆς
κατὰ Τρίπολιν, κατὰ τὸ τοῦ Θεοῦ μάλιστα πρόσωπον, ὁ δ' Ἀντιλίβανος τῆς κατὰ Σιδόνα·
τελευτῶσι δ' ἐγγύς πως τῶν Ἀραβίων ὀρῶν
τῶν ὑπὲρ τῆς Δαμασκηνῆς καὶ τῶν Τραχώνων[2]
ἐκεῖ λεγομένων εἰς ἄλλα ὄρη γεώλοφα καὶ
καλλίκαρπα. ἀπολείπουσι δὲ μεταξὺ πεδίον
κοῖλον· πλάτος μὲν τὸ ἐπὶ τῇ θαλάττῃ διακοσίων σταδίων, μῆκος δὲ τὸ ἀπὸ τῆς θαλάττης εἰς
τὴν μεσόγαιαν ὁμοῦ[3] τι διπλάσιον. διαρρεῖται
δὲ ποταμοῖς ἄρδουσι χώραν εὐδαίμονα καὶ πάμ-
φορον, μεγίστῳ δὲ τῷ Ἰορδάνῃ. ἔχει δὲ καὶ
λίμνην, ἣ φέρει τὴν ἀρωματῖτιν σχοῖνον[4] καὶ
κάλαμον, ὡς δ' αὕτως καὶ ἕλη· καλεῖται δ' ἡ
λίμνη Γεννησαρῖτις. φέρει δὲ καὶ βάλσαμον.
τῶν δὲ ποταμῶν ὁ μὲν Χρυσορρόας, ἀρξάμενος
ἀπὸ τῆς Δαμασκηνῶν πόλεως καὶ χώρας, εἰς τὰς
ὀχετείας ἀναλίσκεται σχεδόν τι· πολλὴν γὰρ
ἐπάρδει καὶ βαθεῖαν σφόδρα·[5] τὸν δὲ Λύκον καὶ
τὸν Ἰορδάνην ἀναπλέουσι φορτίοις, Ἀράδιοι δὲ
μάλιστα.

17. Τῶν δὲ πεδίων τὸ μὲν πρῶτον, τὸ ἀπὸ
τῆς θαλάττης, Μάκρας καλεῖται καὶ Μάκρα
πεδίον· ἐν τούτῳ δὲ Ποσειδώνιος ἱστορεῖ τὸν
δράκοντα πεπτωκότα ὁραθῆναι νεκρόν, μῆκος[6]

---

[1] Συρίαν FE, Γωνίαν and Γονίαν other MSS. and in margin
of F.

[2] Τραχώνων, Tzschucke, for Τραχανῶν.

[3] Instead of ὁμοῦ, E reads σχεδόν.

[4] σχοῖνον ("rush"), Tzschucke and Corais emend to σχῖνον
(the mastich-tree).

banus, which form Coelê-Syria, as it is called, and
are approximately parallel to each other. They
both begin slightly above the sea—Libanus above
the sea near Tripolis and nearest to Theuprosopon,
and Antilibanus above the sea near Sidon; and
somewhere in the neighbourhood of the Arabian
mountains above Damascenê and the Trachones,[1]
as they are called, the two mountains terminate in
other mountains that are hilly and fruitful. They
leave a hollow plain between them, the breadth of
which, near the sea, is two hundred stadia, and the
length, from the sea into the interior, is about twice
that number. It is intersected by rivers, the Jordan
being the largest, which water a country that is
fertile and all-productive. It also contains a lake,
which produces the aromatic rush [2] and reed; and
likewise marshes. The lake is called Gennesaritis.
The plain also produces balsam. Among the rivers
is the Chrysorrhoas, which begins at the city and
country of the Damasceni and is almost wholly
used up in the conduits, for it irrigates a large
territory that has a very deep soil; but the Lycus
and the Jordan are navigated inland with vessels
of burden, mostly by the Aradians.

17. As for the plains, the first, beginning at the
sea, is called Macras, or Macra-Plain. Here, as
reported by Poseidonius, was seen the fallen dragon,

[1] " Trachones " means " Rugged, strong tracts " (see
16. 2. 20).
[2] See critical note.

---

[5] Instead of σφόδρα, E reads χθόνα.
[6] After μῆκος Dhi read μέν ; so Corais.

σχεδόν τι καὶ πλεθριαῖον, πάχος δ᾽, ὥσθ᾽
ἱππέας ἑκατέρωθεν παραστάντας ἀλλήλους μὴ
καθορᾶν, χάσμα δέ, ὥστ᾽ ἔφιππον δέξασθαι,
τῆς δὲ φολίδος λεπίδα ἑκάστην ὑπεραίρουσαν
θυρεοῦ.

18. Μετὰ δὲ τὸν Μάκραν ἐστὶν ὁ Μασσύας,
ἔχων τινὰ καὶ ὀρεινά, ἐν οἷς ἡ Χαλκίς, ὥσπερ
ἀκρόπολις τοῦ Μασσύου· ἀρχὴ δ᾽ αὐτοῦ Λαοδίκεια ἡ πρὸς Λιβάνῳ. τὰ μὲν οὖν ὀρεινὰ ἔχουσι
πάντα Ἰτουραῖοί τε καὶ Ἄραβες, κακοῦργοι
πάντες, οἱ δ᾽ ἐν τοῖς πεδίοις γεωργοί· κακούμενοι
δ᾽ ὑπ᾽ ἐκείνων ἄλλοτε ἄλλης βοηθείας δέονται.
ὁρμητηρίοις δ᾽ ἐρυμνοῖς χρῶνται, καθάπερ οἱ
τὸν Λίβανον ἔχοντες ἄνω μὲν ἐν τῷ ὄρει Σιννᾶν,
καὶ Βόρραμα καὶ ἄλλα τοιαῦτα ἔχουσι τείχη,
κάτω δὲ Βότρυν καὶ Γίγαρτον καὶ τὰ ἐπὶ τῆς
θαλάττης σπήλαια καὶ τὸ ἐπὶ τῷ Θεοῦ προ-
σώπῳ φρούριον ἐπιτεθέν, ἃ κατέσπασε Πομπήιος, ἀφ᾽ ὧν τήν τε Βύβλον κατέτρεχον[1] καὶ
τὴν ἐφεξῆς ταύτῃ Βηρυτόν, αἱ μεταξὺ κεῖνται
Σιδόνος καὶ τοῦ Θεοῦ προσώπου. ἡ μὲν οὖν
Βύβλος, τὸ τοῦ Κινύρου βασίλειον, ἱερά ἐστι
τοῦ Ἀδώνιδος· ἣν τυραννουμένην ἠλευθέρωσε
Πομπήιος πελεκίσας ἐκεῖνον· κεῖται δ᾽ ἐφ᾽ ὕψους
τινὸς μικρὸν ἄπωθεν τῆς θαλάττης.

19. Εἶτα μετὰ ταύτην Ἄδωνις ποταμὸς καὶ
ὄρος Κλῖμαξ καὶ Παλαίβυβλος· εἶθ᾽ ὁ Λύκος
C 756 ποταμὸς καὶ Βηρυτός· αὕτη δὲ κατεσπάσθη μὲν
ὑπὸ Τρύφωνος, ἀνελήφθη δὲ νῦν ὑπὸ Ῥωμαίων,

---

[1] κατέτρεχον F, κατέτρεχε other MSS.

---

[1] About 100 feet.   [2] Now Beyrout.

the corpse of which was about a plethrum[1] in length, and so bulky that horsemen standing by it on either side could not see one another; and its jaws were large enough to admit a man on horseback, and each flake of its horny scales exceeded an oblong shield in length.

18. After Macras one comes to the Massyas Plain, which contains also some mountainous parts, among which is Chalcis, the acropolis, as it were, of the Massyas. The beginning of this plain is the Laodiceia near Libanus. Now all the mountainous parts are held by Ituraeans and Arabians, all of whom are robbers, but the people in the plains are farmers; and when the latter are harassed by the robbers at different times they require different kinds of help. These robbers use strongholds as bases of operation; those, for example, who hold Libanus possess, high up on the mountain, Sinna and Borrama and other fortresses like them, and, down below, Botrys and Gigartus and the caves by the sea and the castle that was erected on Theuprosopon. Pompey destroyed these places; and from them the robbers overran both Byblus and the city that comes next after Byblus, I mean the city Berytus,[2] which lie between Sidon and Theuprosopon. Now Byblus, the royal residence of Cinyras, is sacred to Adonis; but Pompey freed it from tyranny by beheading its tyrant with an axe; and it is situated on a height only a slight distance from the sea.

19. Then, after Byblus, one comes to the Adonis River and to Mt. Climax and to Palaebyblus; and then to the Lycus River and Berytus. But though Berytus was razed to the ground by Tryphon, it has now been restored by the Romans; and it

δεξαμένη δύο τάγματα, ἃ ἵδρυσεν Ἀγρίππας
ἐνταῦθα, προσθεὶς καὶ τοῦ Μασσύου πολλὴν
μέχρι καὶ τῶν τοῦ Ὀρόντου πηγῶν, αἳ πλησίον
τοῦ τε Λιβάνου καὶ τοῦ Παραδείσου καὶ τοῦ
Αἰγυπτίου τείχους περὶ τὴν Ἀπαμέων γῆν εἰσι,
ταῦτα μὲν οὖν τὰ ἐπὶ θαλάττῃ.

20. Ὑπὲρ δὲ τοῦ Μασσύου ἐστὶν ὁ καλούμενος
Αὐλὼν βασιλικὸς καὶ ἡ Δαμασκηνὴ χώρα,
διαφερόντως ἐπαινουμένη· ἔστι δὲ καὶ ἡ Δα-
μασκὸς πόλις ἀξιόλογος, σχεδόν τι καὶ ἐπιφα-
νεστάτη τῶν ταύτῃ κατὰ τὰ Περσικά· ὑπέρκεινται
δ' αὐτῆς δύο λεγόμενοι Τράχωνες· ἔπειτα πρὸς
τὰ Ἀράβων μέρη καὶ τῶν Ἰτουραίων ἀναμὶξ
ὄρη δύσβατα, ἐν οἷς καὶ σπήλαια βαθύστομα,
ὧν ἓν καὶ τετρακισχιλίους ἀνθρώπους δέξασθαι
δυνάμενον ἐν καταδρομαῖς, αἳ τοῖς Δαμασκηνοῖς
γίνονται πολλαχόθεν. τὸ μέντοι πλέον τοὺς
ἀπὸ τῆς εὐδαίμονος Ἀραβίας ἐμπόρους λεηλα-
τοῦσιν οἱ βάρβαροι· ἧττον δὲ συμβαίνει κατα-
λυθέντων νυνὶ τῶν περὶ Ζηνόδωρον λῃστῶν διὰ
τὴν ἐκ τῶν Ῥωμαίων εὐνομίαν καὶ διὰ τὴν ἐκ
τῶν στρατιωτῶν ἀσφάλειαν τῶν ἐν τῇ Συρίᾳ
τρεφομένων.

21. Ἅπασα μὲν οὖν ἡ ὑπὲρ τῆς Σελευκίδος
ὡς ἐπὶ τὴν Αἴγυπτον καὶ τὴν Ἀραβίαν ἀνί-
σχουσα χώρα Κοίλη Συρία καλεῖται, ἰδίως δ'
ἡ τῷ Λιβάνῳ καὶ τῷ Ἀντιλιβάνῳ ἀφωρισμένη.
τῆς δὲ λοιπῆς ἡ μὲν ἀπὸ Ὀρθωσίας μέχρι
Πηλουσίου παραλία Φοινίκη καλεῖται, στενή τις

---

[1] See 16. 2. 16 and footnote.
[2] i.e. the remainder of Coelê-Syria in the broad sense of
the term.

received two legions, which were settled there by Agrippa, who also added to it much of the territory of Massyas, as far as the sources of the Orontes River. These sources are near Mt. Libanus and Paradeisus and the Aegyptian fortress situated in the neighbourhood of the land of the Apameians. So much, then, for the places on the sea.

20. Above Massyas lies the Royal Valley, as it is called, and also the Damascene country, which is accorded exceptional praise. The city Damascus is also a noteworthy city, having been, I might almost say, even the most famous of the cities in that part of the world in the time of the Persian empire; and above it are situated two Trachones,[1] as they are called. And then, towards the parts inhabited promiscuously by Arabians and Ituraeans, are mountains hard to pass, in which there are deep-mouthed caves, one of which can admit as many as four thousand people in times of incursions, such as are made against the Damasceni from many places. For the most part, indeed, the barbarians have been robbing the merchants from Arabia Felix, but this is less the case now that the band of robbers under Zenodorus has been broken up through the good government established by the Romans and through the security established by the Roman soldiers that are kept in Syria.

21. Now the whole of the country above the territory of Seleuceia, extending approximately to Aegypt and Arabia, is called Coelê-Syria; but the country marked off by the Libanus and the Antilibanus is called by that name in a special sense. Of the remainder[2] the seaboard from Orthosia to Pelusium is called Phoenicia, which is a narrow

καὶ ἀλιτενής, ἡ δ' ὑπὲρ ταύτης μεσόγαια μέχρι
τῶν Ἀράβων ἡ μεταξὺ Γάζης καὶ Ἀντιλιβάνου
Ἰουδαία λέγεται.

22. Ἐπεὶ οὖν τὴν ἰδίως λεγομένην Κοίλην
Συρίαν ἐπεληλύθαμεν, ἐπὶ τὴν Φοινίκην μέτιμεν·
ταύτης δὲ τὰ μὲν ἀπὸ Ὀρθωσίας μέχρι Βηρυτοῦ
λόγου τετύχηκε· μετὰ δὲ Βηρυτόν ἐστι Σιδὼν
ὅσον ἐν τετρακοσίοις[1] σταδίοις· μεταξὺ δὲ ὁ
Ταμύρας ποταμὸς καὶ τὸ τοῦ Ἀσκληπιοῦ ἄλσος
καὶ Λεόντων πόλις. μετὰ δὲ Σιδόνα μεγίστη
τῶν Φοινίκων καὶ ἀρχαιοτάτη Τύρος ἐστίν, ἡ[2]
ἐνάμιλλος αὐτῇ κατά τε μέγεθος καὶ κατὰ τὴν
ἐπιφάνειαν καὶ τὴν ἀρχαιότητα ἐκ πολλῶν μύθων
παραδεδομένην.[3] οἱ μὲν οὖν ποιηταὶ τὴν Σιδόνα
τεθρυλήκασι μᾶλλον (Ὅμηρος δὲ οὐδὲ μέμνηται
τῆς Τύρου), αἱ δ' εἰς τὴν Λιβύην καὶ τὴν Ἰβηρίαν
ἀποικίαι μέχρι καὶ ἔξω Στηλῶν τὴν Τύρον πλέον
ἐξυμνοῦσι.[4] ἀμφότεραι δ' οὖν ἔνδοξοι καὶ λαμπ-
ραὶ καὶ πάλαι καὶ νῦν· ὁποτέραν δ' ἄν τις εἴποι
μητρόπολιν Φοινίκων, ἔρις ἐν ἀμφοτέραις ἐστίν.
ἡ μὲν οὖν Σιδὼν ἐπὶ εὐφνεῖ λιμένι τῆς ἠπείρου τὴν
ἵδρυσιν ἔχει.

23. Τύρος δ' ἐστὶν ὅλη νῆσος σχεδόν τι συνῳ-
κισμένη παραπλησίως, ὥσπερ ἡ Ἄραδος, συνῆπται
C 757 δὲ χώματι πρὸς τὴν ἤπειρον, ὃ κατεσκεύασε
πολιορκῶν Ἀλέξανδρος· δύο δ' ἔχει λιμένας, τὸν

---

[1] τετρακοσίοις (ν') clearly seems to be an error for διακοσίοις (σ').

[2] ἡ is omitted by Corais and Meineke.

[3] παραδεδομένην, Corais, for παραδεδομένη; so the later editors.

[4] μᾶλλον, after ἐξυμνοῦσι, is omitted by Exz, Corais, and Meineke.

country and lies flat along the sea, whereas the interior above Phoenicia, as far as the Arabians, between Gaza and Antilibanus, is called Judaea.

22. Since, then, I have traversed Coelê-Syria in the special sense of that name, I shall pass on to Phoenicia. Of this country, I have already described the parts extending from Orthosia to Berytus; and after Berytus one comes to Sidon, at a distance of about four hundred [1] stadia; but between the two places are the Tamyras River and the grove of Asclepius and a city of Leones.[2] After Sidon one comes to Tyre, the largest and oldest city of the Phoenicians, which rivals Sidon, not only in size, but also in its fame and antiquity, as handed down to us in numerous myths. Now although the poets have referred more repeatedly to Sidon than to Tyre (Homer does not even mention Tyre), yet the colonies sent into Libya and Iberia,[3] as far even as outside the Pillars, hymn rather the praises of Tyre. At any rate, both cities have been famous and illustrious, both in early times and at the present time; and no matter which of the two one might call the metropolis of the Phoenicians, there is a dispute in both cities. Now Sidon is situated on the mainland near a harbour that is by nature a good one.

23. But Tyre is wholly an island, being built up nearly in the same way as Aradus; and it is connected with the mainland by a mole, which was constructed by Alexander when he was besieging it; and it has two harbours, one that can be closed

---

[1] Apparently an error for "two hundred."
[2] i.e. of "Lions." Cf. the "Leontopolis" in Aegypt (17. 1. 19), where the inhabitants worshipped a lion (17. 1. 40).
[3] e.g. Carthage and Gadeira.

μὲν κλειστόν, τὸν δ' ἀνειμένον, ὃν Αἰγύπτιον
καλοῦσιν. ἐνταῦθα δέ φασι πολυστέγους τὰς
οἰκίας ὥστε καὶ τῶν ἐν Ῥώμῃ μᾶλλον· διὸ
καὶ σεισμοὺς γενομένους[1] ἀπολιπεῖν μικρὸν
τοῦ ἄρδην ἀφανίσαι τὴν πόλιν. ἠτύχησε
δὲ καὶ ὑπ' Ἀλεξάνδρου πολιορκίᾳ ληφθεῖσα·
ἀλλὰ τῶν τοιούτων συμφορῶν κατέστη κρείττων
καὶ ἀνέλαβεν αὐτὴν τῇ τε ναυτιλίᾳ, καθ' ἣν
ἁπάντων τῶν ἀεὶ κρείττους εἰσὶ κοινῇ Φοίνικες,
καὶ τοῖς πορφυρείοις· πολὺ γὰρ ἐξήτασται πασῶν
ἡ Τυρία καλλίστη πορφύρα· καὶ ἡ θήρα πλησίον
καὶ τἆλλα εὔπορα τὰ πρὸς βαφὴν ἐπιτήδεια· καὶ
δυσδιάγωγον μὲν ποιεῖ τὴν πόλιν ἡ πολυπληθία
τῶν βαφείων, πλουσίαν δὲ διὰ τὴν τοιαύτην
ἀνδρείαν. οὐχ ὑπὸ τῶν βασιλέων δ' ἐκρίθησαν
αὐτόνομοι μόνον, ἀλλὰ καὶ ὑπὸ τῶν Ῥωμαίων
μικρὰ ἀναλώσαντες, βεβαιωσάντων τὴν ἐκείνων
γνώμην. τιμᾶται δὲ καθ' ὑπερβολὴν Ἡρακλῆς
ὑπ' αὐτῶν. τῆς δὲ περὶ τὰς ναυστολίας[2] δυνάμεως τὸ πλῆθος καὶ τὸ μέγεθος τῶν ἀποικίδων
ἐστὶ πόλεων τεκμήριον· οὗτοι μὲν οὖν τοιοῦτοι.

24. Σιδόνιοι δὲ πολύτεχνοί τινες παραδέδονται
καὶ καλλίτεχνοι, καθάπερ καὶ ὁ ποιητὴς δηλοῖ·
πρὸς δὲ καὶ φιλόσοφοι περί τε ἀστρονομίαν καὶ
ἀριθμητικήν, ἀπὸ τῆς λογιστικῆς ἀρξάμενοι καὶ
τῆς νυκτιπλοίας· ἐμπορικὸν γὰρ καὶ ναυκληρικὸν
ἑκάτερον· καθάπερ καὶ τῶν Αἰγυπτίων εὕρεμα

---

[1] moxz read σεισμῶν γενομένων.
[2] ναυστολίας, the editors, for ναυστολογίας.

---

[1] See 5. 3. 7.
[2] The Phoenician Melcharth.

and the other, called " Aegyptian " harbour, open.
The houses here, it is said, have many stories, even
more than the houses at Rome,[1] and on this account,
when an earthquake took place, it lacked but little
of utterly wiping out the city. The city was also
unfortunate when it was taken by siege by Alexander; but it overcame such misfortunes and restored
itself both by means of the seamanship of its people,
in which the Phoenicians in general have been
superior to all peoples of all times, and by means of
their dye-houses for purple; for the Tyrian purple
has proved itself by far the most beautiful of all;
and the shell-fish are caught near the coast; and
the other things requisite for dyeing are easily got;
and although the great number of dye-works makes
the city unpleasant to live in, yet it makes the city
rich through the superior skill of its inhabitants.
The Tyrians were adjudged autonomous, not only
by the kings, but also, at small expense to them, by
the Romans, when the Romans confirmed the decree
of the kings. Heracles [2] is paid extravagant honours
by them. The number and the size of their colonial
cities is an evidence of their power in maritime
affairs. Such, then, are the Tyrians.

24. The Sidonians, according to tradition, are
skilled in many beautiful arts, as the poet also
points out; [3] and besides this they are philosophers
in the sciences of astronomy and arithmetic, having
begun their studies with practical calculations and
with night-sailings; for each of these branches of
knowledge concerns the merchant and the ship-
owner; as, for example, geometry was invented, it

[3] "Since the Sidonians, skilled in cunning handiwork had
wrought it (the silver mixing bowl) well " (*Iliad* 23. 743).

γεωμετρίαν φασὶν ἀπὸ τῆς χωρομετρίας, ἣν ὁ
Νεῖλος ἀπεργάζεται, συγχέων τοὺς ὅρους κατὰ
τὰς ἀναβάσεις. τοῦτο μὲν οὖν παρ' Αἰγυπτίων
ἥκειν εἰς τοὺς Ἕλληνας πεπιστεύκασιν, ἀστρονομίαν δὲ καὶ ἀριθμητικὴν παρὰ Φοινίκων· νυνὶ
δὲ πάσης καὶ τῆς ἄλλης φιλοσοφίας εὐπορίαν
πολὺ πλείστην λαβεῖν ἔστιν ἐκ τούτων τῶν
πόλεων· εἰ δὲ δεῖ Ποσειδωνίῳ πιστεῦσαι, καὶ
τὸ περὶ τῶν ἀτόμων δόγμα παλαιόν ἐστιν ἀνδρὸς
Σιδονίου Μώχου πρὸ τῶν Τρωικῶν χρόνων
γεγονότος. τὰ μὲν οὖν παλαιὰ ἐάσθω· καθ' ἡμᾶς
δὲ ἐκ Σιδόνος μὲν ἔνδοξοι φιλόσοφοι γεγόνασι
Βοηθός τε, ᾧ συνεφιλοσοφήσαμεν ἡμεῖς τὰ
Ἀριστοτέλεια, καὶ Διόδοτος, ἀδελφὸς αὐτοῦ· ἐκ
Τύρου δὲ Ἀντίπατρος, καὶ μικρὸν πρὸ ἡμῶν
Ἀπολλώνιος ὁ τὸν πίνακα ἐκθεὶς τῶν ἀπὸ Ζήνω-
νος φιλοσόφων καὶ τῶν βιβλίων. διέχει δὲ τῆς
Σιδόνος ἡ Τύρος οὐ πλείους τῶν διακοσίων στα-
C 758 δίων· ἐν δὲ τῷ μεταξὺ πολίχνιον, Ὀρνίθων πόλις
λεγομένη· εἶτα πρὸς Τύρῳ ποταμὸς ἐξίησι· μετὰ
δὲ τὴν Τύρον ἡ Παλαίτυρος ἐν τριάκοντα σταδίοις.

25. Εἶθ' ἡ Πτολεμαΐς ἐστι μεγάλη πόλις, ἣν
Ἄκην ὠνόμαζον πρότερον· ᾗ ἐχρῶντο ὁρμητηρίῳ
πρὸς τὴν Αἴγυπτον οἱ Πέρσαι. μεταξὺ δὲ τῆς
Ἄκης καὶ Τύρου θινώδης αἰγιαλός ἐστιν ὁ φέρων
τὴν ὑαλῖτιν ἄμμον. ἐνταῦθα μὲν οὖν φασι μὴ
χεῖσθαι, κομισθεῖσαν εἰς Σιδόνα δὲ τὴν χωνείαν
δέχεσθαι· τινὲς δὲ καὶ τοῖς Σιδονίοις εἶναι τὴν

---

[1] Cf. 17. 1. 3.
[2] Whether Strabo and Boethus studied together under

is said, from the measurement of lands which is made necessary by the Nile when it confounds the boundaries at the time of its overflows.[1] This science, then, is believed to have come to the Greeks from the Aegyptians; astronomy and arithmetic from the Phoenicians; and at present by far the greatest store of knowledge in every other branch of philosophy is to be had from these cities. And if one must believe Poseidonius, the ancient dogma about atoms originated with Mochus, a Sidonian, born before the Trojan times. However, let us dismiss things ancient. In my time there have been famous philosophers from Sidon; Boethus, with whom I studied the Aristotelian philosophy,[2] and his brother Diodotus; and from Tyre, Antipater, and, a little before my time, Apollonius, who published a tabulated account of the philosophers of the school of Zeno and of their books. Tyre is distant from Sidon not more than two hundred stadia; and between them lies a town called City of Ornithes;[3] and then one comes to a river which empties near Tyre, and after Tyre, to Palae-Tyre,[4] at a distance of thirty stadia.

25. Then one comes to Ptolemaïs, a large city, in earlier times named Acê; this city was used by the Persians as a base of operations against Aegypt. Between Acê and Tyre is a sandy beach, which produces the sand used in making glass. Now the sand, it is said, is not fused here, but is carried to Sidon and there melted and cast. Some say that the Sidonians, among others, have the glass-sand

Andronicus of Rhodes (see 14. 2. 13), or under Xenarchus of Seleuceia in Cilicia (see 14. 5. 4), or both, is uncertain.
[3] Ornithopolis, "City of Birds."   [4] Old Tyre.

ὑαλῖτιν ψάμμον ἐπιτηδείαν εἰς χύσιν, οἱ δὲ πᾶσαν
πανταχοῦ χεῖσθαί[1] φασιν. ἤκουσα δ' ἐν τῇ
Ἀλεξανδρείᾳ παρὰ τῶν ὑαλουργῶν, εἶναί τινα
καὶ κατ' Αἴγυπτον ὑαλῖτιν γῆν, ἧς χωρὶς οὐχ
οἷόν τε τὰς πολυχρόους καὶ πολυτελεῖς κατα-
σκευὰς ἀποτελεσθῆναι, καθάπερ καὶ ἄλλοις
ἄλλων μιγμάτων δεῖν· καὶ ἐν Ῥώμῃ δὲ πολλὰ
παρευρίσκεσθαί φασι καὶ πρὸς τὰς χρόας καὶ
πρὸς τὴν ῥᾳστώνην τῆς κατασκευῆς, καθάπερ ἐπὶ
τῶν κρυσταλλοφανῶν· ὅπου γε καὶ τρυβλίον
χαλκοῦ πρίασθαι καὶ ἐκπωμάτιον ἔστιν.

26. Ἱστορεῖται δὲ παράδοξον πάθος τῶν πάνυ
σπανίων, κατὰ τὸν αἰγιαλὸν τοῦτον τὸν μεταξὺ
τῆς τε Τύρου καὶ τῆς Πτολεμαΐδος. καθ' ὃν γὰρ
καιρὸν οἱ Πτολεμαεῖς, μάχην συνάψαντες πρὸς
Σαρπηδόνα τὸν στρατηγόν, ἐλείφθησαν[2] ἐν τῷ
τόπῳ τούτῳ, τροπῆς γενομένης λαμπρᾶς, ἐπέκλυ-
σεν ἐκ τοῦ πελάγους κῦμα τοὺς φεύγοντας ὅμοιον
πλημμυρίδι, καὶ τοὺς μὲν εἰς τὸ πέλαγος ἀφήρ-
πασε καὶ διέφθειρεν, οἱ δ' ἐν τοῖς κοίλοις τόποις
ἔμειναν νεκροί· διαδεξαμένη δὲ ἡ ἄμπωτις πάλιν
ἀνεκάλυψε καὶ ἔδειξε τὰ σώματα τῶν κειμένων
ἀναμὶξ ἐν νεκροῖς ἰχθύσι. τοιαῦτα δὲ καὶ περὶ
τὸ Κάσιον συμβαίνει τὸ πρὸς Αἰγύπτῳ, σπασμῷ
τινι ὀξεῖ καὶ ἁπλῷ[3] περιπιπτούσης τῆς γῆς καὶ
εἰς ἑκάτερον μεταβαλλομένης ἅπαξ· ὥστε τὸ μὲν
μετεωρισθὲν αὐτῆς μέρος ἀπαγαγεῖν[4] τὴν θάλατ-

---

[1] χεῖσθαι F, κινεῖσθαι other MSS.

[2] ἐλήφθησαν F, omitted by other MSS. (cp. Athenaeus 8.
2, p. 333).

[3] For ἁπλῷ Corais reads παλμῷ (vibration).

[4] ἀπαγαγεῖν, Jones, following suggestion of Capps, for
ἐπαγαγεῖν F, ἐπάγειν other MSS.

that is adapted to fusing, though others say that
any sand anywhere can be fused. I heard at Alexandria from the glass-workers that there was in
Aegypt a kind of vitreous earth without which
many-coloured and costly designs could not be
executed, just as elsewhere different countries
require different mixtures; and at Rome, also, it
is said that many discoveries are made both for
producing the colours and for facility in manu-
facture, as, for example, in the case of glass-ware,
where one can buy a glass beaker or drinking-cup
for a copper.

26. A marvellous occurrence of a very rare kind
is reported as having taken place on this shore
between Tyre and Ptolemaïs: at the time when
the Ptolemaeans, after joining battle with Sarpedon
the general, were left in this place, after a brilliant
rout had taken place, a wave from the sea, like a
flood-tide, submerged the fugitives;[1] and some were
carried off into the sea and destroyed, whereas
others were left dead in the hollow places; and
then, succeeding this wave, the ebb uncovered the
shore again and disclosed the bodies of men lying
promiscuously among dead fish. Like occurrences
take place in the neighbourhood of the Mt. Casius
situated near Aegypt, where the land undergoes a
single quick convulsion, and makes a sudden
change to a higher or lower level, the result being
that, whereas the elevated part repels the sea and

---

[1] The account of Athenaeus (8. 2, p. 333), quoted from
Poseidonius, is clearer: the opposing generals were Tryphon
the Apameian (see 16. 2. 10) and Sarpedon the general of
Demetrius; it was Tryphon who won the fight and his soldiers
who were submerged.

ταν, τὸ δὲ συνιζῆσαν[1] δέξασθαι, τραπομένης δὲ
τὴν ἀρχαίαν πάλιν ἕδραν ἀπολαβεῖν τὸν τόπον,
τοτὲ μὲν οὖν καὶ ἐξαλλάξεώς τινος γενομένης,
τοτὲ δ' οὔ· τάχα καὶ περιόδοις τισὶν ἐνδεδεμένων
τῶν τοιούτων παθῶν ἀδήλοις ἡμῖν, καθάπερ τοῦτο
καὶ ἐπὶ τῶν κατὰ τὸν Νεῖλον ἀναβάσεων λέγεται
διαφόρων γινομένων, ἄδηλον δὲ τὴν τάξιν ἐχουσῶν.

27. Μετὰ δὲ τὴν Ἄκην Στράτωνος πύργος,
πρόσορμον ἔχων. μεταξὺ δὲ ὅ τε Κάρμηλος τὸ
ὄρος καὶ πολιχνίων ὀνόματα, πλέον δ' οὐδέν,
Συκαμίνων πόλις, Βουκόλων καὶ Κροκοδείλων
πόλις καὶ ἄλλα τοιαῦτα· εἶτα δρυμὸς μέγας τις.

C 759   28. Εἶτα Ἰόπη,[2] καθ' ἣν ἡ ἀπὸ τῆς Αἰγύπτου
παραλία σημειωδῶς ἐπὶ τὴν ἄρκτον κάμπτεται,
πρότερον ἐπὶ τὴν ἕω τεταμένη. ἐνταῦθα δὲ
μυθεύουσί τινες τὴν Ἀνδρομέδαν ἐκτεθῆναι τῷ
κήτει· ἐν ὕψει γάρ ἐστιν ἱκανῶς τὸ χωρίον, ὥστ'
ἀφορᾶσθαί φασιν ἀπ' αὐτοῦ τὰ Ἱεροσόλυμα, τὴν
τῶν Ἰουδαίων μητρόπολιν· καὶ δὴ καὶ ἐπινείῳ
τούτῳ κέχρηνται καταβάντες μέχρι θαλάττης οἱ
Ἰουδαῖοι· τὰ δ' ἐπίνεια τῶν λῃστῶν λῃστήρια
δηλονότι ἐστί. τούτων δὲ καὶ ὁ Κάρμηλος ὑπῆρξε
καὶ ὁ δρυμός· καὶ δὴ καὶ εὐάνδρησεν οὗτος ὁ
τόπος, ὥστ' ἐκ τῆς πλησίον κώμης Ἰαμνείας καὶ
τῶν κατοικιῶν τῶν κύκλῳ τέτταρας μυριάδας

_____

[1] συνιζῆσαν, Xylander, for συνίζησιν.
[2] Ἰόπη Emoz, Ἰόππη other MSS.

_____

[1] For an extended discussion of this and similar problems,
see 1. 3–4, 10. 13.
[2] This place was magnificently built up by Herod and
named Caesarea in honour of Augustus.
[3] "Mulberry City."

the sunken part receives it, yet, the land makes a reverse change and the site resumes its old position again, a complete interchange of levels sometimes having taken place and sometimes not.[1] Perhaps such disturbances are subject to periodic principles unknown to us, as is also said to be the case of the overflows of the Nile, which prove to be variant but follow some unknown order.

27. After Acê one comes to the Tower of Strato,[2] which has a landing-place for vessels. Between the two places is Mt. Carmel, as also towns of which nothing more than the names remain—I mean Sycaminopolis,[3] Bucolopolis,[4] Crocodeilopolis,[5] and others like them. And then one comes to a large forest.[6]

28. Then one comes to Iopê,[7] where the seaboard from Aegypt, though at first stretching towards the east, makes a significant bend towards the north. Here it was, according to certain writers of myths, that Andromeda was exposed to the sea-monster; for the place is situated at a rather high elevation —so high, it is said, that Jerusalem, the metropolis of the Judaeans, is visible from it, and indeed the Judaeans have used this place as a seaport when they have gone down as far as the sea; but the seaports of robbers are obviously only robbers' dens.[8] To these people belonged, not only Carmel, but also the forest; and indeed this place was so well supplied with men that it could muster forty thousand men from the neighbouring village Iamneia and

---

[4] " Herdsman City."   [5] "Crocodile City."
[6] Josephus (14. 13. 3) speaks of a place near Mt. Carmel as Δρύμοι (" Forests ").
[7] Now Jaffa.   [8] See § 27 following.

ὁπλίζεσθαι. εἰσὶ δ' ἐντεῦθεν εἰς τὸ Κάσιον τὸ πρὸς Πηλουσίῳ μικρῷ πλείους ἢ χίλιοι στάδιοι, τριακόσιοι δ' ἄλλοι πρὸς αὐτὸ τὸ Πηλούσιον.

29. Ἐν δὲ τῷ μεταξὺ καὶ ἡ Γαδαρίς ἐστιν, ἣν καὶ αὐτὴν ἐξιδιάσαντο οἱ Ἰουδαῖοι· εἶτ' Ἀζωτὸς καὶ Ἀσκάλων. ἀπὸ δὲ Ἰαμνείας εἰς Ἄζωτον καὶ Ἀσκάλωνά εἰσιν ὅσον διακόσιοι στάδιοι. κρομμυών τ' ἀγαθός[1] ἐστιν ἡ χώρα τῶν Ἀσκαλωνιτῶν, πόλισμα δὲ μικρόν. ἐντεῦθεν ἦν Ἀντίοχος ὁ φιλόσοφος, μικρὸν πρὸ ἡμῶν γεγονώς. ἐκ δὲ τῶν Γαδάρων Φιλόδημός τε ὁ Ἐπικούρειος[2] καὶ Μελέαγρος καὶ Μένιππος ὁ σπουδογέλοιος καὶ Θεόδωρος ὁ καθ' ἡμᾶς ῥήτωρ.

30. Εἶθ' ὁ τῶν Γαζαίων λιμὴν πλησίον· ὑπέρκειται δὲ καὶ ἡ πόλις ἐν ἑπτὰ σταδίοις, ἔνδοξός ποτε γενομένη, κατεσπασμένη δ' ὑπὸ Ἀλεξάνδρου καὶ μένουσα ἔρημος. ἐντεῦθεν δ' ὑπέρβασις λέγεται χιλίων διακοσίων ἑξήκοντα σταδίων εἰς Αἴλαν[3] πόλιν ἐπὶ τῷ μυχῷ τοῦ Ἀραβίου κόλπου κειμένην· διττὸς δ' ἐστίν· ὁ μὲν ἔχων εἰς τὸ[4] πρὸς τῇ Ἀραβίᾳ καὶ τῇ Γάζῃ μέρος, ὃν Αἰλανίτην προσαγορεύουσιν ἀπὸ τῆς ἐν αὐτῷ πόλεως, ὁ δ' εἰς τὸ πρὸς Αἰγύπτῳ κατὰ τὴν Ἡρώων πόλιν, εἰς ὃν ἐκ Πηλουσίου ἡ ὑπέρθεσις ἐπιτομωτέρα· δι' ἐρήμων δὲ καὶ ἀμμωδῶν χωρίων αἱ ὑπερβάσεις ἐπὶ καμήλων· πολὺ δὲ καὶ τὸ τῶν ἑρπετῶν ἐν αὐταῖς πλῆθος.

31. Μετὰ δὲ Γάζαν Ῥαφία, ἐν ᾗ μάχη συνέβη

---

[1] κρομυών, Meineke ; κρομμύων MSS. ; κρομμύοις τ' ἀγαθή moz, Tzschucke and Corais.

[2] After Ἐπικούρειος the MSS. add γεγονώς.

[3] Αἴλαν, Meineke emends to Αἴλανα.

[4] ὁ μὲν ἔχων εἰς τό, Kramer, for ὁ μὲν εἶς ἔχων τό.

the settlements all round. Thence to Mt. Casius near Pelusium the distance is a little more than one thousand stadia; and, three hundred stadia farther, one comes to Pelusium itself.

29. But in the interval one comes to Gadaris, which the Judaeans appropriated to themselves; and then to Azotus and Ascalon. The distance from Iamneia to Azotus and Ascalon is about two hundred stadia. The country of the Ascalonitae is a good onion-market, though the town is small. Antiochus the philosopher, who was born a little before my time, was a native of this place. Philodemus, the Epicurean, and Meleager and Menippus, the satirist, and Theodorus, the rhetorician of my own time, were natives of Gadaris.

30. Then, near Ascalon, one comes to the harbour of the Gazaeans. The city of the Gazaeans is situated inland at a distance of seven stadia; it became famous at one time, but was rased to the ground by Alexander and remains uninhabited. Thence there is said to be an overland passage of one thousand two hundred and sixty stadia to Aela, a city situated near the head of the Arabian Gulf. This head consists of two recesses: one extending into the region near Arabia and Gaza, which is called Aelanites, after the city situated on it, and the other, extending to the region near Aegypt in the neighbourhood of the City of Heroes,[1] to which the overland passage from Pelusium is shorter; and the overland journeys are made on camels through desert and sandy places; and on these journeys there are also many reptiles to be seen.

31. After Gaza one comes to Rhaphia, where a

___
[1] Heröonpolis.

Πτολεμαίῳ τε τῷ τετάρτῳ καὶ Ἀντιόχῳ τῷ
Μεγάλῳ. εἶτα Ῥινοκόλουρα,[1] ἀπὸ τῶν εἰσῳ-
κισμένων ἐκεῖ τὸ παλαιὸν ἀνθρώπων ἠκρωτηριασμένων[2] τὰς ῥῖνας οὕτω καλουμένη· τῶν γὰρ
Αἰθιόπων τις, ἐπελθὼν ἐπὶ τὴν Αἴγυπτον, ἀντὶ
τοῦ ἀναιρεῖν[3] τοὺς κακούργους ἀποτέμνων τὰς
ῥῖνας ἐνταῦθα κατῴκιζεν, ὡς οὐκ ἂν ἔτι τολ-
μήσοντας κακουργεῖν διὰ τὴν αἰσχύνην τῆς ὄψεως.

32. Καὶ αὕτη μὲν οὖν ἡ ἀπὸ Γάζης λυπρὰ
πᾶσα καὶ ἀμμώδης· ἔτι δὲ μᾶλλον τοιαύτη ἡ
C 760 ἐφεξῆς ὑπερκειμένη,[4] ἔχουσα τὴν Σιρβωνίδα
λίμνην παράλληλόν πως[5] τῇ θαλάττῃ μικρὰν
δίοδον ἀπολείπουσαν μεταξὺ μέχρι τοῦ Ἐκρήγ-
ματος καλουμένου, μῆκος ὅσον διακοσίων σταδίων, πλάτος δὲ τὸ μέγιστον πεντήκοντα· τὸ δ᾽
Ἔκρηγμα συγκέχωσται. εἶτα συνεχὴς ἄλλη
τοιαύτη[6] ἡ ἐπὶ τὸ Κάσιον, κἀκεῖθεν ἐπὶ τὸ
Πηλούσιον.

33. Ἔστι δὲ τὸ Κάσιον θινώδης τις λόφος
ἀκρωτηριάζων ἄνυδρος, ὅπου τὸ Πομπηίου τοῦ
Μάγνου σῶμα κεῖται καὶ Διός ἐστιν ἱερὸν Κασίου·
πλησίον δὲ καὶ ἐσφάγη ὁ Μάγνος, δολοφονηθεὶς
ὑπὸ τῶν Αἰγυπτίων. εἶθ᾽ ἡ ἐπὶ Πηλούσιον ὁδός,
ἐν ᾗ τὰ Γέρρα καὶ ὁ Χαβρίου λεγόμενος χάραξ
καὶ τὰ πρὸς τῷ Πηλουσίῳ βάραθρα, ἃ ποιεῖ
παρεκχεόμενος ὁ Νεῖλος, φύσει κοίλων καὶ ἑλωδῶν

---

[1] Ῥινοκόλουρα the spelling of the MSS. except E, which
has Ῥινοκόρουρα (cp. readings in 16. 1. 12 and 16. 4. 24).

[2] The words ἐκεῖ . . . ἠκρωτηριασμένων are omitted in EF.

[3] ἀναιρεῖν *moz*, ἀνελθεῖν Xylander, κατελθεῖν Corais ; -εῖν,
with the other letters erased, other MSS.

[4] τοιούτην ἡ ἐφεξῆς ὑπερκειμένη, the editors, for τοιαύτην
ἐφεξῆς ὑπερκειμένην.

battle was fought between Ptolemaeus the Fourth and Antiochus the Great. Then to Rhinocolura,[1] so called from the people with mutilated noses that had been settled there in early times; for some Aethiopian invaded Aegypt and, instead of killing the wrongdoers, cut off their noses and settled them at that place, assuming that on account of their disgraceful faces they would no longer dare do people wrong.

32. Now the whole of this country from Gaza is barren and sandy, but still more so is the country that lies next above it, which contains Lake Sirbonis,[2] a lake which lies approximately parallel to the sea and, in the interval, leaves a short passage as far as the Ecregma,[3] as it is called; the lake is about two hundred stadia in length and its maximum breadth is about sixty stadia; but the Ecregma has become filled up with earth. Then follows another continuous tract of this kind as far as Casius; and then one comes to Pelusium.

33. Casius is a sandy hill without water and forms a promontory; the body of Pompey the Great is buried there; and on it is a temple of Zeus Casius. Near this place Pompey the Great was slain, being treacherously murdered by the Aegyptians. Then comes the road to Pelusium, on which lie Gerrha and the Palisade of Chabrias, as it is called, and the pits near Pelusium. These pits are formed by side-flows from the Nile, the region being by nature

---

[1] " Docked-nose-ville."   [2] See 1. 3. 4 and 17. 1. 35.
[3] *i.e.* " Outbreak " to the sea.

---

[5] πως, Corais, for πρός.
[6] τοιαύτη, Letronne, for τοσαύτην.

ὄντων τῶν τόπων. τοιαύτη μὲν ἡ Φοινίκη. φησὶ δ'
Ἀρτεμίδωρος εἰς τὸ Πηλούσιον ἐκ μὲν Ὀρθωσίας
εἶναι σταδίους τρισχιλίους ἐξακοσίους πεντήκοντα
κατακολπίζοντι· ἐκ δὲ Μελαινῶν ἢ Μελανιῶν
τῆς Κιλικίας τῶν πρὸς Κελένδεριν ἐπὶ μὲν τὰ
μεθόρια τῆς Κιλικίας καὶ Συρίας χιλίους καὶ
ἐννακοσίους· ἐντεῦθεν δ' ἐπὶ τὸν Ὀρόντην πεντακοσίους εἴκοσιν· εἶτ' ἐπὶ Ὀρθωσίαν χιλίους
ἑκατὸν τριάκοντα.

34. Τῆς δ' Ἰουδαίας τὰ μὲν ἑσπέρια ἄκρα τὰ
πρὸς τῷ Κασίῳ κατέχουσιν Ἰδουμαῖοί τε καὶ ἡ
λίμνη. Ναβαταῖοι δ' εἰσὶν οἱ Ἰδουμαῖοι· κατὰ
στάσιν δ' ἐκπεσόντες ἐκεῖθεν προσεχώρησαν τοῖς
Ἰουδαίοις καὶ τῶν νομίμων τῶν αὐτῶν ἐκείνοις
ἐκοινώνησαν· πρὸς θαλάττῃ δὲ ἡ Σιρβωνὶς τὰ
πολλὰ κατέχει[1] καὶ ἡ συνεχὴς μέχρι Ἱεροσο-
λύμων· καὶ γὰρ ταῦτα πρὸς θαλάττῃ ἐστίν· ἀπὸ
γὰρ τοῦ ἐπινείου τῆς Ἰόπης[2] εἴρηται ὅτι ἐστὶν
ἐν ὄψει. ταῦτα μὲν προσάρκτια· τὰ πολλὰ δ' ὡς
ἕκαστά εἰσιν ὑπὸ φύλων οἰκούμενα μικτῶν ἔκ τε
Αἰγυπτίων ἐθνῶν καὶ Ἀραβίων καὶ Φοινίκων·
τοιοῦτοι γὰρ οἱ τὴν Γαλιλαίαν ἔχοντες καὶ τὸν
Ἱερικοῦντα καὶ τὴν Φιλαδελφίαν καὶ Σαμάρειαν,
ἣν Ἡρώδης Σεβαστὴν ἐπωνόμασεν. οὕτω δ'
ὄντων μιγάδων, ἡ κρατοῦσα μάλιστα φήμη τῶν
περὶ τὸ ἱερὸν τὸ ἐν τοῖς Ἱεροσολύμοις πιστευομέ-
νων Αἰγυπτίους ἀποφαίνει τοὺς προγόνους τῶν
νῦν Ἰουδαίων λεγομένων.

---

[1] κατέχει, Casaubon, for κατεῖχε.   [2] Ἰόπης CF.

---

[1] See 14. 5. 3 and footnote.

hollow and marshy. Such is Phoenicia. Artemidorus says that the distance to Pelusium from Orthosia is three thousand six hundred and fifty stadia, including the sinuosities of the gulfs; and from Melaenae, or Melaniae, in Cilicia, near Celenderis, to the common boundaries of Cilicia and Syria, one thousand nine hundred; and thence to the Orontes River, five hundred and twenty; and then to Orthosia one thousand one hundred and thirty.[1]

34. As for Judaea, its western extremities towards Casius are occupied by the Idumaeans and by the lake. The Idumaeans are Nabataeans,[2] but owing to a sedition they were banished from there,[3] joined the Judaeans, and shared in the same customs with them. The greater part of the region near the sea is occupied by Lake Sirbonis and by the country continuous with the lake as far as Jerusalem; for this city is also near the sea; for, as I have already said,[4] it is visible from the seaport of Iopê. This region lies towards the north; and it is inhabited in general, as is each place in particular, by mixed stocks of people from Aegyptian and Arabian and Phoenician tribes; for such are those who occupy Galilee and Hiericus[5] and Philadelphia and Samaria, which last Herod surnamed Sebastê.[6] But though the inhabitants are mixed up thus, the most prevalent of the accredited reports in regard to the temple at Jerusalem represents the ancestors of the present Judaeans, as they are called, as Aegyptians.

---

[2] An Arabian people (see 16. 4. 21).
[3] Arabia Petraea (see 16. 4. 21).
[4] 16. 2. 28.   [5] Jericho.
[6] *i.e.* in Latin, "Augusta," in honour of Augustus Caesar.

35. Μωσῆς γάρ τις τῶν Αἰγυπτίων ἱερέων, ἔχων τι μέρος τῆς κάτω[1] καλουμένης χώρας, ἀπῆρεν ἐκεῖσε ἐνθένδε, δυσχεράνας τὰ καθεστῶτα, καὶ συνεξῆραν αὐτῷ πολλοὶ τιμῶντες τὸ θεῖον. ἔφη γὰρ ἐκεῖνος καὶ ἐδίδασκεν, ὡς οὐκ ὀρθῶς φρονοῖεν οἱ Αἰγύπτιοι θηρίοις εἰκάζοντες καὶ βοσκήμασι τὸ θεῖον, οὐδ' οἱ Λίβυες· οὐκ εὖ δὲ

C 761 οὐδ' οἱ Ἕλληνες, ἀνθρωπομόρφους τυποῦντες· εἴη γὰρ ἓν τοῦτο μόνον θεὸς τὸ περιέχον ἡμᾶς ἅπαντας καὶ γῆν καὶ θάλατταν, ὃ καλοῦμεν οὐρανὸν καὶ κόσμον καὶ τὴν τῶν ὄντων φύσιν. τούτου δὴ τίς ἂν εἰκόνα πλάττειν θαρρήσειε νοῦν ἔχων ὁμοίαν τινὶ[2] τῶν παρ' ἡμῖν; ἀλλ' ἐὰν δεῖν[3] πᾶσαν ξοανοποιΐαν, τέμενος δ'[4] ἀφορίσαντας καὶ σηκὸν ἀξιόλογον τιμᾶν ἕδους[5] χωρίς· ἐγκοι-μᾶσθαι δὲ καὶ αὐτοὺς ὑπὲρ ἑαυτῶν καὶ ὑπὲρ τῶν ἄλλων ἄλλους τοὺς εὐονείρους· καὶ προσδοκᾶν δεῖν ἀγαθὸν παρὰ τοῦ θεοῦ καὶ δῶρον ἀεί τι καὶ σημεῖον τοὺς σωφρόνως ζῶντας καὶ μετὰ δικαιο-σύνης, τοὺς δ' ἄλλους μὴ προσδοκᾶν.

36. Ἐκεῖνος μὲν οὖν τοιαῦτα λέγων ἔπεισεν εὐγνώμονας ἄνδρας οὐκ ὀλίγους καὶ ἀπήγαγεν ἐπὶ τὸν τόπον τοῦτον, ὅπου νῦν ἐστι τὸ ἐν τοῖς Ἱεροσολύμοις κτίσμα. κατέσχε δὲ ῥᾳδίως, οὐκ ἐπίφθονον ὂν τὸ χωρίον, οὐδ' ὑπὲρ οὗ ἄν τις ἐσπουδασμένως μαχέσαιτο· ἔστι γὰρ πετρῶδες,

---

[1] κάτω, Corais inserts.   [2] τινί, Casaubon, for τινά.
[3] δεῖν, Corais, for δεῖ.   [4] δ', Corais inserts.
[5] ἕδους h, αἰδοῦς FD, εἴδους other MSS.

---

[1] Strabo evidently has in mind, among other forms of worship, the bull-worship of the Aegyptians. The bull was

35. Moses, namely, was one of the Aegyptian priests, and held a part of Lower Aegypt, as it is called, but he went away from there to Judaea, since he was displeased with the state of affairs there, and was accompanied by many people who worshipped the Divine Being. For he said, and taught, that the Aegyptians were mistaken in representing the Divine Being by the images of beasts and cattle,[1] as were also the Libyans; and that the Greeks were also wrong in modelling gods in human form; for, according to him, God is this one thing alone that encompasses us all and encompasses land and sea—the thing which we call heaven, or universe, or the nature of all that exists. What man, then, if he has sense, could be bold enough to fabricate an image of God resembling any creature amongst us? Nay, people should leave off all image-carving, and, setting apart a sacred precinct and a worthy sanctuary, should worship God without an image; and people who have good dreams should sleep in the sanctuary, not only themselves on their own behalf, but also others for the rest of the people; and those who live self-restrained and righteous lives should always expect some blessing or gift or sign from God, but no other should expect them.

36. Now Moses, saying things of this kind, persuaded not a few thoughtful men and led them away to this place where the settlement of Jerusalem now is; and he easily took possession of the place, since it was not a place that would be looked on with envy, nor yet one for which anyone would make a serious fight; for it is rocky, and, although it itself

worshipped by them as a symbol of the might and fatherhood of God.

αὐτὸ μὲν εὔυδρον, τὴν δὲ κύκλῳ χώραν ἔχον
λυπρὰν καὶ ἄνυδρον, τὴν δ' ἐντὸς ἑξήκοντα
σταδίων καὶ ὑπόπετρον. ἅμα δ' ἀντὶ τῶν ὅπλων
τὰ ἱερὰ προὐβάλλετο καὶ τὸ θεῖον, ἵδρυσιν τούτου
ζητεῖν ἀξιῶν, καὶ παραδώσειν ὑπισχνούμενος
τοιοῦτον σεβασμὸν καὶ τοιαύτην ἱεροποιίαν, ἥτις
οὔτε δαπάναις ὀχλήσει τοὺς χρωμένους οὔτε
θεοφορίαις οὔτε ἄλλαις πραγματείαις ἀτόποις.
οὗτος μὲν οὖν εὐδοκιμήσας τούτοις συνεστήσατο
ἀρχὴν οὐ τὴν τυχοῦσαν, ἁπάντων προσχωρησάν-
των ῥᾳδίως τῶν κύκλῳ διὰ τὴν ὁμιλίαν καὶ τὰ
προτεινόμενα.

37. Οἱ δὲ διαδεξάμενοι χρόνους μέν τινας ἐν
τοῖς αὐτοῖς διέμενον δικαιοπραγοῦντες καὶ θεο-
σεβεῖς ὡς ἀληθῶς ὄντες· ἔπειτ' ἐφισταμένων ἐπὶ
τὴν ἱερωσύνην τὸ μὲν πρῶτον δεισιδαιμόνων,
ἔπειτα τυραννικῶν ἀνθρώπων, ἐκ μὲν τῆς δεισι-
δαιμονίας αἱ τῶν βρωμάτων ἀποσχέσεις, ὧνπερ
καὶ νῦν ἔθος ἐστὶν αὐτοῖς ἀπέχεσθαι, καὶ αἱ
περιτομαὶ καὶ αἱ ἐκτομαὶ[1] καὶ εἴ τινα τοιαῦτα
ἐνομίσθη, ἐκ δὲ τῶν τυραννίδων τὰ ληστήρια.
οἱ μὲν γὰρ ἀφιστάμενοι τὴν χώραν ἐκάκουν καὶ
αὐτὴν καὶ τὴν γειτνιῶσαν, οἱ δὲ συμπράττοντες
τοῖς ἄρχουσι καθήρπαζον τὰ ἀλλότρια καὶ τῆς
Συρίας κατεστρέφοντο καὶ τῆς Φοινίκης πολλήν.
ἦν δ' ὅμως εὐπρέπειά τις περὶ τὴν ἀκρόπολιν
αὐτῶν, οὐχ ὡς τυραννεῖον[2] βδελυττομένων, ἀλλ'
ὡς ἱερὸν σεμνυνόντων καὶ σεβομένων.

[1] ἐκτομιαί F h.
[2] τύραννον CDFh i; corrected in margin of DF.

[1] So Tozer interprets. The Greek could mean that "the
territory inside" the city, "sixty stadia" (in circumference)
"is also rocky beneath the surface."

is well supplied with water, its surrounding territory is barren and waterless, and the part of the territory within a radius of sixty stadia is also rocky beneath the surface.[1] At the same time Moses, instead of using arms, put forward as defence his sacrifices and his Divine Being, being resolved to seek a seat of worship for Him [2] and promising to deliver to the people a kind of worship and a kind of ritual which would not oppress those who adopted them either with expenses or with divine obsessions or with other absurd troubles. Now Moses enjoyed fair repute with these people, and organised no ordinary kind of government, since the peoples all round, one and all, came over to him, because of his dealings with them and of the prospects he held out to them.

37. His successors for some time abided by the same course, acting righteously and being truly pious toward God; but afterwards, in the first place, superstitious men were appointed to the priesthood, and then tyrannical people; and from superstition arose abstinence from flesh, from which it is their custom to abstain even to-day, and circumcisions and excisions [3] and other observances of the kind. And from the tyrannies arose the bands of robbers;[4] for some revolted and harassed the country, both their own country and that of their neighbours, whereas others, co-operating with the rulers, seized the property of others and subdued much of Syria and Phoenicia. But still they had respect for their acropolis, since they did not loathe it as the seat of tyranny, but honoured and revered it as a holy place.

[2] *i.e.* a city and temple dedicated to His worship.
[3] *i.e.* of females (see 16. 4. 9).   [4] See 16. 2. 28.

38. Πέφυκε γὰρ οὕτω, καὶ κοινόν ἐστι τοῦτο καὶ τοῖς Ἕλλησι καὶ τοῖς βαρβάροις. πολιτικοὶ γὰρ ὄντες ἀπὸ προστάγματος κοινοῦ ζῶσιν· ἄλλως γὰρ οὐχ οἷόν τε τοὺς πολλοὺς ἕν τι καὶ ταὐτό[1] ποιεῖν ἡρμοσμένως ἀλλήλοις, ὅπερ ἦν τὸ πολιτεύεσθαι, καὶ ἄλλως πως νέμειν βίον κοινόν. τὸ δὲ πρόσταγμα διττόν· ἢ γὰρ παρὰ θεῶν ἢ παρὰ ἀνθρώπων· καὶ οἵ γε ἀρχαῖοι τὸ παρὰ τῶν θεῶν ἐπρέσβευον μᾶλλον καὶ ἐσέμνυνον, καὶ διὰ τοῦτο καὶ ὁ χρηστηριαζόμενος ἦν τότε πολὺς καὶ τρέχων εἰς μὲν Δωδώνην, ὅπως

C 762

ἐκ δρυὸς ὑψικόμοιο Διὸς βουλὴν ἐπακούσῃ,[2]

συμβούλῳ τῷ Διὶ χρώμενος, εἰς δὲ Δελφούς,

τὸν ἐκτεθέντα παῖδα μαστεύων μαθεῖν,
εἰ μηκέτ᾽ εἴη·

αὐτὸς δ᾽ ὁ παῖς

ἔστειχε τοὺς τεκόντας ἐκμαθεῖν θέλων
πρὸς δῶμα Φοίβου.

καὶ ὁ Μίνως παρὰ τοῖς Κρησὶν

ἐννέωρος βασίλευε Διὸς μεγάλου ὀαριστής·

δι᾽ ἐννέα ἐτῶν, ὥς φησι Πλάτων, ἀναβαίνων ἐπὶ τὸ ἄντρον τοῦ Διὸς καὶ παρ᾽ ἐκείνου τὰ προστάγματα λαμβάνων καὶ παρακομίζων εἰς τοὺς ἀνθρώπους. τὰ δ᾽ ὅμοια ἐποίει καὶ Λυκοῦργος ὁ ζηλωτὴς αὐτοῦ· πυκνὰ γάρ, ὡς ἔοικεν, ἀποδημῶν ἐπυνθάνετο παρὰ τῆς Πυθίας, ἃ προσῆκεν παραγγέλλειν τοῖς Λακεδαιμονίοις.

---

[1] κατ᾽ αὐτό, CDFh*ir*, κατὰ ταὐτό *moxz*; emended by Corais.

38. For this is natural; and it is common to the Greeks and the barbarians; for, being members of states, they live under common mandates; for otherwise it would be impossible for the mass of people in any country to do one and the same thing in harmony with one another, which is precisely what life in a free state means, or in any other way to live a common life. And the mandates are twofold; for they come either from gods or from men; and the ancients, at least, held those from the gods in greater honour and veneration; and on this account men who consulted oracles were much in evidence at that time—men who ran to Dodona " to hear the will of Zeus from the high-tressed oak," [1] thus using Zeus as their counsellor, and also to Delphi, " seeking to learn whether the child which had been exposed to die was no longer alive; " [2] but the child himself " was on his way to the home of Phoebus, wishing to discover his parents." [3] And among the Cretans Minos " reigned as king, who held converse with great Zeus every ninth year," [4] every nine years, as Plato says, when he would go up to the cave of Zeus and receive decrees from him and carry them to the people. And Lycurgus,[5] his emulator, did likewise; for oftentimes, as it appears, he would go abroad to inquire of the Pythian priestess what ordinances it was proper for him to report to the Lacedaemonians.

---

[1] *Odyssey* 14. 328. [2] Euripides, *Phoen.* 36.
[3] *Ibid.* 34.   [4] See 10. 4. 8 and footnote.
   [5] See 10. 4. 18.

---

[2] ἐπακούσῃ, Corais, for ὑποκούσῃ.

39. Ταῦτα γὰρ ὅπως ποτὲ ἀληθείας ἔχει, παρά γε τοῖς ἀνθρώποις ἐπεπίστευτο καὶ ἐνενόμιστο, καὶ διὰ τοῦτο καὶ οἱ μάντεις ἐτιμῶντο, ὥστε καὶ βασιλείας ἀξιοῦσθαι, ὡς τὰ παρὰ τῶν θεῶν ἡμῖν ἐκφέροντες παραγγέλματα καὶ ἐπανορθώματα καὶ ζῶντες καὶ ἀποθανόντες· καθάπερ καὶ ὁ Τειρεσίας,

τῷ καὶ τεθνηῶτι νόον πόρε Περσεφόνεια
οἴῳ πεπνῦσθαι· τοὶ δὲ σκιαὶ ἀίσσουσι.[1]

τοιοῦτος δὲ καὶ ὁ Ἀμφιάρεως καὶ ὁ Τροφώνιος καὶ ὁ Ὀρφεὺς καὶ ὁ Μουσαῖος καὶ ὁ παρὰ τοῖς Γέταις θεός, τὸ μὲν παλαιὸν Ζάμολξις, Πυθα-γόρειός τις, καθ' ἡμᾶς δὲ ὁ τῷ Βυρεβίστᾳ[2] θεσπίζων, Δεκαίνεος· παρὰ δὲ τοῖς Βοσπορηνοῖς Ἀχαΐκαρος, παρὰ δὲ τοῖς Ἰνδοῖς οἱ γυμνοσο-φισταί, παρὰ δὲ τοῖς Πέρσαις οἱ Μάγοι καὶ νεκυόμαντεις καὶ ἔτι οἱ λεγόμενοι λεκανόμαντεις καὶ ὑδρόμαντεις, παρὰ δὲ τοῖς Ἀσσυρίοις οἱ Χαλδαῖοι, παρὰ δὲ τοῖς Ῥωμαίοις οἱ Τυρρηνικοὶ ὡροσκόποι.[3] τοιοῦτος δέ τις ἦν καὶ ὁ Μωσῆς καὶ οἱ διαδεξάμενοι ἐκεῖνον, τὰς μὲν ἀρχὰς λαβόντες οὐ φαύλας, ἐκτραπόμενοι δ' ἐπὶ τὸ χεῖρον.

40. Ἤδη δ' οὖν φανερῶς τυραννουμένης τῆς Ἰουδαίας, πρῶτος ἀνθ' ἱερέως ἀνέδειξεν ἑαυτὸν βασιλέα Ἀλέξανδρος· τούτου δ' ἦσαν υἱοὶ Ὑρ-κανός τε καὶ Ἀριστόβουλος· διαφερομένων δὲ περὶ τῆς ἀρχῆς, ἐπῆλθε Πομπήιος καὶ κατέλυσεν αὐτοὺς καὶ τὰ ἐρύματα αὐτῶν κατέσπασε καὶ αὐτὰ

---

[1] Meineke ejects the words καθάπερ . . . ἀίσσουσι.
[2] Βυρεβίσθα CDF*h*, Βυρεβίθα *i* (see critical note, 7. 3. 5).

39. For these things, whatever truth there may be in them, have at least been believed and sanctioned among men; and for this reason the prophets too were held in so much honour that they were deemed worthy to be kings, on the ground that they promulgated to us ordinances and amendments from the gods, not only when they were alive, but also when they were dead, as, for example, Teiresias, " to whom even in death Persephone granted reason, that he alone should have understanding, whereas the others flit about as shadows." [1] Such, also, were Amphiaräus, Trophonius, Orpheus, Musaeus, and the god among the Getae, who in ancient times was Zamolxis,[2] a Pythagoreian, and in my time was Decaeneus,[3] the diviner of Byrebistas; and, among the Bosporeni, Achaecarus; and, among the Indians, the Gymnosophists; and, among the Persians, the Magi and the necromancers, as also the dish-diviners and water-diviners, as they are called; and, among the Assyrians, the Chaldaeans; and, among the Romans, the Tyrrhenian nativity-casters.[4] Moses was such a person as these, as also his successors, who, with no bad beginning, turned out for the worse.

40. At any rate, when now Judaea was under the rule of tyrants, Alexander was first to declare himself king instead of priest; and both Hyrcanus and Aristobulus were sons of his; and when they were at variance about the empire, Pompey went over and overthrew them and rased their fortifica-

---

[1] *Odyssey* 10. 494. [2] See 7. 3. 5.
[3] 7. 3. 5. [4] Cf. 17. 1. 43.

---

[3] ἀροσκόποι, Corais emends to οἰωνοσκόποι; Letronne conj. ἱεροσκόποι.

STRABO

ἐν πρώτοις τὰ Ἱεροσόλυμα βίᾳ καταλαβών·[1] ἦν
γὰρ πετρῶδες καὶ εὐερκὲς ἔρυμα, ἐντὸς μὲν
C 763 εὔυδρον, ἐκτὸς δὲ παντελῶς διψηρόν, τάφρον
λατομητὴν ἔχον βάθος μὲν ἑξήκοντα ποδῶν,
πλάτος δὲ πεντήκοντα καὶ διακοσίων· ἐκ δὲ τοῦ
λίθου τοῦ λατομηθέντος ἐπεπύργωτο τὸ τεῖχος
τοῦ ἱεροῦ. κατελάβετο δ᾽, ὥς φασι, τηρήσας τὴν
τῆς νηστείας ἡμέραν, ἡνίκα ἀπείχοντο οἱ Ἰουδαῖοι παντὸς ἔργου, πληρώσας τὴν τάφρον καὶ
ἐπιβαλὼν τὰς διαβάθρας· κατασπάσαι δ᾽ οὖν
ἐκέλευσε τὰ τείχη πάντα καὶ ἀνεῖλεν εἰς δύναμιν
τὰ λῃστήρια καὶ τὰ γαζοφυλάκια τῶν τυράννων.
ἦν δὲ δύο μὲν τὰ ταῖς εἰσβολαῖς ἐπικείμενα τοῦ
Ἱερικοῦντος Θρῆξ τε καὶ Ταῦρος, ἄλλα δὲ Ἀλε-
ξάνδριόν τε καὶ Ὑρκάνιον καὶ Μαχαιροῦς[2] καὶ
Λυσιὰς[3] καὶ τὰ περὶ τὴν Φιλαδελφίαν καὶ ἡ
περὶ Γαλιλαίαν Σκυθόπολις.
41. Ἱερικοῦς δ᾽ ἐστὶ πεδίον κύκλῳ περιεχόμενον
ὀρεινῇ τινι καί που καὶ θεατροειδῶς πρὸς αὐτὸ
κεκλιμένῃ· ἐνταῦθα δ᾽ ἐστὶν ὁ φοινικών, μεμι-
γμένην ἔχων καὶ ἄλλην ὕλην ἥμερον καὶ εὔκαρπον, πλεονάζων δὲ τῷ φοίνικι, ἐπὶ μῆκος σταδίων
ἑκατόν, διάρρυτος ἅπας καὶ μεστὸς κατοικιῶν·
ἔστι δ᾽ αὐτοῦ καὶ βασίλειον καὶ ὁ τοῦ βαλσάμου
παράδεισος· ἔστι δὲ τὸ φυτὸν θαμνῶδες, κυτίσῳ
ἐοικὸς καὶ τερμίνθῳ, ἀρωματίζον· οὗ τὸν φλοιὸν
ἐπισχίσαντες ὑπολαμβάνουσιν ἀγγείοις τὸν ὀπόν,

[1] καταλαβών, Casaubon, for καταβαλών.
[2] After Μαχαιροῦς w adds Λύδας.
[3] After Λυσίας F adds καὶ Λύδας.

[1] i.e. Palm-grove. [2] Built by Herod the Great.

tions, and in particular took Jerusalem itself by force; for it was a rocky and well-walled fortress; and though well supplied with water inside, its outside territory was wholly without water; and it had a trench cut in rock, sixty feet in depth and two hundred and sixty feet in breadth; and, from the stone that had been hewn out, the wall of the temple was fenced with towers. Pompey seized the city, it is said, after watching for the day of fasting, when the Judaeans were abstaining from all work; he filled up the trench and threw ladders across it; moreover, he gave orders to rase all the walls and, so far as he could, destroyed the haunts of robbers and the treasure-holds of the tyrants. Two of these were situated on the passes leading to Hiericus, I mean Threx and Taurus, and others were Alexandrium and Hyrcanium and Machaerus and Lysias and those in the neighbourhood of Philadelphia and Scythopolis in the neighbourhood of Galilaea.

41. Hiericus is a plain surrounded by a kind of mountainous country, which, in a way, slopes towards it like a theatre. Here is the Phoenicon,[1] which is mixed also with other kinds of cultivated and fruitful trees, though it consists mostly of palm trees; it is one hundred stadia in length, and is everywhere watered with streams and full of dwellings. Here are also the palace [2] and the balsam park. The balsam is of the shrub kind, resembling cytisus [3] and terminthus,[4] and has a spicy flavour. The people make incisions in the bark and catch the juice in vessels. This juice is a glutinous, milk-

---

[3] *Medicago Arborea.*
[4] The terebinth tree, *Pistacia terebinthus* (cf. 15. 2. 10).

γλίσχρῳ γάλακτι παραπλήσιον· ἀναληφθεὶς δ᾿
εἰς κογχάρια λαμβάνει πῆξιν· λύει δὲ κεφα-
λαλγίας θαυμαστῶς καὶ ὑποχύσεις ἀρχομένας
καὶ ἀμβλυωπίας· τίμιος οὖν ἐστι, καὶ διότι
ἐνταῦθα μόνον γεννᾶται· καὶ ὁ φοινικὼν δὲ
τοιοῦτος, ἔχων τὸν καρπωτὸν φοίνικα ἐνταῦθα
μόνον, πλὴν τοῦ Βαβυλωνίου καὶ τοῦ ἐπέκεινα
πρὸς τὴν ἕω· μεγάλη οὖν ἀπ᾿ αὐτῶν ἡ πρόσοδος.
καὶ τῷ ξυλοβαλάμῳ δὲ ὡς ἀρώματι χρῶνται.

42. Ἡ δὲ Σιρβωνὶς λίμνη πολλὴ μέν ἐστι· καὶ
γὰρ χιλίων σταδίων εἰρήκασί τινες τὸν κύκλον·
τῇ μέντοι παραλίᾳ παρεκτέταται μικρῷ τι πλέον
τῶν διακοσίων σταδίων μῆκος ἐπιλαμβάνουσα,
ἀγχιβαθής, βαρύτατον ἔχουσα ὕδωρ, ὥστε μὴ
δεῖν κολύμβου, ἀλλὰ τὸν ἐμβάντα καὶ μέχρις
ὀμφαλοῦ προβάντα[1] εὐθὺς ἐξαίρεσθαι· μεστὴ δ᾿
ἐστὶν ἀσφάλτου· αὕτη[2] δὲ ἀναφυσᾶται κατὰ
καιροὺς ἀτάκτους ἐκ μέσου τοῦ βάθους μετὰ
πομφολύγων, ὡς ἂν ζέοντος ὕδατος· κυρτουμένη
δ᾿ ἡ ἐπιφάνεια λόφου φαντασίαν παρέχει· συνανα-
φέρεται δὲ καὶ ἄσβολος[3] πολλή, καπνώδης μέν,
πρὸς δὲ τὴν ὄψιν ἄδηλος, ὑφ᾿ ἧς κατιοῦται καὶ
χαλκὸς καὶ ἄργυρος καὶ πᾶν τὸ στιλπνὸν μέχρι
καὶ χρυσοῦ· ἀπὸ δὲ τοῦ κατιοῦσθαι τὰ σκεύη
γνωρίζουσιν οἱ περιοικοῦντες ἀρχομένην τὴν
ἀναβολὴν τοῦ ἀσφάλτου, καὶ παρασκευάζονται
πρὸς τὴν μεταλλείαν αὐτοῦ, ποιησάμενοι σχεδίας

---

[1] προεμβάντα CDF*hi*, προελθόντα *x*. προβάντα is omitted by
the Epit. and Meineke.

[2] τοῦτο, after αὕτη, is ejected by Groskurd and Meineke.

[3] Instead of ἄσβολος, E reads ἄσβαλος, F ἀσβῶλος, and the
Epit. βῶλος.

white substance; and when it is put up in small
quantities it solidifies; and it is remarkable for its
cure of headache and of incipient cataracts and of
dimness of sight. Accordingly, it is costly; and
also for the reason that it is produced nowhere else.
Such is also the case with the Phoenicon, which
alone has the caryotic palm,[1] excepting the Babylonian and that beyond Babylonia towards the east.
Accordingly, the revenue derived from it is great.
And they use the xylo-balsam [2] as spice.

42. Lake Sirbonis [3] is large; in fact some state
that it is one thousand stadia in circuit; however,
it extends parallel to the coast to a length of slightly
more than two hundred stadia, is deep to the very
shore, and has water so very heavy that there is no
use for divers, and any person who walks into it
and proceeds no farther than up to his navel is
immediately raised afloat. It is full of asphalt.
The asphalt is blown to the surface at irregular
intervals from the midst of the deep, and with it
rise bubbles, as though the water were boiling;
and the surface of the lake, being convex, presents
the appearance of a hill. With the asphalt there
arises also much soot, which, though smoky, is
imperceptible to the eye; and it tarnishes copper
and silver and anything that glistens, even gold;
and when their vessels are becoming tarnished the
people who live round the lake know that the asphalt
is beginning to rise; and they prepare to collect

[1] Palma caryota, with walnut-like fruit.
[2] Apparently the liquid obtained from the branches when
cut off.
[3] Strabo seems obviously to be confusing the Asphaltites
Lacus (the Dead Sea) with Lake Sirbonis, which latter " broke
through to the Mediterranean Sea " (see 1. 3. 4 and 1. 4. 7).

C 764 καλαμίνας. ἔστι δ᾽ ἡ ἄσφαλτος γῆς βῶλος,
ὑγραινομένη μὲν ὑπὸ θερμοῦ καὶ ἀναφυσωμένη
καὶ διαχεομένη, πάλιν δὲ μεταβάλλουσα εἰς
πάγον ἰσχυρὸν ὑπὸ τοῦ ψυχροῦ ὕδατος, οἷόν
ἐστι τὸ τῆς λίμνης ὕδωρ, ὥστε τομῆς καὶ κοπῆς
δεῖσθαι· εἶτ᾽ ἐπιπολάζουσα διὰ τὴν φύσιν τοῦ
ὕδατος, καθ᾽ ἣν ἔφαμεν μηδὲ κολύμβου δεῖσθαι,
μηδὲ βαπτίζεσθαι τὸν ἐμβάντα, ἀλλ᾽ ἐξαίρεσθαι·
προσπλεύσαντες δὲ ταῖς σχεδίαις κόπτουσι καὶ
φέρονται τῆς ἀσφάλτου ὅσον ἕκαστος δύναται.
43. Τὸ μὲν οὖν συμβαῖνον τοιοῦτον· γόητας δὲ
ὄντας σκήπτεσθαί φησιν ἐπῳδὰς ὁ Ποσειδώνιος
τοὺς ἀνθρώπους καὶ οὖρα καὶ ἄλλα δυσώδη ὑγρά,
ἃ¹ περικαταχέαντας καὶ ἐκπιάσαντας πήττειν
τὴν ἄσφαλτον, εἶτα τέμνειν· εἰ μή τίς ἐστιν
ἐπιτηδειότης τῶν οὔρων τοιαύτη, καθάπερ καὶ
ἐν ταῖς κύστεσι τῶν λιθιώντων, καὶ ἐκ τῶν
παιδικῶν οὔρων ἡ χρυσόκολλα συνίσταται· ἐν
μέσῃ δὲ τῇ λίμνῃ τὸ πάθος συμβαίνειν εὔλογον,
ὅτι καὶ ἡ πηγὴ τοῦ πυρὸς καὶ τῆς ἀσφάλτου
κατὰ μέσον ἐστὶ καὶ τὸ πλῆθος· ἄτακτος δὲ ἡ
ἀναφύσησις, ὅτι καὶ ἡ τοῦ πυρὸς κίνησις οὐκ
ἔχει τάξιν ἡμῖν φανεράν, ὥσπερ καὶ ἄλλων
πνευμάτων πολλῶν. τοιαῦτα δὲ καὶ τὰ ἐν
Ἀπολλωνίᾳ τῇ Ἠπειρώτιδι.

¹ ἅ, Corais brackets.

---

¹ On a recent visit to the Dead Sea (December, 1929), the
translator found that Strabo's whole account is substantially
correct. As for floating, a very corpulent person could walk
out only up to the navel before floating, but a very lean
person up to the shoulders.

it by means of rafts made of reed. The asphalt is a clod of earth, which at first is liquefied by heat, and is blown up to the surface and spreads out; and then again, by reason of the cold water, the kind of water the lake in question has, it changes to a firm, solidified substance, and therefore requires cutting and chopping; and then it floats, because of the nature of the water, owing to which, as I was saying, there is no use for divers; and no person who walks into it can immerse himself either, but is raised afloat.[1] They reach the asphalt on rafts and chop it and carry off as much as they each can.

43. Such, then, is the fact in the case; but according to Poseidonius the people are sorcerers and pretend to use incantations, as also urine and other malodorous liquids, which they first pour all over the solidified substance, and squeeze out the asphalt and harden it, and then cut it into pieces; unless there is some suitable element of this kind in urine, such, for example, as chrysocolla,[2] which forms in the bladder of people who have bladder-stones and is derived from the urine of children. It is reasonable that this behaviour should occur in the middle of the lake, because the source of the fire and also the greater part of the asphalt is at the middle of it; but the bubbling up is irregular, because the movement of the fire, like that of many other subterranean blasts, follows no order known to us. Such, also, are the phenomena at Apollonia in Epirus.[3]

---

[2] Literally, " gold-solder." The translator does not know what the word means in the above passage, whether malachite (carbonate of copper), or borate of soda, or what.

[3] See 7. 5. 8.

44. Τοῦ δ᾽ ἔμπυρον τὴν χώραν εἶναι καὶ ἄλλα
τεκμήρια φέρουσι πολλά· καὶ γὰρ πέτρας τινὰς
ἐπικεκαυμένας δεικνύουσι τραχείας περὶ Μοα-
σάδα καὶ σήραγγας πολλαχοῦ καὶ γῆν τεφρώδη,
σταγόνας τε πίσσης ἐκ λισσάδων λειβομένας
καὶ δυσώδεις πόρρωθεν ποταμοὺς ζέοντας, κατοικίας τε ἀνατετραμμένας σποράδην· ὥστε πιστεύειν τοῖς θρυλουμένοις ὑπὸ τῶν ἐγχωρίων, ὡς
ἄρα ᾠκοῦντό ποτε τρισκαίδεκα πόλεις ἐνταῦθα,
ὧν τῆς μητροπόλεως Σοδόμων σώζοιτο κύκλος
ἑξήκοντά που σταδίων· ὑπὸ δὲ σεισμῶν καὶ
ἀναφυσημάτων πυρὸς καὶ θερμῶν ὑδάτων ἀσφαλ-
τωδῶν τε καὶ θειωδῶν ἡ λίμνη προπέσοι καὶ
πέτραι πυρίληπτοι γένοιντο, αἵ τε πόλεις αἱ μὲν
καταποθεῖεν, ἃς δ᾽ ἐκλίποιεν οἱ δυνάμενοι φυγεῖν.
Ἐρατοσθένης δέ φησι τἀναντία, λιμναζούσης τῆς
χώρας, ἐκρήγμασιν ἀνακαλυφθῆναι τὴν πλείστην, καθάπερ τὴν θάλατταν.[1]

45. Ἔστι δὲ καὶ ἐν τῇ Γαδαρίδι ὕδωρ μοχθηρὸν
λιμναῖον, οὗ τὰ γευσάμενα κτήνη τρίχας καὶ
ὁπλὰς καὶ κέρατα ἀποβάλλει. ἐν δὲ ταῖς κα-
λουμέναις Ταριχέαις[2] ἡ λίμνη μὲν ταριχείας
ἰχθύων ἀστείας παρέχει, φύει δὲ δένδρα καρπο-
φόρα, μηλέαις ἐμφερῆ· χρῶνται δ᾽ Αἰγύπτιοι τῇ
ἀσφάλτῳ πρὸς τὰς ταριχείας τῶν νεκρῶν.

46. Πομπήιος μὲν οὖν περικόψας τινὰ τῶν
C 765 ἐξιδιασθέντων ὑπὸ τῶν Ἰουδαίων κατὰ βίαν

[1] θάλατταν, Corais emends to Θετταλίαν.
[2] Ταριχίαις F, Ταριχείας; emended by Tzschucke.

44. Many other evidences are produced to show that the country is fiery; for near Moasada are to be seen rugged rocks that have been scorched, as also, in many places, fissures and ashy soil, and drops of pitch dripping from smooth cliffs, and boiling rivers that emit foul odours to a great distance, and ruined settlements here and there; and therefore people believe the oft-repeated assertions of the local inhabitants, that there were once thirteen inhabited cities in that region of which Sodom was the metropolis, but that a circuit of about sixty stadia of that city escaped unharmed; and that by reason of earthquakes and of eruptions of fire and of hot waters containing asphalt and sulphur, the lake burst its bounds, and rocks were enveloped with fire; and, as for the cities, some were swallowed up and others were abandoned by such as were able to escape. But Eratosthenes says, on the contrary, that the country was a lake, and that most of it was uncovered by outbreaks, as was the case with the sea.[1]

45. In Gadaris, also, there is noxious lake water; and when animals taste it they lose hair and hoofs and horns. At the place called Taricheae the lake supplies excellent fish for pickling; and on its banks grow fruit-bearing trees resembling apple trees. The Aegyptians use the asphalt for embalming the bodies of the dead.

46. Now Pompey clipped off some of the territory that had been forcibly appropriated by the Judaeans,

[1] *i.e.* the lake burst its bounds in a number of places, as did the Mediterranean at the Pillars (see 1. 2. 31), if the text is correct. But it is most probable that Strabo wrote "as was the case with *Thessaly*" (see 9. 5. 2, and Herodotus 7. 129), as suggested by Corais and Kramer (see critical note).

ἀπέδειξεν Ἡρώδῃ[1] τὴν ἱερωσύνην· τῶν δ' ἀπὸ
γένους τις[2] ὕστερον Ἡρώδης, ἀνὴρ ἐπιχώριος,
παραδὺς εἰς τὴν ἱερωσύνην, τοσοῦτον διήνεγκε
τῶν πρὸ αὐτοῦ, καὶ μάλιστα τῇ πρὸς Ῥωμαίους
ὁμιλίᾳ καὶ πολιτείᾳ, ὥστε καὶ βασιλεὺς ἐχρη-
μάτισε, δόντος τὸ μὲν πρῶτον Ἀντωνίου τὴν
ἐξουσίαν, ὕστερον δὲ καὶ Καίσαρος τοῦ Σεβαστοῦ·
τῶν δ' υἱῶν τοὺς μὲν αὐτὸς ἀνεῖλεν, ὡς ἐπιβουλεύ-
σαντας αὐτῷ, τοὺς δὲ τελευτῶν διαδόχους ἀπέ-
λιπε, μερίδας αὐτοῖς ἀποδούς. Καῖσαρ δὲ καὶ
τοὺς υἱοὺς ἐτίμησε τοῦ Ἡρώδου καὶ τὴν ἀδελφὴν
Σαλώμην καὶ τὴν ταύτης θυγατέρα Βερενίκην· οὐ
μέντοι εὐτύχησαν οἱ παῖδες, ἀλλ' ἐν αἰτίαις
ἐγένοντο, καὶ ὁ μὲν ἐν φυγῇ διετέλει, παρὰ τοῖς
Ἀλλόβριξι Γαλάταις λαβὼν οἴκησιν, οἱ δὲ
θεραπείᾳ πολλῇ μόλις εὕροντο κάθοδον, τετραρ-
χίας ἀποδειχθείσης ἑκατέρῳ.

III

1. Ὑπέρκειται δὲ τῆς Ἰουδαίας καὶ τῆς Κοίλης
Συρίας μέχρι Βαβυλωνίας καὶ τῆς τοῦ Εὐφράτου
ποταμίας πρὸς νότον Ἀραβία πᾶσα χωρὶς τῶν ἐν
τῇ Μεσοποταμίᾳ Σκηνιτῶν. περὶ μὲν οὖν τῆς
Μεσοποταμίας καὶ τῶν νεμομένων αὐτὴν ἐθνῶν
εἴρηται· τὰ δὲ πέραν τοῦ Εὐφράτου τὰ μὲν πρὸς ταῖς
ἐκβολαῖς αὐτοῦ νέμονται Βαβυλώνιοι καὶ τὸ τῶν

---

[1] Ἡρώδῃ, Corais emends to Ὑρκανῷ.
[2] τις hz, τισίν, other MSS.

and appointed Herod [1] to the priesthood; but later
a certain Herod, a descendant of his and a native
of the country, who slinked into the priesthood,
was so superior to his predecessors, particularly
in his intercourse with the Romans and in his
administration of affairs of state, that he received
the title of king, being given that authority first
by Antony and later by Augustus Caesar. As for
his sons, he himself put some of them to death, on
the ground that they had plotted against him; and
at his death left others as his successors, having
assigned to them portions of his kingdom. Caesar
also honoured the sons of Herod and his sister Salomê
and her daughter Berenicê. However, his sons
were not successful, but became involved in accusa-
tions; and one of them [2] spent the rest of his life
in exile, having taken up his abode among the
Allobrogian Gauls, whereas the others, [3] by much
obsequiousness, but with difficulty, found leave to
return home, with a tetrarchy assigned to each.

III

1. Above Judaea and Coelê-Syria, as far as
Babylonia and the river-country of the Euphrates
towards the south, lies the whole of Arabia, with
the exception of the Scenitae in Mesopotamia.
Now I have already spoken of Mesopotamia and
the tribes that occupy it; [4] but as for the parts on
the far side of the Euphrates, those near its outlets
are occupied by Babylonians and the tribe of the

---

[1] Hyrcanus, apparently.　　　[2] Archeläus.
[3] Antipas and Philip.　　　[4] 16. 1. 26 ff.

Χαλδαίων ἔθνος (εἴρηται δὲ καὶ[1] περὶ τούτων),
τὰ δ' ἑξῆς τῆς Μεσοποταμίας μέχρι Κοίλης
Συρίας, τὸ μὲν πλησιάζον τῷ ποταμῷ καὶ τὴν
Μεσοποταμίαν Σκηνῖται κατέχουσιν Ἄραβες,
δυναστείας ἀποτετμημένοι μικρὰς ἐν λυπροῖς
χωρίοις διὰ τὰς ἀνυδρίας, γεωργοῦντες μὲν ἢ
οὐδὲν ἢ μικρά, νομὰς δὲ ἔχοντες παντοδαπῶν
θρεμμάτων, καὶ μάλιστα καμήλων· ὑπὲρ δὲ τούτων ἔρημός ἐστι πολλή· τὰ δὲ τούτων ἔτι νοτιώτερα ἔχουσιν οἱ τὴν εὐδαίμονα καλουμένην Ἀραβίαν οἰκοῦντες. ταύτης δὲ τὸ μὲν προσάρκτιον
πλευρὸν ἡ λεχθεῖσά ἐστιν ἔρημος, τὸ δ' ἑῷον
ὁ Περσικὸς κόλπος, τὸ δὲ ἑσπέριον ὁ Ἀράβιος,
τὸ δὲ νότιον ἡ μεγάλη θάλαττα ἡ ἔξω τῶν κόλπων
ἀμφοῖν, ἣν ἅπασαν Ἐρυθρὰν καλοῦσιν.

2. Ὁ μὲν οὖν Περσικὸς κόλπος λέγεται καὶ ἡ
κατὰ Πέρσας θάλαττα· φησὶ δὲ περὶ αὐτῆς
Ἐρατοσθένης οὕτως, ὅτι τὸ μὲν στόμα φησὶν
εἶναι στενὸν οὕτως, ὥστ' ἐξ Ἁρμόζων, τοῦ τῆς
Καρμανίας ἀκρωτηρίου, τῆς Ἀραβίας ἀφορᾶται
τὸ ἐν Μάκαις· ἀπὸ δὲ τοῦ στόματος ἡ ἐν δεξιᾷ
παραλία περιφερὴς οὖσα κατ' ἀρχὰς μὲν ἀπὸ τῆς
Καρμανίας πρὸς ἕω μικρόν, εἶτα πρὸς ἄρκτον
νεύει, καὶ μετὰ ταῦτα πρὸς τὴν ἑσπέραν μέχρι
Τερηδόνος καὶ τῆς ἐκβολῆς τοῦ Εὐφράτου· περιέ-
χει δὲ τήν τε Καρμανίων παραλίαν καὶ τὴν
C 766 Περσῶν καὶ Σουσίων καὶ Βαβυλωνίων ἀπὸ
μέρους, ὅσον μυρίων οὖσα[2] σταδίων· περὶ ὧν καὶ
ἡμεῖς εἰρήκαμεν· τὸ δ' ἐντεῦθεν ἑξῆς ἐπὶ τὸ στόμα
πάλιν ἄλλοι τοσοῦτοι, καθάπερ καὶ Ἀνδροσθένη

---

[1] καί is omitted by all MSS. except x.

Chaldaeans, of whom I have already spoken;[1] and of those parts that follow after Mesopotamia as far as Coelê-Syria, the part that lies near the river, as well as Mesopotamia, is occupied by Arabian Scenitae, who are divided off into small sovereignties and live in tracts that are barren for want of water. These people till the land either little or none, but they keep herds of all kinds, particularly of camels. Above these people lies an extensive desert; but the parts lying still farther south than their country are held by the people who inhabit Arabia Felix, as it is called. The northern side of Arabia Felix is formed by the above-mentioned desert, the eastern by the Persian Gulf, the western by the Arabian Gulf, and the southern by the great sea that lies outside both gulfs, which as a whole is called Erythra.[2]

2. Now the Persian Gulf is also called the Persian Sea; and Eratosthenes describes it as follows: its mouth, he says, is so narrow that from Harmozi, the promontory of Carmania, one can see the promontory at Macae in Arabia; and from its mouth the coast on the right, being circular, inclines at first, from Carmania, slightly towards the east, and then towards the north, and, after this, towards the west as far as Teredon and the outlet of the Euphrates; and it comprises the coast of the Carmanians and in part that of the Persians and Susians and Babylonians, a distance of about ten thousand stadia. I have already spoken of these peoples.[3] And thence next to its mouth it extends another ten thousand stadia, as stated, Eratosthenes says, by

[1] 16. 1. 6.   [2] *i.e.* " Red " Sea.   [3] 15. 2. 14 ff.

---

[2] οὖσα D, οὖσαν other MSS.

λέγειν φησὶ τὸν Θάσιον, τὸν καὶ Νεάρχῳ συμ
πλεύσαντα καὶ¹ καθ' αὑτόν· ὥστε δῆλον ἐκ
τούτων εἶναι, διότι μικρὸν ἀπολείπεται τῷ μεγέθει
τῆς κατὰ τὸν Εὔξεινον θαλάττης αὕτη ἡ θάλαττα·
λέγειν δέ φησιν ἐκεῖνον περιπεπλευκότα στόλῳ
τὸν κόλπον, ὅτι ἀπὸ Τερηδόνος ἐξῆς ἐν δεξιᾷ
ἔχοντι τὴν ἤπειρον ὁ παράπλους ἔχει προκειμένην
νῆσον Ἴκαρον,² καὶ ἱερὸν Ἀπόλλωνος ἅγιον ἐν
αὐτῇ καὶ μαντεῖον Ταυροπόλου.

3. Παραπλεύσαντι δὲ τῆς Ἀραβίας εἰς δισχιλί
ους καὶ τετρακοσίους σταδίους ἐν βαθεῖ κόλπῳ κεῖ
ται πόλις Γέρρα, Χαλδαίων φυγάδων ἐκ Βαβυλῶνος
οἰκούντων γῆν³ ἁλμυρίδα καὶ ἐχόντων ἁλίνας τὰς
οἰκίας, ἅς, ἐπειδὴ λεπίδες τῶν ἁλῶν ἀφιστάμεναι
κατὰ τὴν ἐπίκαυσιν τὴν ἐκ τῶν ἡλίων συνεχεῖς
ἀποπίπτουσι, καταρραίνοντες ὕδασι πυκνὰ τοὺς
τοίχους συνέχουσι· διέχει δὲ τῆς θαλάττης
διακοσίους σταδίους ἡ πόλις· πεζέμποροι δ' εἰσὶν
οἱ Γερραῖοι τὸ πλέον τῶν Ἀραβίων φορτίων καὶ
ἀρωμάτων.⁴ Ἀριστόβουλος δὲ τοὐναντίον φησὶ
τοὺς Γερραίους τὰ πολλὰ σχεδίαις εἰς τὴν Βαβυ
λωνίαν ἐμπορεύεσθαι, ἐκεῖθεν δὲ τῷ Εὐφράτῃ τὰ
φορτία ἀναπλεῖν εἰς Θάψακον, εἶτα πεζῇ κομί
ζεσθαι πάντῃ.

4. Πλεύσαντι δ' ἐπὶ πλέον ἄλλαι νῆσοι, Τύρος
καὶ Ἄραδος, εἰσίν, ἱερὰ ἔχουσαι τοῖς Φοινικικοῖς⁵
ὅμοια· καί φασί γε οἱ ἐν αὐταῖς οἰκοῦντες τὰς
ὁμωνύμους τῶν Φοινίκων νήσους καὶ πόλεις
ἀποίκους ἑαυτῶν. διέχουσι δὲ αἱ νῆσοι αὗται

¹ καί, Tyrwhitt inserts before καθ'.
² Ἴκαρον E. Ἴκαριον other MSS.
³ γῆν, Meineke, for τήν.
⁴ ἀρωμάτων i, ἀρωματικῶν other MSS.

Androsthenes the Thasian, who made the voyage,
not only with Nearchus but also on his own account;
so that it is clear from this that this sea is but little
short of the Euxine in size; and Eratosthenes says
that Androsthenes, who sailed round the gulf with
a fleet, states that in making the coasting voyage,
with the continent on the right, one sees next after
Teredon the island Icarus and a temple sacred to
Apollo in it and an oracle of Tauropolus.[1]

3. After sailing along the coast of Arabia for a
distance of two thousand four hundred stadia, one
comes to Gerrha,[2] a city situated on a deep gulf;
it is inhabited by Chaldaeans, exiles from Babylon;
the soil contains salt and the people live in houses
made of salt; and since flakes of salt continually
scale off, owing to the scorching heat of the rays of
the sun, and fall away, the people frequently sprinkle
the houses with water and thus keep the walls firm.
The city is two hundred stadia distant from the sea;
and the Gerrhaeans traffic by land, for the most part,
in the Arabian merchandise and aromatics, though
Aristobulus says, on the contrary, that the Gerrhaeans
import most of their cargoes on rafts to Babylonia,
and thence sail up the Euphrates with them, and
then convey them by land to all parts of the country.

4. On sailing farther, one comes to other islands,
I mean Tyre and Aradus, which have temples like
those of the Phoenicians. It is asserted, at least
by the inhabitants of the islands, that the islands
and cities of the Phoenicians which bear the same
name are their own colonies. These islands are

---

[1] *i.e.* Artemis Tauropolus.   [2] Now Adjer.

---

[5] φοινικοῖς CD*h*, φοινικικίοις *o*, φοινικίοις *xz*.

Τερηδόνος μὲν δεχήμερον πλοῦν, τῆς δὲ κατὰ τὸ στόμα ἄκρας τῆς ἐν Μάκαις ἡμερήσιον.

5. Ἀπὸ δὲ τῆς Καρμανίας εἰρήκασι καὶ Νέαρχος καὶ Ὀρθαγόρας νῆσον Ὤγυριν[1] κεῖσθαι πρὸς νότον πελαγίαν ἐν δισχιλίοις σταδίοις, ἐν ᾗ τάφος Ἐρύθρα δείκνυται, χῶμα μέγα ἀγρίοις φοίνιξι κατάφυτον· τοῦτον δὲ βασιλεῦσαι τῶν τόπων καὶ ἀπ᾽ αὐτοῦ τὴν θάλατταν ἐπώνυμον καταλιπεῖν· δηλῶσαι δὲ ταῦτά φησιν αὐτοῖς Μιθρωπάστην τὸν Ἀρσίτου[2] τοῦ Φρυγίας σατράπου, φυγόντα μὲν Δαρεῖον, διατρίψαντα δ᾽ ἐν τῇ νήσῳ, συμμίξαντα δὲ αὐτοῖς καταχθεῖσιν εἰς τὸν Περσικὸν κόλπον καὶ ζητοῦντα κάθοδον δι᾽ αὐτῶν εἰς τὴν οἰκείαν.

6. Καθ᾽ ὅλην δὲ τὴν τῆς Ἐρυθρᾶς παραλίαν κατὰ βυθοῦ φύεται δένδρα ὅμοια δάφνῃ καὶ ἐλαίᾳ, ταῖς μὲν ἀμπώτισιν ὅλα ὑπερφανῆ γιγνόμενα, ταῖς δὲ πλημμυρίσιν ἔσθ᾽ ὅτε ὅλα καλυπτόμενα, καὶ ταῦτα τῆς ὑπερκειμένης γῆς ἀδένδρου οὔσης, ὥστε C 767 ἐπιτείνεσθαι[3] τὸ παράδοξον. περὶ μὲν οὖν τῆς κατὰ Πέρσας θαλάττης, ἣν ἑῴαν πλευρὰν ἔφαμεν εἶναι τῆς εὐδαίμονος Ἀραβίας, τοιαῦτα εἴρηκεν Ἐρατοσθένης.

7. Φησὶ δ᾽ ὁ Νέαρχος τὸν Μιθρωπάστην ἐντυχεῖν αὐτοῖς μετὰ Μαζήνου· τὸν δὲ Μαζήνην ἐπάρχειν νήσου τινὸς τῶν ἐν τῷ Περσικῷ κόλπῳ· καλεῖσθαι δὲ τὴν νῆσον Ὀάρακτα·[4] εἰς ταύτην δὲ τὸν Μιθρωπάστην καταφυγόντα ξενίας τυχεῖν

[1] Ὤγυριν, Kramer, for Τυρίνην CDF h i x z, Τυρρηνήν E, Ὤγυρον Corais.
[2] Ἀρσίτου, Meineke, for Ἀρητίνου.
[3] ἐπιτείνεσθαι, Corais, for ἐπιγίνεσθαι.

distant a ten days' sail from Teredon and a one day's sail from the promontory near the mouth of the gulf at Macae.

5. Both Nearchus and Orthagoras state that the island Ogyris lies in the high sea at a distance of two thousand stadia from Carmania, and that on it is to be seen the grave of Erythras, a large mound planted with wild palm trees; and that Erythras reigned as king over that region and left the sea named after himself.[1] Nearchus says that these things were pointed out to them by Mithropastes, the son of Aristes, which latter was satrap of Phrygia; and that the former was banished by Dareius, took up his residence in the island, joined them when they landed in the Persian Gulf, and sought through them to be restored to his homeland.

6. Along the whole of the coast of the Red Sea, down in the deep, grow trees like the laurel and the olive, which at the ebb tides are wholly visible above the water but at the full tides are sometimes wholly covered;[2] and while this is the case, the land that lies above the sea has no trees, and therefore the peculiarity is all the greater. Such are the statements of Eratosthenes concerning the Persian Sea, which, as I was saying, forms the eastern side of Arabia Felix.

7. Nearchus says that they were met by Mithropastes, in company with Mazenes; that Mazenes was ruler of an island in the Persian Gulf; that the island was called Oaracta; that Mithropastes took refuge, and obtained hospitality, in this island upon

[1] i.e. the "Erythraean" (Red) Sea.
[2] Coral Reefs, apparently.

---

[4] Ὀάρακτα, Corais and Meineke, for Δύρακτα *moxz*, Δώρακτα other MSS., Δῶρα Stephanus.

κατὰ τὴν ἐξ Ὠγύριος[1] γενομένην ἄφοδον, καὶ δὴ καὶ συνελθεῖν τῷ Μαζήνῃ[2] συσταθησόμενον τοῖς ἐν τῷ στόλῳ Μακεδόσι, τὸν δὲ Μαζήνην καὶ καθηγεμόνα τοῦ πλοῦ γενέσθαι. λέγει δὲ καὶ ἐν ἀρχῇ τοῦ Περσικοῦ παράπλου νῆσον, ἐν ᾗ μαργαρίτης πολὺς καὶ πολυτίμητός ἐστιν, ἐν ἄλλαις δὲ ψῆφοι τῶν διαυγῶν καὶ λαμπρῶν· ἐν δὲ ταῖς πρὸ τοῦ Εὐφράτου νήσοις δένδρα φύεσθαι λιβάνου πνέοντα, ὧν τὰς ῥίζας κλωμένων ὀπὸν ῥεῖν· παγούρων δὲ καὶ ἐχίνων μεγέθη, ὅπερ κοινὸν ἐν πάσῃ τῇ ἔξω θαλάττῃ· τοὺς μὲν γὰρ εἶναι μείζους καυσίων, τοὺς δὲ καὶ δικοτύλους· ἐποκεῖλαν δὲ κῆτος ἰδεῖν πεντήκοντα πηχῶν.

IV

1. Ἀρχὴ δὲ τῆς Ἀραβίας ἀπὸ τῆς Βαβυλωνίας ἐστὶν ἡ Μαικηνή·[3] πρόκειται δὲ ταύτης τῇ μὲν ἡ ἔρημος τῶν Ἀράβων, τῇ δὲ τὰ ἕλη τὰ κατὰ Χαλδαίους, ἃ ποιεῖ παρεκχεόμενος ὁ Εὐφράτης, τῇ δὲ ἡ κατὰ Πέρσας θάλαττα, δυσάερος[4] οὖσα καὶ ὁμιχλώδης καὶ ἔπομβρος ἅμα καὶ καυματηρά, καλλίκαρπος[5] ἐστιν ὅμως· ἡ δ᾽ ἄμπελος ἐν ἕλεσι

[1] Ὠγύριος, Tzschucke and Kramer and Meineke, for Ὠγύρου.

[2] Μαζήνῃ, Tzschucke, for Ἀμαζήνῃ.

[3] Μαικηνή appears to be an error for Μαισηνή (or Μεσηνή). Cp. Μεσήνης (2. 1. 31) and Μεσηνῶν (16. 1. 8).

[4] δέ, after δυσάερος, Corais deletes.

his departure from Ogyris; that, furthermore, Mithropastes had a conference with Mazenes for the purpose of being recommended by him to the Macedonians in the fleet; and that Mazenes became guide in their voyage. Nearchus goes on to say that there is an island at the beginning of the Persian Gulf where quantities of valuable pearls are to be found; and that in other islands there are pebbles of transparent and brilliant stones; and that in the islands off the mouth of the Euphrates there are trees which smell like frankincense, and that juice flows from their roots when they are broken in pieces. And he speaks of the large size of the crabs and sea-urchins, which is a common thing in the whole of the exterior sea; for, he adds, some are larger than hats [1] and others as large as a vessel holding two cotylae; [2] and he says that he saw a whale stranded on the beach that was fifty cubits [3] in length.

IV

1. Arabia commences on the side of Babylonia with Maecenê. In front of Maecenê, on one side, lies the desert of the Arabians; and on another side lie the marshes opposite the Chaldaeans, which are formed by diversions of water from the Euphrates; and on another side lies the Persian Sea. The country has foul air, is misty, and is subject both to rains and to scorching heat; but still its products are excellent. The vine grows in the marshes, as

[1] The Greek word implies the broad-brimmed felt hats worn by the Macedonians.
[2] *i.e.* nearly a pint.   [3] About 100 feet.

---

[5] δέ, Corais inserts.

φύεται, καλαμίναις ῥιψὶν ἐπιβαλλομένης γῆς,
ὅση δέξαιτ᾽ ἂν τὸ φυτόν, ὥστε φορητὴν γίνεσθαι
πολλάκις, εἶτα κοντοῖς ἀπωθεῖσθαι πάλιν εἰς τὴν
οἰκείαν ἕδραν.

2. Ἐπάνειμι δὲ ἐπὶ τὰς Ἐρατοσθένους ἀποφάσεις, ἃς ἑξῆς περὶ τῆς Ἀραβίας ἐκτίθεται. φησὶ
δὲ περὶ τῆς προσαρκτίου καὶ ἐρήμης, ἥτις ἐστὶ
μεταξὺ τῆς τε εὐδαίμονος Ἀραβίας καὶ τῆς
Κοιλοσύρων καὶ τῶν Ἰουδαίων, μέχρι τοῦ μυχοῦ
τοῦ Ἀραβίου κόλπου, διότι ἀπὸ Ἡρώων πόλεως,
ἥτις ἐστὶ πρὸς τῷ Νείλῳ μυχὸς[1] τοῦ Ἀραβίου
κόλπου, πρὸς μὲν τὴν Ναβαταίων Πέτραν εἰς
Βαβυλῶνα πεντακισχίλιοι ἑξακόσιοι, πᾶσα μὲν
πρὸς ἀνατολὰς θερινάς, διὰ δὲ τῶν παρακειμένων
Ἀραβίων ἐθνῶν Ναβαταίων τε καὶ Χαυλοταίων
καὶ Ἀγραίων· ὑπὲρ δὲ τούτων ἡ Εὐδαίμων ἐστίν,
ἐπὶ μυρίους καὶ δισχιλίους ἐκκειμένη σταδίους πρὸς
νότον μέχρι τοῦ Ἀτλαντικοῦ πελάγους. ἔχουσι δ᾽
αὐτὴν οἱ μὲν πρῶτοι μετὰ τοὺς Σύρους καὶ τοὺς
Ἰουδαίους ἄνθρωποι γεωργοί· μετὰ δὲ τούτους
δίαμμός ἐστι γῆ καὶ λυπρά, φοίνικας ἔχουσα ὀλίγους καὶ ἄκανθαν καὶ μυρίκην καὶ ὀρυκτὰ ὕδατα,
καθάπερ καὶ ἡ Γεδρωσία· σκηνῖται δ᾽ ἔχουσιν αὐτὴν
C 768 Ἄραβες καὶ καμηλοβοσκοί. τὰ δ᾽ ἔσχατα πρὸς
νότον καὶ ἀνταίροντα τῇ Αἰθιοπίᾳ βρέχεταί τε
θερινοῖς ὄμβροις καὶ δισπορεῖται παραπλησίως τῇ
Ἰνδικῇ, ποταμοὺς δ᾽ ἔχει καταναλισκομένους εἰς
πεδία καὶ λίμνας. εὐκαρπία δ᾽ ἐστὶν ἥ τε ἄλλη

---

[1] Corais and Meineke insert ἐν τῷ after ἐστί, and emend
μυχός to μυχῷ, but cp. ἔστι δ᾽ ἡ Ἄλωρος τὸ μυχαίτατον τοῦ
Θερμαίου κόλπου (Book VII, Frag. 20), and οὗτος (i.e. the
recess of the Arabian Gulf referred to) ὀνομάζεται Ποσείδιον.

much earth being thrown on hurdles of reeds as the
plant may require; so that the vine is often carried
away, and then is pushed back again to its proper
place by means of poles.

2. But I return to Eratosthenes, who next sets
forth his opinions concerning Arabia. He says concerning the northerly, or desert, part of Arabia, which
lies between Arabia Felix and Coelê-Syria and Judaea,
extending as far as the recess of the Arabian Gulf,
that from the City of Heroes,[1] which forms a recess
of the Arabian Gulf near the Nile, the distance in the
direction of the Petra of the Nabataeans to Babylon
is five thousand six hundred stadia, the whole of the
journey being in the direction of the summer sunrise[2]
and through the adjacent countries of the Arabian
tribes, I mean the Nabataeans and the Chaulotaeans
and the Agraeans. Above these lies Arabia Felix,
which extends for a distance of twelve thousand stadia
towards the south, to the Atlantic Sea. The first
people who occupy Arabia Felix, after the Syrians
and Judaeans, are farmers. After these the soil is
sandy and barren, producing a few palm-trees and
a thorny tree[3] and the tamarisk, and affording
water by digging, as is the case in Gedrosia;[4] and
it is occupied by tent-dwellers and camel-herds.
The extreme parts towards the south, lying opposite
to Aethiopia, are watered by summer rains and are
sowed twice, like India;[5] and the rivers there are
used up in supplying plains and lakes. The country

[1] Heröonpolis.
[2] *i.e.* north-east (cf. Vol. I, p. 105, note 1).
[3] Apparently the *Mimosa Nilotica.*
[4] *i.e.* well-water (see 15. 2. 3).
[5] See 15. 1. 20 and 17. 3. 11.

καὶ μελιτουργεῖα δαψιλῆ, βοσκημάτων τε ἀφθονία
πλὴν ἵππων καὶ ἡμιόνων καὶ ὑῶν, ὄρνεά τε
παντοῖα πλὴν χηνῶν καὶ ἀλεκτορίδων. κατοικεῖ
δὲ τὰ μέγιστα τέτταρα ἔθνη τὴν ἐσχάτην λεχθεῖσαν χώραν· Μιναῖοι [1] μὲν ἐν τῷ πρὸς τὴν Ἐρυθρὰν
μέρει, πόλις δ’ αὐτῶν ἡ μεγίστη Κάρνα ἢ Κάρ-
νανα· [2] ἐχόμενοι δὲ τούτων Σαβαῖοι, μητρόπολις
δ’ αὐτῶν Μαρίαβα· τρίτοι δὲ Κατταβανεῖς, καθή-
κοντες πρὸς τὰ στενὰ καὶ τὴν διάβασιν τοῦ
Ἀραβίου κόλπου, τὸ δὲ βασίλειον αὐτῶν Τάμνα
καλεῖται· πρὸς ἔω δὲ μάλιστα Χατραμωτῖται,
πόλιν δ’ ἔχουσι Σάβαταν.

3. Μοναρχοῦνται δὲ πᾶσαι καί εἰσιν εὐδαίμονες,
κατεσκευασμέναι καλῶς ἱεροῖς τε καὶ βασιλείοις·
αἵ τε οἰκίαι ταῖς Αἰγυπτίαις ἐοίκασι κατὰ τὴν
τῶν ξύλων ἔνδεσιν· χώραν δ’ ἐπέχουσιν οἱ τέτταρες
νομοὶ μείζω τοῦ κατ’ Αἴγυπτον Δέλτα· διαδέχε-
ται δὲ τὴν βασίλειαν οὐ παῖς παρὰ πατρός, ἀλλ’
ὃς ἂν πρῶτος γεννηθῇ τινι τῶν ἐπιφανῶν παῖς
μετὰ τὴν κατάστασιν τοῦ βασιλέως· ἅμα γὰρ τῷ
κατασταθῆναί τινα εἰς τὴν ἀρχὴν ἀναγράφονται
τὰς ἐγκύους γυναῖκας τῶν ἐπιφανῶν ἀνδρῶν,
καὶ ἐφιστᾶσι φύλακας· ἥτις δ’ [3] ἂν πρώτη τέκῃ,
τὸν ταύτης [4] υἱὸν νόμος ἐστὶν ἀναληφθέντα
τρέφεσθαι βασιλικῶς, ὡς διαδεξόμενον.

4. Φέρει δὲ λιβανωτὸν μὲν ἡ Κατταβανία,
σμύρναν δὲ ἡ Χατραμωτῖτις· καὶ ταῦτα δὲ καὶ τὰ
ἄλλα ἀρώματα μεταβάλλονται τοῖς ἐμπόροις.

---

[1] Μιναῖοι E, Μηναῖοι Dhi, Μειναῖοι other MSS.
[2] F has ἢ Καρανᾶν, CDh Καρανὰ, ωχ ἢ Καρανά ; Emoz omit.
[3] δ’, after ἥτις, Corais inserts.
[4] ταύτης, the editors, for αὐτῆς.

is in general fertile, and abounds in particular with places for making honey; and, with the exception of horses and mules and hogs, it has an abundance of domesticated animals; and, with the exception of geese and chickens, has all kinds of birds. The extreme part of the country above-mentioned is occupied by the four largest tribes; by the Minaeans, on the side towards the Red Sea, whose largest city is Carna or Carnana; next to these, by the Sabaeans, whose metropolis is Mariaba;[1] third, by the Catta-banians, whose territory extends down to the straits and the passage across the Arabian Gulf, and whose royal seat is called Tamna; and, farthest toward the east, the Chatramotitae, whose city is Sabata.[2]

3. All these cities are ruled by monarchs and are prosperous, being beautifully adorned with both temples and royal palaces. And the houses are like those of the Aegyptians in respect to the manner in which the timbers are joined together. The four jurisdictions cover more territory than the Aegyptian Delta; and no son of a king succeeds to the throne of his father, but the son of some notable man who is born first after the appointment of the king; for at the same time that some one is appointed to the throne, they register the pregnant wives of their notable men and place guards over them; and by law the wife's son who is born first is adopted and reared in a royal manner as future successor to the throne.

4. Cattabania produces frankincense,[3] and Chatra-motitis produces myrrh; and both these and the other aromatics are bartered to merchants. These

---

[1] Now Marib.   [2] Also spelled Sabattha; now Sawa.
[3] The gum of the libanus tree.

ἔρχονται δὲ πρὸς αὐτοὺς ἐξ Αἰλάνων μὲν εἰς
Μιναίαν ἐν ἑβδομήκοντα ἡμέραις· ἔστι δ' ἡ Αἴλανα
πόλις ἐν θατέρῳ μυχῷ τοῦ Ἀραβίου κόλπου, τῷ
κατὰ Γάζαν τῷ Αἰλανίτῃ καλουμένῳ, καθάπερ
εἰρήκαμεν· Γερραῖοι [1] δ' εἰς τὴν Χατραμωτῖτιν ἐν
τετταράκοντα ἡμέραις ἀφικνοῦνται. τοῦ δ'
Ἀραβίου κόλπου τὸ μὲν παρὰ τὴν Ἀραβίαν
πλευρὸν ἀρχομένοις ἀπὸ τοῦ Αἰλανίτου μυχοῦ,
καθάπερ οἱ περὶ Ἀλέξανδρον ἀνέγραψαν καὶ
Ἀναξικράτη, μυρίων καὶ τετρακισχιλίων σταδίων
ἐστίν· εἴρηται δὲ ἐπὶ πλέον. τὸ δὲ κατὰ τὴν
Τρωγλοδυτικήν, ὅπερ ἐστὶν ἐν δεξιᾷ ἀποπλέουσιν
ἀπὸ Ἡρώων πόλεως, μέχρι μὲν Πτολεμαΐδος καὶ
τῆς τῶν ἐλεφάντων θήρας, ἐννακισχίλιοι πρὸς
μεσημβρίαν στάδιοι καὶ μικρὸν ἐπὶ τὴν ἕω·
ἐντεῦθεν δὲ μέχρι τῶν στενῶν, ὡς τετρακισχίλιοι
C 769 καὶ πεντακόσιοι πρὸς τὴν ἕω μᾶλλον. ποιεῖ δὲ
ἄκρα τὰ στενὰ πρὸς τὴν Αἰθιοπίαν, Δειρὴ καλουμένη, καὶ πολίχνιον ὁμώνυμον αὐτῇ· κατοικοῦσι
δὲ Ἰχθυοφάγοι. καί φασιν ἐνταῦθα στήλην εἶναι
Σεσώστριος τοῦ Αἰγυπτίου, μηνύουσαν ἱεροῖς γράμ-
μασι τὴν διάβασιν αὐτοῦ. φαίνεται γὰρ τὴν
Αἰθιοπίδα καὶ τὴν Τρωγλοδυτικὴν πρῶτος καταστρεψάμενος οὗτος, εἶτα διαβὰς εἰς τὴν Ἀραβίαν,
κἀντεῦθεν τὴν Ἀσίαν ἐπελθὼν τὴν σύμπασαν· διὸ
δὴ πολλαχοῦ Σεσώστριος χάρακες προσαγορεύονται, καὶ ἀφιδρύματά ἐστιν Αἰγυπτίων θεῶν
ἱερῶν. τὰ δὲ κατὰ Δειρὴν στενὰ συνάγεται εἰς
σταδίους ἑξήκοντα· οὐ μὴν ταῦτά γε καλεῖται
νυνὶ στενά, ἀλλὰ προσπλεύσασιν ἀπωτέρω, καθὸ
τὸ μὲν διαρμά ἐστι τὸ μεταξὺ τῶν ἠπείρων δια-

_____
[1] Γερραῖοι EF*mgo*, Γαβαῖοι other MSS.

arrive there in seventy days from Aelana [1] (Aelana is a city on the other recess of the Arabian Gulf, the recess near Gaza [2] called Aelanites, as I have said before),[3] but the Gerrhaeans arrive at Chatramotitis in forty days. The part of the Arabian Gulf along the side of Arabia, beginning at the Aelanites recess, is, as recorded by Alexander's associates and by Anaxicrates, fourteen thousand stadia, though this figure is excessive; and the part opposite the Troglodytic country (which is on the right as one sails from the City of Heroes), as far as Ptolemaïs and the country where elephants are captured, extends nine thousand stadia towards the south and slightly in the direction of the east; and thence, as far as the straits, four thousand five hundred stadia, in a direction more towards the east. The straits are formed towards Aethiopia by a promontory called Deirê,[4] and by a town bearing the same name, which is inhabited by the Ichthyophagi.[5] And here, it is said, there is a pillar of Sesostris the Aegyptian, which tells in hieroglyphics of his passage across the gulf; for manifestly he was the first man to subdue the countries of the Aethiopians and the Troglodytes; and he then crossed into Arabia, and thence invaded the whole of Asia; and accordingly, for this reason, there are in many places palisades of Sesostris, as they are called, and reproductions of temples of Aegyptian gods. The straits at Deirê contract to a width of sixty stadia. However, it is not these that are called straits now, but a place farther along on the voyage, where the voyage across the gulf between

---

[1] Now Kasr-el-Akaba. [2] Now Azzah.
[3] 16. 2. 30. [4] " Neck."
[5] Fish-eaters.

κοσίων που σταδίων, ἓξ δὲ νῆσοι συνεχεῖς ἀλλή-
λαις τὸ δίαρμα ἐκπληροῦσαι στενοὺς τελέως
διάπλους ἀπολείπουσι, δι᾽ ὧν σχεδίαις τὰ φορτία
κομίζουσι δεῦρο κἀκεῖσε, καὶ λέγουσι ταῦτα
στενά. μετὰ δὲ τὰς νήσους ὁ ἑξῆς πλοῦς ἐστιν
ἐγκολπίζουσι παρὰ τὴν σμυρνοφόρον ἐπὶ τὴν
μεσημβρίαν ἅμα καὶ τὴν ἕω μέχρι πρὸς τὴν τὸ
κιννάμωμον φέρουσαν, ὅσον πεντακισχιλίων στα-
δίων· πέρα δὲ ταύτης οὐδένα ἀφῖχθαί φασι
μέχρι νῦν. πόλεις δ᾽ ἐν μὲν τῇ παραλίᾳ μὴ
πολλὰς εἶναι, κατὰ δὲ τὴν μεσόγαιαν πολλὰς
οἰκουμένας καλῶς. τὰ μὲν δὴ τοῦ Ἐρατοσθένους
περὶ τῆς Ἀραβίας τοιαῦτα· προσθετέον δὲ καὶ τὰ
παρὰ τῶν ἄλλων.

ō. Φησὶ δ᾽ Ἀρτεμίδωρος τὸ ἀντικείμενον ἐκ
τῆς Ἀραβίας ἀκρωτήριον τῇ Δειρῇ καλεῖσθαι
Ἀκίλαν· τοὺς δὲ περὶ τὴν Δειρὴν κολοβοὺς εἶναι
τὰς βαλάνους. ἀπὸ δὲ Ἡρώων πόλεως πλέουσι
κατὰ τὴν Τρωγλοδυτικὴν πόλιν εἶναι Φιλωτέραν
ἀπὸ τῆς ἀδελφῆς τοῦ δευτέρου Πτολεμαίου
προσαγορευθεῖσαν, Σατύρου κτίσμα τοῦ πεμφθέντος ἐπὶ τὴν διερεύνησιν τῆς τῶν ἐλεφάντων
θήρας καὶ τῆς Τρωγλοδυτικῆς· εἶτα ἄλλην πόλιν
Ἀρσινόην· εἶτα θερμῶν ὑδάτων ἐκβολὰς πικρῶν
καὶ ἁλμυρῶν, κατὰ πέτρας τινὸς ὑψηλῆς ἐκδι-
δόντων εἰς τὴν θάλατταν, καὶ πλησίον ὄρος ἐστὶν
ἐν πεδίῳ μιλτῶδες· εἶτα Μυὸς ὅρμον, ὃν [1] καὶ
Ἀφροδίτης ὅρμον καλεῖσθαι, λιμένα μέγαν, τὸν
εἴσπλουν ἔχοντα σκολιόν· προκεῖσθαι δὲ νήσους
τρεῖς, δύο μὲν ἐλαίαις κατασκίους, μίαν δ᾽ ἧττον

---

[1] ὃν is omitted by all MSS. except E.

the two continents is about two hundred stadia, and where are six islands, which follow one another in close succession, fill up the channel, and leave between them extremely narrow passages; through these merchandise is transported from one continent to the other; and for these the name " straits " is used. After the islands, the next voyage, following the sinuosities of the bays, along the myrrh-bearing country in the direction of south and east as far as the cinnamon-bearing country, is about five thousand stadia; and to the present time, it is said, no one has arrived beyond that country; and though there are not many cities on the coast, there are many in the interior that are beautifully settled. Such, then, is Eratosthenes' account of Arabia; but I must also add the accounts of the other writers.

5. Artemidorus says that the promontory on the Arabian side opposite to Deirê is called Acila; and that the males in the neighbourhood of Deirê have their sexual glands mutilated.[1] As one sails from the City of Heroes along the Troglodytic country, one comes to a city Philotera, which was named after the sister of the second Ptolemy, having been founded by Satyrus, who had been sent for the purpose of investigating the Troglodytic country and the hunting of elephants. Then to another city, Arsinoê. Then to springs of hot water, salty and bitter, which flow down a high rock and empty into the sea. Near by, in a plain, is a mountain that is red as ruddle. Then one comes to Myus Harbour, which is also called Aphrodite's Harbour; it is a large harbour with a winding entrance, off which lie three islands; two of these are densely shaded with olive trees, while

---

[1] See 16. 2. 37, and 16. 4. 9, 10.

κατάσκιον, μελεαγρίδων μεστήν· εἶθ' ἑξῆς τὸν
Ἀκάθαρτον κόλπον, καὶ αὐτὸν κατὰ τὴν Θηβαΐδα
κείμενον, καθάπερ τὸν Μυὸς ὅρμον, ὄντως [1] δὲ
ἀκάθαρτον· καὶ γὰρ ὑφάλοις χοιράσι καὶ ῥαχίαις
ἐκτετράχυνται καὶ πνοαῖς καταιγιζούσαις τὸ
C 770 πλέον. ἐνταῦθα δὲ ἱδρῦσθαι Βερενίκην πόλιν ἐν
βάθει τοῦ κόλπου.

6. Μετὰ δὲ τὸν κόλπον ἡ Ὀφιώδης καλουμένη
νῆσος ἀπὸ τοῦ συμβεβηκότος, ἣν ἠλευθέρωσε
τῶν ἑρπετῶν ὁ βασιλεύς, ἅμα καὶ διὰ τὰς φθορὰς
τῶν προσορμιζομένων ἀνθρώπων τὰς ἐκ τῶν
θηρίων καὶ διὰ τὰ τοπάζια. λίθος δέ ἐστι
διαφανὴς χρυσοειδὲς ἀποστίλβων [2] φέγγος, ὅσον
μεθ' ἡμέραν μὲν οὐ ῥάδιον ἰδεῖν ἐστι (περιαυγεῖται [3] γάρ), νύκτωρ δ' ὁρῶσιν οἱ συλλέγοντες·
περικαθάψαντες δὲ ἀγγεῖον σημείου χάριν μεθ'
ἡμέραν ἀνορύττουσι· καὶ ἦν σύστημα ἀνθρώπων
ἀποδεδειγμένων εἰς τὴν φυλακὴν τῆς λιθείας
ταύτης καὶ τὴν συναγωγήν, σιταρκούμενον [4] ὑπὸ
τῶν τῆς Αἰγύπτου βασιλέων.

7. Μετὰ δὲ τὴν νῆσον ταύτην πολλά ἐστιν
Ἰχθυοφάγων γένη καὶ Νομάδων· εἶθ' ὁ τῆς
Σωτείρας λιμήν, ὃν ἐκ κινδύνων μεγάλων τινὲς
σωθέντες τῶν ἡγεμόνων ἀπὸ τοῦ συμβεβηκότος
οὕτως ἐκάλεσαν. μετὰ δὲ ταῦτα ἐξάλλαξις πολλὴ
τῆς παραλίας καὶ τοῦ κόλπου· τὸν γὰρ παράπλουν οὐκέτι συμβαίνει τραχὺν εἶναι, συνάπτειν
τέ πως τῇ Ἀραβίᾳ, καὶ τὸ πέλαγος ταπεινὸν

---

[1] ὄντως F, οὕτως Dh, οὕτω other MSS.
[2] ἀπολάμπων CEmoxz.
[3] ὑπεραυγεῖται E (Kramer approving); περιαυγεῖται other
MSS.

the third is less so and is full of guinea-fowls.[1] Then, next, one comes to the Acathartus [2] Gulf, which also, like Myus Harbour, lies opposite Thebaïs, and is really " acarthartus," for it is roughened by reefs and submarine rocks, and, most of the time, by tempestuous winds. And here, deep inland on the recess of the gulf, lies a city Berenicê.

6. After the gulf, one comes to the island Ophiodes,[3] so called from the fact in the case; but it was freed from the serpents by the king, both because of their destruction of the people who landed there and on account of the topazes found there. Topaz is a transparent stone that sparkles with a golden lustre—so dimly in the day-time, however, that one cannot easily see it (for it is outshone by the rays of the sun), but those who collect it see it at night, place a vessel over it as a sign and dig it up in the day-time. There was an organisation of people who were appointed by the kings of Aegypt to keep guard over this stone and the collecting of it; and this organisation was supplied by them with provisions.

7. After this island one comes to many tribes of Ichthyophagi and Nomads. And then to the Harbour of Soteira,[4] which was so called from the fact in the case by certain commanders who had been saved from great dangers. After this there is a great change in the coast and the gulf; for the coasting voyage is no longer rough, and in a way closely approaches Arabia; and the sea is as low, I

---

[1] *Numida Meleagris.*   [2] *i.e.* " Foul."
[3] *i.e.* " Snaky."   [4] *i.e.* " Saviour " (some goddess).

---

[4] σιταρκούμενον, Corais, for σιταρχούμενον.

STRABO

εἶναι, σχεδόν τι καὶ ἐπὶ δύο ὀργυιάς, ποάζειν τε
τὴν ἐπιφάνειαν διαφαινομένου τοῦ μνίου καὶ τοῦ
φύκους, ὅπερ πλεονάζει κατὰ τὸν πόρον· ὅπου γε
καὶ δένδρα φύεται καθ' ὕδατος παρὰ τοῖς ἐνταῦθα·
ἔχει δὲ καὶ κυνῶν πλῆθος τῶν θαλαττίων ὁ
πόρος· εἶθ' οἱ Ταῦροι, δύο ὄρη τύπον τινὰ
πόρρωθεν δεικνύντα τοῖς ζῴοις ὅμοιον. εἶτ' ἄλλο
ὄρος ἱερὸν ἔχον τῆς Ἴσιδος, Σεσώστριος ἀφίδρυμα·
εἶτα νῆσος ἐλαίᾳ κατάφυτος ἐπικλυζομένη· μεθ'
ἣν ἡ Πτολεμαῒς πρὸς τῇ θήρᾳ τῶν ἐλεφάντων,
κτίσμα Εὐμήδους τοῦ πεμφθέντος ἐπὶ τὴν θήραν
ὑπὸ Φιλαδέλφου, λάθρα περιβαλομένου[1] χερ-
ρονήσῳ τινὶ τάφρον καὶ περίβολον, εἶτ' ἐκθερα-
πεύσαντος τοὺς κωλύοντας καὶ κατεσκευασμένου[2]
φίλους ἀντὶ δυσμενῶν.

8. Ἐν δὲ τῷ μεταξὺ ἐκδίδωσιν ἀπόσπασμα τοῦ
Ἀσταβόρα καλουμένου ποταμοῦ, ὃς ἐκ λίμνης
τὴν ἀρχὴν ἔχων μέρος μέν τι ἐκδίδωσι, τὸ δὲ
πλέον συμβάλλει τῷ Νείλῳ· εἶτα νῆσοι ἐξ Λατο-
μίαι καλούμεναι· καὶ μετὰ ταῦτα τὸ Σαβαϊτικὸν
στόμα λεγόμενον καὶ ἐν τῇ μεσογαίᾳ φρούριον,
Τοσούχου[3] ἵδρυμα· εἶτα λιμὴν καλούμενος
Ἐλαία[4] καὶ ἡ Στράτωνος νῆσος· εἶτα λιμὴν
Σαβὰ καὶ κυνήγιον ἐλεφάντων, ὁμώνυμον αὐτῷ.
ἡ δ' ἐν βάθει τούτων χώρα Τηνεσσὶς λέγεται·

[1] περιβαλομένου, Corais, for περιβαλλομένου.
[2] κατεσκευασμένους CDF hx.
[3] Τοσούχου E, Corais, Kramer, and Meineke; τὸ Σούχοι
other MSS. C. Müller plausibly conj. φρούριόν τι, Σούχοι
ἵδρυμα (cp. Σοῦχος, 17. 1. 38).
[4] Ἐλεα FDh, and E has αι above ε.

<hr>

[1] " Tauri " means " Bulls."

318

might almost say, as two fathoms in depth; and the surface is covered, grass-like, with sea-weeds and rock-weeds that are visible below the surface—a thing still more in evidence at the strait, where, among the plants, even trees grow down below the water; and the strait has also a large number of sea-dogs. Then one comes to the Tauri, two mountains which from a distance present the outlines of the animals.[1] Then to another mountain, which has a temple sacred to Isis, a reproduction[2] built by Sesostris. Then to an island planted with olive trees and subject to inundation; and after this to Ptolemaïs, near the hunting-grounds for elephants, a city founded by Eumedes, who had been sent to the hunting-grounds by Philadelphus;[3] Eumedes secretly enclosed a kind of peninsula with a ditch and wall, and then, by courteous treatment of those who tried to hinder the work, actually won them over as friends instead of foes.

8. In the interval there empties a branch of the Astaboras River, as it is called, which, having its source in a lake, empties a part of its waters,[4] but for the most part joins the Nile. Then one comes to six islands called Latomiae;[5] and then to the Sabaïtic mouth, as it is called, and to a fortress in the interior which was founded by Tosuches. And then to a harbour called Elaea and to the island of Strato. And then to a harbour called Saba and to a hunting-ground for elephants of the same name. The country deep in the interior is called Tenessis;

[2] *i.e.* of an Aegyptian temple.
[3] Ptolemy Philadelphus.
[4] *i.e.* into the gulf.
[5] Quarries.

ἔχουσι δ' αὐτὴν οἱ παρὰ Ψαμμιτίχου φυγάδες
C 771 Αἰγυπτίων· ἐπονομάζονται δὲ Σεμβρῖται,¹ ὡς ἂν
ἐπήλυδες· βασιλεύονται δ' ὑπὸ γυναικός, ὑφ' ἥν²
ἐστι καὶ ἡ Μερόη, πλησίον τῶν τόπων οὖσα
τούτων ἐν τῷ Νείλῳ νῆσος, ὑπὲρ ἧς ἄλλη ἐστὶ
νῆσος οὐ πολὺ ἄπωθεν ἐν τῷ ποταμῷ, κατοικία
τῶν αὐτῶν τούτων φυγάδων. ἀπὸ δὲ Μερόης
ἐπὶ τήνδε τὴν θάλατταν εὐζώνῳ ὁδὸς ἡμερῶν
πεντεκαίδεκα. περὶ δὲ τὴν Μερόην καὶ ἡ
συμβολὴ τοῦ τε Ἀσταβόρα καὶ τοῦ Ἀστάπου
καὶ ἔτι τοῦ Ἀστασόβα³ πρὸς τὸν Νεῖλον.

9. Παροικοῦσι δὲ τούτοις οἱ Ῥιζοφάγοι καὶ
Ἕλειοι προσαγορευόμενοι διὰ τὸ ἐκ τοῦ παρα-
κειμένου ῥιζοτομοῦντας ἕλους κόπτειν λίθοις καὶ
ἀναπλάσσειν μάζας, ἡλιάσαντες δὲ σιτεῖσθαι·
λεοντόβατα δ' ἐστὶ τὰ χωρία· ταῖς θ' ὑπὸ κυνὸς
ἐπιτολὴν ἡμέραις ὑπὸ κωνώπων μεγάλων ἐξελαύ-
νεται τὰ θηρία ἐκ τῶν τόπων. εἰσὶ δὲ καὶ
Σπερμοφάγοι πλησίον, οἳ τῶν σπερμάτων ἐπιλι-
πόντων ἀπὸ⁴ τῶν ἀκροδρύων τρέφονται, σκευά-
ζοντες παραπλησίως, ὥσπερ τὰς ῥίζας οἱ Ῥιζοφάγοι. μετὰ δὲ τὴν Ἐλαίαν⁵ αἱ Δημητρίου⁶ σκο-
πιαὶ καὶ βωμοὶ Κόνωνος· ἐν δὲ τῇ μεσογαίᾳ
καλάμων Ἰνδικῶν φύεται πλῆθος· καλεῖται δὲ ἡ
χώρα Κορακίου. ἦν δέ τις ἐν βάθει Ἐνδέρα,
γυμνητῶν ἀνθρώπων κατοικία, τόξοις χρωμένων
καλαμίνοις καὶ πεπυρακτωμένοις ὀιστοῖς· ἀπὸ

¹ Σεμβρῖται, Corais, for Σαβρῖται F, Σεβρῖται other MSS.
² ἧς DF*hrw*.
³ Ἀστασόβα Corais, for Ἀστοσόβα margin of F, Ἀσταγάβα
other MSS.
⁴ ἀπό, Meineke, for ὑπό.

and it is occupied by the Aegyptians who went there as exiles from Psammitichus. They are called Sembritae, as being foreigners.[1] They are governed by a queen, to whom also Meroê, an island in the Nile near that region, is subject; and above this island, at no great distance, is another island in the river, a settlement of these same exiles. The journey from Meroê to this sea,[2] for a well-girded traveller, requires fifteen days. Near Meroê is the confluence of the Astaboras and the Astapus, as also of the Astasobas with the Nile.

9. Along these rivers live the Rhizophagi[3] and the Heleii,[4] who are so called because they cut roots from the adjacent marsh, crush them with stones, form them into cakes, and then heat the cakes in the sun's rays and use them for food. This region is the haunt of lions; and the beasts are driven out of this region by large gnats on the days of the rising of the dog-star. Near by are also the Spermophagi,[5] who, when the seeds fail, live on nuts, preparing them for eating in the same manner as the Rhizophagi prepare roots. After Elaea one comes to the Lookouts of Demetrius and the Altars of Conon; and in the interior grows an abundance of Indian reeds; and the country is called the country of Coracius. Deep in the interior was a place called Endera, a settlement of naked people, who use bows made of reeds and arrows hardened by fire; and generally

---

[1] Cf. 17. 1. 2 and Herodotus 2. 30.
[2] *i.e.* the Red Sea, in the neighbourhood of Saba.
[3] Root-eaters.   [4] Marsh-men.   [5] Seed-eaters.

---

[5] Ἐλαίαν E (with ε above αι) ; Ἐλέαν other MSS. except *ix.*
[6] Δημήτρου F, Δήμητρος Ptolemaeus.

δένδρων δὲ τοξεύουσι τὰ θηρία τὸ πλέον, ἔστι δ᾽
ὅτε καὶ ἀπὸ γῆς· πολὺ δ᾽ ἐστὶ παρ᾽ αὐτοῖς
πλῆθος τῶν ἀγρίων βοῶν· ἀπὸ δὲ τῆς τούτων
καὶ τῶν ἄλλων θηρίων κρεοφαγίας [1] ζῶσιν, ἐπὰν
δὲ μηδὲν θηρεύσωσι, τὰ ξηρὰ δέρματα ἐπ᾽ ἀνθρα-
κιᾶς ὀπτῶντες ἀρκοῦνται τῇ τοιαύτῃ τροφῇ.
ἔθος δ᾽ ἐστὶν αὐτοῖς ἀγῶνα τοξείας προτιθέναι
τοῖς ἀνήβοις παισί. μετὰ δὲ τοὺς Κόνωνος
βωμοὺς ὁ Μήλινος λιμήν· ὑπέρκειται δ᾽ αὐτοῦ
φρούριον Κοράου καλούμενον καὶ κυνήγιον τοῦ
Κοράου καὶ ἄλλο φρούριον [2] καὶ κυνήγια πλείω·
εἶτα ὁ Ἀντιφίλου λιμὴν καὶ οἱ ὑπὲρ τούτου
Κρεοφάγοι,[3] κολοβοὶ τὰς βαλάνους καὶ αἱ γυναῖκες Ἰουδαϊκῶς ἐκτετμημέναι.

10. Ἔτι δ᾽ ὑπὲρ τούτων ὡς πρὸς μεσημβρίαν
οἱ Κυναμολγοί, ὑπὸ δὲ τῶν ἐντοπίων Ἄγριοι
καλούμενοι, κατάκομοι, καταπώγωνες, κύνας
ἐκτρέφοντες εὐμεγέθεις, οἷς θηρεύουσι τοὺς
ἐπερχομένους ἐκ τῆς πλησιοχώρου βόας Ἰνδικούς,
εἴθ᾽ ὑπὸ θηρίων ἐξελαυνομένους εἴτε σπάνει νομῆς·
ἡ δ᾽ ἔφοδος αὐτῶν ἀπὸ θερινῶν τροπῶν μέχρι
μέσου χειμῶνος. τῷ δ᾽ Ἀντιφίλου λιμένι ἑξῆς
ἐστι λιμὴν καλούμενος Κολοβῶν ἄλσος καὶ
Βερενίκη πόλις ἡ κατὰ Σαβὰς καὶ Σαβαί, πόλις
εὐμεγέθης· εἶτα τὸ τοῦ Εὐμένους ἄλσος. ὑπέρκειται δὲ πόλις Δάραβα [4] καὶ κυνήγιον ἐλεφάντων

---

[1] κρεοφαγίας CF, κρεωφαγίας other MSS.
[2] The words Κοράου . . . φρούριον are omitted by all MSS.
except EF.
[3] Κρεόφαγοι F, Κρεώφαγοι other MSS.
[4] Δαραβά moxz, Δίραδα other MSS.

---

[1] Meat-eaters. [2] See 16. 4. 5. [3] Milkers of bitches.

they shoot wild animals from trees, but sometimes
from the ground; and they have in their country a
great multitude of wild cattle; and they live on the
flesh of these and the other wild animals, but when
they take nothing in the chase they bake dried skins
on hot coals and are satisfied with such food as that.
It is their custom to propose contests in archery for
boys who are in their teens. After the Altars of
Conon one comes to the Melinus Harbour, above
which lie a Fortress of Coraüs, as it is called, and a
Hunting-ground of Coraüs and another fortress and
several hunting-grounds. And then to the Harbour
of Antiphilus, and, above this, to the Creophagi,[1] of
whom the males have their sexual glands mutilated
and the women are excised in the Jewish fashion.[2]

10. Also above these, approximately towards the
south, are the Cynamolgi,[3] by the natives called
Agrii, who have long hair and long beards and raise
good-sized dogs. With these dogs they hunt Indian
cattle which come in from the neighbouring territory,
whether driven thither by wild beasts or by scarcity
of pasturage. The time of their incursion is from the
summer solstice to mid-winter. Next after the
Harbour of Antiphilus one comes to the Grove of the
Colobi,[4] and to Berenicê, a Sabaean city, and to
Sabae, a good-sized city; and then to the Grove of
Eumenes. Above the grove lie a city Daraba and
the hunting-ground for elephants called " The one

[4] " Colobi " means " persons " (who have their sexual
glands) "mutilated." Cp. 16. 2. 37 and 16. 3. 5, 9. Diodorus
Siculus (3. 32) says: "All the Troglodytes are circumcised
like the Aegyptians except those who, from the fact in the
case, are called 'Colobi'; for these alone, who live this side
the Strait, have all the part that is merely circumcised by the
others cut off with razors in infancy."

τὸ πρὸς τῷ φρέατι καλούμενον· κατοικοῦσι δ'
Ἐλεφαντοφάγοι, τὴν θήραν ποιούμενοι τοιαύτην·
C 772 ἀπὸ τῶν δένδρων ἰδόντες ἀγέλην διὰ τοῦ δρυμοῦ
φερομένην, τῇ μὲν οὐκ ἐπιτίθενται, τοὺς δ'
ἀποπλανηθέντας ἐκ τῶν ὄπισθεν λάθρα προσιόντες νευροκοποῦσι· τινὲς δὲ καὶ τοξεύμασιν
ἀναιροῦσιν αὐτοὺς χολῇ βεβαμμένοις ὄφεων· ἡ δὲ
τοξεία διὰ τριῶν ἀνδρῶν συντελεῖται, τῶν μὲν
κατεχόντων τὸ τόξον καὶ προβεβηκότων τοῖς
ποσί, τοῦ δ' ἕλκοντος τὴν νευράν· ἄλλοι δὲ
σημειωσάμενοι τὰ δένδρα, οἷς εἰώθασι προσανα-
παύεσθαι, προσιόντες ἐκ θατέρου μέρους τὸ στέ-
λεχος ὑποκόπτουσιν· ἐπὰν οὖν προσιὸν τὸ θηρίον
ἀποκλίνῃ πρὸς αὐτό, πεσόντος τοῦ δένδρου πίπτει
καὶ αὐτό, ἀναστῆναι δὲ μὴ δυναμένου διὰ τὸ τὰ
σκέλη διηνεκὲς ὀστοῦν ἔχειν καὶ ἀκαμπές, κατα-
πηδήσαντες ἀπὸ τῶν δένδρων ἀνατέμνουσιν αὐτό·
τοὺς δὲ κυνηγοὺς οἱ Νομάδες ἀκαθάρτους καλοῦσιν.
11. Ὑπέρκειται δὲ τούτων ἔθνος οὐ μέγα
Στρουθοφάγων, παρ' οἷς ὄρνεις εἰσὶ μέγεθος
ἐλάφων ἔχοντες, πετᾶσθαι μὲν οὐ δυνάμενοι,
θέοντες δὲ ὀξέως, καθάπερ οἱ στρουθοκάμηλοι·
θηρεύουσι δ' αὐτοὺς οἱ μὲν τόξοις, οἱ δὲ ταῖς
δοραῖς τῶν στρουθῶν σκεπασθέντες τὴν μὲν
δεξιὰν καλύπτουσι τῷ τραχηλιμαίῳ μέρει καὶ
κινοῦσιν οὕτως, ὥσπερ τὰ ζῷα κινεῖται τοῖς
τραχήλοις, τῇ δὲ ἀριστερᾷ σπέρμα προχέουσιν
ἀπὸ πήρας παρηρτημένης, καὶ τούτῳ δελεάσαντες
τὰ ζῷα εἰς φάραγγας συνωθοῦσιν· ἐνταῦθα δ'
ἐφεστῶτες ξυλοκόποι κατακόπτουσι· καὶ ἀμπέ-
χονται δὲ καὶ ὑποστόρνυνται[1] τὰ δέρματα ταῦτα.

[1] Cmoxz read ὑποστρώννυνται.

near the well "; they are inhabited by the Elephanto-
phagi,[1] who engage in the chase of elephants. When
from trees they first see a herd of elephants moving
through the forest they do not then attack them, but
stealthily follow the herd and hamstring those
that have wandered from the rear of the herd. Some,
however, kill them with arrows dipped in the gall of
serpents. But the shooting of the bow is performed
by three persons; two of these step to the front and
hold the bow, and the third draws the string. Others,
noting the trees against which the elephants are
wont to rest, approach them from the other side
and cut the trunks of these trees low down. So when
the elephant approaches and leans against it, the
tree falls and the elephant falls too; and since the
elephant is unable to arise, because its legs have only
a continuous and unbending bone, they leap down
from the trees and cut the animal to pieces. The
Nomads call the hunters " Acatharti."[2]

11. Above these is situated a tribe of no large size,
that of the Struthophagi,[3] in whose country there
are birds of the size of deer, which, though unable to
fly, run swiftly, like ostriches. Some hunt them
with bows and arrows, whereas others, covered with
the skins of birds, conceal the right hand in the
neck of the skin and move it in the same way as the
birds move their necks, and with the left hand they
pour forth seeds from a bag suspended to the side,
and with these seeds they bait the creatures and run
them together into gullies, where men with cudgels,
standing over them, slaughter them. And their
skins are used both for clothing and for bed-covers.

---

[1] Elephant-eaters.   [2] *i.e.* " Unclean."
[3] Bird-eaters.

πολεμοῦσι δὲ τούτοις οἱ Σιμοὶ [1] καλούμενοι Αἰθίοπες, κέρασιν ὀρύγων ὅπλοις χρώμενοι.

12. Πλησιόχωροι δὲ τούτοις εἰσὶ μελανώτεροί τε τῶν ἄλλων καὶ βραχύτεροι καὶ βραχυβιώτατοι Ἀκριδοφάγοι· [2] τὰ γὰρ τετταράκοντα ἔτη σπανίως ὑπερτιθέασιν, ἀποθηριουμένης αὐτῶν τῆς σαρκός· ζῶσι δ᾽ ἀπὸ ἀκρίδων, ἃς οἱ ἐαρινοὶ λίβες καὶ ζέφυροι, πνέοντες μεγάλοι, συνελαύνουσιν εἰς τοὺς τόπους τούτους· ἐν ταῖς χαράδραις δὲ ἐμβαλόντες ὕλην καπνώδη καὶ ὑφάψαντες μικρὸν [3] . . . . ὑπερπετάμεναι [4] γὰρ [5] τὸν καπνὸν σκοτοῦνται καὶ πίπτουσι· [6] συγκόψαντες δ᾽ αὐτὰς μεθ᾽ ἁλμυρίδος μάζας ποιοῦνται καὶ χρῶνται. τούτων δ᾽ ἔρημος ὑπέρκειται μεγάλη, νομὰς δαψιλεῖς ἔχουσα, ἐκλειφθεῖσα δ᾽ ὑπὸ πλήθους σκορπίων καὶ φαλαγγίων τῶν τετραγνάθων καλουμένων, ἐπιπολάσαντός ποτε καὶ ἀπεργασαμένου τοῖς ἀνθρώποις φυγὴν παντελῆ.

13. Μετὰ δὲ Εὐμένους λιμένα μέχρι Δειρῆς [7] καὶ τῶν κατὰ τὰς ἐξ νήσους στενῶν Ἰχθυοφάγοι καὶ Κρεοφάγοι [8] κατοικοῦσι καὶ Κολοβοὶ μέχρι τῆς μεσογαίας. εἰσὶ δὲ καὶ θῆραι πλείους ἐλεφάντων καὶ πόλεις ἄσημοι καὶ νησία πρὸ τῆς παραλίας. νομάδες δ᾽ οἱ πλείους, ὀλίγοι δ᾽ οἱ

C 773

---

[1] Σιμοί, the editors, for Σίλλοι ; E has μοί written above, first hand.
[2] Ἀκριδοφάγοι is omitted by the MSS. but is added by first hand in margin of F.
[3] Here the MSS. have a lacuna of about ten letters.
[4] ὑπερπετώμεναι Dhi, ὑπερπετόμεναι E, ὑπερπετασθέντων z (first hand), ὑπερπετασθεισῶν mo and z (second hand).
[5] γάρ, omitted by moz.
[6] moz have εἶτα σκοτουμένων καὶ πιπτουσῶν.

The Aethiopians called "Simi" carry on war with these people; they use as weapons the horns of gazelles.

12. Neighbouring this people are the Acridophagi,[1] who are blacker than the rest and shorter in stature and the shortest-lived; for they rarely live beyond forty years, since their flesh is infested with parasites.[2] They live on locusts, which are driven into this region in the spring-time by strong-blowing south-west and western winds. They cast smoking timber in the ravines, lighting it slightly (and thus easily catch the locusts),[3] for when they fly above the smoke they are blinded and fall. The people pound them with salt, make them into cakes, and use them for food. Above these people lies a large uninhabited region, which has pastures in abundance. It was abandoned by reason of the multitude of scorpions and tarantulas, the tetragnathi,[4] as they are called; these once prevailed and caused a complete desertion by the inhabitants.

13. After the Harbour of Eumenes, as far as Deirê and the straits opposite the six islands,[5] the country is inhabited by the Ichthyophagi and the Creophagi and the Colobi,[6] who extend as far as the interior. In this region are several hunting-grounds for elephants, and insignificant cities, and islands lying off the coast. The greater part of the people

---

[1] Locust-eaters.   [2] Literally "wild creatures."
[3] This is obviously the meaning of certain Greek words lost from the MSS. (see critical note).
[4] *i.e.* four-jawed.   [5] 16. 4. 4.
[6] *i.e.* "Mutilated" people (see 16. 4. 5).

---

[7] Δηρῆς E.
[8] Κρεοφάγοι CF, Κρεωφάγοι other MSS.

γεωργοῦντες· παρά τισι δὲ τούτων φύεται στύραξ
οὐκ ὀλίγος. συνάγουσι δὲ ταῖς ἀμπώτισιν οἱ
Ἰχθυοφάγοι τοὺς ἰχθῦς· ἐπιρρίψαντες δὲ ταῖς
πέτραις κατοπτῶσι πρὸς τὸν ἥλιον, εἶτ' ἐξοπτή-
σαντες τὰς ἀκάνθας μὲν σωρεύουσι, τὴν δὲ σάρκα
πατήσαντες μάζας ποιοῦνται, πάλιν δὲ ταύτας
ἡλιάζοντες σιτοῦνται· χειμῶνος δ' ἀδυνατήσαντες
συνάγειν τοὺς ἰχθῦς, τὰς σεσωρευμένας ἀκάνθας
κόψαντες μάζας ἀναπλάττονται καὶ χρῶνται,
τὰς δὲ νεαρὰς ἐκμυζῶσιν. ἔνιοι δὲ τὰς κόγχας
ἐχούσας τὴν σάρκα σιτεύουσι καταβάλλοντες εἰς
χαράδρια καὶ συστάδας θαλάττης, εἶτ' ἰχθύδια
παραρριπτοῦντες [1] τροφήν, αὐταῖς χρῶνται ἐν τῇ
τῶν ἰχθύων σπάνει· ἔστι δ' αὐτοῖς καὶ ἰχθυοτρο-
φεῖα παντοῖα, ἀφ' ὧν ταμιεύονται. ἔνιοι δὲ τῶν
τὴν ἄνυδρον παραλίαν οἰκούντων διὰ πέντε
ἡμερῶν ἐπὶ τὰ ὑδρεῖα ἀναβαίνουσι πανοικὶ [2] μετὰ
παιανισμοῦ, ῥιφέντες δὲ πρηνεῖς πίνουσι βοῶν
δίκην ἕως ἐκτυμπανώσεως τῆς γαστρός, εἶτ' ἀπίασιν ἐπὶ θάλατταν πάλιν· οἰκοῦσι δ' ἐν σπηλαίοις
ἢ μάνδραις στεγασταῖς ἀπὸ δοκῶν μὲν καὶ στρω-
τήρων τῶν κητείων ὀστέων καὶ ἀκανθῶν, φυλλάδος
δ' ἐλαΐνης.

14. Οἱ δὲ Χελωνοφάγοι τοῖς ὀστράκοις αὐτῶν
σκεπάζονται μεγάλοις οὖσιν, ὥστε καὶ πλεῖσθαι
ἐν αὐτοῖς· ἔνιοι δὲ τοῦ φύκους ἀποβεβλημένου
πολλοῦ καὶ θῖνας ὑψηλὰς καὶ λοφώδεις ποιοῦντος,

[1] παροπτῶντες CEFr (περιρριπτοῦντες, second hand in F).
[2] F reads πανοικειοῦ, Meineke πανοίκιοι.

---

[1] The "styrax" (or "storax") shrub, or tree, produces a
sweet-smelling gum or resin used in frankincense.
[2] i.e. fish-ponds and the like.

are nomads; and those who till the soil are few in number. And in some parts of their country styrax [1] grows in no small quantities. The Ichthyophagi collect the fish at the ebb-tides, throw them upon the rocks, and bake them in the sun; and then, when they have thoroughly baked them, they pile up the bones, tread the flesh with their feet and make it into cakes; and again they bake these cakes and use them for food. But in stormy weather, when they are unable to collect the fish, they pound the bones which they have piled up and mould them into cakes and use them for food; and they suck the bones when fresh. But some, who have shell-fish, fatten them by throwing them down into gullies and pools of sea-water, and then, throwing in minnows as food for them, use them for food when there is a scarcity of fish. They also have all kinds of places for hatching and feeding fish,[2] from which they parcel them out. Some of the people who inhabit the part of the coast that is without water go inland every five days, families and all, with a shouting of pæans, to the water-reservoirs, throw themselves upon the ground face downwards, drink like cattle until their stomachs are filled out as tight as drums, and then return to the sea again. They live in caves, or in pens roofed over with beams and cross-beams, consisting of the bones of whales and small fish,[3] as also with olive branches.

14. The Chelonophagi [4] live under cover of turtle-shells, which are so large that they are used as boats; but some of these people, since the sea-weed is thrown ashore in great quantities and forms high and hill-like heaps, dig beneath these and dwell

[3] Cf. 15. 2. 2.   [4] Turtle-eaters.

ὑπορύττοντες ταύτας ὑποικοῦσι. τοὺς δὲ νεκροὺς
ῥίπτουσι τροφὴν τοῖς ἰχθύσιν, ἀναλαμβανομένους
ὑπὸ τῶν πλημμυρίδων. τῶν δὲ νήσων τινὲς
τρεῖς ἐφεξῆς κεῖνται, ἡ μὲν Χελωνῶν, ἡ δὲ Φωκῶν,
ἡ δ᾽ Ἱεράκων λεγομένη· πᾶσα δ᾽ ἡ παραλία
φοίνικάς[1] τε ἔχει καὶ ἐλαιῶνας καὶ δαφνῶνας,
οὐχ ἡ ἐντὸς τῶν στενῶν μόνον, ἀλλὰ καὶ τῆς
ἐκτὸς πολλή. ἔστι δέ τις καὶ Φιλίππου νῆσος,
καθ᾽ ἣν ὑπέρκειται τὸ Πυθαγγέλου καλούμενον
τῶν ἐλεφάντων κυνήγιον· εἶτ᾽ Ἀρσινόη πόλις καὶ
λιμήν, καὶ μετὰ ταῦτα ἡ Δειρή· καὶ τούτων
ὑπέρκειται θήρα τῶν ἐλεφάντων. ἀπὸ δὲ τῆς
Δειρῆς ἡ ἐφεξῆς ἐστιν ἀρωματοφόρος, πρώτη μὲν
ἡ τὴν σμύρναν φέρουσα (καὶ αὕτη μὲν Ἰχθυοφάγων καὶ Κρεοφάγων), φύει δὲ καὶ περσέαν[2] καὶ
συκάμινον Αἰγύπτιον· ὑπέρκειται δὲ ἡ Λίχα
θήρα τῶν ἐλεφάντων· πολλαχοῦ δ᾽ εἰσὶ συστάδες
τῶν ὀμβρίων ὑδάτων, ὧν ἀναξηρανθεισῶν οἱ
ἐλέφαντες ταῖς προβοσκίσι καὶ τοῖς ὀδοῦσι
C 774 φρεωρυχοῦσι καὶ ἀνευρίσκουσιν ὕδωρ. ἐν δὲ τῇ
παραλίᾳ ταύτῃ μέχρι τοῦ[3] Πυθολάου[4] ἀκρωτηρίου[5] δύο λίμναι εἰσὶν εὐμεγέθεις· ἡ μὲν ἁλμυ-
ροῦ ὕδατος, ἣν καλοῦσι θάλατταν, ἡ δὲ γλυκέος,
ἣ τρέφει καὶ ἵππους ποταμίους καὶ κροκοδείλους,
περὶ τὰ χείλη δὲ πάπυρον· ὁρῶνται δὲ καὶ ἴβεις
περὶ τὸν τόπον. ἤδη δὲ καὶ οἱ πλησίον τῆς
ἄκρας τῆς Πυθολάου[6] τὰ σώματα ὁλόκληροί

---

[1] φοινικῶνας E.   [2] περσέαν the editors, for περσαίαν.
[3] τά D.   [4] Πιθολάου xz.
[5] ἀκρωτήρια Dhixz.   [6] Πιθολάου Dxz.

330

under them. They throw out their dead as food for the fish, the bodies being caught up by the flood-tides. Some of the islands, three of them, follow in succession: Tortoise Island, Seal Island, and Hawk Island, as it is called; and the whole of the coast has palm-trees, olive groves, and laurel groves, not only the part inside the straits, but also most of the part outside. And there is also an island called Philip's Island, opposite which, above the coast, lies the hunting-ground for elephants called the Hunting-ground of Pythangelus. Then one comes to Arsinoê, a city and harbour; and, after these, to Deirê; and above these lies a hunting-ground for elephants. The next country after Deirê produces aromatics, the first that produces myrrh (this country belongs to the Icthyophagi and Creophagi), and it also produces both persea [1] and the Aegyptian sycaminus.[2] Above this country lies a hunting-ground for elephants, called the Hunting-ground of Lichas. In many places there are pools of rain-water; and when these dry up, the elephants, with their trunks and tusks, dig wells and find water. On this coast, extending as far as the promontory of Pytholäus, there are two lakes of fair size, one of which has salt water and is called a sea, whereas the other has fresh water, supports both hippopotamus and crocodiles, and has papyrus round its edges; and the ibis is also to be seen in the neighbourhood of this place. Beginning with those who live near the promontory of Pytholäus, the people are wholly free from mutilation [3] of the body. After these, one

[1] A tree with such luscious fruit that Cambyses transplanted it to Persia (see Diodorus Siculus 1. 34).

[2] Mulberry tree.

[3] See 16. 4. 5, 9.

STRABO

εἰσι· μετὰ δὲ τούτους ἡ λιβανωτοφόρος· ἐνταῦθα
ἄκρα ἐστὶ καὶ ἱερὸν αἰγειρῶνα ἔχον. ἐν δὲ τῇ
μεσογαίᾳ ποταμία τις Ἴσιδος λεγομένη καὶ
ἄλλη τις Νεῖλος, ἄμφω καὶ σμύρναν καὶ λίβανον παραπεφυκότα ἔχουσαι. ἔστι δὲ καὶ δεξα-
μενή τις τοῖς ἐκ τῶν ὀρῶν ὕδασι πληρουμένη καὶ
μετὰ ταῦτα Λέοντος σκοπὴ[1] καὶ Πυθαγγέλου
λιμήν· ἡ δ' ἑξῆς ἔχει καὶ ψευδοκασσίαν.[2] συνεχῶς δ' εἰσὶ ποτάμιαί τε πλείους ἔχουσαι λίβανον παραπεφυκότα καὶ ποταμοὶ μέχρι τῆς Κιννα-
μωμοφόρου· ὁ δ' ὁρίζων ταύτην ποταμὸς φέρει
καὶ φλοῦν πάμπολυν· εἶτ' ἄλλος ποταμὸς καὶ
Δαφνοῦς λιμὴν καὶ ποταμία Ἀπόλλωνος καλουμένη, ἔχουσα πρὸς τῷ λιβάνῳ καὶ σμύρναν καὶ
κιννάμωμον· τοῦτο δὲ πλεονάζει[3] μᾶλλον περὶ
τοὺς ἐν βάθει τόπους· εἶθ' ὁ Ἐλέφας τὸ ὄρος,
ἐκκείμενον εἰς θάλατταν, καὶ διῶρυξ καὶ ἐφεξῆς
Ψυγμοῦ[4] λιμὴν μέγας καὶ ὕδρευμα, τὸ Κυνο-
κεφάλων καλούμενον, καὶ τελευταῖον ἀκρωτήριον
τῆς παραλίας ταύτης, τὸ Νότου κέρας. κάμ-
ψαντι δὲ τοῦτο ὡς ἐπὶ μεσημβρίαν οὐκέτι,
φησίν, ἔχομεν λιμένων ἀναγραφὰς οὐδὲ τόπων
διὰ τὸ μηκέτι εἶναι γνώριμον, ἐν δὲ τῇ ἑξῆς
παραλίᾳ.

[1] Λέοντος σκοπή, Corais, for λεοντοσκόπη CDF h, λεοντοσκοπή E, Λέοντος κώπη s, Λέοντος κώμη Casaubon.
[2] ψευδοκασίαν F.
[3] πλεονάζει F (first hand in margin); πλέον ἀκμάζει other MSS.
[4] γυμνοῦ CDEF h ir ; but ψυγμοῦ first hand in F r.

332

comes to the country that bears frankincense; and here is a promontory and a temple that has a grove of poplars. In the interior lie the river-land of Isis, as it is called, and another river-land called Neilus, both of which produce both myrrh and frankincense along their banks. Here, too, there is a kind of reservoir which is filled by waters from the mountains; and after this one comes to the Lookout of Leon and the Harbour of Pythangelus; and the next country has, among other things, pseudo-cassia. And one comes to several river-lands in succession that produce frankincense along the rivers, and to rivers that extend as far as the cinnamon-bearing country; and the river which bounds this country produces also the flowering rush in very great quantities. Then to another river and to the Daphnus Harbour and to the River-land of Apollo, as it is called, which produces, in addition to frankincense, both myrrh and cinnamon; but the cinnamon is more abundant in the neighbourhood of the places that are deep in the interior. Then to Elephas,[1] the mountain, which juts out into the sea, and to a trench, and, next thereafter, to the large Harbour of Psygmus, and to a watering-place [2] called the Watering-place of the Cynocephali,[3] and to the last promontory of this coast, Notu-ceras.[4] After rounding this promontory approximately towards the south, we no longer, he says, have any record of harbours or places, because the promontory is not known from here on, and the same is true of the coast next after it.

---

[1] Elephant.   [2] A well, apparently.
[3] *i.e.* the " Dog-headed " people.
[4] *i.e.* Horn of the South.

STRABO

15. Εἰσὶ δὲ[1] καὶ στῆλαι καὶ βωμοὶ Πυθολάου καὶ Λίχα καὶ Πυθαγγέλου καὶ Λέοντος καὶ Χαριμόρτου κατὰ τὴν γνώριμον παραλίαν τὴν ἀπὸ Δειρῆς μέχρι Νότου κέρως, τὸ δὲ διάστημα οὐ γνώριμον. πληθύει δ' ἐλέφασιν ἡ χώρα καὶ λέουσι τοῖς καλουμένοις μύρμηξιν· ἀπεστραμμένα δ' ἔχουσι τὰ αἰδοῖα, καὶ χρυσοειδεῖς τὴν χρόαν, ψιλότεροι δὲ τῶν κατὰ τὴν Ἀραβίαν· φέρει δὲ καὶ παρδάλεις ἀλκίμους καὶ ῥινοκέρωτας. οὗτοι δὲ μικρὸν ἀπολείπονται τῶν ἐλεφάντων οἱ ῥινοκέρωτες, οὐχ,[2] ὥσπερ Ἀρτεμίδωρός φησιν, ἐπὶ σειρὰν τῷ μήκει, καίπερ ἑωρακέναι φήσας ἐν Ἀλεξανδρείᾳ, ἀλλὰ σχεδόν τι ὅσον . . .[3] τῷ ὕψει, ἀπό γε τοῦ ὑφ' ἡμῶν ὁραθέντος· οὔτε πύξῳ τὸ χρῶμα ἐμφερές, ἀλλ' ἐλέφαντι μᾶλλον· μέγεθος δ' ἐστὶ ταύρου· μορφὴ δ' ἐγγυτάτω συάγρου, καὶ μάλιστα κατὰ τὴν προτομήν, πλὴν τῆς ῥινός, ὅτι ἔστι κέρας σιμὸν στερεώτερον ὀστέου παντός· χρῆται δ' ὅπλῳ, καθάπερ καὶ
C 775 τοῖς ὀδοῦσιν ὁ σύαγρος· ἔχει δὲ καὶ τύλους δύο, ὡς ἂν σπείρας δρακόντων ἀπὸ τῆς ῥάχεως μέχρι τῆς γαστρὸς περικειμένας, τὴν μὲν πρὸς τῷ λόφῳ, τὴν δὲ πρὸς τῇ ὀσφύι. ἐκ μὲν δὴ τοῦ ὑφ' ἡμῶν ὁραθέντος ταῦτά φαμεν ἡμεῖς, ἐκεῖνος δὲ προσδιασαφεῖ, διότι καὶ ἐλεφαντομάχον ἰδίως ἐστὶ τὸ ζῷον περὶ τῆς νομῆς, ὑποδῦνον τῇ προτομῇ καὶ ἀνακεῖρον τὴν γαστέρα, ἐὰν μὴ προληφθῇ τῇ προβοσκίδι καὶ τοῖς ὀδοῦσι.

---

[1] δέ, Corais inserts.   [2] οὐχ, Corais inserts.
[3] Obviously some number of cubits (πῆχυς) or spans (σπιθαμή) has fallen out of the MSS.

[1] See the description of "gold-mining ants" in 15. 1. 44.

334

15. One comes also to pillars and altars of Pytholäus and Lichas and Pythangelus and Leon and Charimortus along the known coast, extending from Deirê as far as Notu-ceras, but the distance is unknown. The country abounds in elephants, and also in lions called ants,[1] which have their genital organs reversed, and are golden in colour, but are less hairy than those in Arabia. It also produces fierce leopards and the rhinoceros. The latter, the rhinoceros, is but little short of the elephant in size, not, as Artemidorus says, " in length to the tail "[2] (although he says that he saw the animal at Alexandria), but falls short, I might almost say, only about . . . in height,[3] judging at least from the one I saw; nor does their colour resemble that of box-wood, but rather that of the elephant; and it is of the size of a bull; and its shape is most nearly like that of the wild boar, particularly in its foreparts, except its nose, which has a snub horn harder than any bone; and it uses its horn as a weapon, just as the wild boar uses its tusks; and it also has two hard welts extending round from its chine to its belly, like the coils of serpents, one of which is on its withers and the other on its loins. Now I am giving this description from the one I saw; but Artemidorus goes on to explain that the creature is especially inclined to fight with the elephant for places of pasture, thrusting its forehead under the elephant and ripping up its stomach, unless it is prevented from so doing by the proboscis and tusks of the elephant.

[2] *i.e.* from head to tail.
[3] The measure of the difference in height is missing from the manuscripts. Artemidorus must have given it in terms of either cubit or span (see critical note).

16. Γίνονται δ' ἐν τούτοις τοῖς τόποις καὶ αἱ
καμηλοπαρδάλεις, οὐδὲν ὅμοιον ἔχουσαι παρδάλει·
τὸ γὰρ ποικίλον τῆς χρόας νεβρίσι μᾶλλον ἔοικε
ῥαβδωτοῖς σπίλοις κατεστιγμέναις· τελέως δὲ τὰ
ὀπίσθια ταπεινότερα τῶν ἐμπροσθίων ἐστίν, ὥστε
δοκεῖν συγκαθῆσθαι τῷ οὐραίῳ μέρει, τὸ ὕψος
βοὸς ἔχοντι, τὰ δὲ ἐμπρόσθια σκέλη τῶν καμη-
λείων οὐ λείπεται· τράχηλος δ' εἰς ὕψος ἐξηρμένος
ὀρθός, τὴν κορυφὴν δὲ πολὺ ὑπερπετεστέραν ἔχει
τῆς καμήλου· διὰ δὲ τὴν ἀσυμμετρίαν ταύτην
οὐδὲ τάχος οἶμαι τοσοῦτον εἶναι περὶ τὸ ζῷον,
ὅσον εἴρηκεν Ἀρτεμίδωρος, ἀνυπέρβλητον φήσας·
ἀλλ' οὐδὲ θηρίον ἐστίν, ἀλλὰ βόσκημα μᾶλλον·
οὐδεμίαν γὰρ ἀγριότητα ἐμφαίνει. γίνονται δέ,
φησί, καὶ σφίγγες καὶ κυνοκέφαλοι καὶ κῆβοι
λέοντος μὲν πρόσωπον ἔχοντες, τὸ δὲ λοιπὸν
σῶμα πάνθηρος, μέγεθος δὲ δορκάδος· καὶ ταῦροι
δ' εἰσὶν ἄγριοι καὶ σαρκοφάγοι, μεγέθει πολὺ
τοὺς παρ' ἡμῖν ὑπερβεβλημένοι καὶ τάχει, πυρροὶ
τὴν χρόαν. κροκούττας δ' ἐστὶ μίγμα λύκου
καὶ κυνός, ὥς φησιν οὗτος. ἃ δ' ὁ Σκήψιος λέγει
Μητρόδωρος ἐν τῷ περὶ συνηθείας βιβλίῳ μύθοις
ἔοικε καὶ οὐ φροντιστέον αὐτῶν. καὶ δρακόντων
δ' εἴρηκε μεγέθη τριάκοντα πηχῶν ὁ Ἀρτεμίδωρος
ἐλέφαντας καὶ ταύρους χειρουμένων, μετριάσας
ταύτῃ γε· οἱ γὰρ Ἰνδικοὶ μυθωδέστεροι καὶ οἱ
Λιβυκοί, οἷς γε καὶ πόα ἐπιπεφυκέναι λέγεται.

17. Νομαδικὸς μὲν οὖν ὁ βίος τῶν Τρωγλο-

---

[1] i.e. camel-leopards.
[2] The Papio sphinx, a large baboon.
[3] i.e. "Dog-heads" (the Papio hamadryas, a sacred baboon).
[4] The Papio cebus (also referred to in 17. 1. 40).

16. In this region, also, are found camelopards,[1] though they are in no respect like leopards; for the dappled marking of their skin is more like that of a fawnskin, which latter is flecked with spots, and their hinder parts are so much lower than their front parts that they appear to be seated on their tail-parts, which have the height of an ox, although their forelegs are no shorter than those of camels; and their necks rise high and straight up, their heads reaching much higher up than those of camels. On account of this lack of symmetry the speed of the animal cannot, I think, be so great as stated by Artemidorus, who says that its speed is not to be surpassed. Furthermore, it is not a wild beast, but rather a domesticated animal, for it shows no signs of wildness. And in this country are also found, he says, sphinxes [2] and cynocephali [3] and cebi,[4] which last have the face of a lion, and a body otherwise like that of a panther and with the size of a gazelle. The country also has bulls that are wild, carnivorous, and far surpass those in our part of the world in size and speed; and their colour is red. The crocuttas [5] is a mixed progeny of wolf and dog, as Artemidorus says. But what Metrodorus of Scepsis says in his book on *Habits* is like a myth and should be disregarded. Artemidorus also speaks of serpents thirty cubits in length which overpower elephants and bulls; and his measurement is moderate, at least for serpents in this part of the world, for the Indian serpents are rather fabulous,[6] as also those in Libya, which are said to grow grass on their backs.[7]

17. Now the Troglodytes live a nomadic life; and

[5] Apparently a species of hyena.
[6] See 2. 1. 9 and 15. 1. 28.   [7] See 17. 3. 5.

δυτῶν, τυραννοῦνται δὲ καθ' ἕκαστα, κοιναὶ δὲ
καὶ γυναῖκες καὶ τέκνα πλὴν τοῖς τυράννοις, τῷ
δὲ τὴν τυράννου φθείραντι πρόβατον ἢ ζημία
ἐστί. στιβίζονται[1] δ' ἐπιμελῶς αἱ γυναῖκες,
περίκεινται δὲ τοῖς τραχήλοις κογχία ἀντὶ
βασκανίων. πολεμοῦσι δὲ περὶ τῆς νομῆς, κατ'
ἀρχὰς μὲν διωθούμενοι ταῖς χερσίν, εἶτα λίθοις,
ὅταν δὲ τραῦμα γένηται, καὶ τοξεύμασι καὶ
μαχαιρίσι· διαλύουσι δὲ γυναῖκες, εἰς μέσους
προϊοῦσαι καὶ δεήσεις προσενέγκασαι· τροφὴ δ'
ἔκ τε σαρκῶν καὶ τῶν ὀστέων κοπτομένων ἀναμὶξ
καὶ εἰς τὰς δορὰς ἐνειλουμένων,[2] εἶτ' ὀπτωμένων
καὶ ἄλλως πολλαχῶς σκευαζομένων ὑπὸ τῶν
C 776 μαγείρων, οὓς καλοῦσιν ἀκαθάρτους· ὥστε μὴ
κρεοφαγεῖν μόνον, ἀλλὰ καὶ ὀστοφαγεῖν καὶ
δερματοφαγεῖν· χρῶνται δὲ καὶ τῷ αἵματι καὶ
τῷ γάλακτι καταμίξαντες. ποτὸν δὲ τοῖς μὲν
πολλοῖς ἀπόβρεγμα παλιούρου, τοῖς δὲ τυράννοις
μελίκρατον, ἀπ' ἄνθους τινὸς ἐκπιεζομένου τοῦ
μέλιτος. ἔστι δ' αὐτοῖς χειμὼν μέν, ἡνίκα οἱ
ἐτησίαι πνέουσι (κατομβροῦνται γάρ), θέρος δ'
ὁ λοιπὸς χρόνος. γυμνῆται δὲ καὶ δερματοφόροι
καὶ σκυταληφόροι διατελοῦσιν· εἰσὶ δ' οὐ κολοβοὶ
μόνον, ἀλλὰ καὶ περιτετμημένοι τινές, καθάπερ
Αἰγύπτιοι. οἱ δὲ Μεγάβαροι Αἰθίοπες τοῖς ῥοπά-
λοις καὶ τύλους προστιθέασι σιδηροῦς, χρῶνται
δὲ καὶ λόγχαις καὶ ἀσπίσιν ὠμοβυρσίναις, οἱ δὲ
λοιποὶ Αἰθίοπες τόξοις καὶ λόγχαις. θάπτουσι

---

[1] στιμμίζονται E.
[2] ἐνειλουμένων, Corais, for ἀνιλουμένων CF, ἀνειλουμένων
other MSS.

their several tribes are ruled by tyrants; and both wives and children are held in common except those of the tyrants; and the fine for anyone who corrupts the wife of a tyrant consists of a sheep. The women paint their eyelids carefully with stibi;[1] and they wear shells for amulets round their necks. The Troglodytes go to war about pasturage, at first pushing their way through with their hands and then with stones, and also, when a wound is inflicted, with arrows and daggers; but the fighters are reconciled by the women, who advance into the midst of the combatants and ply them with entreaties. Their food consists of flesh and bones which are first chopped up together and wrapped in skins and then baked, or prepared in numerous other ways by the cooks (whom they call "unclean"), so that they not only eat the flesh, but also the bones and the skin; and they also use the blood mixed with milk. As for beverages, most of the people drink a brew of buckthorn,[2] but the tyrants drink a mixture of honey and water, the honey being pressed out of some kind of flower. They have winter when the Etesian winds blow (for they have rains); but the rest of the time is summer. They always go lightly clad, wear skins, and carry clubs; and they not only mutilate their bodies,[3] but some of them are also circumcised, like the Aegyptians. The Aethiopian Megabari have iron knobs on their clubs, and also use spears and shields made of rawhide, but the rest of the Aethiopians use the bow and arrow and lances. Before burying their

---

[1] Lat. *stibium*, *i.e.* the sesquisulphide of antimony, a dark pigment. [2] *Rhamnus paliurus.*
[3] See 16. 4. 5 and Diodorus Siculus 3. 32.

δέ τινες τῶν Τρωγλοδυτῶν, ῥάβδοις παλιουρίναις δήσαντες τὸν αὐχένα τῶν νεκρῶν πρὸς τὰ σκέλη· ἔπειτα εὐθὺς καταλεύουσιν[1] ἱλαροί, γελῶντες ἅμα, ἕως ἂν τοῦ σώματος τὴν ὄψιν ἀποκρύψωσιν· εἶτ᾽ ἐπιθέντες κέρας αἴγειον ἀπίασιν. ὁδοιποροῦσι δὲ νύκτωρ ἐκ τῶν ἀρρένων θρεμμάτων κώδωνας ἐξάψαντες, ὥστ᾽ ἐξίστασθαι τὰ θηρία τῷ ψόφῳ· καὶ λαμπάσι δὲ[2] καὶ τόξοις ἐπὶ τὰ θηρία χρῶνται, καὶ διαγρυπνοῦσι δὲ τῶν ποιμνίων χάριν, ᾠδῇ τινι χρώμενοι πρὸς τῷ πυρί.

18. Ταῦτ᾽ εἰπὼν περὶ τῶν Τρωγλοδυτῶν καὶ τῶν προσχώρων Αἰθιόπων ἐπάνεισιν ἐπὶ τοὺς Ἄραβας· καὶ πρώτους ἔπεισι τοὺς τὸν Ἀράβιον κόλπον ἀφορίζοντας καὶ ἀντικειμένους τοῖς Τρωγλοδύταις, ἀρξάμενος ἀπὸ τοῦ Ποσειδίου. φησὶ δὲ ἐνδοτέρω κεῖσθαι τοῦτο τοῦ Αἰλανίτου μυχοῦ· συνεχῆ δὲ τοῦ Ποσειδίου φοινικῶνα εἶναι εὔυδρον, τιμᾶσθαί τε κομιδῇ διὰ τὸ πᾶσαν τὴν κύκλῳ καυματηράν τε καὶ ἄνυδρον καὶ ἄσκιον ὑπάρχειν, ἐνταῦθα δὲ καὶ τὴν εὐκαρπίαν τῶν φοινίκων εἶναι θαυμαστήν· προεστήκασι δὲ τοῦ ἄλσους ἀνὴρ καὶ γυνή, διὰ γένους ἀποδεδειγμένοι, δερματοφόροι, τροφὴν ἀπὸ τῶν φοινίκων ἔχοντες. κοιτάζονται δ᾽ ἐπὶ δένδρων καλυβοποιησάμενοι διὰ τὸ πλῆθος τῶν θηρίων. εἶθ᾽ ἑξῆς ἐστι νῆσος Φωκῶν, ἀπὸ τοῦ πλήθους τῶν θηρίων τούτων ὠνομασμένη. πλησίον δ᾽ αὐτῆς ἀκρωτήριον, ὃ διατείνει πρὸς τὴν Πέτραν τὴν τῶν Ναβαταίων καλουμένων

---

[1] καταλεύουσιν, Tzschucke, for καταλέγουσιν.
[2] δέ Eoz, τε other MSS.

---

[1] So Diodorus Siculus (3. 33).

dead, some of the Troglodytes bind the neck of the corpses to the legs with twigs of the buckthorn, and then immediately, with merriment and laughter,[1] throw stones upon them until the body is hidden from sight; and then they place a ram's horn on the barrow and go away. They travel by night, first fastening bells to the male cattle, so as to drive away the wild beasts with the noise; and they also use torches and bows to repel the wild beasts; and, for the sake of their flocks, they also keep watch during the night, singing a kind of song near the fire.

18. After saying all this about the Troglodytes and the neighbouring Aethiopians, Artemidorus returns to the Arabians; and first, beginning at Poseidium, he describes the Arabians who border on the Arabian Gulf and live opposite the Troglodytes. He says that Poseidium lies farther in than the Aelanites Gulf; and that contiguous to Poseidium there is a grove of palm trees, which is well supplied with water and is highly valued because all the country around is hot and waterless and shadeless; and that here the fertility of the palms is wonderful; and that a man and a woman have charge of the grove, being appointed to that charge through hereditary right. They wear skins, and live on dates from the palm trees; but on account of the number of wild beasts they build huts in trees and sleep there. Then, next, one comes to the Island of Phocae,[2] which was so named from the number of seals there. Near the island is a promontory, which extends to the Rock of the Nabataean Arabians, as they are called, and

[2] Seals.

Ἀράβων καὶ τὴν Παλαιστίνην χώραν, εἰς ἣν
Μιναῖοί τε καὶ Γερραῖοι καὶ πάντες οἱ πλησιόχωροι τὰ τῶν ἀρωμάτων φορτία κομίζουσιν. εἶτ'
ἄλλη παραλία, πρότερον μὲν Μαρανιτῶν καλουμένη, ὧν οἱ μὲν ἦσαν γεωργοί, τινὲς δὲ σκηνῖται,
C 777 νῦν δὲ Γαρινδαίων, ἀνελόντων ἐκείνους δόλῳ·
ἐπέθεντο γὰρ αὐτοῖς, πενταετηρικήν τινα πανή-
γυριν ἐπιτελοῦσι, καὶ τούτους τε διέφθειραν καὶ
τοὺς ἄλλους ἐπελθόντες ἄρδην διελυμήναντο.
εἶθ' ὁ Αἰλανίτης [1] κόλπος καὶ ἡ Ναβαταία, πολύ-
ανδρος οὖσα [2] χώρα καὶ εὔβοτος· οἰκοῦσι δὲ καὶ
νήσους προκειμένας πλησίον· οἳ πρότερον μὲν
καθ' ἡσυχίαν ἦσαν, ὕστερον δὲ σχεδίαις ἐληίζοντο
τοὺς ἐκ τῆς Αἰγύπτου πλέοντας· δίκας δ' ἔτισαν,
ἐπελθόντος στόλου καὶ ἐκπορθήσαντος αὐτούς.
ἑξῆς δ' ἐστὶ πεδίον εὔδενδρόν τε καὶ εὔυδρον καὶ [3]
βοσκημάτων παντοίων μεστόν, ἄλλων τε καὶ
ἡμιόνων· καὶ καμήλων ἀγρίων [4] καὶ ἐλάφων καὶ
δορκάδων πλῆθος ἐν αὐτῷ, λέοντές τε καὶ παρδάλεις καὶ λύκοι συχνοί. πρόκειται δὲ νῆσος
καλουμένη Δία· εἶτα κόλπος ὅσον πεντακοσίων
σταδίων, ὄρεσι περικλειόμενος καὶ δυσεισβόλῳ
στόματι· περιοικοῦσι δὲ θηρευτικοὶ ἄνδρες τῶν
χερσαίων ἀγρευμάτων. εἶτ' ἔρημοι τρεῖς νῆσοι
πλήρεις ἐλαιῶν, οὐ τῶν παρ' ἡμῖν, ἀλλὰ τῶν
ἐντοπίων, ἃς καλοῦμεν Αἰθιοπικάς, ὧν τὸ δάκρυον
καὶ ἰατρικῆς δυνάμεώς ἐστιν. ἐφεξῆς δ' ἐστὶν

---

[1] Αἰλανίτης E, Ἐλανίτης other MSS.
[2] ἤ, before χώρα, moz omit.
[3] καί, after εὔυδρον, Dh omit.
[4] The MSS. read ἡμιόνων ἀγρίων καὶ καμήλων. Kramer,
citing Diodorus Siculus 3. 42, transposes ἀγρίων as above.

to the Palaestine country, whither Minaeans and Gerrhaeans and all the neighbouring peoples convey their loads of aromatics. Then one comes to another coast, which was formerly called the coast of the Maranitae, some of whom were farmers and others tent-dwellers, but is now called the coast of the Garindaeans, who destroyed the Maranitae by treachery; for the Garindaeans attacked them while they were celebrating some quadrennial festival, and not only destroyed all the people at the festival but also overran and exterminated the rest of the tribe. Then to the Aelanites Gulf, and to Nabataea, a country with a large population and well supplied with pasturage. They also dwell on islands situated off the coast near by; and these Nabataeans formerly lived a peaceful life, but later, by means of rafts, went to plundering the vessels of people sailing from Aegypt. But they paid the penalty when a fleet went over and sacked their country. One comes next to a plain which is well supplied with trees and water and is full of all kinds of domestic animals— mules among others; and it has a multitude of wild camels, deer, and gazelles, as also numerous lions, leopards, and wolves.[1] Off this plain lies an island called Dia. Then one comes to a gulf about five hundred stadia in extent, which is enclosed all round by mountains and a mouth that is difficult to enter; and round it live men who hunt the land animals. Then to three uninhabited islands, full of olive trees, not the kind in our country, but the indigenous kind, called Aethiopic, the sap of which has medicinal power. Next in order one comes to a stony beach,

---

[1] Jackals, perhaps.

αἰγιαλὸς λιθώδης, καὶ μετὰ τοῦτον τραχεῖα καὶ
δυσπαράπλευστος ὅσον χιλίων σταδίων παραλία
σπάνει λιμένων καὶ ἀγκυροβολίων· ὄρος γὰρ
παρατείνει τραχὺ καὶ ὑψηλόν· εἶθ᾽ ὑπώρειαι
σπιλαδώδεις¹ μέχρι τῆς θαλάττης, τοῖς ἐτησίαις
μάλιστα καὶ ταῖς τότε ἐπομβρίαις ἀβοήθητον
παρέχουσαι τὸν κίνδυνον. ἑξῆς δ᾽ ἐστὶ κόλπος
νήσους ἔχων σποράδας, καὶ συνεχῶς² θῖνες ψάμμου μελαίνης τρεῖς ἄγαν ὑψηλοί, καὶ μετὰ τούτους
Χαρμόθας³ λιμὴν ὅσον σταδίων τὸν κύκλον ἑκατόν,
στενὸν καὶ ἐπικίνδυνον ἔχων τὸν εἴσπλουν παντὶ
σκάφει. ῥεῖ δὲ καὶ ποταμὸς εἰς αὐτόν· ἐν μέσῳ
δὲ νῆσος εὔδενδρος καὶ γεωργήσιμος. εἶτ᾽ ἐστὶ
παραλία τραχεῖα, καὶ μετὰ ταύτην κόλποι τινὲς
καὶ χώρα Νομάδων ἀπὸ καμήλων ἐχόντων τὸν
βίον· καὶ γὰρ πολεμοῦσιν ἀπ᾽ αὐτῶν καὶ ὁδεύουσι
καὶ τρέφονται τῷ τε γάλακτι χρώμενοι καὶ ταῖς
σαρξί. ῥεῖ δὲ ποταμὸς δι᾽ αὐτῶν ψῆγμα χρυσοῦ
καταφέρων, οὐκ ἴσασι δ᾽ αὐτὸ κατεργάζεσθαι·
καλοῦνται δὲ Δέβαι, οἱ μὲν νομάδες, οἱ δὲ καὶ
γεωργοί. οὐ λέγω δὲ τῶν ἐθνῶν τὰ ὀνόματα τὰ
πολλὰ⁴ διὰ τὴν ἀδοξίαν καὶ ἅμα ἀτοπίαν τῆς
ἐκφορᾶς αὐτῶν. ἐχόμενοι δ᾽ εἰσὶν ἡμερώτεροι
τούτων ἄνδρες, εὐκρατοτέραν οἰκοῦντες γῆν· καὶ
γὰρ εὔυδρός⁵ ἐστι καὶ εὔομβρος· χρυσός τε
C 778 ὀρυκτὸς γίνεται παρ᾽ αὐτοῖς οὐ ψήγματος, ἀλλὰ
βωλαρίων χρυσοῦ καθάρσεως οὐ πολλῆς δεομέ-

---

¹ σπηλαιώδεις *moxz*, Tzschucke, Corais.
² συνεχεῖς CEx.
³ E reads Χαρμόλας, F Χαρμοθᾶς.
⁴ πολλά, Meineke, for παλαιά. Letronne conj. ἄλλα,
Kramer πλείω.

344

and after that to a stretch of coast about one thousand
stadia in length which is rugged and difficult for
vessels to pass, for lack of harbours and anchoring-
places, since a rugged and lofty mountain stretches
along it. Then one comes to foot-hills, which are
rocky and extend to the sea; and these, especially at
the time of the Etesian winds and the rains, present to
sailors a danger that is beyond all help. Next is a
gulf with scattered islands; and continuous with the
gulf are three exceedingly high banks of black sand;
and after these lies Charmothas Harbour, about one
hundred stadia in circuit, with an entrance that is
narrow and dangerous for all kinds of boats. A river
flows into it; and there is an island in the middle
of it which is well supplied with trees and fit for
tillage. Then one comes to a rugged stretch of
coast; and after that to certain gulfs and to a country
of nomads who get their livelihood from camels; for
they carry on war from the backs of camels, travel
upon them, and subsist upon their milk and flesh.
A river flows through their country that brings down
gold-dust, but the inhabitants do not know how to
work it. They are called Debae; and some of them
are nomads, whereas others are also farmers. I am
not giving most of the names of the tribes because
of their insignificance and at the same time because
of the oddity of the pronunciations. Next to the
Debae are men more civilised than they; and the
country these live in has a more temperate climate;
for it is well watered, and well supplied with rains.
Gold obtained by digging is found in their country
—not gold-dust, but gold nuggets, which do not
require much purification; the smallest nuggets

STRABO

νων,[1] μέγεθος δ' ἐχόντων ἐλάχιστον μὲν πυρῆνος, μέσον δὲ μεσπίλου, μέγιστον δὲ καρύου· τρήσαντες δὲ ταῦτα ἐναλλὰξ λίθοις διαφανέσιν ὅρμους ποιοῦνται διείροντες λίνον,[2] περιτίθενται δὲ περὶ τοὺς τραχήλους καὶ καρπούς· πωλοῦσι δὲ καὶ πρὸς τοὺς ἀστυγείτονας εὔωνον τὸν χρυσόν, τριπλάσιον ἀντιδιδόντες[3] τοῦ χαλκοῦ, διπλάσιον δὲ τοῦ ἀργύρου διά τε τὴν ἀπειρίαν τῆς ἐργασίας καὶ τὴν σπάνιν τῶν ἀντιλαμβανομένων, ὧν ἡ χρεία πρὸς τοὺς βίους ἀναγκαιοτέρα.

19. Συνάπτει δ' ἡ τῶν Σαβαίων εὐδαιμονεστάτη, μεγίστου ἔθνους, παρ' οἷς καὶ σμύρνα καὶ λίβανος καὶ κιννάμωμον· ἐν δὲ τῇ παραλίᾳ καὶ βάλσαμον καὶ ἄλλη τις πόα σφόδρα εὐώδης, ταχὺ δ' ἐξίτηλον τὴν ὀδμὴν ἔχουσα· εἰσὶ δὲ καὶ φοίνικες εὐώδεις καὶ κάλαμος, ὄφεις δὲ σπιθαμιαῖοι, φοινικοῖ τὴν χρόαν, προσαλλόμενοι καὶ μέχρι λαγόνος, τὸ δῆγμα ἔχοντες ἀνήκεστον. διὰ δὲ τὴν ἀφθονίαν τῶν καρπῶν ἀργοὶ καὶ ῥάθυμοι τοῖς βίοις εἰσὶν οἱ ἄνθρωποι. κοιτάζονται δὲ ἐπὶ τῶν ῥιζῶν τῶν δένδρων ἐκτέμνοντες οἱ πολλοὶ καὶ δημοτικοί.[4] διαδεχόμενοι δ' οἱ σύνεγγυς ἀεὶ τὰ φορτία, τοῖς μετ' αὐτοὺς παραδιδόασι μέχρι Συρίας καὶ Μεσοποταμίας· καρούμενοι δ' ὑπὸ τῶν εὐωδιῶν, αἴρουσι

---

[1] δεομέγων ux, δεομένου other MSS.
[2] λίνῳ E.
[3] ἀντιδίδοντες Ex, ἀντιδόντες other MSS.
[4] The words οἱ . . . δημοτικοί are omitted by moz.

346

have the size of a fruit-stone, the medium that
of a medlar, and the largest that of a walnut.
They make collars with these nuggets, perforating
them and stringing them alternately with transparent stones by means of thread; and they
wear them round their necks and wrists. They
also sell the gold at a cheap price to their
neighbours, giving it in exchange for three times the
quantity of brass and double the quantity of silver,
because of their lack of experience in working gold
and because of the scarcity of the things received
in exchange, which are more important for the
necessities of life.

19. Bordering upon these people is the very fertile
country of the Sabaeans, a very large tribe, in
whose country myrrh and frankincense and cinnamon
are produced; and on the coast is found balsam, as
also another kind of herb of very fragrant smell,
which quickly loses its fragrance. There are also
sweet-smelling palms, and reeds; and serpents a
span in length, which are dark-red in colour, can
leap even as far as a hare, and inflict an incurable
bite. On account of the abundance of fruits the
people are lazy and easy-going in their modes of life.
Most of the populace sleep on the roots of trees
which they have cut out of the ground.[1] Those who
live close to one another receive in continuous
succession the loads of aromatics and deliver them
to their next neighbours, as far as Syria and Mesopotamia; and when they are made drowsy by the sweet
odours they overcome the drowsiness by inhaling

---

[1] Surely a strange sort of bed—if the Greek text is correct.
In 16. 4. 18, Strabo says that the Arabians, "on account of
the number of wild beasts, build huts in trees and sleep there."

τὸν κάρον ἀσφάλτου θυμιάματι καὶ τράγου πώγ-
ωνος. ἡ δὲ πόλις τῶν Σαβαίων, ἡ Μαρίαβα,[1]
κεῖται μὲν ἐπ' ὄρους εὐδένδρου, βασιλέα δ' ἔχει
κύριον τῶν κρίσεων καὶ τῶν ἄλλων· ἐκ δὲ τῶν
βασιλείων[2] οὐ θέμις ἐξιέναι,[3] ἢ καταλεύουσιν[4]
αὐτὸν παραχρῆμα οἱ ὄχλοι κατά τι λόγιον· ἐν
χλιδῇ δ' ἐστὶ γυναικείᾳ καὶ αὐτὸς καὶ οἱ περὶ
αὐτόν· τὰ δὲ πλήθη τὰ μὲν γεωργεῖ, τὰ δ' ἐμπο-
ρεύεται τὰ ἀρώματα τά τε ἐπιχώρια καὶ τὰ ἀπὸ
τῆς Αἰθιοπίας, πλέοντες ἐπ' αὐτὰ διὰ τῶν στενῶν
δερματίνοις πλοίοις· τοσαῦτα δ' ἐστὶ τὸ πλῆθος,
ὥστ' ἀντὶ φρυγάνων καὶ τῆς καυσίμου ὕλης
χρῆσθαι κινναμώμῳ καὶ κασσίᾳ[5] καὶ τοῖς ἄλλοις.
γίνεται δ' ἐν τοῖς Σαβαίοις καὶ τὸ λάριμνον,
εὐωδέστατον θυμίαμα. ἐκ δὲ τῆς ἐμπορίας οὗτοί
τε καὶ Γερραῖοι πλουσιώτατοι πάντων εἰσίν,
ἔχουσί τε παμπληθῆ κατασκευὴν χρυσωμάτων
τε καὶ ἀργυρωμάτων, κλινῶν τε καὶ τριπόδων
καὶ κρατήρων σὺν ἐκπώμασι καὶ τῇ τῶν οἴκων
πολυτελείᾳ· καὶ γὰρ θυρώματα καὶ τοῖχοι καὶ
ὀροφαὶ δι' ἐλέφαντος καὶ χρυσοῦ καὶ ἀργύρου
λιθοκολλήτου τυγχάνει διαπεποικιλμένα. ταῦτα
μὲν περὶ τούτων εἴρηκε, τἆλλα δὲ τὰ μὲν παραπλησίως τῷ Ἐρατοσθένει λέγει· τὰ δὲ καὶ παρὰ
τῶν ἄλλων ἱστορικῶν παρατίθησι.

C 779   20. Ἐρυθρὰν γὰρ λέγειν τινὰς τὴν θάλατταν
ἀπὸ τῆς χροιᾶς τῆς ἐμφαινομένης κατ' ἀνάκλασιν,
εἴτε ἀπὸ τοῦ ἡλίου κατὰ κορυφὴν ὄντος εἴτε ἀπὸ

---

[1] Μαρίαβα, Tzschucke, for Μερίαβα CFmowxz, Μεριάβα E, Μέρια Dhi.

[2] βασιλείων, the editors, instead of ἄλλων Βασιλέων.

[3] ἐξιέναι, Kramer, for ἐξεῖναι.

348

the incense of asphalt and goats' beard. The city
of the Sabaeans, Mariaba, is situated upon a well-
wooded mountain; and it has a king who is authority
in lawsuits and everything else; but it is not lawful
for him to leave the palace, or, if he does, the rabble,
in accordance with some oracle, stone him to death
on the spot. Both he himself and those about him
live in effeminate luxury; but the masses engage
partly in farming and partly in the traffic in aromatics,
both the local kinds and those from Aethiopia; to
get the latter they sail across the straits in leathern
boats. They have these aromatics in such abundance
that they use cinnamon and cassia and the others
instead of sticks and firewood. In the country of
the Sabaeans is also found larimnum, a most fragrant
incense. From their trafficking both the Sabaeans
and the Gerrhaeans have become richest of all; and
they have a vast equipment of both gold and silver
articles, such as couches and tripods and bowls,
together with drinking-vessels and very costly
houses; for doors and walls and ceilings are variegated with ivory and gold and silver set with precious
stones. This is Artemidorus' account of these
peoples, but the rest of his statements are partly
similar to those of Eratosthenes and partly quoted
from the other historians.

20. For example, he says that some writers call
the sea " Erythra "[1] from the colour it presents as
the result of reflection, whether from the rays of the
sun when it is in the zenith, or from the mountains,

---

[1] *i.e.* the Erythraean (Red) sea.

---

⁴ καταλεύουσιν, Leopardi, for καταλύουσιν.
⁵ κασία Diaz.

τῶν ὀρῶν ἐρυθραινομένων ἐκ τῆς ἀποκαύσεως·[1]
ἀμφοτέρως γὰρ εἰκάζειν·[2] Κτησίαν δὲ τὸν Κνίδιον
πηγὴν ἱστορεῖν ἐκδιδοῦσαν εἰς τὴν θάλατταν
ἐρευθὲς καὶ μιλτῶδες ὕδωρ· Ἀγαθαρχίδην δὲ τὸν
ἐκείνου πολίτην παρά τινος Βόξου,[3] Πέρσου[4] τὸ
γένος, ἱστορῆσαι, διότι Πέρσης τις Ἐρύθρας,
ἱπποφορβίου τινὸς ὑπὸ λεαίνης οἴστρῳ κατασχομένης[5] ἐξελαθέντος μέχρι θαλάττης κἀκεῖθεν εἰς
νῆσόν τινα διάραντος, σχεδίαν πηξάμενος πρῶτος
περαιωθείη πρὸς τὴν νῆσον· ἰδὼν δὲ καλῶς οἰκήσιμον, τὴν μὲν ἀγέλην εἰς τὴν Περσίδα ἀπαγάγοι
πάλιν, ἀποίκους δ' ἐκεῖ στείλαι τε καὶ τὰς ἄλλας
νήσους καὶ τὴν παραλίαν, ἐπώνυμον δὲ ποιήσειεν
ἑαυτοῦ τὸ πέλαγος. τοὺς δὲ Περσέως υἱὸν ἀπο-
φαίνεσθαι τὸν Ἐρύθραν, ἡγήσασθαί τε τῶν τόπων.
λέγεται δ' ὑπό τινων τὰ ἀπὸ τῶν στενῶν τοῦ
Ἀραβίου κόλπου μέχρι τῆς κινναμωμοφόρου τῆς
ἐσχάτης πεντακισχιλίων σταδίων, οὐκ εὐκρινῶς,
εἴτ' ἐπὶ νότον εἴτ'[6] ἐπὶ τὰς ἀνατολάς. λέγεται
δὲ καὶ διότι ὁ σμάραγδος καὶ ὁ βήρυλλος ἐν τοῖς
τοῦ χρυσίου μετάλλοις ἐγγίνεται. εἰσὶ δὲ καὶ
ἅλες εὐώδεις ἐν Ἀραψιν, ὥς φησι Ποσειδώνιος.

21. Πρῶτοι δ' ὑπὲρ τῆς Συρίας Ναβαταῖοι καὶ
Σαβαῖοι τὴν εὐδαίμονα Ἀραβίαν νέμονται καὶ
πολλάκις κατέτρεχον αὐτῆς, πρὶν ἢ Ῥωμαίων
γενέσθαι· νῦν δὲ κἀκεῖνοι Ῥωμαίοις εἰσὶν ὑπήκοοι
καὶ Σύροι. μητρόπολις δὲ τῶν Ναβαταίων ἐστὶν

---

[1] Instead of ἀποκαύσεως, x reads ἐκκαύσεως, Eustathius
(*Ad. Dionys.* 31) καύσεως, Corais ἐπικαύσεως.
[2] εἰκάζει *moz*; so Corais.
[3] Βόξου *Dh*, Ἐ3όσου C and *marg.* F.
[4] Πέρσου, Casaubon inserts.
[5] κατασχομένης *moz*, κατασχομένου other MSS.

which have been reddened by the scorching heat;
for, he continues, conjecture runs both ways about
the cause; but Ctesias the Cnidian reports a
spring, consisting of red and ochre-coloured water,
as emptying into the sea; and Agatharcides, a
fellow-citizen of Ctesias, reports from a certain
Boxus, of Persian descent, that when a herd of
horses had been driven out of the country by a
passion-frenzied lioness as far as the sea and from
there the herd had crossed over to a certain island,
a certain Persian, Erythras by name, built a raft and
was the first man to cross to the island; and that
when he saw that it was beautifully adapted to
habitation, he drove the herd back to Persis, sent
forth colonists to that island and to the others and
to the coast, and caused the sea to be named after
himself; but other writers, he says, declare that
Erythras was the son of Perseus, and that he ruled
over this region. Some writers say that the distance
from the straits of the Arabian Gulf to the extremity
of the cinnamon-bearing country is five thousand
stadia, without distinguishing clearly whether they
mean towards the south or towards the east. It is
said also that the emerald and the beryl are found in
the gold mines. And there are also fragrant salts
in the country of the Arabians, as Poseidonius says.

21. The first people above Syria who dwell in
Arabia Felix are the Nabataeans and the Sabaeans.
They often overran Syria before they became
subject to the Romans; but at present both they
and the Syrians are subject to the Romans. The
metropolis of the Nabataeans is Petra,[1] as it is

---

[1] Rock.

---

[6] εἶτ' . . . εἶτ' E, οὔτ . . . οὔτ' other MSS.

ἡ Πέτρα καλουμένη· κεῖται γὰρ ἐπὶ χωρίου
τἆλλα ὁμαλοῦ καὶ ἐπιπέδου, κύκλῳ δὲ πέτρᾳ
φρουρουμένου, τὰ μὲν ἐκτὸς ἀποκρήμνου καὶ
ἀποτόμου, τὰ δ' ἐντὸς πηγὰς ἀφθόνους ἔχοντος
εἴς τε ὑδρείαν καὶ κηπείαν. ἔξω δὲ τοῦ περιβόλου
χώρα ἔρημος ἡ πλείστη, καὶ μάλιστα ἡ πρὸς
Ἰουδαίᾳ· ταύτῃ δὲ καὶ ἐγγυτάτω ἐστὶ τριῶν ἢ
τεττάρων ὁδὸς ἡμερῶν εἰς Ἱερικοῦντα,[1] εἰς δὲ τὸν
φοινικῶνα πέντε. βασιλεύεται μὲν οὖν ὑπό τινος
ἀεὶ τῶν ἐκ τοῦ βασιλικοῦ γένους, ἔχει δ' ὁ
βασιλεὺς ἐπίτροπον τῶν ἑταίρων τινά, καλούμενον ἀδελφόν· σφόδρα δ' εὐνομεῖται. γενόμενος
γοῦν παρὰ τοῖς Πετραίοις[2] Ἀθηνόδωρος, ἀνὴρ
φιλόσοφος καὶ ἡμῖν ἑταῖρος, διηγεῖτο θαυμάζων·
εὑρεῖν γὰρ ἐπιδημοῦντας ἔφη πολλοὺς μὲν Ῥωμαίων, πολλοὺς δὲ καὶ τῶν ἄλλων ξένων· τοὺς
μὲν οὖν ξένους ὁρᾶν κρινομένους πολλάκις καὶ
πρὸς ἀλλήλους καὶ πρὸς τοὺς ἐπιχωρίους, τῶν δ'
ἐπιχωρίων οὐδένας ἀλλήλοις ἐγκαλοῦντας, ἀλλὰ
τὴν πᾶσαν εἰρήνην ἄγοντας πρὸς ἑαυτούς.

C 780   22. Πολλὰ δὲ καὶ ἡ τῶν Ῥωμαίων ἐπὶ τοὺς
Ἄραβας στρατεία νεωστὶ γενηθεῖσα ἐφ' ἡμῶν, ὧν
ἡγεμὼν ἦν Αἴλιος Γάλλος, διδάσκει τῶν τῆς χώρας
ἰδιωμάτων. τοῦτον δ' ἔπεμψεν ὁ Σεβαστὸς Καῖσαρ διαπειρασόμενον τῶν ἐθνῶν καὶ τῶν τόπων
τούτων τε καὶ τῶν Αἰθιοπικῶν, ὁρῶν[3] τήν τε
Τρωγλοδυτικὴν τὴν προσεχῆ τῇ Αἰγύπτῳ γει-
τονεύουσαν τούτοις, καὶ τὸν Ἀράβιον κόλπον

---

[1] Ἱερικοῦντα E (with χ above κ), Ἐρικοῦντα CDFhw, Ἱερι-
χοῦντα moz.
[2] πετραίοις marg. i, πετρίοις EFz, πατρίοις other MSS.
[3] ὁρῶν F, ὀρῶν other MSS.

called; for it lies on a site which is otherwise smooth
and level, but it is fortified all round by a rock, the
outside parts of the site being precipitous and sheer,
and the inside parts having springs in abundance,
both for domestic purposes and for watering gardens.
Outside the circuit of the rock most of the territory
is desert, in particular that towards Judaea. Here,
too, is the shortest road to Hiericus,[1] a journey of
three or four days, as also to the grove of palm
trees,[2] a journey of five days. Petra is always ruled
by some king from the royal family; and the king
has as Administrator one of his companions, who is
called " brother." It is exceedingly well-governed;
at any rate, Athenodorus, a philosopher and com-
panion of mine, who had been in the city of the
Petraeans, used to describe their government with
admiration, for he said that he found both many
Romans and many other foreigners sojourning there,
and that he saw that the foreigners often engaged in
lawsuits, both with one another and with the natives,
but that none of the natives prosecuted one another,
and that they in every way kept peace with one
another.

22. Many of the special characteristics of Arabia
have been disclosed by the recent expedition of the
Romans against the Arabians, which was made in
my own time under Aelius Gallus as commander.
He was sent by Augustus Caesar to explore the
tribes and the places, not only in Arabia, but also in
Aethiopia, since Caesar saw that the Troglodyte
country which adjoins Aegypt neighbours upon
Arabia, and also that the Arabian Gulf, which

[1] Jericho.   [2] See 16. 4. 18.

στενὸν ὄντα τελέως τὸν διείργοντα ἀπὸ τῶν Τρωγλοδυτῶν τοὺς Ἄραβας· προσοικειοῦσθαι δὴ διενοήθη τούτους ἢ καταστρέφεσθαι. ἦν δέ τι[1] καὶ τὸ πολυχρημάτους ἀκούειν ἐκ παντὸς χρόνου, πρὸς ἄργυρον καὶ χρυσὸν τὰ ἀρώματα διατιθεμένους καὶ τὴν πολυτελεστάτην λιθίαν,[2] ἀναλίσκοντας τῶν λαμβανομένων τοῖς ἔξω μηδέν· ἢ γὰρ φίλοις ἤλπιζε πλουσίοις χρήσεσθαι[3] ἢ ἐχθρῶν κρατήσειν πλουσίων. ἐπῆρε δ' αὐτὸν καὶ ἡ παρὰ τῶν Ναβαταίων ἐλπίς, φίλων ὄντων καὶ συμπράξειν ἅπανθ' ὑπισχνουμένων.

23. Ἐπὶ τούτοις μὲν οὖν ἔστειλε τὴν στρατείαν ὁ Γάλλος· ἐξηπάτησε δ' αὐτὸν ὁ τῶν Ναβαταίων ἐπίτροπος Συλλαῖος, ὑποσχόμενος μὲν ἡγήσεσθαι[4] τὴν ὁδὸν καὶ χορηγήσειν ἅπαντα καὶ συμπράξειν, ἅπαντα δ' ἐξ ἐπιβουλῆς πράξας, καὶ οὔτε παράπλουν ἀσφαλῆ μηνύων, οὔθ' ὁδόν, ἀλλὰ ἀνοδίαις καὶ κυκλοπορίαις καὶ πάντων ἀπόροις χωρίοις, ἢ ῥαχίαις ἀλιμένοις παραβάλλων ἢ χοιράδων ὑφάλων μεσταῖς ἢ τεναγώδεσι· πλεῖστον δὲ αἱ πλημμυρίδες ἐλύπουν, ἐν τοιούτοις καὶ ταῦτα χωρίοις, καὶ αἱ ἀμπώτεις. πρῶτον μὲν δὴ τοῦθ' ἁμάρτημα συνέβη τὸ μακρὰ κατασκευάσασθαι πλοῖα, μηδενὸς ὄντος μηδ' ἐσομένου κατὰ θάλατταν πολέμου. οὐδὲ γὰρ κατὰ γῆν σφόδρα πολεμισταί εἰσιν, ἀλλὰ κάπηλοι μᾶλλον οἱ Ἄραβες καὶ ἐμπορικοί, μήτι γε κατὰ θάλατταν. ὁ δ' οὐκ ἔλαττον ὀγδοήκοντα ἐναυπηγήσατο δίκροτα καὶ

---

[1] Instead of δέ τι, CDF*h* read δ' ἔτι.
[2] λιθείαν Ε*oxz*.
[3] χρήσεσθαι Ε, χρήσασθαι other MSS.
[4] ἡγήσεσθαι, Corais, for ἡγήσασθαι.

separates the Arabians from the Troglodytes, is extremely narrow. Accordingly he conceived the purpose of winning the Arabians over to himself or of subjugating them. Another consideration was the report, which had prevailed from all time, that they were very wealthy, and that they sold aromatics and the most valuable stones for gold and silver, but never expended with outsiders any part of what they received in exchange; for he expected either to deal with wealthy friends or to master wealthy enemies. He was encouraged also by the expectation of assistance from the Nabataeans, since they were friendly and promised to co-operate with him in every way.

23. Upon these considerations, therefore, Gallus set out on the expedition; but he was deceived by the Nabataean Administrator, Syllaeus, who, although he had promised to be guide on the march and to supply all needs and to co-operate with him, acted treacherously in all things, and pointed out neither a safe voyage along the coast nor a safe journey by land, misguiding him through places that had no roads and by circuitous routes and through regions destitute of everything, or along rocky shores that had no harbours or through waters that were shallow or full of submarine rocks; and particularly in places of that kind the flood-tides, as also the ebb-tides, caused very great distress. Now this was the first mistake of Gallus, to build long boats, since there was no naval war at hand, or even to be expected; for the Arabians are not very good warriors even on land, rather being hucksters and merchants, to say nothing of fighting at sea. But Gallus built not less than eighty boats, biremes and

τριήρεις καὶ φασήλους κατὰ Κλεοπατρίδα τὴν
πρὸς τῇ παλαιᾷ διώρυγι τῇ ἀπὸ τοῦ Νείλου.
γνοὺς δὲ διεψευσμένος ἐναυπηγήσατο σκευαγωγὰ
ἑκατὸν καὶ τριάκοντα, οἷς ἔπλευσεν ἔχων περὶ
μυρίους πεζοὺς τῶν ἐκ τῆς Αἰγύπτου Ῥωμαίων
καὶ τῶν συμμάχων, ὧν ἦσαν Ἰουδαῖοι μὲν πεντακόσιοι, Ναβαταῖοι δὲ χίλιοι μετὰ τοῦ Συλλαίου.
πολλὰ δὲ παθὼν καὶ ταλαιπωρηθεὶς πεντεκαιδεκαταῖος ἧκεν εἰς Λευκὴν κώμην τῆς Ναβαταίων γῆς,
ἐμπόριον μέγα, πολλὰ τῶν πλοίων ἀποβαλών, ὧν
ἔνια καὶ αὔτανδρα ὑπὸ δυσπλοίας, πολεμίου δ᾽
οὐδενός· τοῦτο δ᾽ ἀπειργάσατο ἡ τοῦ Συλλαίου
C 781 κακία τοῦ μεζῇ φήσαντος ἀνόδευτα εἶναι στρατο-
πέδοις εἰς τὴν Λευκὴν κώμην, εἰς ἣν καὶ ἐξ ἧς οἱ
καμηλέμποροι τοσούτῳ πλήθει ἀνδρῶν καὶ καμήλων ὁδεύουσιν ἀσφαλῶς καὶ εὐπόρως εἰς Πέτραν
καὶ[1] ἐκ Πέτρας, ὥστε μὴ διαφέρειν μηδὲν στρα-
τοπέδου.

24. Συνέβαινε δὲ τοῦτο τοῦ μὲν βασιλέως τοῦ
Ὀβόδα μὴ πολὺ φροντίζοντος τῶν κοινῶν, καὶ
μάλιστα τῶν κατὰ πόλεμον (κοινὸν δὲ τοῦτο πᾶσι
τοῖς Ἀράβων βασιλεῦσιν), ἅπαντα δὲ ἐπὶ τῇ τοῦ
ἐπιτρόπου ποιουμένου ἐξουσίᾳ[2] τοῦ Συλλαίου·
τούτου δ᾽ ἅπαντα δόλῳ στρατηγοῦντος καὶ
ζητοῦντος, ὡς οἶμαι, κατοπτεῦσαι μὲν τὴν χώραν
καὶ συνεξελεῖν τινας αὐτῶν πόλεις καὶ ἔθνη μετὰ
τῶν Ῥωμαίων, αὐτὸν δὲ καταστῆναι κύριον
ἁπάντων, ἀφανισθέντων ἐκείνων ὑπὸ λιμοῦ καὶ
κόπου καὶ νόσων καὶ ἄλλων, ὅσων δόλῳ παρε-
σκεύασεν ἐκεῖνος. εἰς γοῦν τὴν Λευκὴν κώμην

---

[1] καί, before ἐκ, Casaubon inserts.
[2] ἐξουσίᾳ omitted by MSS. except moz.

triremes and light boats, at Cleopatris,[1] which is near
the old canal which extends[2] from the Nile. But
when he realised that he had been thoroughly deceived, he built one hundred and thirty vessels of
burden, on which he set sail with about ten thousand
infantry, consisting of Romans in Aegypt, as also of
Roman allies, among whom were five hundred Jews
and one thousand Nabataeans under Syllaeus. After
many experiences and hardships he arrived in fourteen days at Leucê Comê[3] in the land of the Nabataeans, a large emporium, although he had lost many
of his boats, some of these being lost, crews and all,
on account of difficult sailing, but not on account of
any enemy. This was caused by the treachery of
Syllaeus, who said that there was no way for an
army to go to Leucê Comê by land; and yet camel-
traders travel back and forth from Petra to this place
in safety and ease, and in such numbers of men and
camels that they differ in no respect from an army.

24. This came to pass because Obodas, the king,
did not care much about public affairs, and particularly military affairs (this is a trait common to all the
Arabian kings), and because he put everything in the
power of Syllaeus; and because Syllaeus treacherously out-generalled Gallus in every way, and
sought, as I think, to spy out the country and, along
with the Romans, to destroy some of its cities and
tribes, and then to establish himself lord of all,
after the Romans were wiped out by hunger and
fatigue and diseases and any other evils which he
had treacherously contrived for them. However,
Gallus put in at Leucê Comê, his army now being

---

[1] Also called Arsinoê (Suez); see 17. 1. 25.
[2] i.e. to the gulf.   [3] i.e. " White Village."

κατῆρεν, ἤδη στομακάκκῃ τε καὶ σκελοτύρβῃ [1]
πειραζομένης τῆς στρατιᾶς, ἐπιχωρίοις πάθεσι,
τῶν μὲν περὶ τὸ στόμα, τῶν δὲ περὶ τὰ σκέλη
παράλυσίν τινα δηλούντων ἔκ τε τῶν ὑδρείων καὶ
βοτανῶν. ἠναγκάσθη γοῦν τό τε θέρος καὶ τὸν
χειμῶνα διατελέσαι αὐτόθι, τοὺς ἀσθενοῦντας
ἀνακτώμενος. ἐκ μὲν οὖν τῆς Λευκῆς κώμης εἰς
Πέτραν, ἐντεῦθεν δ' εἰς Ῥινοκόλουρα [2] τῆς πρὸς
Αἰγύπτῳ Φοινίκης τὰ φορτία κομίζεται, κἀντεῦθεν
εἰς τοὺς ἄλλους· νυνὶ δὲ τὸ πλέον εἰς τὴν Ἀλεξάνδρειαν τῷ Νείλῳ· κατάγεται δ' [3] ἐκ τῆς
Ἀραβίας καὶ τῆς Ἰνδικῆς εἰς Μυὸς ὅρμον· εἶθ'
ὑπέρθεσις [4] εἰς Κοπτὸν τῆς Θηβαΐδος καμήλοις
ἐν διώρυγι τοῦ Νείλου κειμένην· [5] εἶτ' [6] εἰς
Ἀλεξάνδρειαν. πάλιν ἐκ τῆς Λευκῆς κώμης ὁ
Γάλλος ἀναζεύξας τὴν στρατιὰν διὰ τοιούτων
ᾔει χωρίων, ὥστε καὶ ὕδωρ καμήλοις κομίζειν
μοχθηρίᾳ τῶν ἡγεμόνων τῆς ὁδοῦ· διόπερ πολλαῖς
ἡμέραις ἧκεν εἰς τὴν Ἀρέτα γῆν, συγγενοῦς τῷ
Ὀβόδα· ἐδέξατο μὲν οὖν αὐτὸν Ἀρέτας φιλικῶς
καὶ δῶρα προσήνεγκεν, ἡ δὲ τοῦ Συλλαίου προ-
δοσία κἀκείνην ἐποίησε τὴν χώραν δυσπόρευτον·
τριάκοντα γοῦν ἡμέραις διῆλθεν αὐτήν, ζειὰς καὶ
φοίνικας ὀλίγους παρέχουσαν καὶ βούτυρον ἀντ'
ἐλαίου, διὰ τὰς ἀνοδίας· ἡ δ' ἐξῆς, ἣν ἐπῄει,
Νομάδων ἦν καὶ ἔρημος [7] τὰ πολλὰ ὡς ἀληθῶς,

---

[1] σκελοτύρβῃ, Casaubon, for σκελοτίρβη.
[2] Ῥινοκολούρα, the reading of all MSS. here (cp. readings in
16. 1. 12 and 16. 2. 31).
[3] Νείλῳ· κατάγεται δ', Groskurd, for Νείλῳ κατάγεται τὰ δ'.
[4] ὑπέρθεσις, Tzschucke, for ὑπερθέσεις.
[5] κειμένην E, κειμένη other MSS.

sorely tried both with scurvy and with lameness in
the leg, which are native ailments, the former dis-
closing a kind of paralysis round the mouth and the
latter round the legs, both being the result of the
native water and herbs. At all events, he was
forced to spend both the summer and the winter
there, waiting for the sick to recover. Now the
loads of aromatics are conveyed from Leucê Comê
to Petra, and thence to Rhinocolura, which is in
Phoenicia near Aegypt, and thence to the other
peoples; but at the present time they are for the
most part transported by the Nile to Alexandria;
and they are landed from Arabia and India at Myus
Harbour; and then they are conveyed by camels
over to Coptus in Thebaïs, which is situated on a
canal of the Nile, and then to Alexandria. Again
Gallus moved his army from Leucê Comê and
marched through regions of such a kind that water
had to be carried by camels, because of the baseness
of the guides; and therefore it took many days
to arrive at the land of Aretas, a kinsman of Obodas.
Now Aretas received him in a friendly way and
offered him gifts, but the treason of Syllaeus made
difficult the journey through that country too; at
any rate, it took thirty days to traverse the country,
which afforded only zeia,[1] a few palm trees, and
butter instead of oil, because they passed through
parts that had no roads. The next country which
he traversed belonged to nomads and most of it was

---

[1] Or zea, a kind of coarse grain.

---

[6] ἐιτ᾽, Kramer inserts, from conj. of Letronne.
[7] ἔρημος *moz*, ἔρημα other MSS.

ἐκαλεῖτο δὲ Ἀραρηνή· βασιλεὺς δ᾽ ἦν Σάβως·[1]
καὶ ταύτην ἀνοδίαις διῆλθε κατατρίψας ἡμέρας
πεντήκοντα μέχρι πόλεως Νεγράνων[2] καὶ χώρας
εἰρηνικῆς τε καὶ ἀγαθῆς. ὁ μὲν οὖν βασιλεὺς
ἔφυγεν, ἡ δὲ πόλις ἐξ ἐφόδου κατελήφθη· ἐκεῖθεν
ἡμέραις ἓξ ἧκεν ἐπὶ τὸν ποταμόν. συναψάντων
δ᾽ αὐτόθι τῶν βαρβάρων εἰς μάχην, περὶ μυρίους
C 782 αὐτῶν ἔπεσον, τῶν δὲ Ῥωμαίων δύο· ἐχρῶντο
γὰρ ἀπείρως τοῖς ὅπλοις, ἀπόλεμοι τελέως ὄντες,
τόξοις τε καὶ λόγχαις καὶ[3] ξίφεσι καὶ σφενδόναις,
οἱ πλεῖστοι δ᾽ αὐτῶν ἀμφιστόμοις πελέκεσιν·
εὐθὺς δὲ καὶ τὴν πόλιν εἷλε καλουμένην Ἀσκᾶ,
ἀπολειφθεῖσαν[4] ὑπὸ τοῦ βασιλέως. ἐντεῦθεν εἰς
Ἄθρουλα πόλιν ἧκε, καὶ[5] κρατήσας αὐτῆς
ἀκονιτί, φρουρὰν ἐμβαλὼν καὶ παρασκευάσας
ἐφόδια[6] σίτου καὶ φοινίκων εἰς πόλιν Μαρσίαβα[7]
προῆλθεν ἔθνους τοῦ Ῥαμμανιτῶν,[8] οἳ ἦσαν ὑπὸ
Ἰλασάρῳ. ἓξ μὲν οὖν ἡμέρας προσβαλὼν ἐπο-
λιόρκει, λειψυδρίας δ᾽ οὔσης ἀπέστη· δύο μὲν οὖν
ἡμερῶν ὁδὸν ἀπέσχε τῆς ἀρωματοφόρου, καθάπερ
τῶν αἰχμαλώτων ἀκούειν ἦν· ἓξ δὲ μηνῶν χρόνον
ἐν ταῖς ὁδοῖς κατέτριψε, φαύλως ἀγόμενος· ἔγνω
δ᾽ ἀναστρέφων, ὀψὲ[9] τὴν ἐπιβουλὴν καταμαθὼν
καὶ καθ᾽ ἑτέρας ὁδοὺς ἐπανελθών· ἐνναταῖος μὲν

---

[1] Instead of Σάβως, Dh read Σάβᾶς, Σάβος morwxz.
[2] Instead of Νεγράνων, F has Ἀγράνων, CDhix Ἀγρανῶν, moz Νεγρανῶν.
[3] καί, Corais inserts.
[4] ἀπολειφθεῖσαν, Corais, from conj. of Casaubon, for συλλη-φθεῖσαν.
[5] καί, Corais inserts.
[6] ἐφόδια moz, omitted by other MSS. except x, which has τροφάς.

truly desert; and it was called Ararenê; and its king was Sabos; and in passing through this country, through parts that had no roads, he spent fifty days, arriving at the city of the Negrani [1] and at a country which was both peaceable and fertile. Now the king had fled and the city was seized at the first onset; and from there he arrived at the river in six days. Here the barbarians joined battle with the Romans, and about ten thousand of them fell, but only two Romans; for they used their weapons in an inexperienced manner, being utterly unfit for war, using bows and spears and swords and slings, though most of them used a double-edged axe; and immediately afterwards he took the city called Asca, which had been forsaken by its king; and thence he went to a city called Athrula; and, having mastered it without a struggle, he placed a garrison in it, arranged for supplies of grain and dates for his march, advanced to a city called Marsiaba, which belonged to the tribe of the Rhammanitae, who were subject to Ilasarus. Now he assaulted and besieged this city for six days, but for want of water desisted. He was indeed only a two days' journey from the country that produced aromatics, as informed by his captives, but he had used up six months' time on his marches because of bad guidance, and he realised the fact when he turned back, when at last he had learned the plot against him and had gone back by other roads;

[1] Negrana.

---

[7] Μαρσναβαί CDh, Μαρσύαβα moxz.   Kramer conj. Μαρίαβα.
[8] 'Ραμβανειτῶν F, 'Ραμανιτῶν Cwx.
[9] ὀψέ, Xylander, for ὕψει.

γὰρ εἰς Νέγρανα[1] ἧκεν, ὅπου ἡ μάχη συμβεβή-
κει, ἑνδεκαταῖος δ' ἐκεῖθεν εἰς Ἑπτὰ φρέατα
καλούμενα ἀπὸ τοῦ συμβεβηκότος· ἐντεῦθεν ἤδη
δι' εἰρηνικῆς[2] εἰς Χάαλλα κώμην καὶ πάλιν ἄλλην
Μαλόθαν πρὸς ποταμῷ κειμένην ἀφικνεῖται· εἶτα
δι' ἐρήμης ὀλίγα ὑδρεῖα ἐχούσης ὁδὸς μέχρι
Ἐγρᾶς[3] κώμης. ἔστι δὲ τῆς Ὀβόδα·[4] κεῖται δ'
ἐπὶ θαλάττης. τὴν δὲ πᾶσαν ὁδὸν ἑξηκοσταῖος[5]
ἐξήνυσε κατὰ τὴν ἐπάνοδον, ἀναλώσας ἓξ μῆνας
ἐν τῇ ἐξ ἀρχῆς ὁδῷ. ἐντεῦθεν δ' ἐπεραίωσε τὴν
στρατιὰν ἑνδεκαταῖος εἰς Μυὸς ὅρμον, εἶθ'
ὑπερθεὶς[6] εἰς Κοπτὸν μετὰ τῶν ὀνηθῆναι[7] δυνα-
μένων κατῆρεν εἰς Ἀλεξάνδρειαν· τοὺς δ' ἄλλους
ἀπέβαλεν, οὐχ ὑπὸ πολεμίων, ἀλλὰ νόσων καὶ
κόπων καὶ λιμοῦ καὶ μοχθηρίας τῶν ὁδῶν· ἐπεὶ
κατὰ πόλεμον ἑπτά γε μόνους[8] διαφθαρῆναι
συνέβη. δι' ἃς αἰτίας οὐδ' ἐπὶ πολὺ πρὸς τὴν
γνῶσιν τῶν τόπων ὤνησεν ἡ στρατεία αὕτη·
μικρὰ δ' ὅμως συνήργησεν. ὁ δ' αἴτιος τούτων ὁ Συλλαῖος ἔτισε δίκας ἐν Ῥώμῃ, προσποιού-
μενος μὲν φιλίαν, ἐλεγχθεὶς δὲ πρὸς ταύτῃ[9] τῇ
πονηρίᾳ καὶ ἄλλα κακουργῶν καὶ ἀποτμηθεὶς τὴν
κεφαλήν.

25. Τὴν μὲν οὖν ἀρωματοφόρον διαιροῦσιν εἰς
τέτταρας μερίδας, ὥσπερ εἰρήκαμεν· τῶν ἀρωμά-

---

[1] Νέγρανα F, Ἀνάγραν w, Ἀνάγρανα other MSS.
[2] εἰρηνικῆς, Corais, for εἰρήνης.
[3] iw have Ὑγρᾶς, moz Νεγρᾶς (cp. Steph. Byz. s.v. Ἰάθριππα).
[4] Ὀβάδα CDhx.
[5] ἑξηκοσταῖος, Casaubon, for ἑξηκοστήν moz, ἑξηκοστόν other MSS.
[6] ὑπερθεὶς, Corais, for ὑπέρθεσις.
[7] ὀνηθῆναι E, ὠνηθῆναι other MSS., σωθῆναι Meineke, from conj. of Kramer.

for on the ninth day he arrived at Negrana, where the battle had taken place, and thence on the eleventh day at Hepta Phreata, as the place is called, from the fact that it has seven wells; and thence, at last, marching through a peaceable country, he arrived at a village called Chaalla, and again at another village called Malotha, which is situated near a river; and then through a desert country, which had only a few watering-places, as far as a village called Egra. The village is in the territory of Obodas; and it is situated on the sea. On his return he accomplished the whole journey within sixty days, although he had used up six months in his first journey. Thence he carried his army across the Myus Harbour within eleven days, and marched by land over to Coptus, and, with all who had been fortunate enough to survive, landed at Alexandria. The rest he had lost, not in wars, but from sickness and fatigue and hunger and bad roads; for only seven men perished in war. For these reasons, also, this expedition did not profit us to a great extent in our knowledge of those regions, but still it made a slight contribution. But the man who was responsible for this failure, I mean Syllaeus, paid the penalty at Rome, since, although he pretended friendship, he was convicted, in addition to his rascality in this matter, of other offences too, and was beheaded.

25. Now writers divide the country that produces aromatics into four parts, as I have said before;[1]

[1] 16. 4. 2.

<hr>

[8] γε μόνους E, omitted by moz, γει ομένον F, γενομένων other MSS.

[9] ταύτῃ, Casaubon, for αὐτῇ.

των δὲ λίβανον μὲν καὶ σμύρναν ἐκ δένδρων
γίνεσθαί φασι [1] κασσίαν [2] δὲ καὶ ἐκ λιμνῶν.[3] τινὲς
δὲ τὴν πλείω ἐξ Ἰνδῶν εἶναι, τοῦ δὲ λιβάνου
βέλτιστον τὸν πρὸς τῇ Περσίδι. κατ' ἄλλην δὲ
διαίρεσιν σύμπασαν τὴν Εὐδαίμονα πενταχῇ
σχίζουσιν εἰς βασιλείας, ὧν ἡ μὲν τοὺς μαχίμους
ἔχει καὶ προαγωνιστὰς ἁπάντων, ἡ δὲ τοὺς γεωρ-
γούς, παρ' ὧν ὁ σῖτος εἰς τοὺς ἄλλους εἰσάγεται,
ἡ δὲ τοὺς βαναυσοτεχνοῦντας, καὶ ἡ μὲν σμυρνο-
C 783 φόρος, ἡ δὲ λιβανωτοφόρος, αἱ δ' αὐταὶ καὶ τὴν
κασσίαν [4] καὶ τὸ κιννάμωμον καὶ τὴν νάρδον
φέρουσι. παρ' ἀλλήλων δ' οὐ μεταφοιτᾷ τὰ ἐπι-
τηδεύματα, ἀλλ' ἐν τοῖς πατρίοις διαμένουσιν
ἕκαστοι. οἶνος δ' ἐκ φοινίκων ὁ πλείων. ἀδελφοὶ
τιμιώτεροι τῶν τέκνων. κατὰ πρεσβυγένειαν καὶ
βασιλεύουσιν οἱ ἐκ τοῦ γένους καὶ ἄλλας ἀρχὰς
ἄρχουσι· κοινὴ κτῆσις ἅπασι τοῖς συγγενέσι,
κύριος δὲ ὁ πρεσβύτατος· μία δὲ καὶ γυνὴ πᾶσιν,
ὁ δὲ φθάσας εἰσιὼν μίγνυται, προθεὶς τῆς θύρας
τὴν ῥάβδον· ἑκάστῳ γὰρ δεῖν ῥαβδοφορεῖν ἔθος·
νυκτερεύει δὲ παρὰ τῷ πρεσβυτάτῳ. διὸ καὶ
πάντες ἀδελφοὶ πάντων εἰσί. μίγνυνται δὲ καὶ
μητράσι· μοιχῷ δὲ ζημία θάνατος· μοιχὸς δ'

---

[1] After φασί, Meyer (*Bot. Erleut. zur Strabo's Geog.* p. 130),
would add the words κιννάμωμον δὲ ἐκ θάμνων.
[2] κασσίαν, Jones, following the MSS., instead of κασίαν,
the spelling adopted here and elsewhere by Kramer and
Meineke.
[3] λιμνῶν, Corais emends to θάμνων ; so Groskurd, Kramer
and Meineke, who cite Theophrastus *Hist. Plant.* 9. 5,
Pliny *Hist. Nat.* 12. 43, Celsus 5. 23. 1, 2, but not Arrian
(*Exped.* 7. 20. 4), who (cited by C. Müller) says: ἤκουεν ἐκ
μὲν τῶν λιμνῶν τὴν κασίαν γίνεσθαι αὐτοῖς, ἀπὸ δὲ τῶν δένδρων

and, among the aromatics, they say that frankincense
and myrrh are produced from trees [1] and that cassia
is produced also from marshes.[2] Some say that
most of the latter comes from India and that the best
frankincense is produced near Persis. But, according to another division, Arabia Felix is split up into
five kingdoms, one of which comprises the warriors,
who fight for all; another, the farmers, who supply
food to all the rest; another, those who engage in
the mechanical arts; another, the myrrh-bearing
country, and another the frankincense-bearing
country, although the same countries produce cassia,
cinnamon, and nard. Occupations are not changed
from one class to another, but each and all keep to
those of their fathers. The greater part of their
wine is made from the palm. Brothers are held in
higher honour than children. The descendants of
the royal family not only reign as kings, but also
hold other offices, in accordance with seniority of
birth; and property is held in common by all kinsmen, though the eldest is lord of all. One woman
is also wife for all; and he who first enters the house
before any other has intercourse with her, having
first placed his staff before the door, for by custom
each man must carry a staff; but she spends the
night with the eldest. And therefore all children
are brothers. They also have intercourse with their
mothers; and the penalty for an adulterer is death;

---

[1] Possibly the Greek for " and cinnamon is produced from
bushes " has fallen out of the text here (see critical note).

[2] *i.e.* as well as from bushes (but see critical note).

τὴν σμύρναν τε καὶ τὸν λιβανωτόν, ἐκ δὲ τῶν θάμνων τὸ κιννάμωμον τέμνεσθαι.

[4] κασσίαν all MSS. except F, which has κασίαν.

ἐστὶν ὁ ἐξ ἄλλου γένους. θυγάτηρ δὲ τῶν βασιλέων τινὸς θαυμαστὴ τὸ κάλλος, ἔχουσα ἀδελφοὺς
πεντεκαίδεκα ἐρῶντας αὐτῆς πάντας, καὶ διὰ
τοῦτ᾿ ἀδιαλείπτως ἄλλον ἐπ᾿ ἄλλῳ παριόντα ὡς
αὐτήν, κάμνουσα ἤδη, παραδέδοται νοήματι χρήσασθαι τοιούτῳ· ποιησαμένη ῥάβδους ὁμοίας ταῖς
ἐκείνων, ὅτ᾿ ἐξίοι[1] παρ᾿ αὐτῆς τις, ἀεί τινα προὐ-
τίθει τῆς θύρας τὴν ὁμοίαν ἐκείνῃ, καὶ μικρὸν
ὕστερον ἄλλην, εἶτ᾿ ἄλλην,[2] στοχαζομένη, ὅπως
μὴ ἐκείνῃ τὴν παραπλησίαν ἔχοι ὁ μέλλων προ-
σιέναι· καὶ δὴ πάντων ποτὲ κατ᾿ ἀγορὰν ὄντων,
ἕνα προσιόντα τῇ θύρᾳ καὶ ἰδόντα τὴν ῥάβδον, ἐκ
μὲν ταύτης εἰκάσαι, διότι παρ᾿ αὐτήν τις εἴη· ἐκ
δὲ τοῦ τοὺς ἀδελφοὺς πάντας ἐν τῇ ἀγορᾷ κατα-
λιπεῖν ὑπονοῆσαι μοιχόν· δραμόντα δὲ πρὸς τὸν
πατέρα καὶ ἐπαγαγόντα[3] ἐκεῖνον ἐλεγχθῆναι
καταψευσάμενον τῆς ἀδελφῆς.

26. Σώφρονες δ᾿ εἰσὶν οἱ Ναβαταῖοι καὶ κτητι-
κοί, ὥστε καὶ δημοσίᾳ τῷ μὲν μειώσαντι τὴν
οὐσίαν ζημία κεῖται, τῷ δ᾿ αὐξήσαντι τιμαί.
ὀλιγόδουλοι δ᾿ ὄντες ὑπὸ τῶν συγγενῶν δια-
κονοῦνται τὸ πλέον ἢ ὑπ᾿ ἀλλήλων ἢ αὐτοδιά-
κονοι, ὥστε καὶ μέχρι τῶν βασιλέων διατείνειν τὸ
ἔθος. συσσίτια δὲ ποιοῦνται κατὰ τρισκαίδεκα
ἀνθρώπους, μουσουργοὶ δὲ δύο τῷ συμποσίῳ
ἑκάστῳ. ὁ δὲ βασιλεὺς ἐν ὄγκῳ[4] μεγάλῳ πολλὰ
συνέχει[5] συμπόσια· πίνει δ᾿ οὐδεὶς πλέον τῶν

---

[1] ἐξῃει *moz.*
[2] εἶτ᾿ ἄλλην omitted by MSS. except F.
[3] ἐπαγαγόντα, Corais, for ἀπαγαγότα.
[4] ὄγκῳ, Jones hesitates to emend to οἴκῳ, the emendation
of Tyrwhitt generally accepted by later editors.
[5] συνέχει Ex, συνεχῆ other MSS., συνεχῆ ποιεῖ *moz.*

but only the person from another family is an adulterer.[1] A daughter of one of the kings who was admired for her beauty had fifteen brothers, who were all in love with her, and therefore visited her unceasingly, one after another. At last, being tired out by their visits, she used the following device: she had staves made like theirs, and, when one of them left her, she always put a staff like his in front of the door, and a little later another, and then another—it being her aim that the one who was likely to visit her next might not have a staff similar to the one in front of the door; and so once, when all the brothers were together at the market-place, one of them, going to her door and seeing the staff in front of it, surmised that someone was with her; and, from the fact that he had left all his brothers in the market-place, he suspected that her visitor was an adulterer; but after running to his father and bringing him to the house, he was proved to have falsely accused his sister.

26. The Nabataeans are a sensible people, and are so much inclined to acquire possessions that they publicly fine anyone who has diminished his possessions and also confer honours on anyone who has increased them. Since they have but few slaves, they are served by their kinsfolk for the most part, or by one another, or by themselves; so that the custom extends even to their kings. They prepare common meals together in groups of thirteen persons; and they have two girl-singers for each banquet. The king holds many drinking-bouts in magnificent style, but no one drinks more than eleven cupfuls,

---

[1] The Greek indicates merely the *male* adulterer.

ἕνδεκα ποτηρίων ἄλλῳ καὶ ἄλλῳ χρυσῷ ἐκπώματι.
οὕτω δ' ὁ βασιλεύς ἐστι δημοτικός, ὥστε πρὸς τῷ
αὐτοδιακόνῳ καὶ ποτε[1] ἀντιδιάκονον τοῖς ἄλλοις
καὶ αὐτὸν γίνεσθαι· πολλάκις δὲ καὶ ἐν τῷ δήμῳ
δίδωσιν εὐθύνας, ἔσθ' ὅτε καὶ ἐξετάζεται τὰ περὶ
τὸν βίον· οἰκήσεις δὲ διὰ λίθου πολυτελεῖς, αἱ δὲ
πόλεις ἀτείχιστοι δι' εἰρήνην· εὔκαρπος ἡ πολλὴ
πλὴν ἐλαίου, χρῶνται δὲ σησαμίνῳ. πρόβατα
C 784 λευκότριχα, βόες μεγάλοι, ἵππων ἄφορος ἡ χώρα·
κάμηλοι δὲ τὴν ὑπουργίαν ἀντ' ἐκείνων παρέχον-
ται· ἀχίτωνες δ' ἐν περιζώμασι καὶ βλαυτίοις
προΐασι, καὶ οἱ βασιλεῖς, ἐν πορφύρᾳ δ' οὗτοι·
εἰσαγώγιμα δ' ἐστὶ τὰ μὲν τελέως, τὰ δ' οὐ
παντελῶς, ἄλλως τε καὶ ἐπιχωριάζει,[2] καθάπερ
χρυσὸς καὶ ἄργυρος[3] καὶ τὰ πολλὰ τῶν ἀρωμάτων, χαλκὸς δὲ καὶ σίδηρος καὶ ἔτι πορφυρᾶ
ἐσθής, στύραξ, κρόκος, κοστάρια, τόρευμα, γραφή,
πλάσμα οὐκ ἐπιχώρια· ἴσα κοπρίαις ἡγοῦνται
τὰ νεκρὰ σώματα, καθάπερ Ἡράκλειτός φησι·
Νέκυες κοπρίων ἐκβλητότεροι· διὸ καὶ παρὰ τοὺς
κοπρῶνας κατορύττουσι καὶ τοὺς βασιλεῖς.
ἥλιον τιμῶσιν ἐπὶ τοῦ δώματος ἱδρυσάμενοι
βωμόν, σπένδοντες ἐν αὐτῷ καθ' ἡμέραν καὶ
λιβανωτίζοντες.

27. Τοῦ δὲ ποιητοῦ λέγοντος,

Αἰθίοπάς θ' ἱκόμην καὶ Σιδονίους καὶ
Ἐρεμβούς,

---

[1] ποτε, Corais, for τό.

each time using a different golden cup. The king is so democratic that, in addition to serving himself, he sometimes even serves the rest himself in his turn. He often renders an account of his kingship in the popular assembly; and sometimes his mode of life is examined. Their homes, through the use of stone, are costly; but, on account of peace, the cities are not walled. Most of the country is well supplied with fruits except the olive; they use sesame-oil instead. The sheep are white-fleeced and the oxen are large, but the country produces no horses. Camels afford the service they require instead of horses. They go out without tunics, with girdles about their loins, and with slippers on their feet—even the kings, though in their case the colour is purple. Some things are imported wholly from other countries, but others not altogether so, especially in the case of those that are native products, as, for example, gold and silver and most of the aromatics, whereas brass and iron, as also purple garb, styrax, crocus, costaria, embossed works, paintings, and moulded works are not produced in their country. They have the same regard for the dead as for dung, as Heracleitus says: " Dead bodies more fit to be cast out than dung "; and therefore they bury even their kings beside dung-heaps. They worship the sun, building an altar on the top of the house, and pouring libations on it daily and burning frankincense.

27. When the poet says, " I came to Aethiopians and Sidonians and Erembians," [1] historians are

_____
[1] *Od.* 4. 84.
_____

[2] ἐπιχωριάζει E, ἐπιχωριάζειν other MSS. Kramer conj. ὅτι before the verb, Corais τά.

[3] χρυσὸς καὶ ἄργυρος E, χρύσον καὶ ἄργυρον.

διαποροῦσι, καὶ περὶ τῶν Σιδονίων μέν, εἴτε τινὰς
χρὴ λέγειν τῶν ἐν τῷ Περσικῷ κόλπῳ κατοι-
κούντων, ὧν ἄποικοι οἱ παρ' ἡμῖν Σιδόνιοι, καθάπερ καὶ Τυρίους τινὰς ἐκεῖ νησιώτας ἱστοροῦσι
καὶ Ἀραδίους, ὧν ἀποίκους τοὺς παρ' ἡμῖν φασιν,
εἴτ' αὐτοὺς τοὺς Σιδονίους· ἀλλὰ μᾶλλον περὶ
τῶν Ἐρεμβῶν ἡ ζήτησις, εἴτε τοὺς Τρωγλοδύτας
ὑπονοητέον λέγεσθαι, καθάπερ οἱ τὴν ἐτυμολογίαν
βιαζόμενοι ἀπὸ τοῦ εἰς τὴν ἔραν ἐμβαίνειν, ὅπερ
ἐστὶν εἰς τὴν γῆν, εἴτε τοὺς Ἄραβας. ὁ μὲν οὖν
Ζήνων ὁ ἡμέτερος μεταγράφει οὕτως·

καὶ Σιδονίους Ἄραβάς τε.

πιθανώτερον δὲ Ποσειδώνιος γράφει τῷ παρὰ
μικρὸν ἀλλάξαι

καὶ Σιδονίους καὶ Ἀραμβούς,[1]

ὡς τοῦ ποιητοῦ τοὺς νῦν Ἄραβας οὕτω καλέ-
σαντος, καθάπερ καὶ ὑπὸ τῶν ἄλλων ὠνομάζοντο
κατ' αὐτόν. φησὶ δὲ ταῦτα τρία ἔθνη, συνεχῆ
ἀλλήλοις ἱδρυμένα, ὁμογένειάν τινα ἐμφαίνειν
πρὸς ἄλληλα, καὶ διὰ τοῦτο[2] παρακειμένοις
ὀνόμασι κεκλῆσθαι, τοὺς μὲν Ἀρμενίους, τοὺς δὲ
Ἀραμαίους,[3] τοὺς δὲ Ἀραμβούς·[4] ὥσπερ δὲ ἀπὸ
ἔθνους[5] ἑνὸς[6] ὑπολαμβάνειν ἔστιν εἰς τρία διῃρῆσθαι κατὰ τὰς τῶν κλιμάτων διαφορὰς ἀεὶ καὶ
μᾶλλον ἐξαλλαττομένων, οὕτω καὶ τοῖς ὀνόμασι

[1] Ἀραμβούς, Corais, for Ἐρεμβούς.
[2] τοῦτο, Groskurd, for τό.
[3] Ἀραμαίους marg. F, Kramer; Ἀριμίους F, Ἀράβους i,
Ἀραβίους other MSS.
[4] Ἀραμβούς marg. F, Ἐρεμβούς elsewhere in MSS.
[5] For ἀπὸ ἔθνους, Corais reads πιθανῶς.

entirely at loss to know, in the first place, in regard
to the Sidonians, whether one should call them a
certain people who dwelt on the Persian Gulf, from
whom the Sidonians in our part of the world [1] were
colonists, just as they speak of Tyrians there,
islanders, as also of Aradians, from whom they say
those in our part of the world were colonists, or
whether one should call them the Sidonians themselves; but, secondly, the inquiry about the Erembians is more doubtful, whether one should suspect
that the Troglodytes are meant, as do those who
force the etymology of " Erembi " from *eran
embainein*,[2] that is, *go into the earth*, or the Arabians.
Now our [3] Zeno alters the text thus : " and to
Sidonians and Arabians "; but Poseidonius more
plausibly writes, with only a slight alteration of the
text, " and Sidonians and Arambians," on the ground
that the poet so called the present Arabians, just as
they were named by all others in his time.   Poseidonius says that the Arabians consist of three tribes,
that they are situated in succession, one after another,
and that this indicates that they are homogeneous
with one another, and that for this reason they were
called by similar names—one tribe " Armenians,"
another " Aramaeans," and another " Arambians."
And just as one may suppose that the Arabians were
divided into three tribes, according to the differences
in the latitudes, which ever vary more and more, so
also one may suppose that they used several names

---

[1] *i.e.* those on the Mediterranean.
[2] See Vol. I, p. 153, and footnote 1.
[3] *i.e.* of our Stoic School.

---

[6] ἑνός, inserted by editors from conj. of Tyrwhitt.

χρήσασθαι πλείοσιν ἀνθ᾽ ἑνός. οὐδ᾽ οἱ Ἐρεμνοὺς
γράφοντες πιθανοί· τῶν γὰρ Αἰθιόπων μᾶλλον
ἴδιον. λέγει δὲ καὶ τοὺς Ἀρίμους ὁ ποιητής, οὕς
φησι Ποσειδώνιος δέχεσθαι δεῖν μὴ τόπον τινὰ
τῆς Συρίας ἢ τῆς Κιλικίας ἢ ἄλλης τινὸς γῆς,
C 785 ἀλλὰ τὴν Συρίαν αὐτήν· Ἀραμαῖοι[1] γὰρ οἱ ἐν
αὐτῇ, τάχα δ᾽ οἱ Ἕλληνες Ἀριμαίους[2] ἐκάλουν
ἢ Ἀρίμους. αἱ δὲ τῶν ὀνομάτων μεταπτώσεις,
καὶ μάλιστα τῶν βαρβαρικῶν, πολλαί· καθάπερ
τὸν Δαριήκην Δαρεῖον ἐκάλεσαν, τὴν δὲ Φάρζιριν[3]
Παρύσατιν,[4] Ἀταργάτιν[5] δὲ τὴν Ἀθάραν,[6] Δερ-
κετὼ δ᾽ αὐτὴν Κτησίας καλεῖ. τῆς δὲ τῶν
Ἀράβων εὐδαιμονίας καὶ Ἀλέξανδρον ἄν τις
ποιήσαιτο μάρτυρα τὸν διανοηθέντα, ὥς φασι,
καὶ βασίλειον αὐτὴν ποιήσασθαι μετὰ τὴν ἐξ
Ἰνδῶν ἐπάνοδον. πᾶσαι μὲν οὖν αἱ ἐπιχειρήσεις
αὐτοῦ κατελύθησαν, τελευτήσαντος παραχρῆμα
τὸν βίον· μία δ᾽ οὖν καὶ αὕτη τῶν ἐπιχειρήσεων
ἦν, εἰ μὲν ἑκόντες παραδέχοιντο αὐτόν· εἰ δὲ μή,
ὡς πολεμήσοντος· καὶ δὴ ὁρῶν μήτε πρότερον
μήθ᾽ ὕστερον πέμψαντας ὡς αὐτὸν πρέσβεις,
παρεσκευάζετο πρὸς τὸν πόλεμον, ὥσπερ εἰρή-
καμεν ἐν τοῖς ἔμπροσθεν.

---

[1] Ἀραμαῖοι, Corais, for Ἀριμαῖοι.
[2] Ἀριμαίους, Corais, for Ἀραμαίους.
[3] Φάρζηριν F.
[4] Παρυσάτην D first hand.
[5] Ἀταργάτην D first hand.
[6] Ἀθάραν Dhi., Ἀθάρα other MSS.

instead of one. Neither are those who write
" Eremni "[1] plausible; for that name is more
peculiarly applicable to the Aethiopians. The poet
also mentions " Arimi, "[2] by which, according to
Poseidonius, we should interpret the poet as meaning, not some place in Syria or in Cilicia or in some
other land, but Syria itself; for the people in Syria
are Aramaeans, though perhaps the Greeks called
them Arimaeans or Arimi. The changes in names,
and particularly in those of the barbarians, are
numerous: for example, they called Dareius
" Darieces," Parysatis " Pharziris," and Athara
" Atargatis," though Ctesias calls her " Derceto."
As for the blest lot of Arabia,[3] one might make even
Alexander a witness thereof, since he intended, as
they say, even to make it his royal abode after his
return from India. Now all his enterprises were
broken up because of his sudden death; but, at any
rate, this too was one of his enterprises, to see whether
they would receive him voluntarily, and if they did
not, to go to war with them; and accordingly, when
he saw that they had not sent ambassadors to him,
either before or after,[4] he set about making prepara-
tions for war, as I have stated heretofore in this
work.[5]

---

[1] Black (people).   [2] *Iliad* 2. 783.
[3] It was called " Arabia the Blest," " Arabia Felix."
[4] *i.e.* his expedition to India.   [5] 16. 1. 11.

A PARTIAL DICTIONARY OF
PROPER NAMES[1]

---

[1] A complete index of the whole work will appear in the next volume.

A PARTIAL DICTIONARY OF PROPER NAMES

A PARTIAL DICTIONARY OF PROPER NAMES

A PARTIAL DICTIONARY OF PROPER NAMES

O

Omanus, temple of, 177
Onesicritus (see *Dictionary* in vol. i), on India, 17, 21, 29, 31, 33, 39, 49, 53, 91, 111, 113, 115, 135, 153, 163, 167
Ophiodes, the island, 317
Opis, 205
Oreitae, the, 129, 139
Orontes River, the, 155, 163, 245, 251

P

Pacorus, invaded Syria, 237; 247
Palaestine, 343
Palibothra, 17, 63, 125
Pandion, Indian King, 5
Paraetaceni, 173, 221
Parmenio, father of Philotas. 145
Paropamisadae, the, 141, 143
Paropamisus Mountain, the, 141, 143, 147
Parthians, the, 173, 219, 225, 233, 237
Pasargadae, 159, 165, 169
Pasitigris River, the, 161
Patalenê, 19, 23, 57, 59
Patrocles, on India, 17
Pelusium, 279
Persepolis, 159, 165
Persian Gates, the, 163
Persian Gulf, the, 155, 301
Persians, the, 173, 179, 187, 189, 195, 205, 271
Persis, 155, 161, 163, 169, 171
Petra, 351, 353, 357, 359
Peucolaïtis, 47
Pharnapates (*see* Phranicates), 247
Philodemus the Epicurean, native of Gadaris, 277
Philotas, son of Parmenio, 145
Phoenicia, 239, 265, 267, 285
Phraates, 237
Phranicates (Pharnapates?), 247
Pindar, on the Hyperboreans, 97
Plato, myths of, 103; on King Minos, 287
Polycleitus (see *Dictionary* in vol. v), 159, 161, 213
Polycritus (Polycleitus?), 185
Pompey, 231, 241, 249, 263, 279, 289, 291, 297
Porticanus, country of, 59
Porus, country of, 5, 49, 51, 127

Poseidonius (see *Dictionary* in vol. i), on the springs of naphtha in Babylonia, 217; native of Apameia, 255; on the fallen dragon in the Macras Plain, 261; on the dogma about atoms, 271; on the sorcerers about the Dead Sea, 295; on Arabian salts, 351
Pramnae, the, Indian sophists, 123
Prasii, the, 63
Prometheus, story of, 13
Psammitichus, 321
Ptolemaïs (Acê), 271, 319
Ptolemy Philadelphus, 319
Ptolemy Philometor, conqueror of Alexander Balas, 247
Pythagoras, doctrines of, 113
Pytholaïs, promontory of, 331; pillars and altars of, 335

S

Sabaeans, the, 347, 349, 351
Sabata (Sawa), 311
Sabus, country of, 57
Salomê, Herod's sister, 299
Samaria, 281
Samosata, 241
Sandracae, 197
Sandrocottus, the King, 63, 95, 143
Sarpedon, the general, 273
Scenae, near Babylon, 235
Selenê (Cleopatra), 241
Seleuceia in Pieria, 241
Seleuceia on the Tigris, 201, 219, 243
Seleucis, 241
Seleucus Callinicus, 243, 259
Seleucus the Chaldaean, 203
Seleucus Nicator, Syrian King, 5, 143, 201, 241, 243, 251
Semiramis, the queen, 7, 135, 195
Seres, the, 61, 63
Sesostris the Aegyptian, 7, 313, 319
Sibae, the, 57
Sidon, 257, 267, 269
Silas River, the, 67
Simonides, on the Hyperboreans, 97; on the burial-places of Memnon, 159
Sinnaca, 231
Sirbonis, Lake, 279, 281, 293
Sitacenê (Apolloniatis), 173, 221
Socrates, on abstaining from meat, 113
Sopeithes, country of, 51
Sophocles, on Mt. Nysa, 9

378

A PARTIAL DICTIONARY OF PROPER NAMES

379

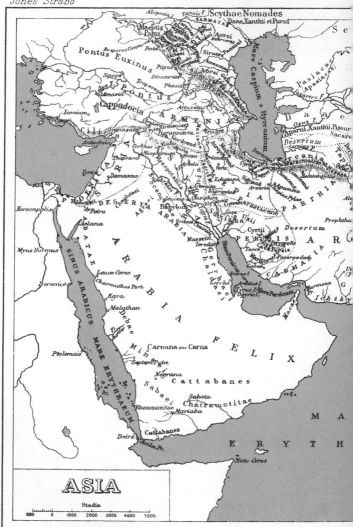

ASIA

Stadia
1000 0 1000 2000 3000 4000 5000

Map XII

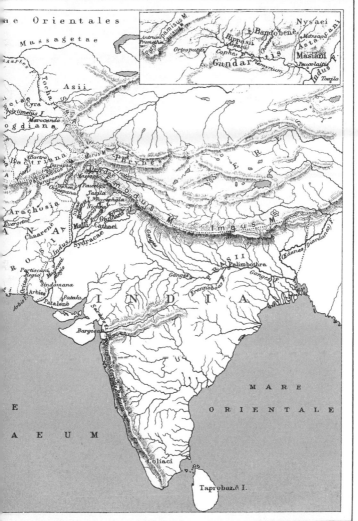

ae Orientales

Mussagetae

Nysaei

Bandobene

Antrum
Promethea

Hippasii

Matsaca
Astacani

Ortospana

Cophas

Masiani

Gandaritis

Proclais

Gandaris

Peucolaitis

Indus

Taxila

Asii

Iaxartes
Tocharii

Cyra

Maracanda

Oxus

Polytimetus F.

ogdiana

Bactriana

Bactra
Darapsa

Merdus

Pryges

Paropanisus

Daraspa

Cophen

Ordae

Oxus

Adespana

Paucalis

Nysa

Ola

Taxila

Imaus M.

Arachosia

Sigal

Nicaea

Euergetae

Chaarene

Ophthea

Malli

Cathaei

Sydracae

Ganges

Odanes (Iuardanes?)

Ganges

Palimbothra

R

Particscara
Regia

Sindomana

Indus

Ganges

Eraunoboas

Ganges F.

Arbis

Patala

I N D I A

Abis

Oritae

Patalene

Saronas

Bargosa

U

M A R E

E

O R I E N T A L E

A E U M

Coliaci

Taprobaze I.